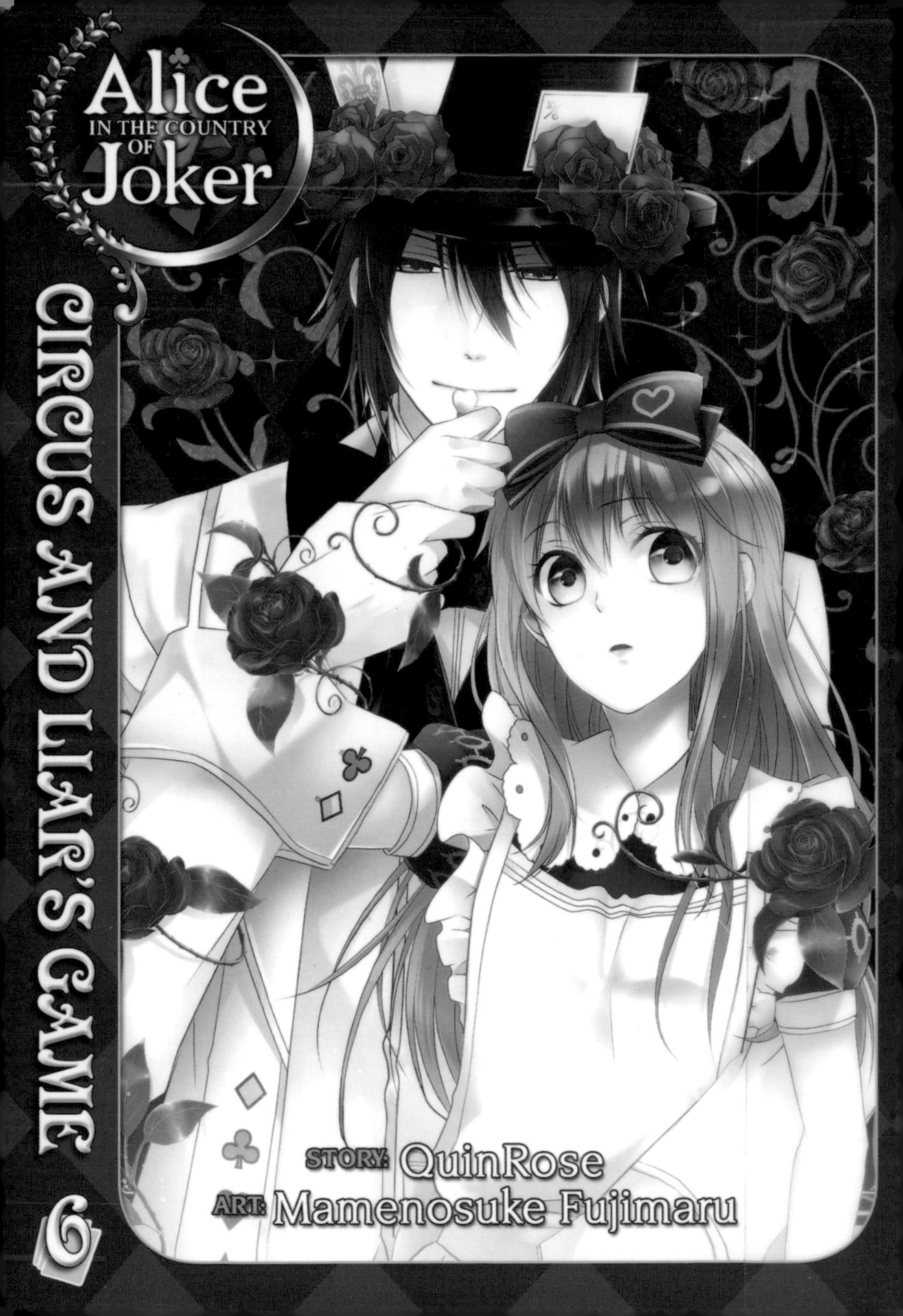
Alice
IN THE COUNTRY
OF
Joker
CIRCUS AND LIAR'S GAME
STORY: QuinRose
ART: Mamenosuke Fujimaru
6

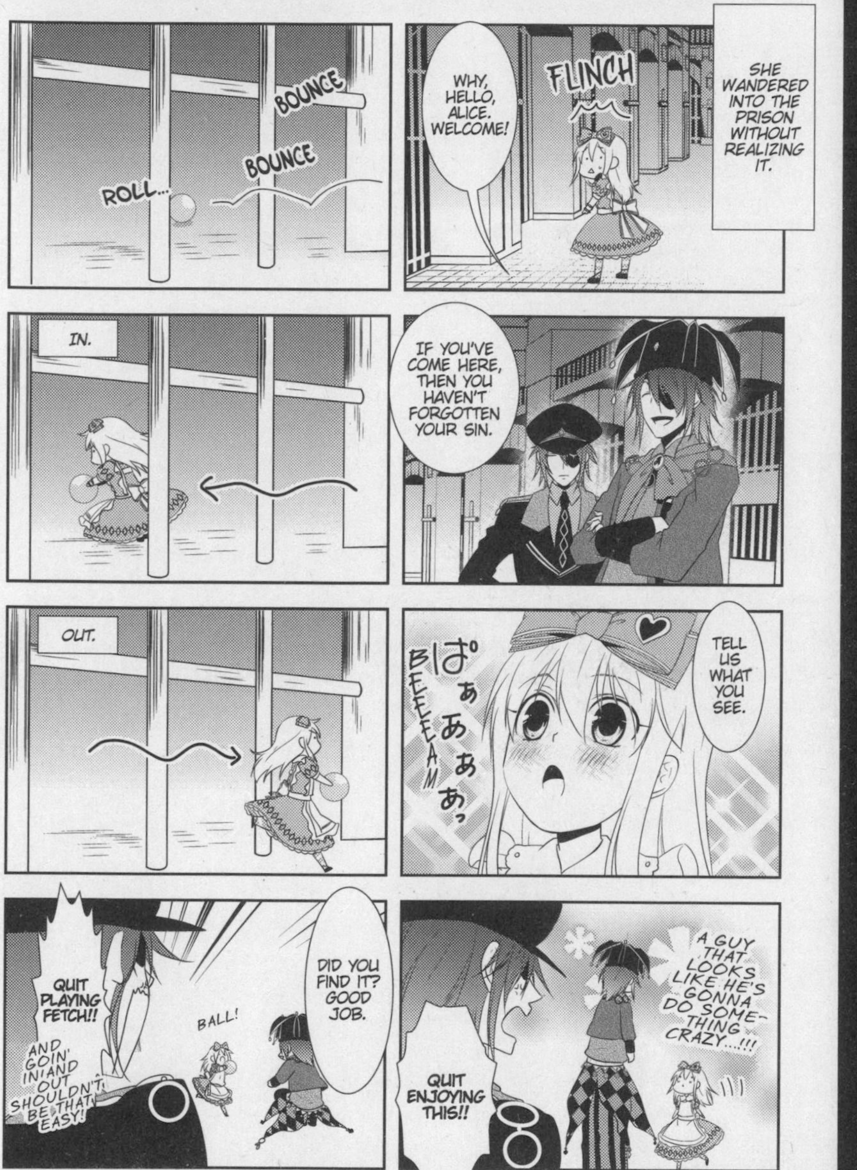
SHE WANDERED INTO THE PRISON WITHOUT REALIZING IT.
FLINCH
WHY, HELLO, ALICE. WELCOME!
BOUNCE
BOUNCE
ROLL...
IF YOU'VE COME HERE, THEN YOU HAVEN'T FORGOTTEN YOUR SIN.
IN.
TELL US WHAT YOU SEE.
ぱぁあああっ
BEEEEAM
OUT.
A GUY THAT LOOKS LIKE HE'S GONNA DO SOME-THING CRAZY...!!!
QUIT ENJOYING THIS!!
DID YOU FIND IT? GOOD JOB.
BALL!
QUIT PLAYING FETCH!!
AND GOIN' IN AND OUT SHOULDN'T BE THAT EASY!

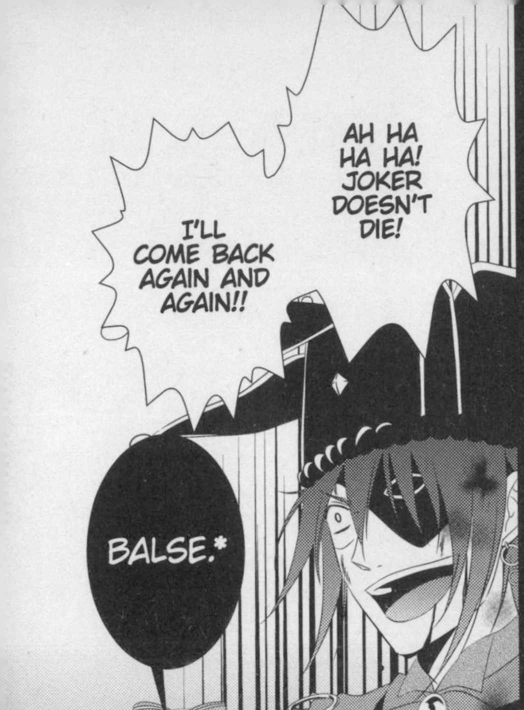
AH HA HA HA! JOKER DOESN'T DIE!
I'LL COME BACK AGAIN AND AGAIN!!
BALSE.*

*"Balse," or "Barusu," is the ultimate destruction spell that destroys the flying castle Laputa in Hayao Miyazaki's film *Castle in the Sky*. The simultaneous tweeting of the word during a broadcast of the movie in Japan broke a Twitter world record for the most tweets in a single second. The more you know!

THANK YOU VERY MUCH!

To everyone who helped me with this project...

Friends & Family
QuinRose-sama
The Publishers

And most importantly-- the readers.

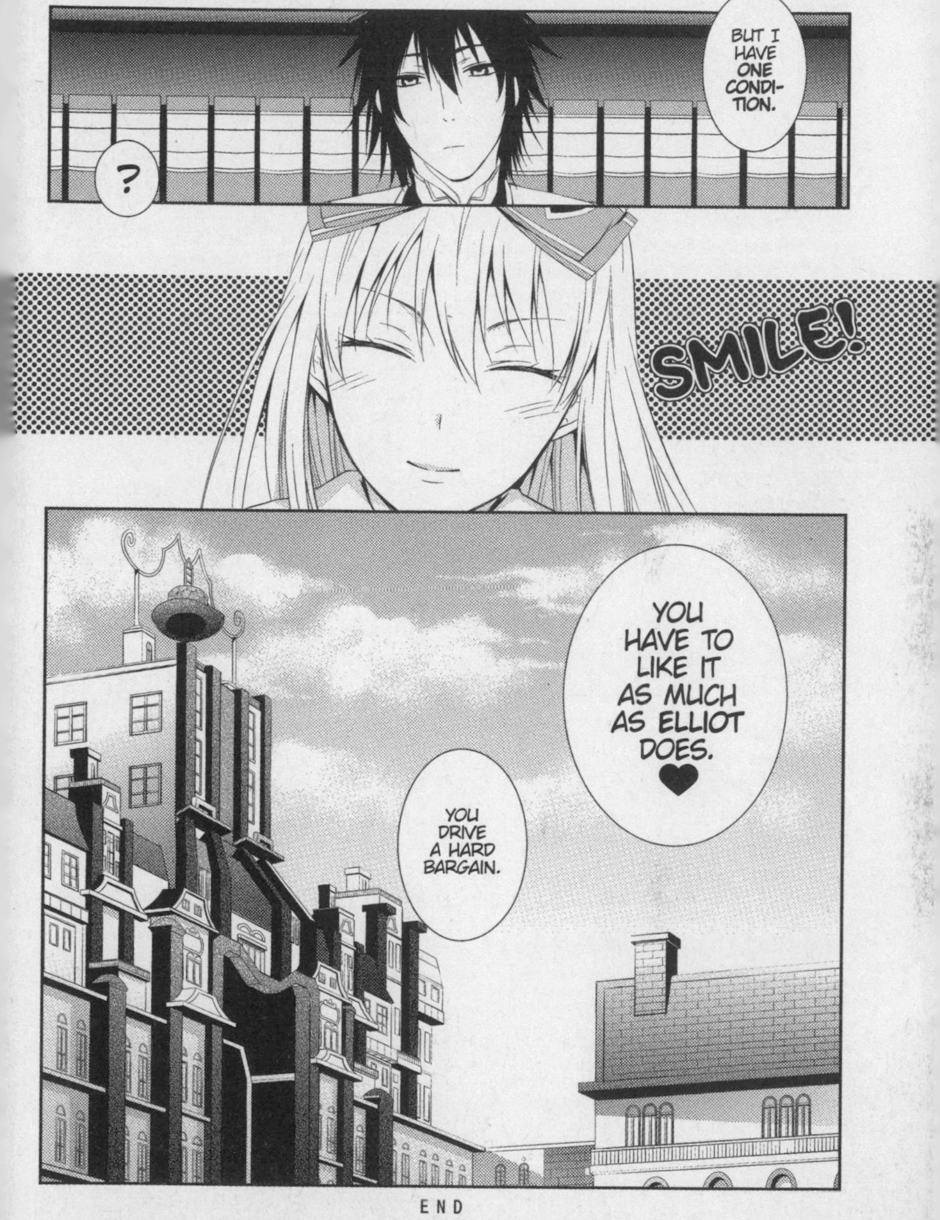
BUT I HAVE ONE CONDITION.
?
SMILE!
YOU HAVE TO LIKE IT AS MUCH AS ELLIOT DOES. ♥
YOU DRIVE A HARD BARGAIN.

END

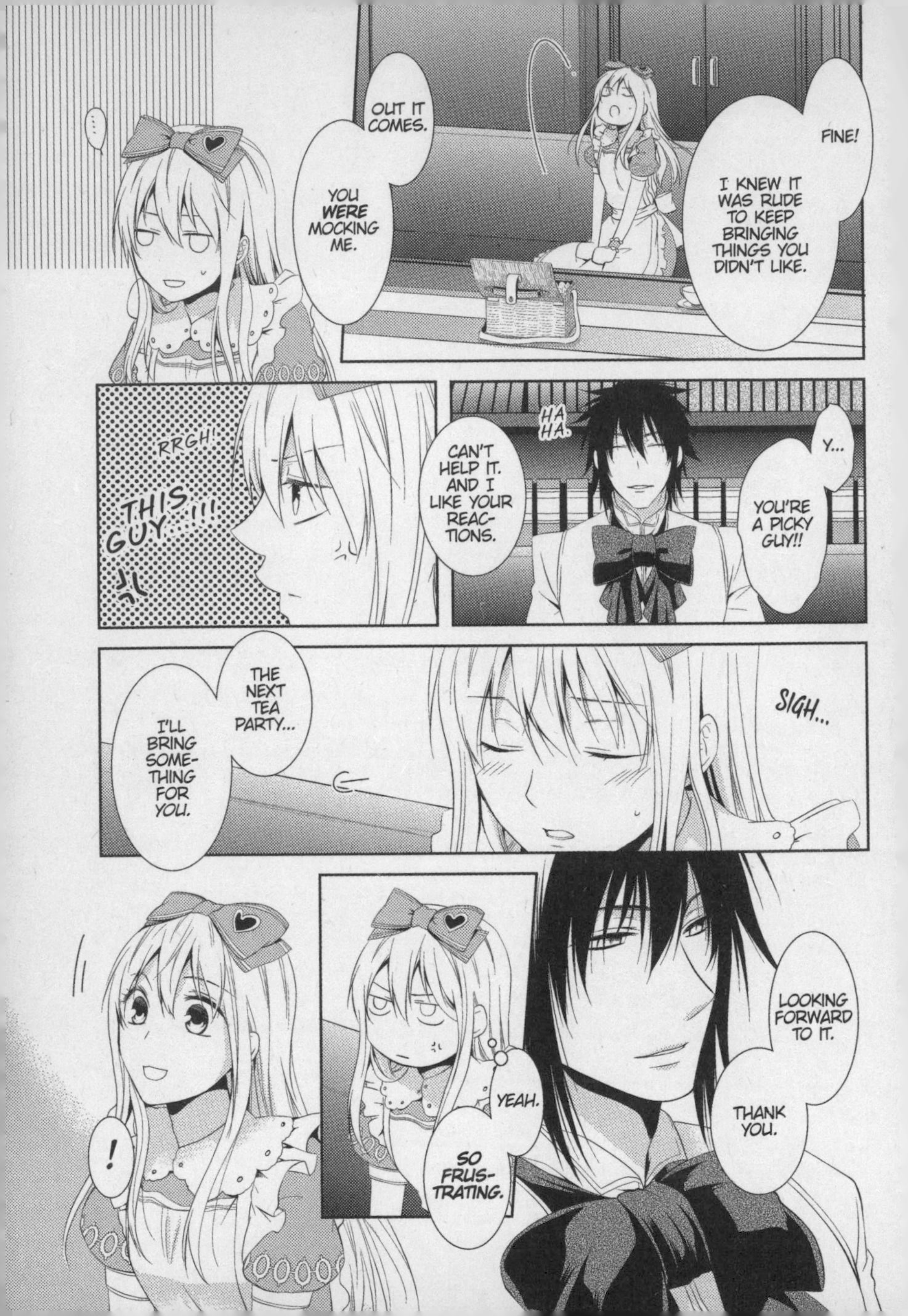
FINE!
I KNEW IT WAS RUDE TO KEEP BRINGING THINGS YOU DIDN'T LIKE.
OUT IT COMES.
YOU WERE MOCKING ME.
...
Y...
YOU'RE A PICKY GUY!!
HA HA.
CAN'T HELP IT. AND I LIKE YOUR REAC-TIONS.
RRGH!
THIS GUY...!!!
SIGH...
THE NEXT TEA PARTY...
I'LL BRING SOME-THING FOR YOU.
LOOKING FORWARD TO IT.
THANK YOU.
YEAH.
SO FRUS-TRATING.
!

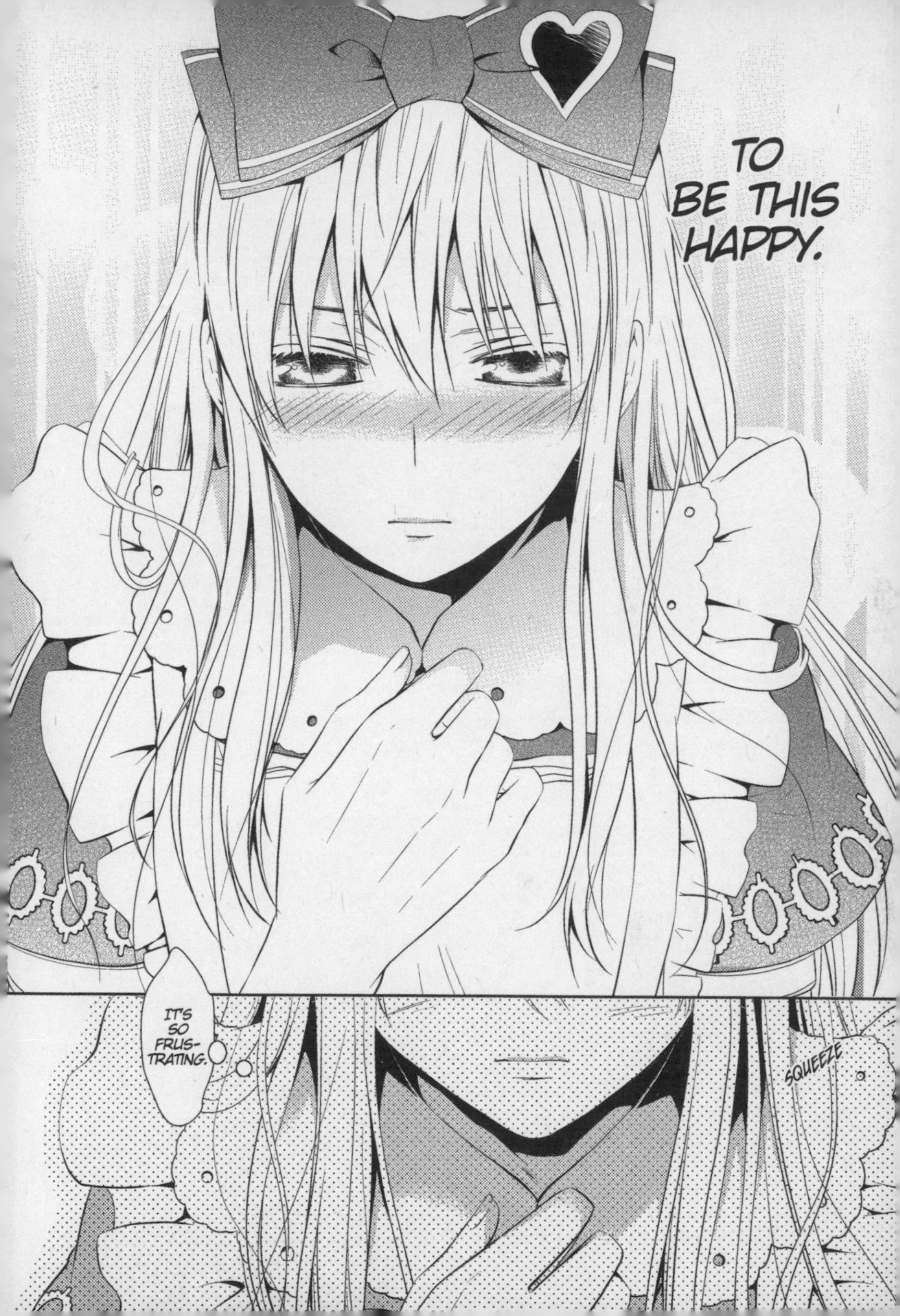
TO BE THIS HAPPY.
SQUEEZE
IT'S SO FRUS-TRATING.

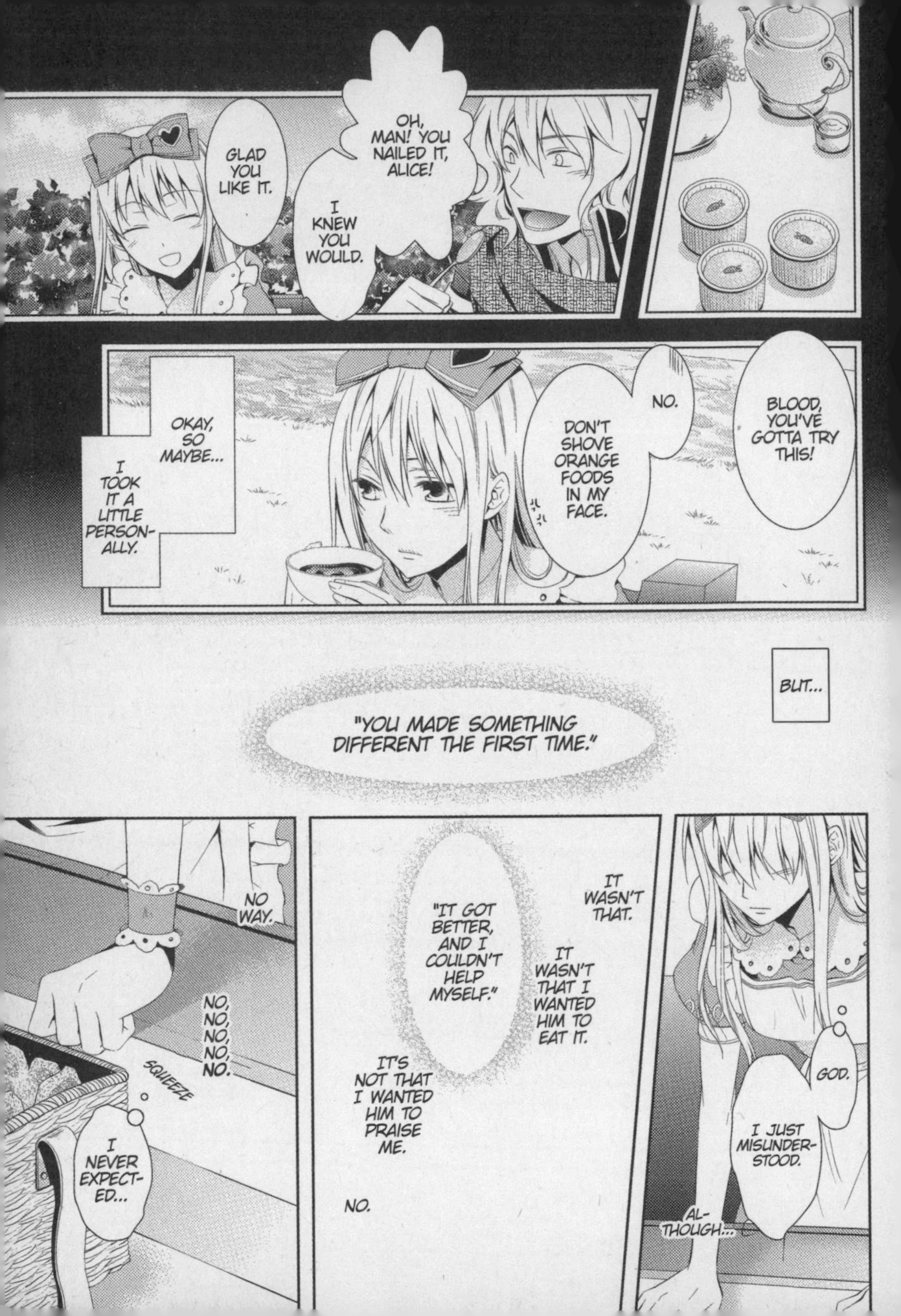
OH, MAN! YOU NAILED IT, ALICE!
I KNEW YOU WOULD.
GLAD YOU LIKE IT.
BLOOD, YOU'VE GOTTA TRY THIS!
NO.
DON'T SHOVE ORANGE FOODS IN MY FACE.
OKAY, SO MAYBE...
I TOOK IT A LITTLE PERSON-ALLY.
BUT...
"YOU MADE SOMETHING DIFFERENT THE FIRST TIME."
GOD.
I JUST MISUNDER-STOOD.
AL-THOUGH...
IT WASN'T THAT.
IT WASN'T THAT I WANTED HIM TO EAT IT.
"IT GOT BETTER, AND I COULDN'T HELP MYSELF."
IT'S NOT THAT I WANTED HIM TO PRAISE ME.
NO.
NO WAY.
NO, NO, NO, NO, NO.
SQUEEZE
I NEVER EXPECT-ED...

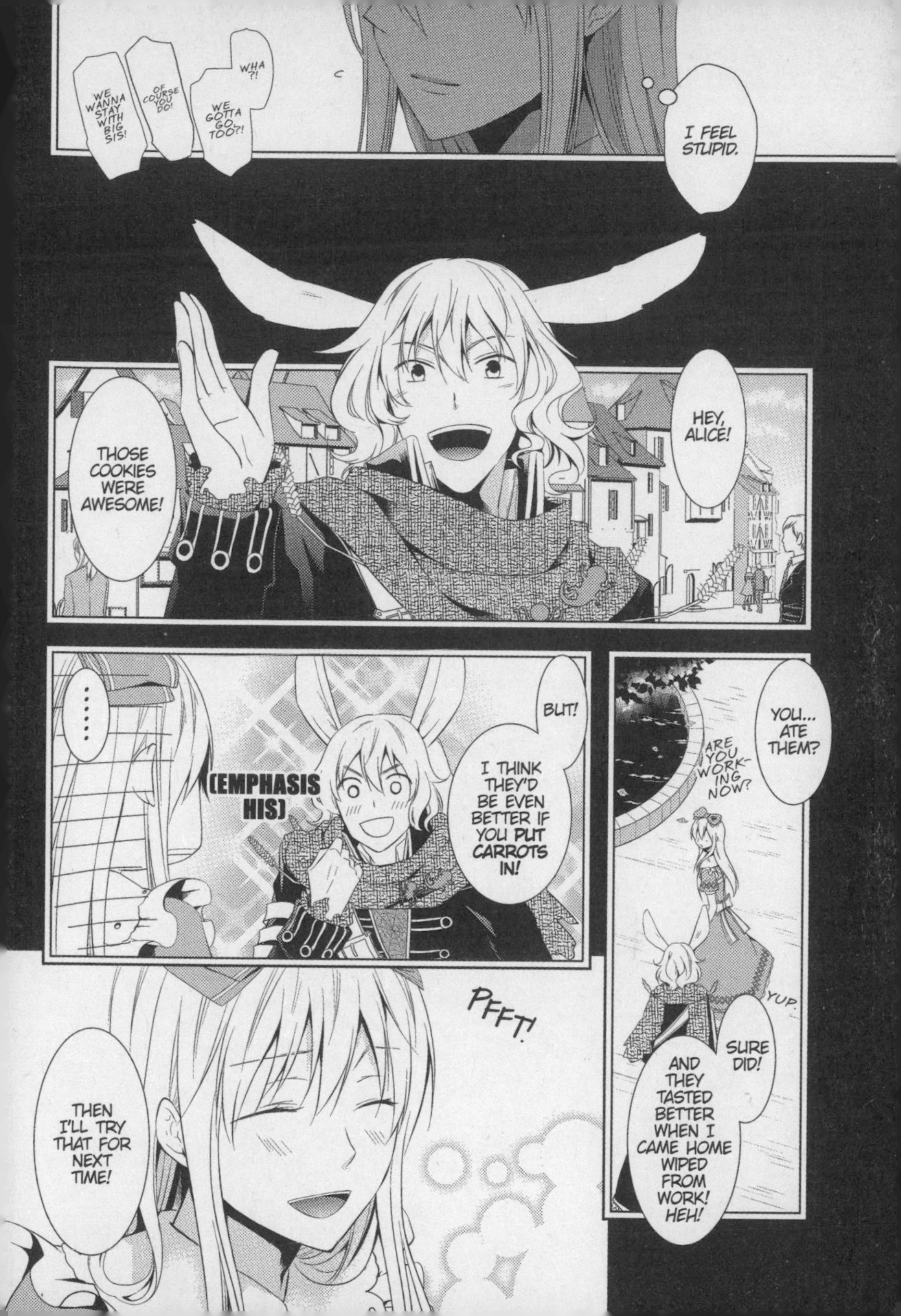
I FEEL STUPID.
WHA?!
WE GOTTA GO, TOO?!
OF COURSE YOU DO!
WE WANNA STAY WITH BIG SIS!
HEY, ALICE!
THOSE COOKIES WERE AWESOME!
YOU... ATE THEM?
ARE YOU WORKING NOW?
YUP.
SURE DID!
AND THEY TASTED BETTER WHEN I CAME HOME WIPED FROM WORK! HEH!
BUT!
I THINK THEY'D BE EVEN BETTER IF YOU PUT CARROTS IN!
(EMPHASIS HIS)
......
PFFT!
THEN I'LL TRY THAT FOR NEXT TIME!

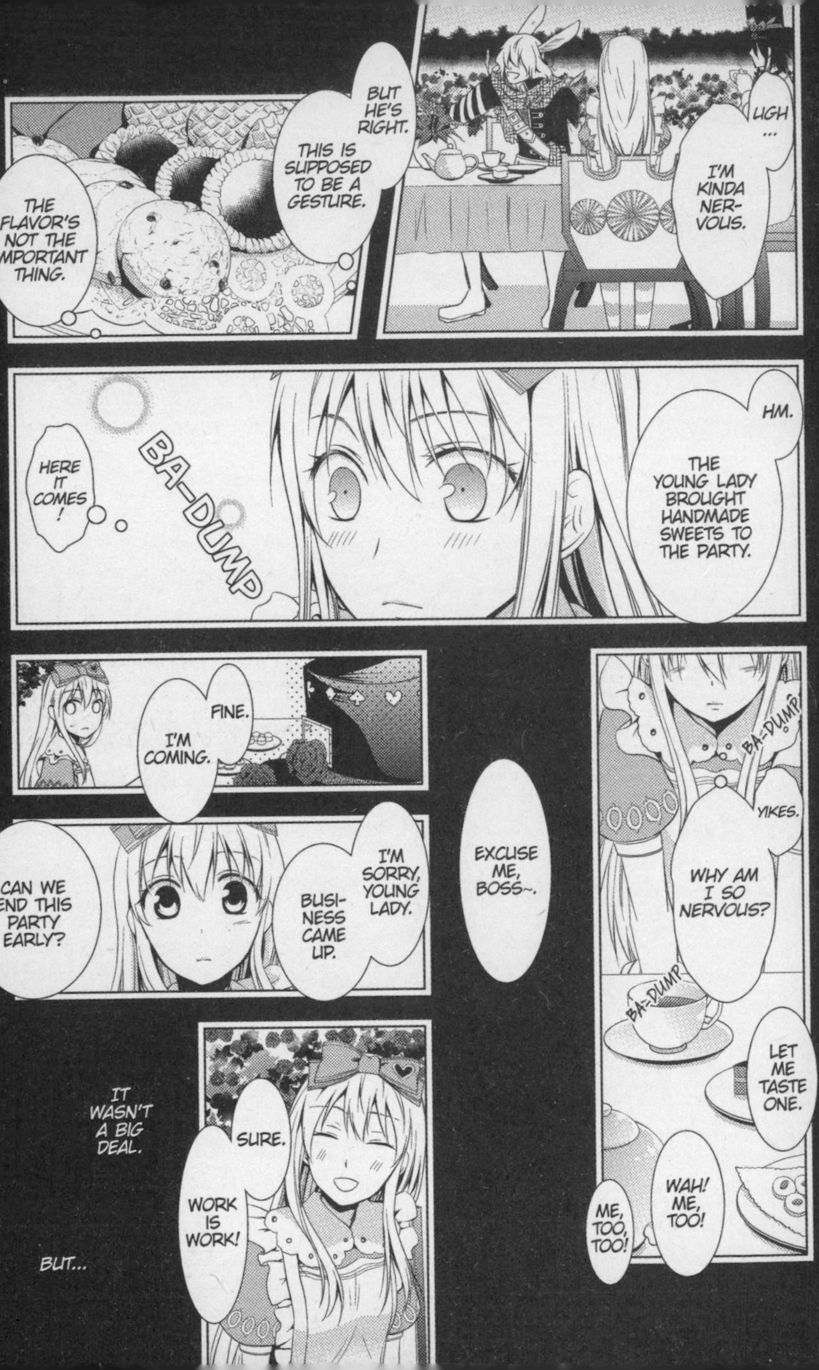
UGH... I'M KINDA NERVOUS.
BUT HE'S RIGHT. THIS IS SUPPOSED TO BE A GESTURE.
THE FLAVOR'S NOT THE IMPORTANT THING.
HM.
THE YOUNG LADY BROUGHT HANDMADE SWEETS TO THE PARTY.
BA-DUMP
HERE IT COMES!
BA-DUMP
YIKES.
WHY AM I SO NERVOUS?
BA-DUMP
LET ME TASTE ONE.
WAH! ME, TOO!
ME, TOO, TOO!
FINE.
I'M COMING.
EXCUSE ME, BOSS~.
I'M SORRY, YOUNG LADY.
BUSINESS CAME UP.
CAN WE END THIS PARTY EARLY?
SURE.
WORK IS WORK!
IT WASN'T A BIG DEAL.
BUT...

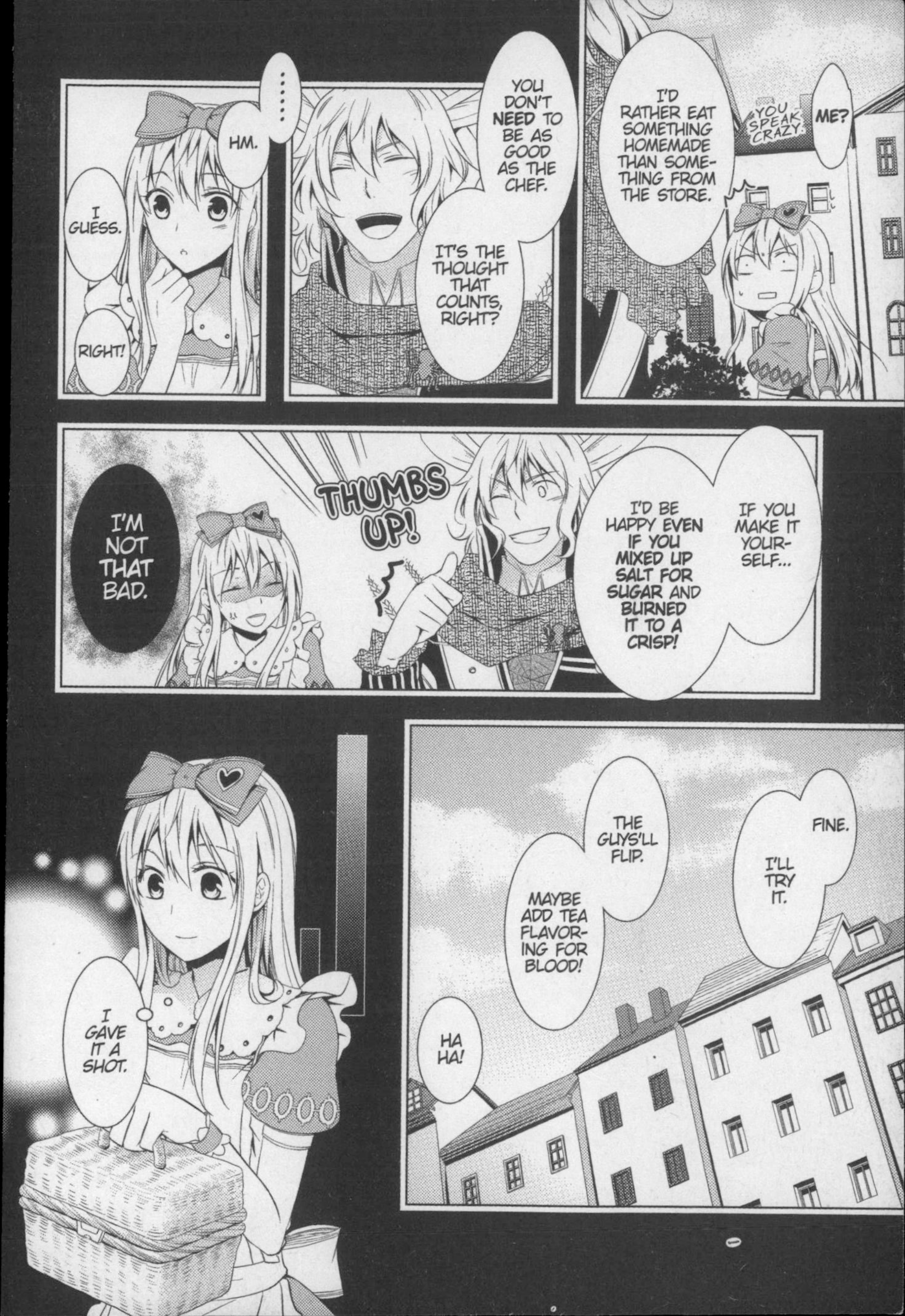
ME?
YOU SPEAK CRAZY.
I'D RATHER EAT SOMETHING HOMEMADE THAN SOMETHING FROM THE STORE.
YOU DON'T NEED TO BE AS GOOD AS THE CHEF.
IT'S THE THOUGHT THAT COUNTS, RIGHT?
……
HM.
I GUESS.
RIGHT!
IF YOU MAKE IT YOURSELF...
I'D BE HAPPY EVEN IF YOU MIXED UP SALT FOR SUGAR AND BURNED IT TO A CRISP!
THUMBS UP!
I'M NOT THAT BAD.
FINE.
I'LL TRY IT.
THE GUYS'LL FLIP.
MAYBE ADD TEA FLAVORING FOR BLOOD!
HA HA!
I GAVE IT A SHOT.

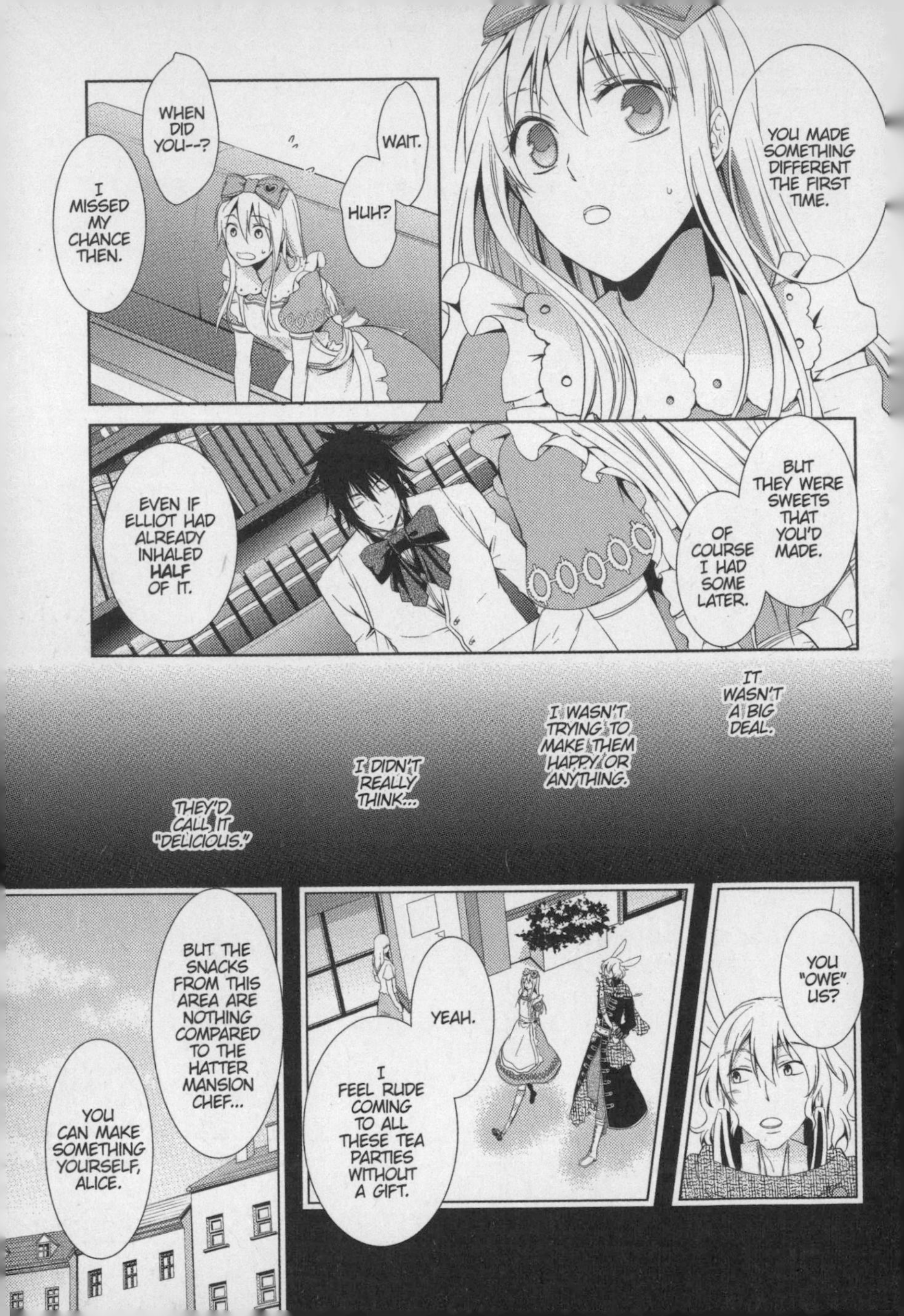
YOU MADE SOMETHING DIFFERENT THE FIRST TIME.
WAIT.
HUH?
WHEN DID YOU--?
I MISSED MY CHANCE THEN.
BUT THEY WERE SWEETS THAT YOU'D MADE.
OF COURSE I HAD SOME LATER.
EVEN IF ELLIOT HAD ALREADY INHALED HALF OF IT.
IT WASN'T A BIG DEAL.
I WASN'T TRYING TO MAKE THEM HAPPY OR ANYTHING.
I DIDN'T REALLY THINK...
THEY'D CALL IT "DELICIOUS."
YOU "OWE" US?
YEAH.
I FEEL RUDE COMING TO ALL THESE TEA PARTIES WITHOUT A GIFT.
BUT THE SNACKS FROM THIS AREA ARE NOTHING COMPARED TO THE HATTER MANSION CHEF...
YOU CAN MAKE SOMETHING YOURSELF, ALICE.

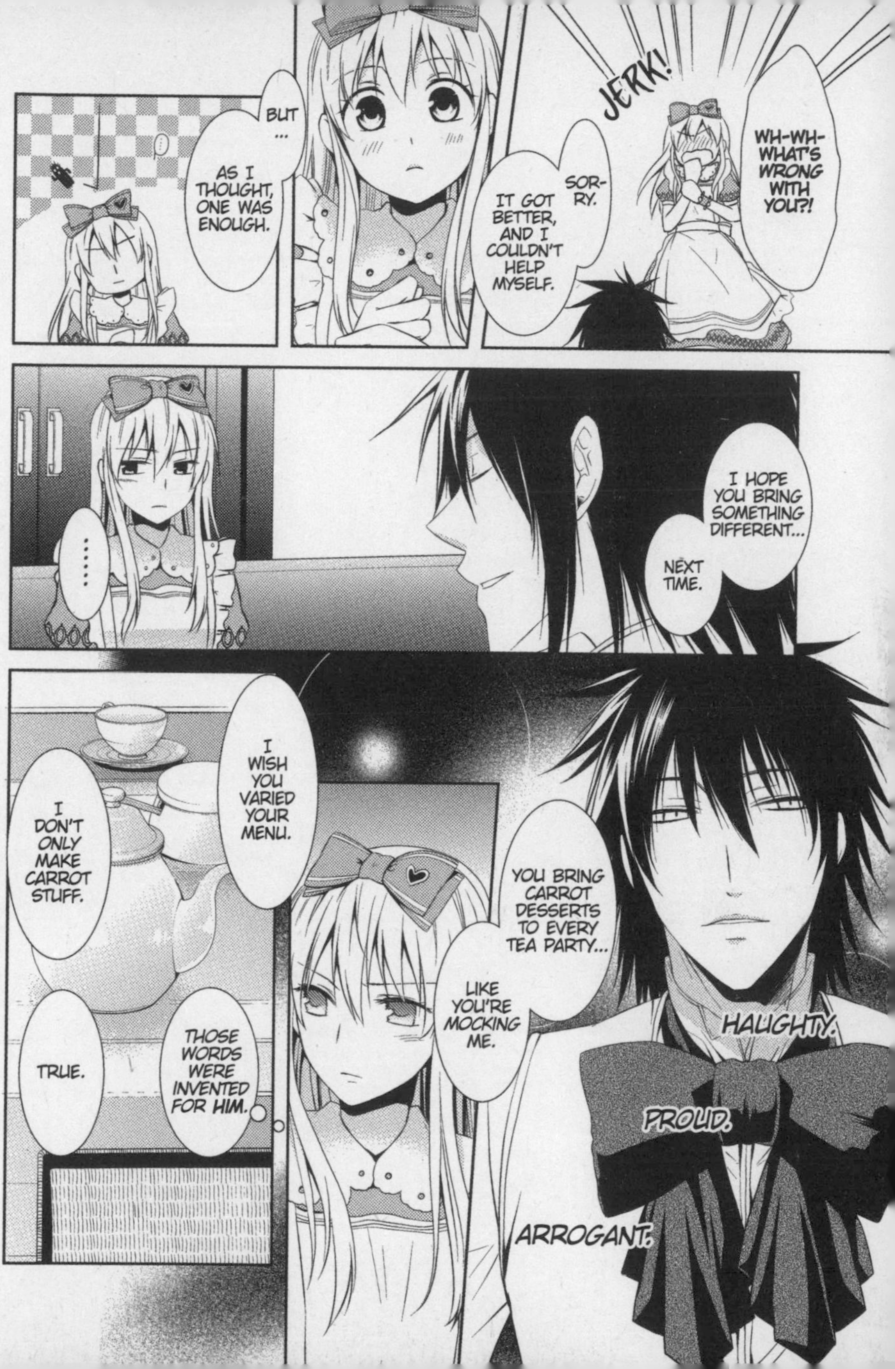
JERK!
WH-WH-WHAT'S WRONG WITH YOU?!
SOR-RY.
IT GOT BETTER, AND I COULDN'T HELP MYSELF.
BUT ...
AS I THOUGHT, ONE WAS ENOUGH.
!
I HOPE YOU BRING SOMETHING DIFFERENT...
NEXT TIME.
......
YOU BRING CARROT DESSERTS TO EVERY TEA PARTY...
LIKE YOU'RE MOCKING ME.
HAUGHTY.
PROUD.
ARROGANT.
THOSE WORDS WERE INVENTED FOR HIM.
TRUE.
I WISH YOU VARIED YOUR MENU.
I DON'T ONLY MAKE CARROT STUFF.

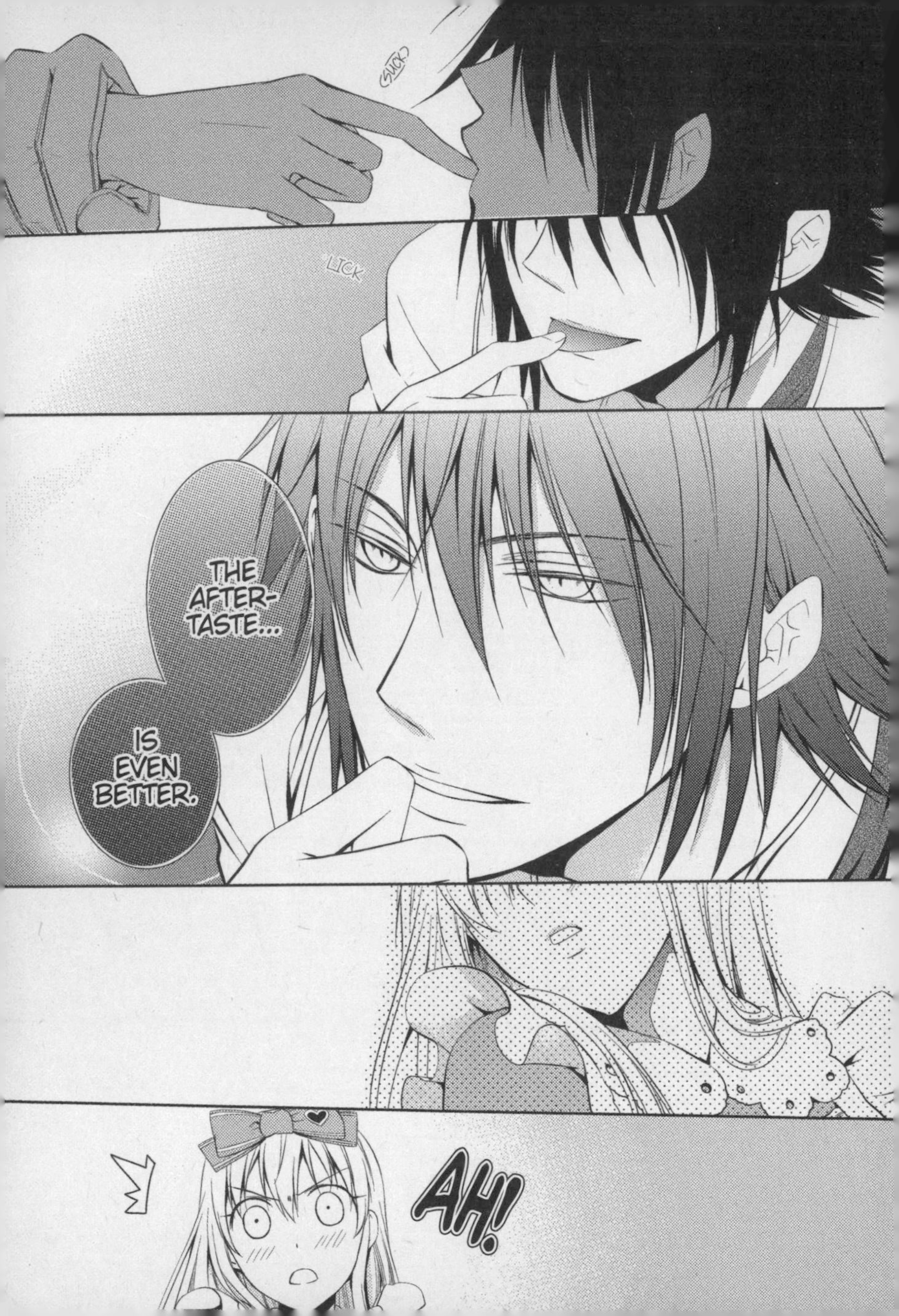

SUCK
LICK
THE AFTER-TASTE...
IS EVEN BETTER.
AH!

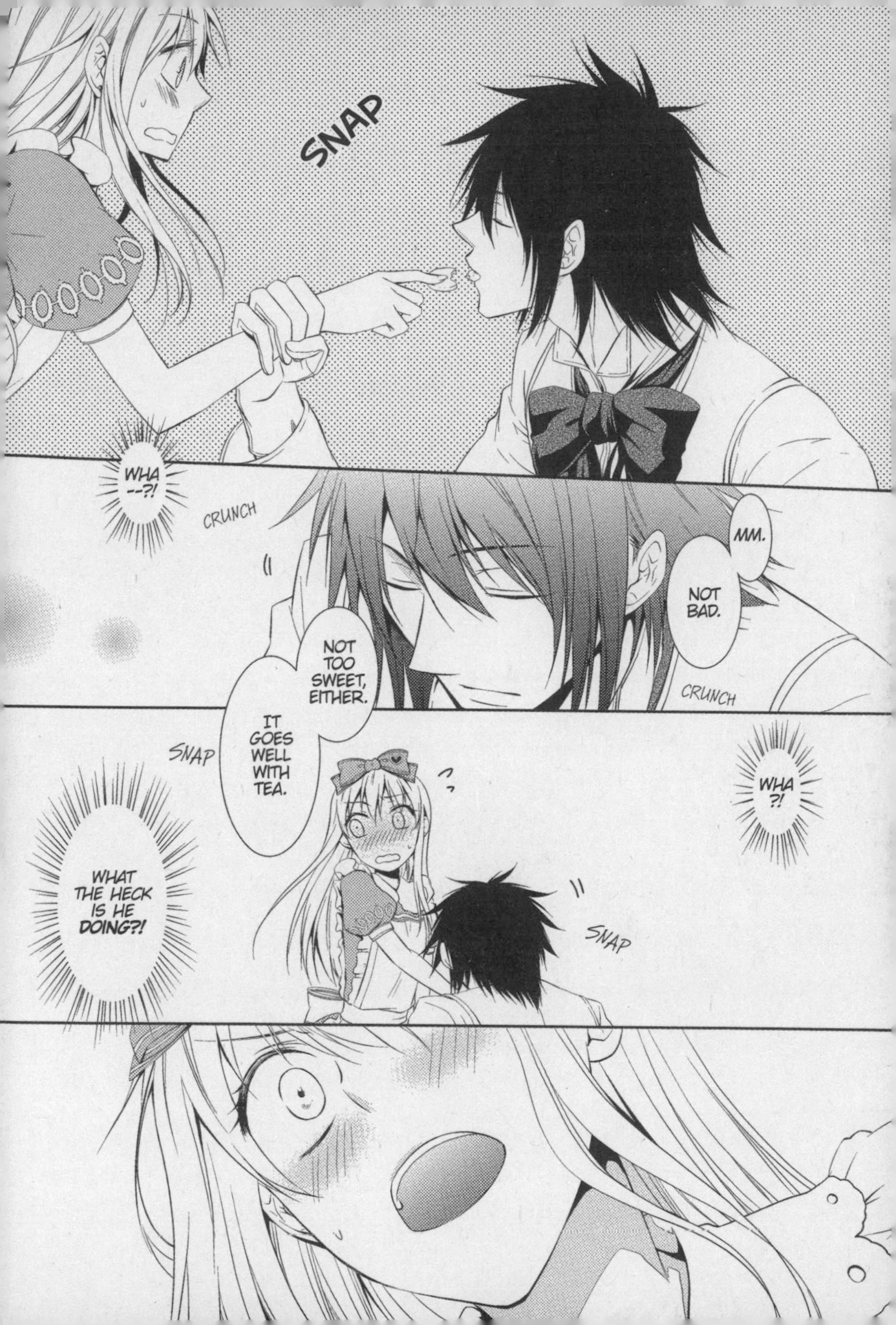
SNAP
MM.
NOT BAD.
NOT TOO SWEET, EITHER.
CRUNCH
CRUNCH
WHA--?!
WHA?!
IT GOES WELL WITH TEA.
SNAP
SNAP
WHAT THE HECK IS HE DOING?!

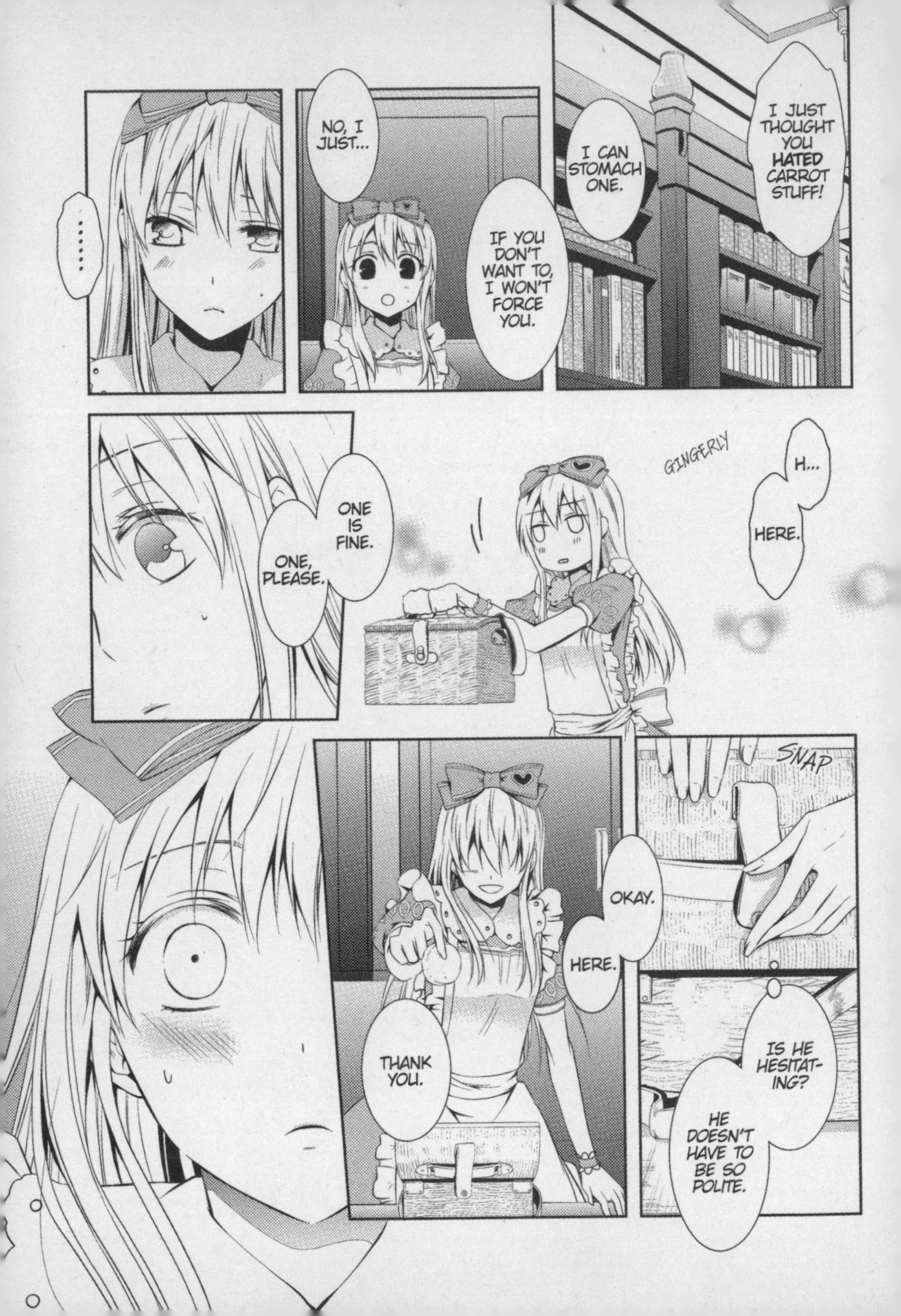
I JUST THOUGHT YOU HATED CARROT STUFF!
I CAN STOMACH ONE.
IF YOU DON'T WANT TO, I WON'T FORCE YOU.
NO, I JUST...
......
GINGERLY
H...
HERE.
ONE IS FINE.
ONE, PLEASE.
SNAP
IS HE HESITATING?
HE DOESN'T HAVE TO BE SO POLITE.
OKAY.
HERE.
THANK YOU.

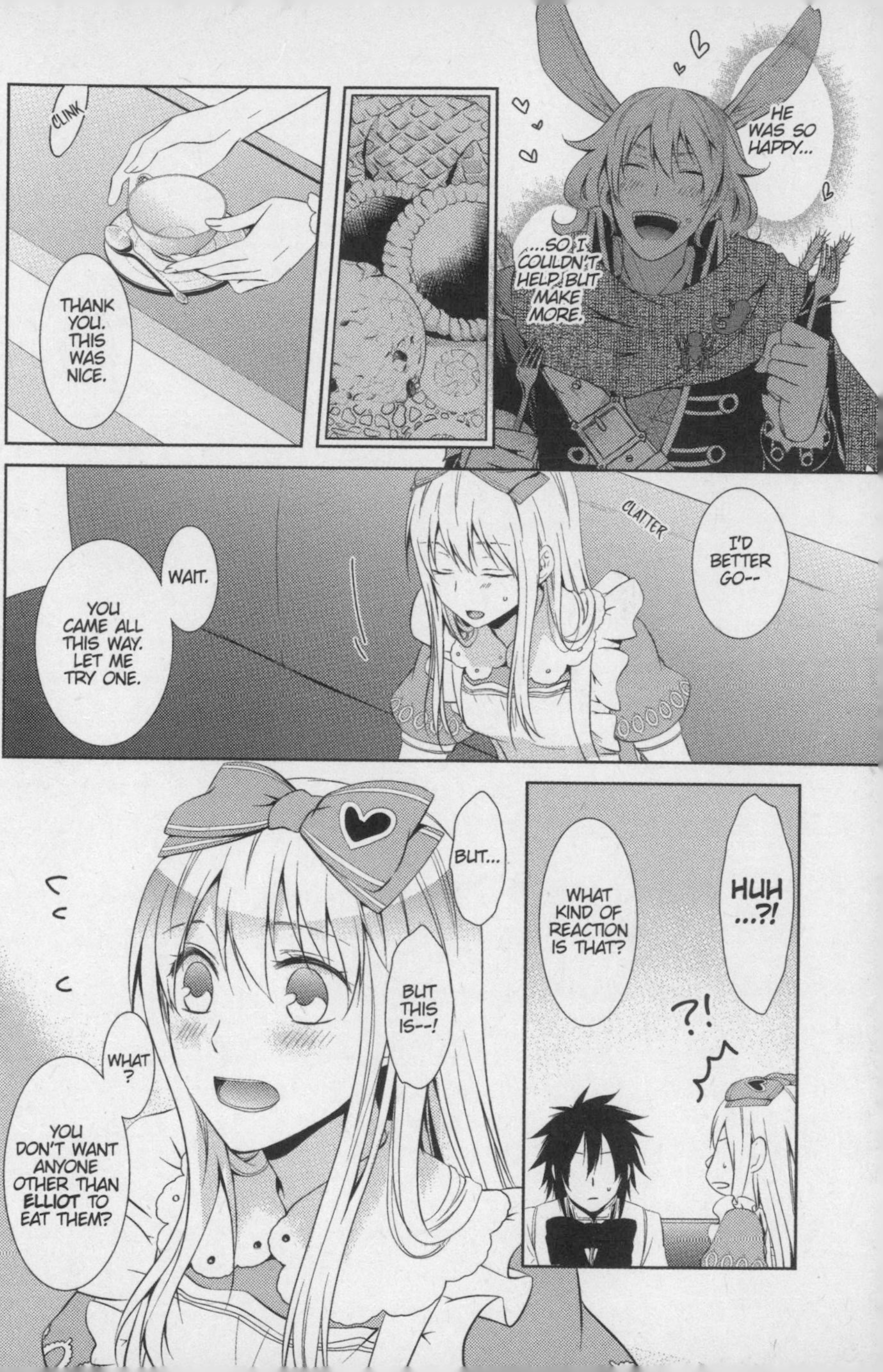
HE WAS SO HAPPY...
...SO I COULDN'T HELP BUT MAKE MORE.
CLINK
THANK YOU. THIS WAS NICE.
I'D BETTER GO--
CLATTER
WAIT.
YOU CAME ALL THIS WAY. LET ME TRY ONE.
HUH ...?!
WHAT KIND OF REACTION IS THAT?
?!
BUT...
BUT THIS IS--!
WHAT?
YOU DON'T WANT ANYONE OTHER THAN ELLIOT TO EAT THEM?

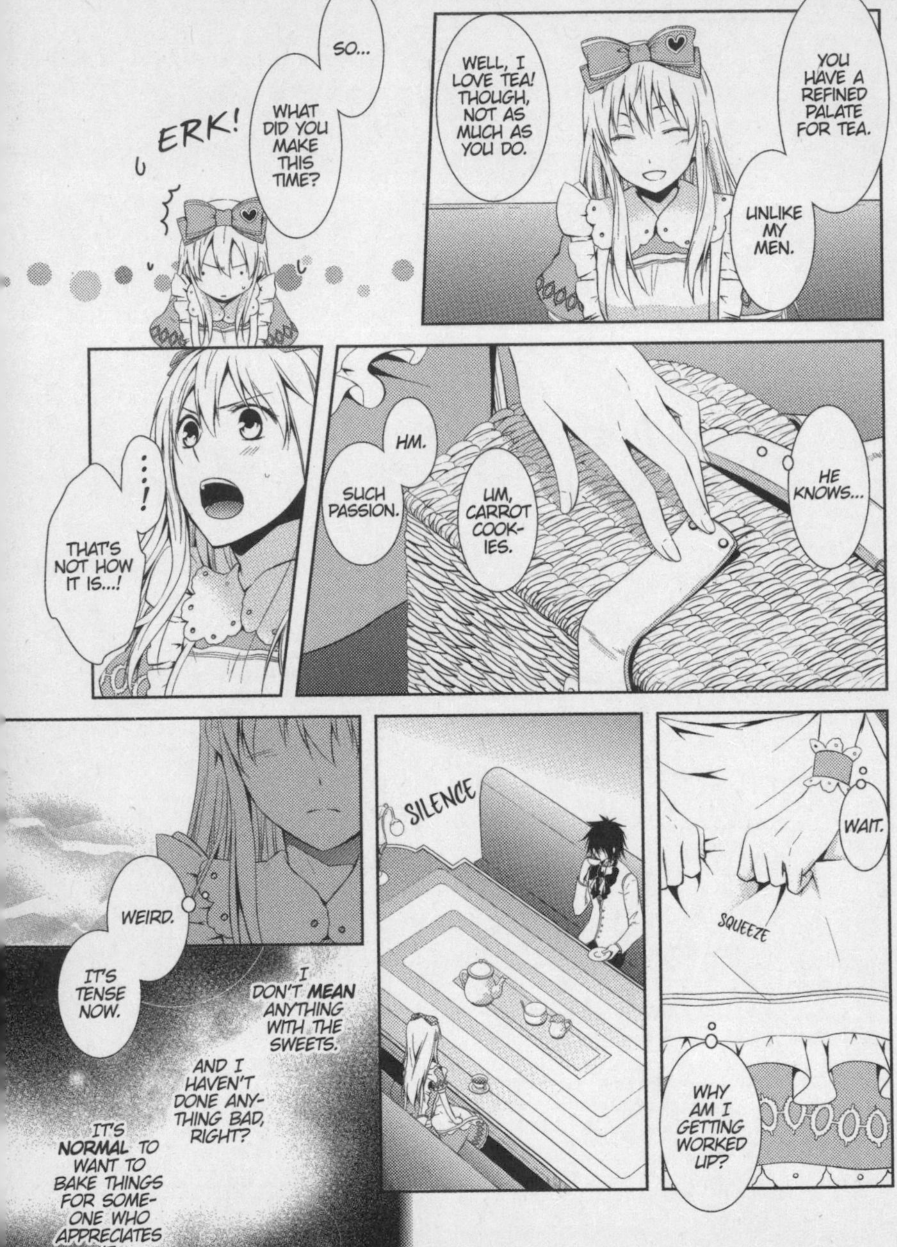
YOU HAVE A REFINED PALATE FOR TEA.
UNLIKE MY MEN.
WELL, I LOVE TEA! THOUGH, NOT AS MUCH AS YOU DO.
SO...
WHAT DID YOU MAKE THIS TIME?
ERK!
HE KNOWS...
UM, CARROT COOK-IES.
HM.
SUCH PASSION.
...!
THAT'S NOT HOW IT IS...!
WAIT.
SQUEEZE
WHY AM I GETTING WORKED UP?
SILENCE
WEIRD.
IT'S TENSE NOW.
I DON'T MEAN ANYTHING WITH THE SWEETS.
AND I HAVEN'T DONE ANY-THING BAD, RIGHT?
IT'S NORMAL TO WANT TO BAKE THINGS FOR SOME-ONE WHO APPRECIATES IT.

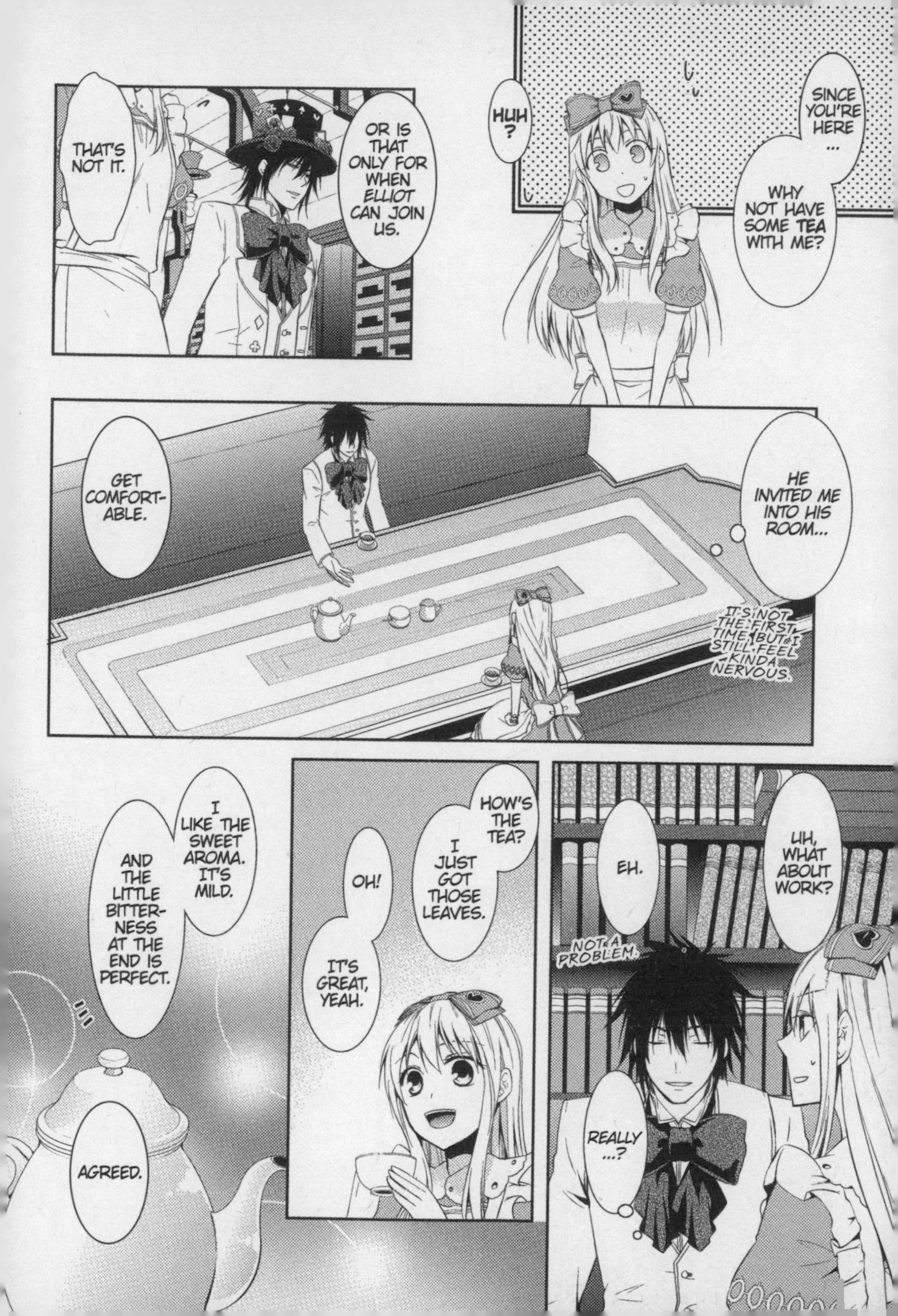
SINCE YOU'RE HERE ...
WHY NOT HAVE SOME TEA WITH ME?
HUH?
OR IS THAT ONLY FOR WHEN ELLIOT CAN JOIN US.
THAT'S NOT IT.
HE INVITED ME INTO HIS ROOM...
IT'S NOT THE FIRST TIME, BUT I STILL FEEL KINDA NERVOUS.
GET COMFORTABLE.
UH, WHAT ABOUT WORK?
EH.
NOT A PROBLEM.
REALLY ...?
HOW'S THE TEA?
I JUST GOT THOSE LEAVES.
OH!
IT'S GREAT, YEAH.
I LIKE THE SWEET AROMA. IT'S MILD.
AND THE LITTLE BITTERNESS AT THE END IS PERFECT.
AGREED.

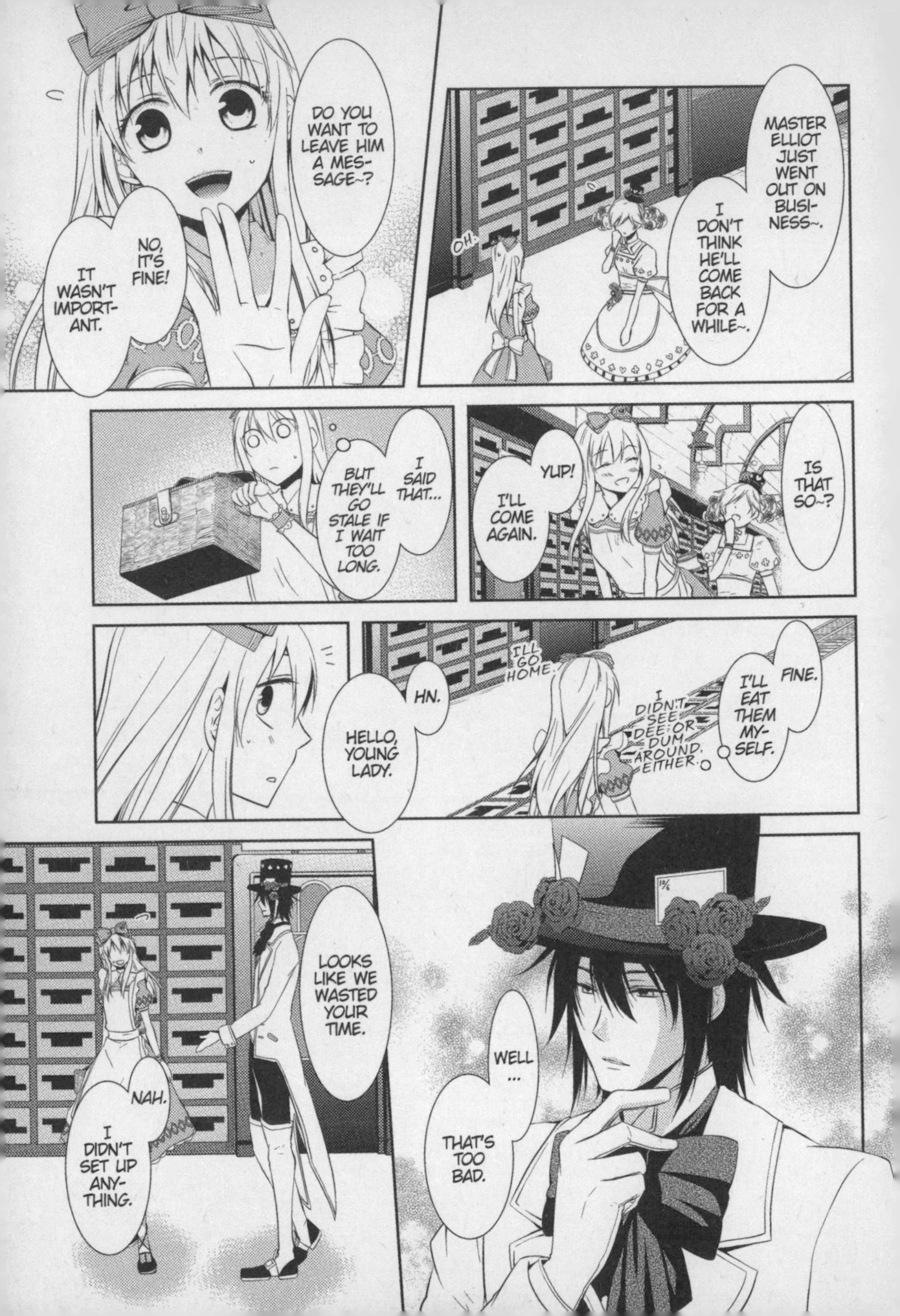
MASTER ELLIOT JUST WENT OUT ON BUSINESS~.
I DON'T THINK HE'LL COME BACK FOR A WHILE~.
OH.
DO YOU WANT TO LEAVE HIM A MESSAGE~?
NO, IT'S FINE!
IT WASN'T IMPORTANT.
IS THAT SO~?
YUP!
I'LL COME AGAIN.
I SAID THAT...
BUT THEY'LL GO STALE IF I WAIT TOO LONG.
FINE.
I'LL EAT THEM MYSELF.
I'LL GO HOME...
I DIDN'T SEE DEE OR DUM AROUND, EITHER.
HN.
HELLO, YOUNG LADY.
WELL...
THAT'S TOO BAD.
LOOKS LIKE WE WASTED YOUR TIME.
NAH.
I DIDN'T SET UP ANYTHING.

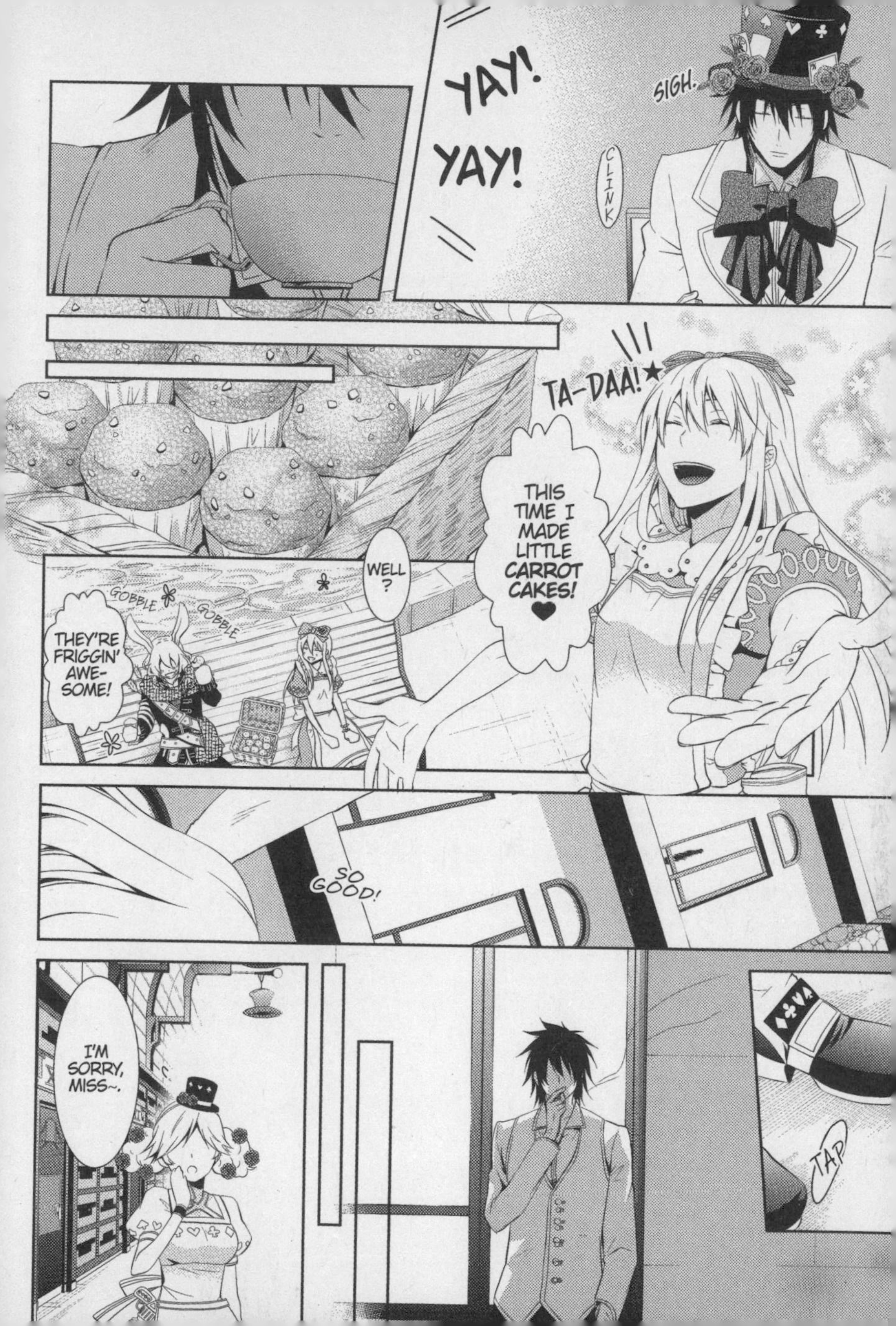
SIGH.
CLINK
YAY!
YAY!
TA-DAA!★
THIS TIME I MADE LITTLE CARROT CAKES! ♥
WELL?
GOBBLE
GOBBLE
THEY'RE FRIGGIN' AWESOME!
SO GOOD!
TAP
I'M SORRY, MISS~.

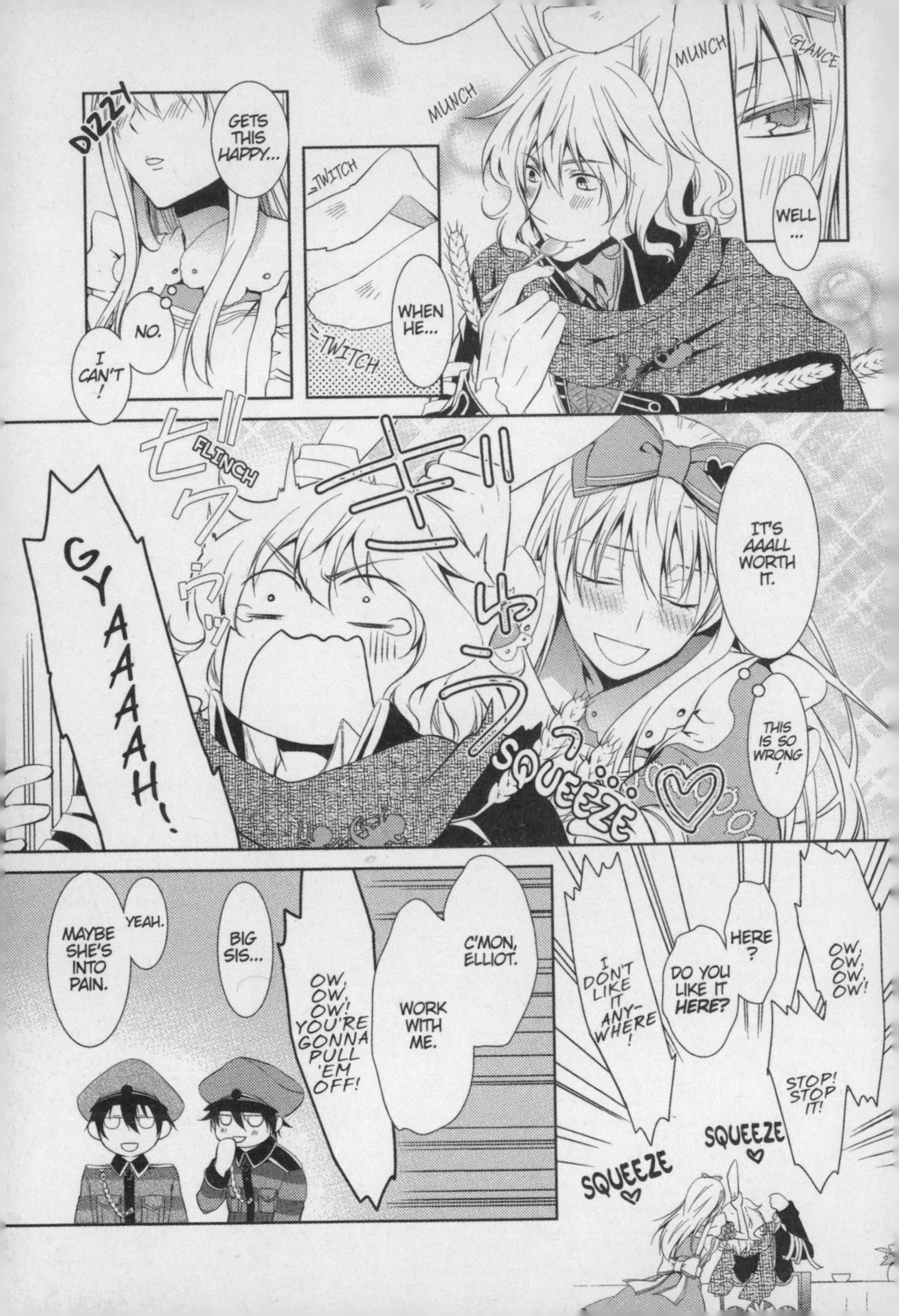
GLANCE
WELL ...
MUNCH
MUNCH
TWITCH
WHEN HE...
TWITCH
GETS THIS HAPPY...
DIZZY
NO.
I CAN'T!
IT'S AAALL WORTH IT.
THIS IS SO WRONG!
SQUEEZE
FLINCH
GYAAAAH!
OW, OW, OW, OW!
HERE?
DO YOU LIKE IT HERE?
I DON'T LIKE IT ANYWHERE!
STOP! STOP IT!
SQUEEZE
SQUEEZE
C'MON, ELLIOT.
WORK WITH ME.
OW, OW, OW! YOU'RE GONNA PULL 'EM OFF!
BIG SIS...
YEAH.
MAYBE SHE'S INTO PAIN.

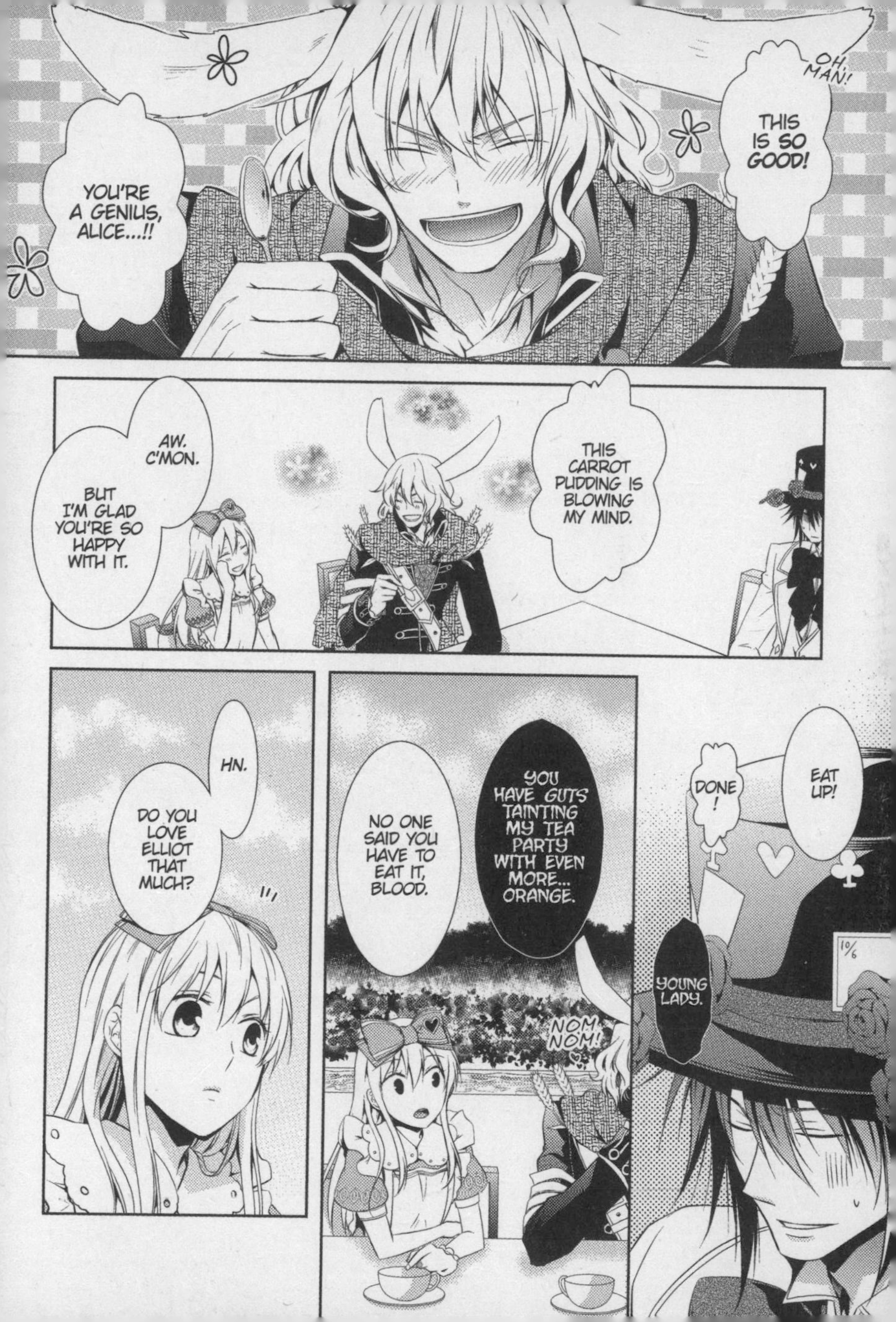
OH MAN!
THIS IS SO GOOD!
YOU'RE A GENIUS, ALICE...!!
THIS CARROT PUDDING IS BLOWING MY MIND.
AW. C'MON.
BUT I'M GLAD YOU'RE SO HAPPY WITH IT.
EAT UP!
DONE!
10/6
YOUNG LADY.
YOU HAVE GUTS TAINTING MY TEA PARTY WITH EVEN MORE... ORANGE.
NO ONE SAID YOU HAVE TO EAT IT, BLOOD.
NOM NOM!
HN.
DO YOU LOVE ELLIOT THAT MUCH?
!!

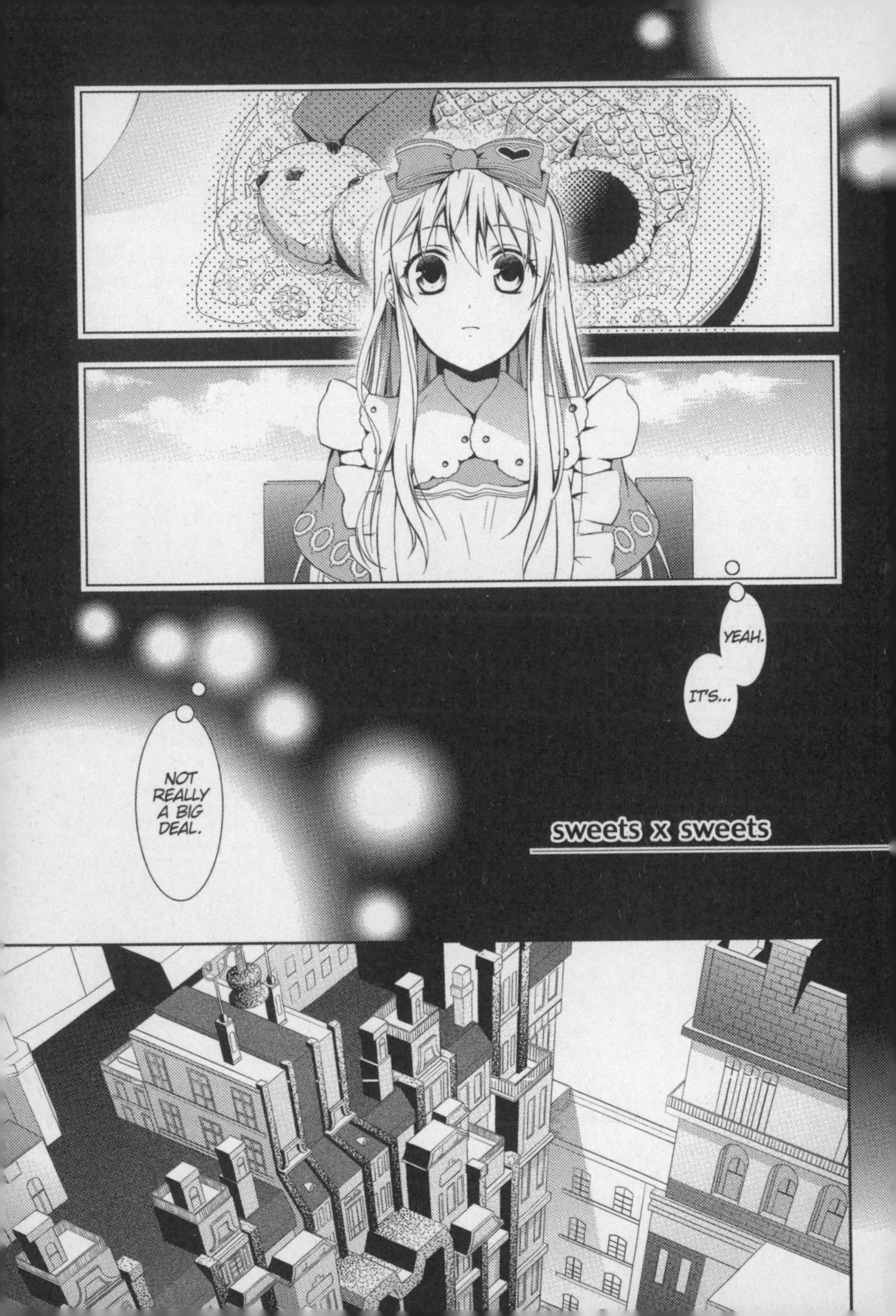
YEAH.
IT'S...
NOT REALLY A BIG DEAL.
sweets x sweets

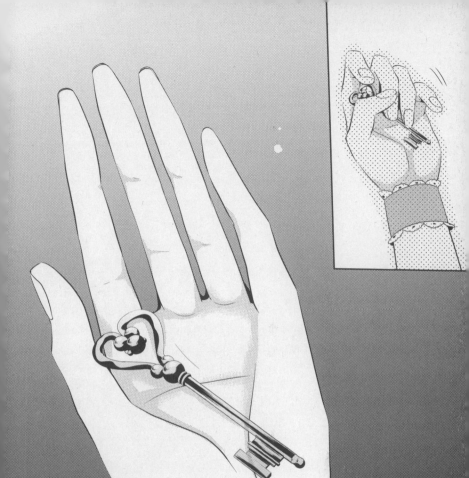

TO BE CONTINUED...

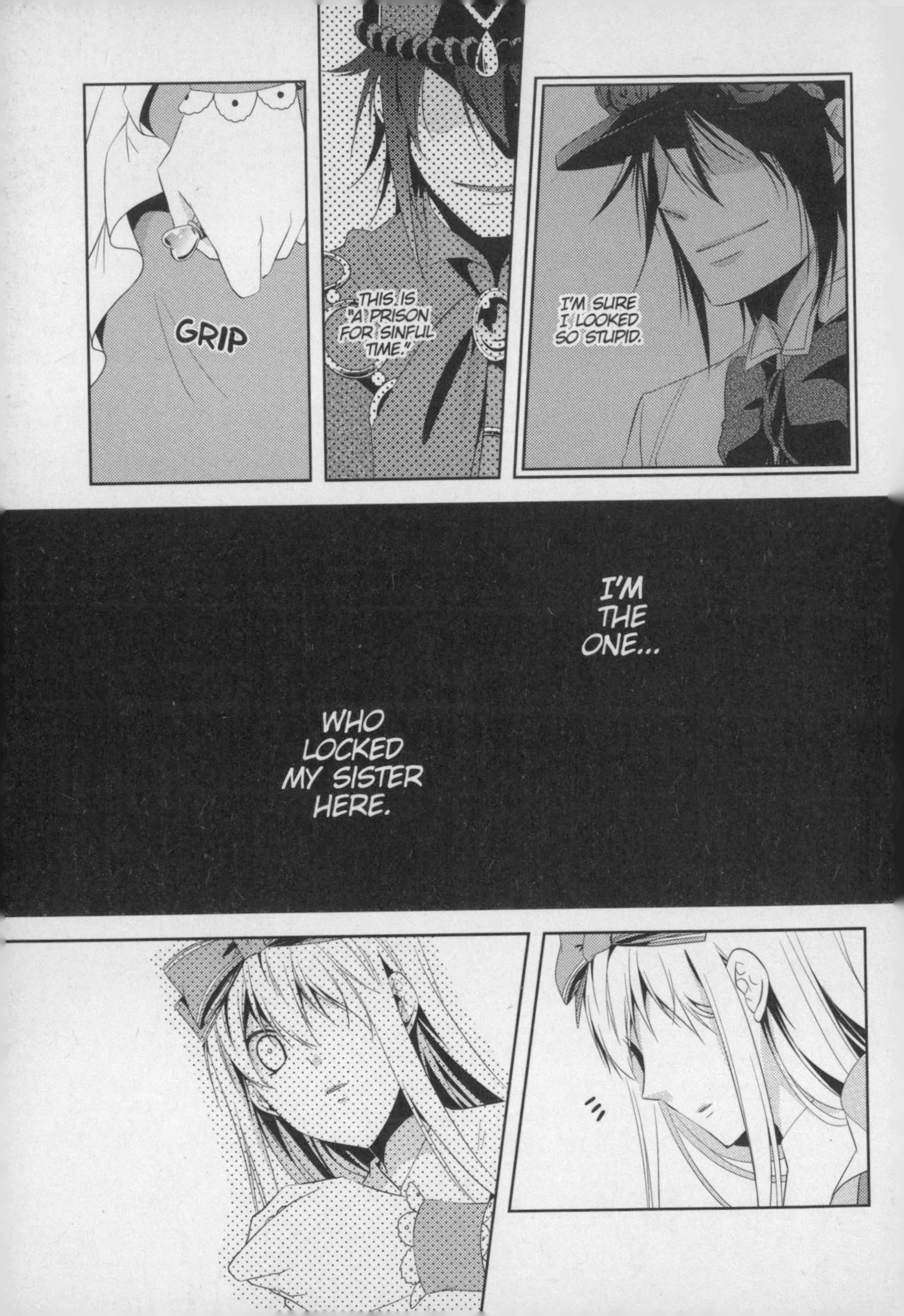
I'M SURE I LOOKED SO STUPID.
THIS IS "A PRISON FOR SINFUL TIME."
GRIP
I'M THE ONE...
WHO LOCKED MY SISTER HERE.

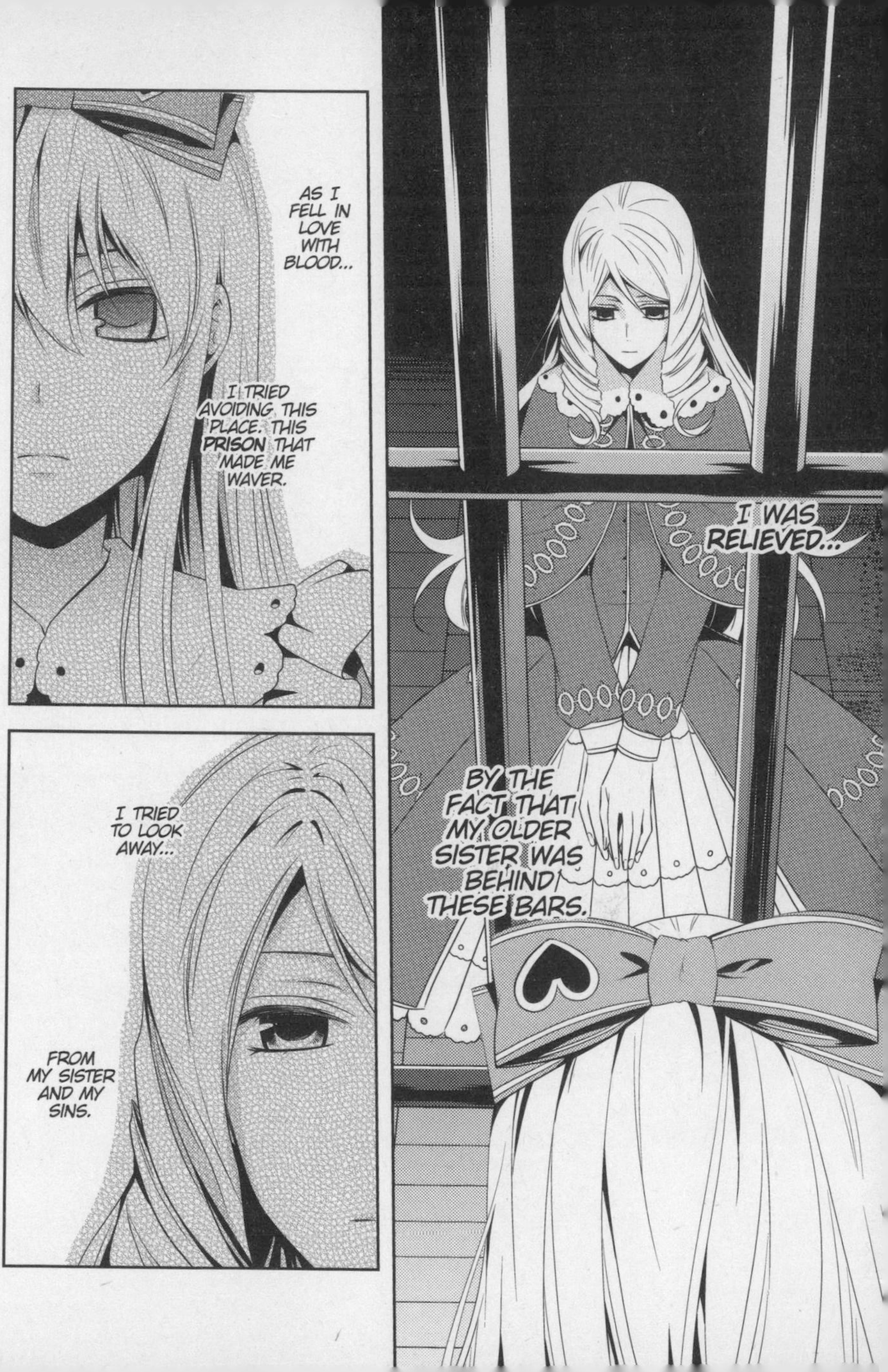
AS I FELL IN LOVE WITH BLOOD...
I TRIED AVOIDING THIS PLACE. THIS PRISON THAT MADE ME WAVER.
I WAS RELIEVED...
BY THE FACT THAT MY OLDER SISTER WAS BEHIND THESE BARS.
I TRIED TO LOOK AWAY...
FROM MY SISTER AND MY SINS.

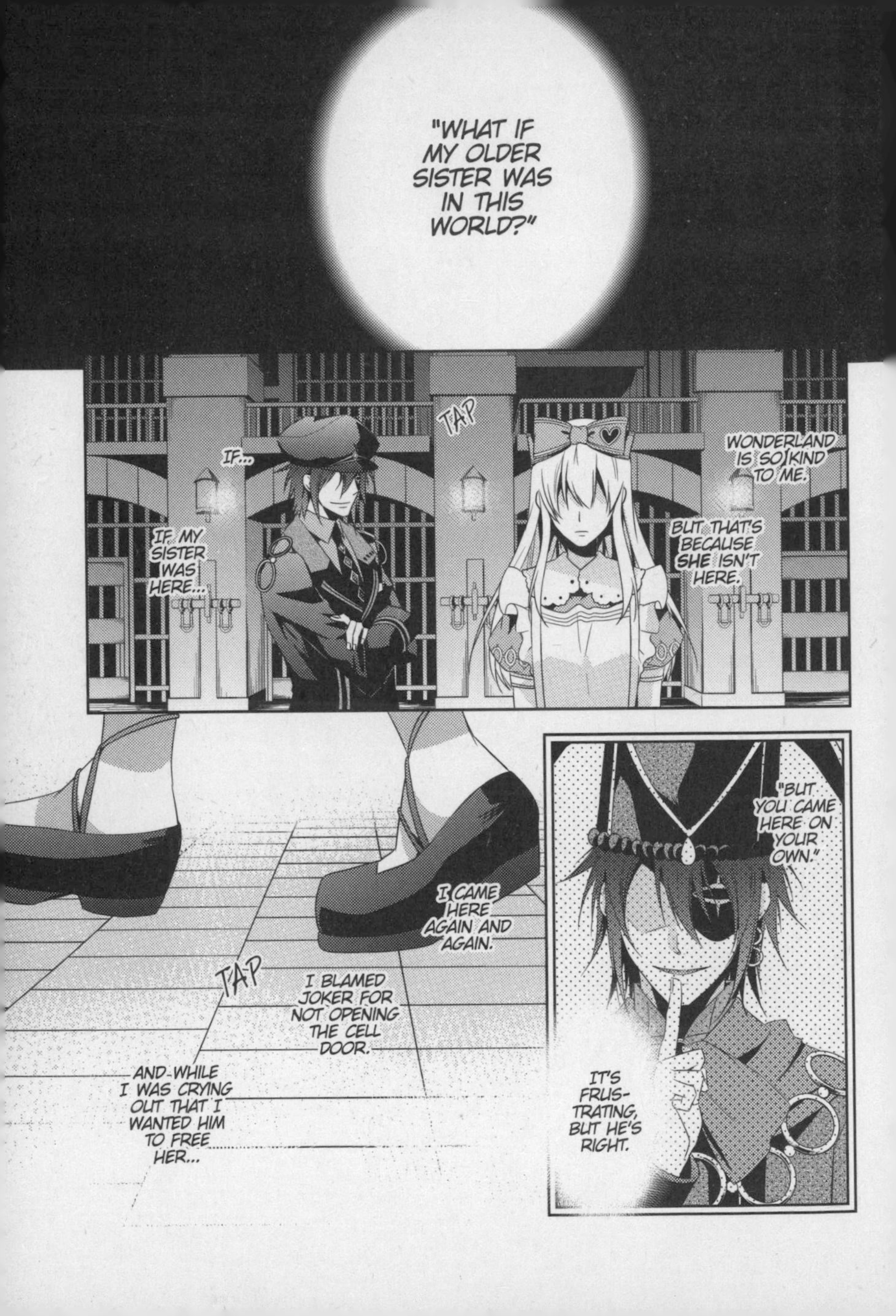
"WHAT IF MY OLDER SISTER WAS IN THIS WORLD?"
WONDERLAND IS SO KIND TO ME.
BUT THAT'S BECAUSE SHE ISN'T HERE.
TAP
IF...
IF MY SISTER WAS HERE...
"BUT YOU CAME HERE ON YOUR OWN."
IT'S FRUS-TRATING, BUT HE'S RIGHT.
I CAME HERE AGAIN AND AGAIN.
TAP
I BLAMED JOKER FOR NOT OPENING THE CELL DOOR.
AND WHILE I WAS CRYING OUT THAT I WANTED HIM TO FREE HER...

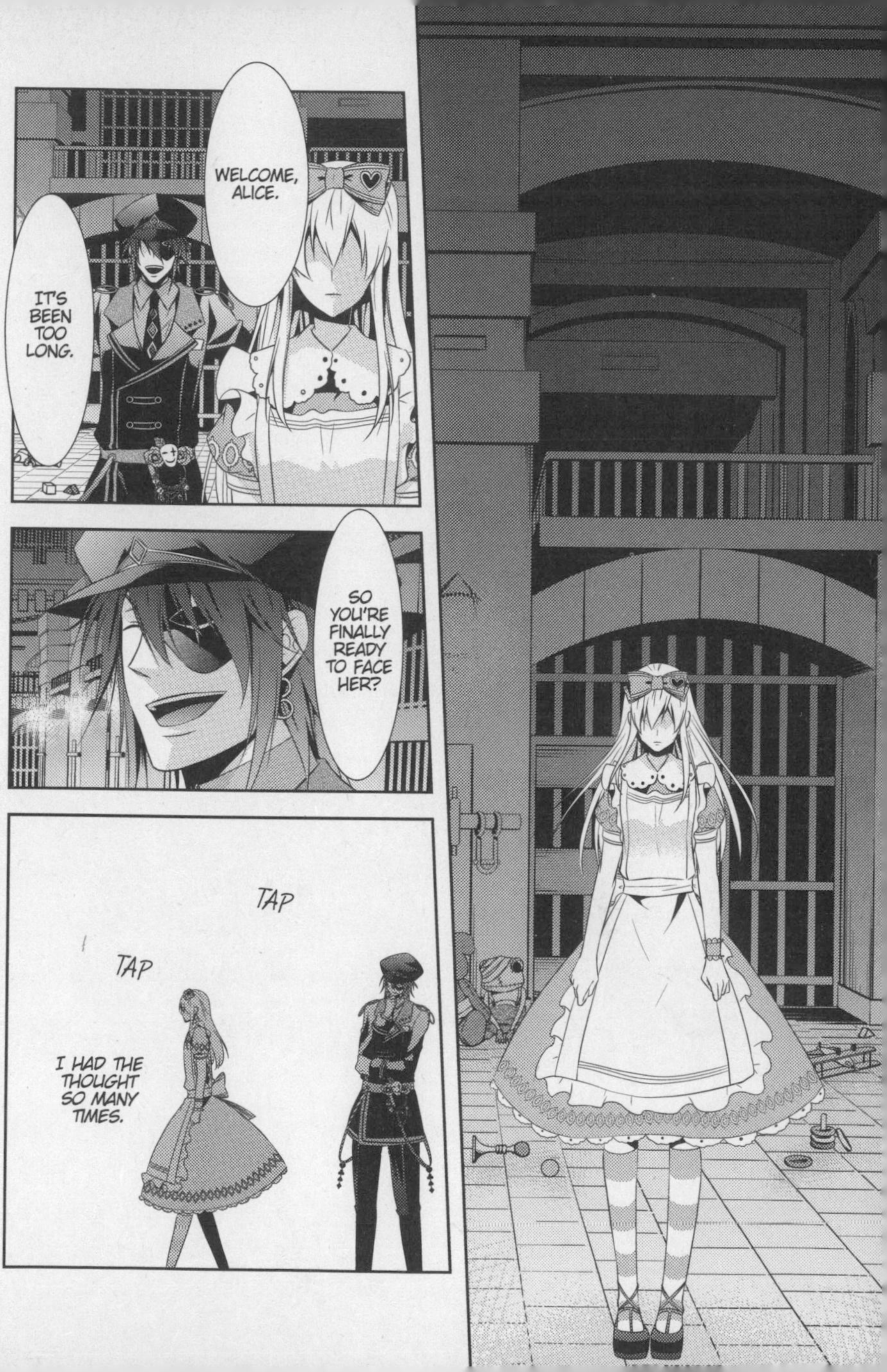
WELCOME, ALICE.
IT'S BEEN TOO LONG.
SO YOU'RE FINALLY READY TO FACE HER?
TAP
TAP
I HAD THE THOUGHT SO MANY TIMES.

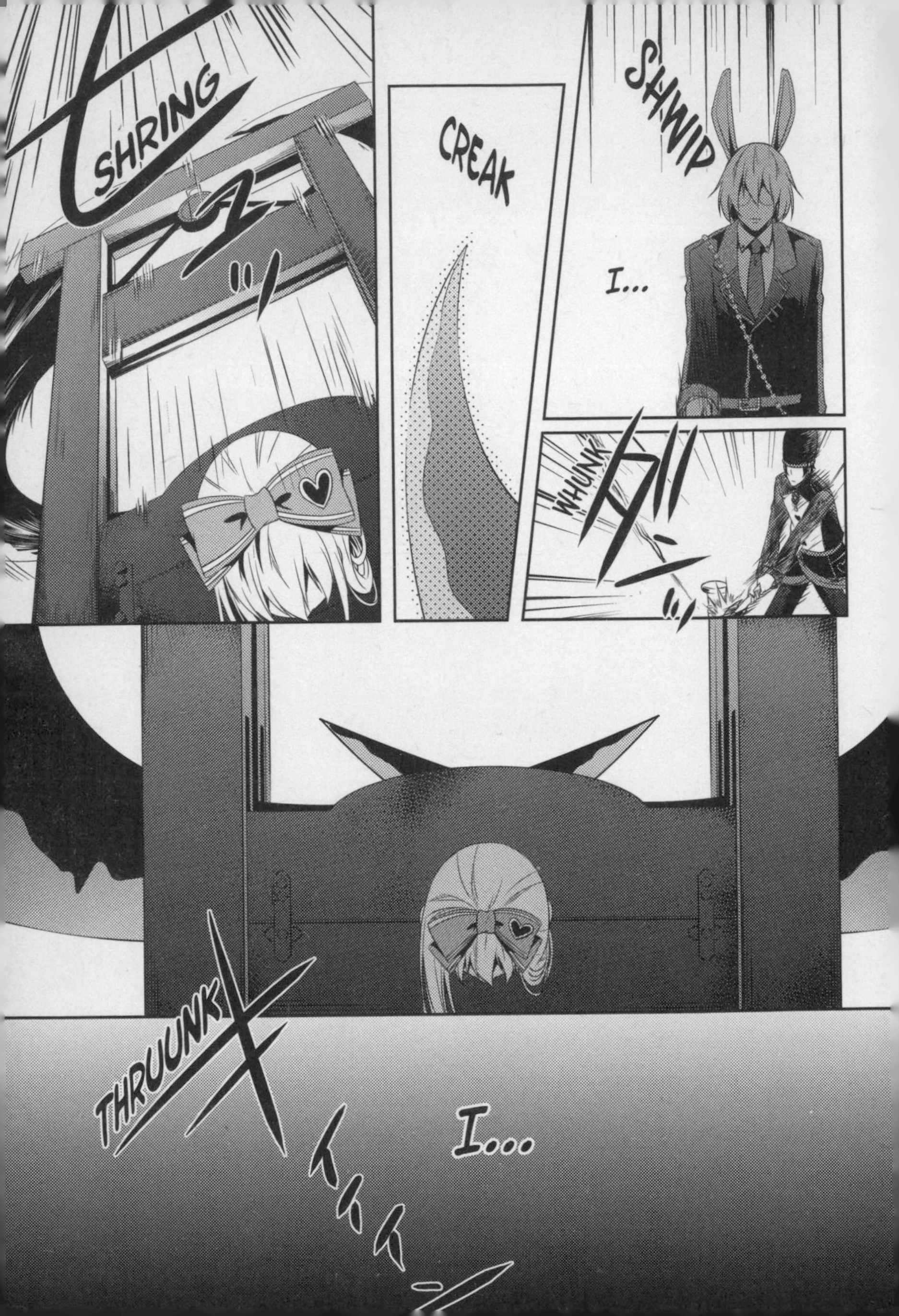
SHWIP
I...
WHUNK
CREAK
SHRING
THRUUNK
I...

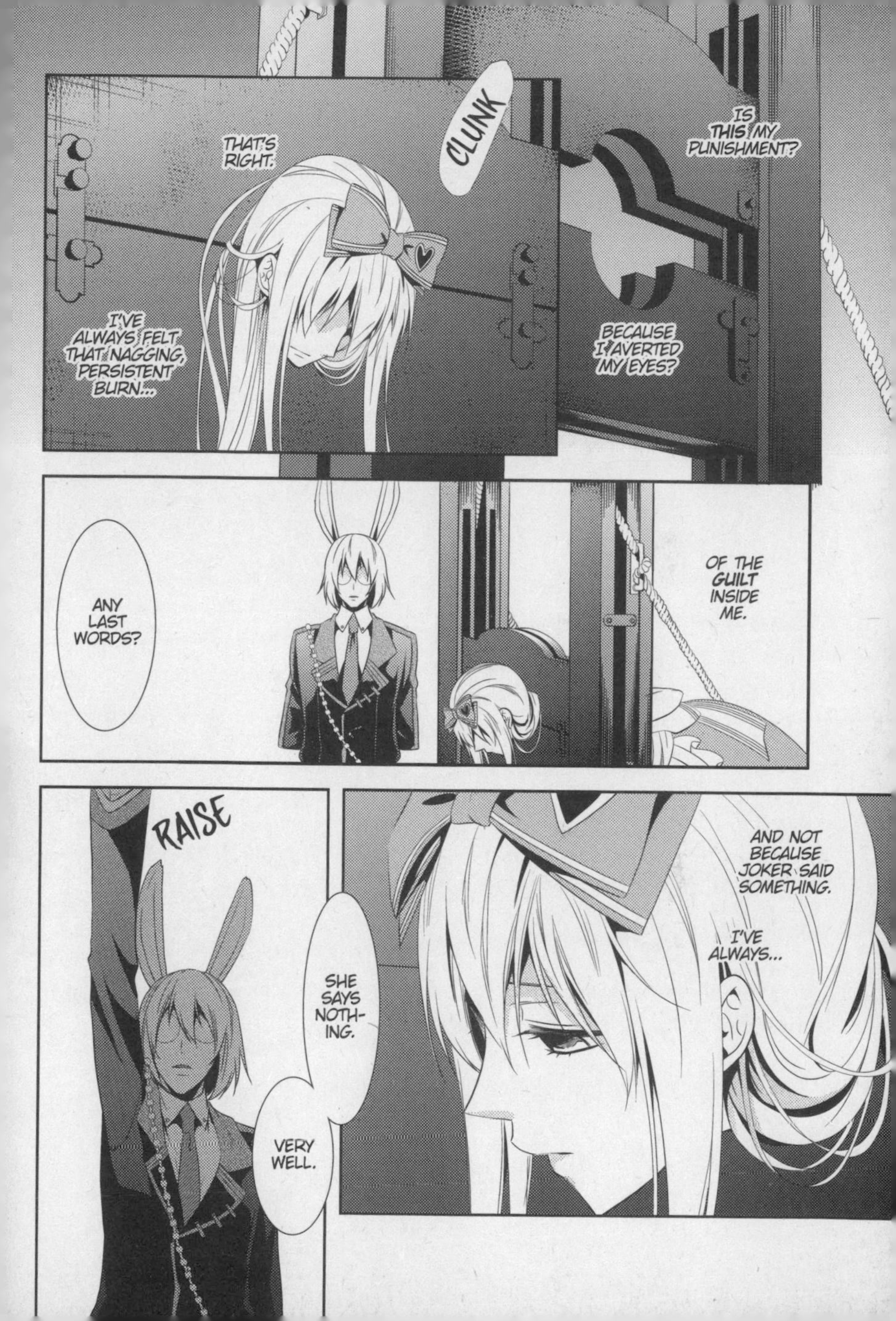
IS THIS MY PUNISHMENT?
BECAUSE I AVERTED MY EYES?
CLUNK
THAT'S RIGHT.
I'VE ALWAYS FELT THAT NAGGING, PERSISTENT BURN...
OF THE GUILT INSIDE ME.
ANY LAST WORDS?
AND NOT BECAUSE JOKER SAID SOMETHING.
I'VE ALWAYS...
RAISE
SHE SAYS NOTHING.
VERY WELL.

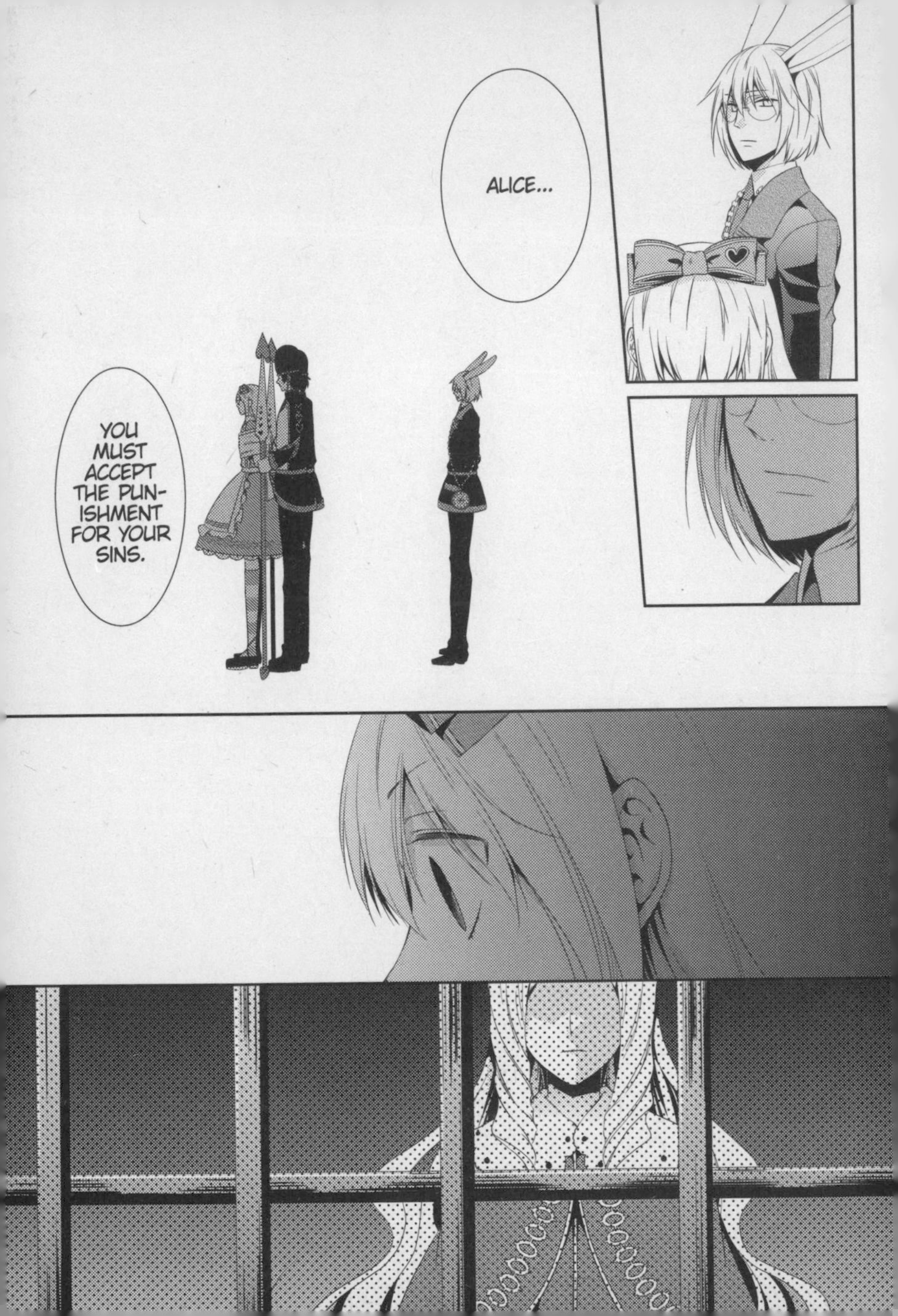
ALICE...
YOU MUST ACCEPT THE PUN-ISHMENT FOR YOUR SINS.

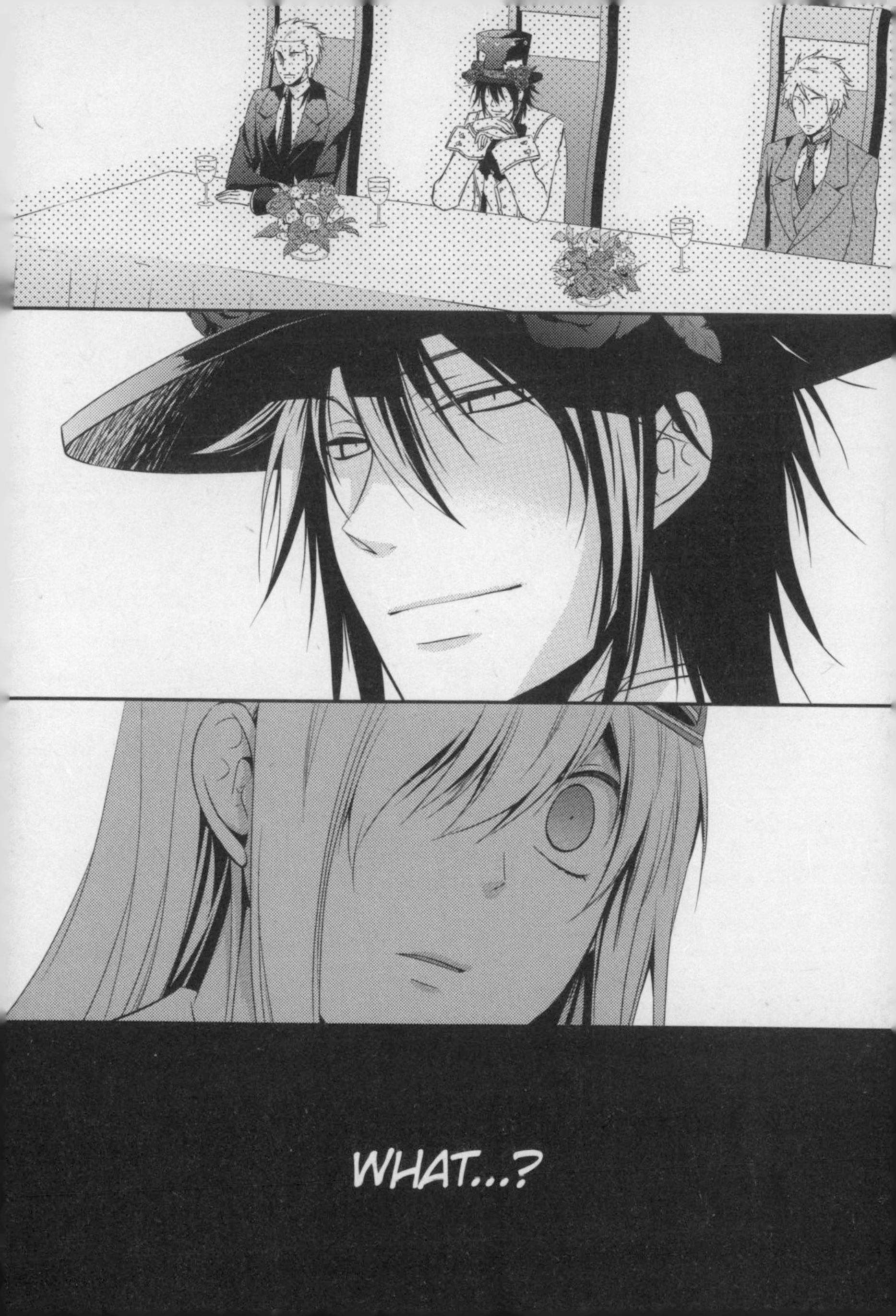
WHAT...?

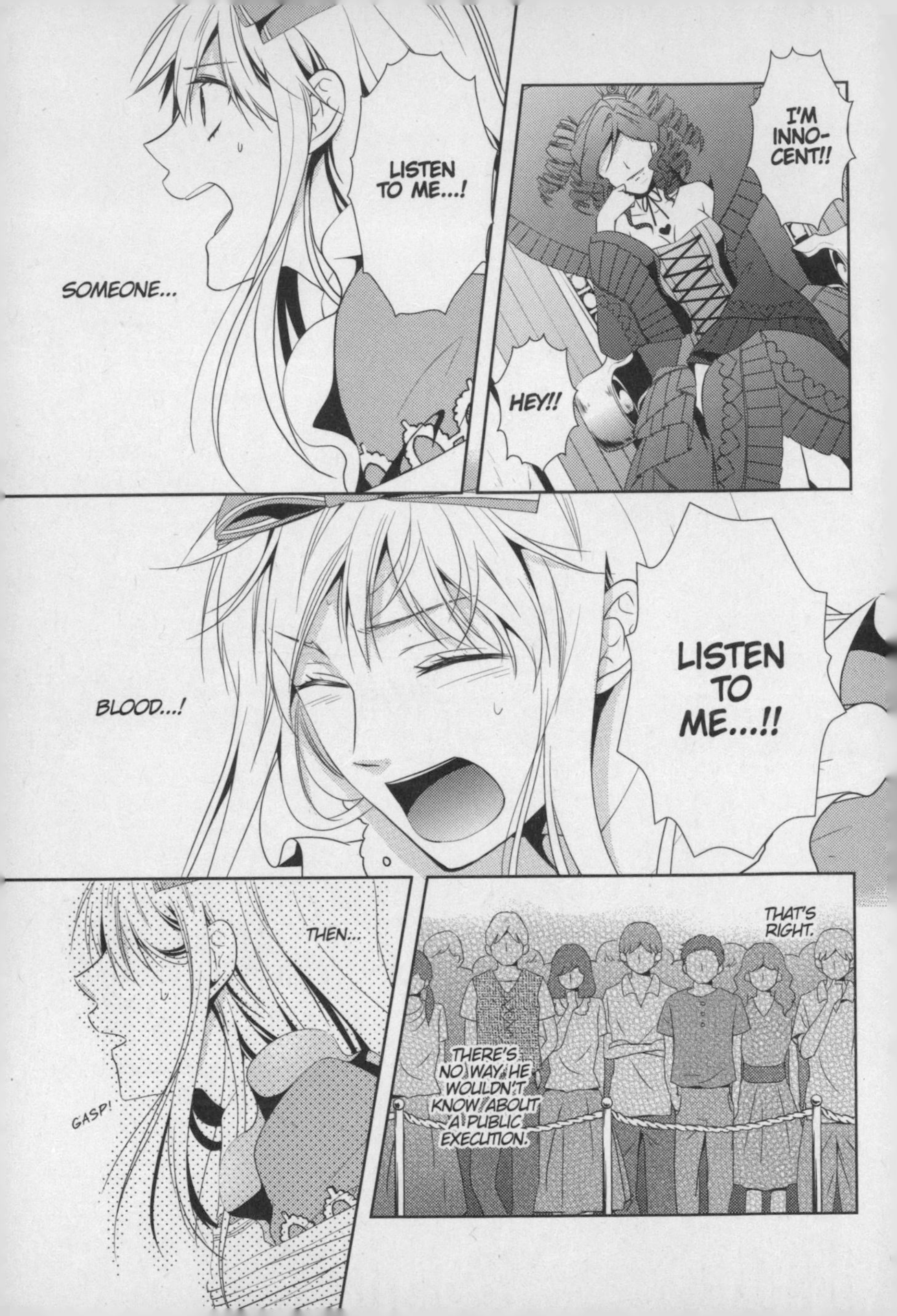
I'M INNO-CENT!!
HEY!!
LISTEN TO ME...!
SOMEONE...
LISTEN TO ME...!!
BLOOD...!
THAT'S RIGHT.
THERE'S NO WAY HE WOULDN'T KNOW ABOUT A PUBLIC EXECUTION.
THEN...
GASP!

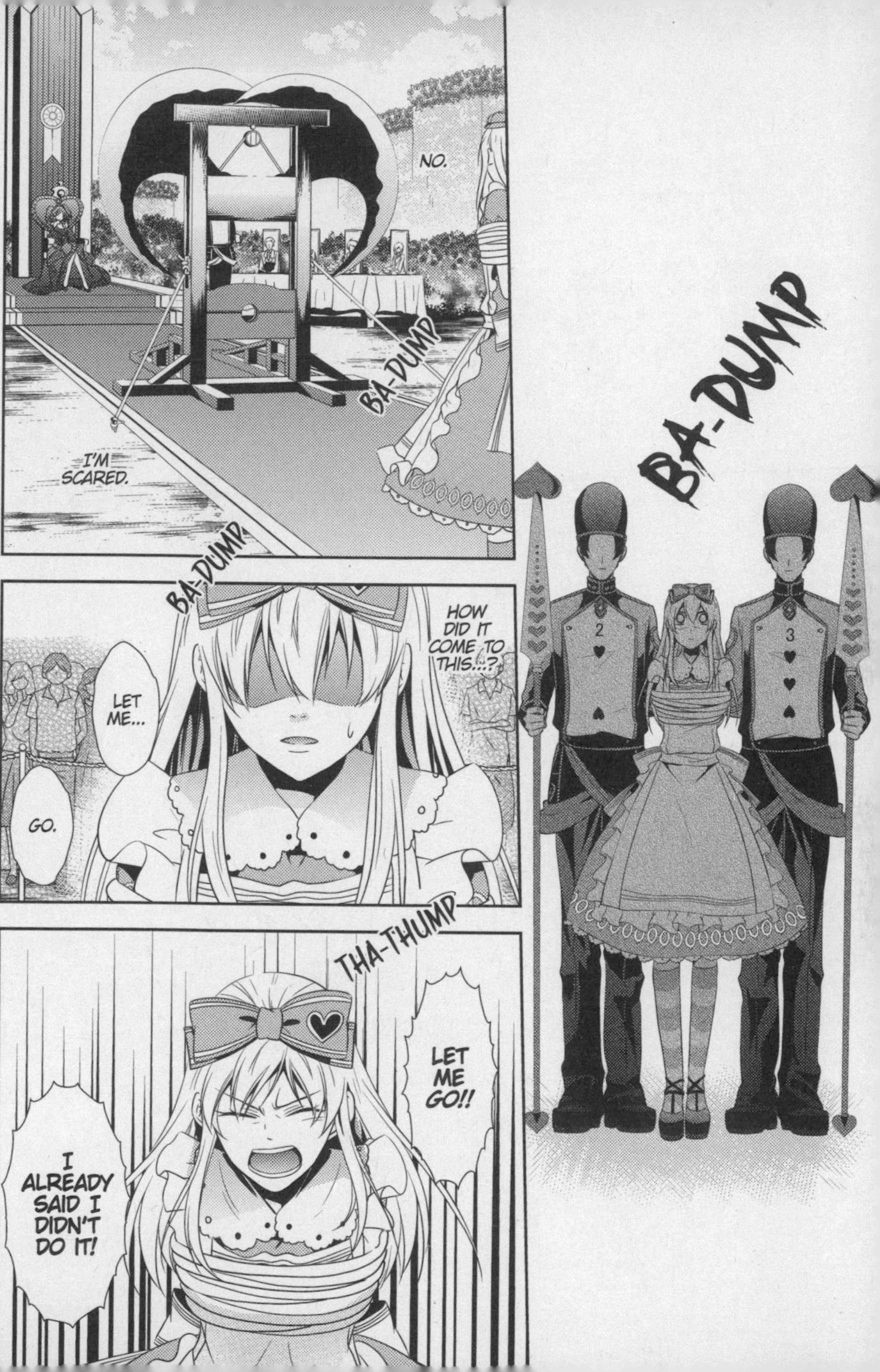
BA-DUMP
NO.
I'M SCARED.
BA-DUMP
BA-DUMP
HOW DID IT COME TO THIS...?
LET ME...
GO.
THA-THUMP
LET ME GO!!
I ALREADY SAID I DIDN'T DO IT!

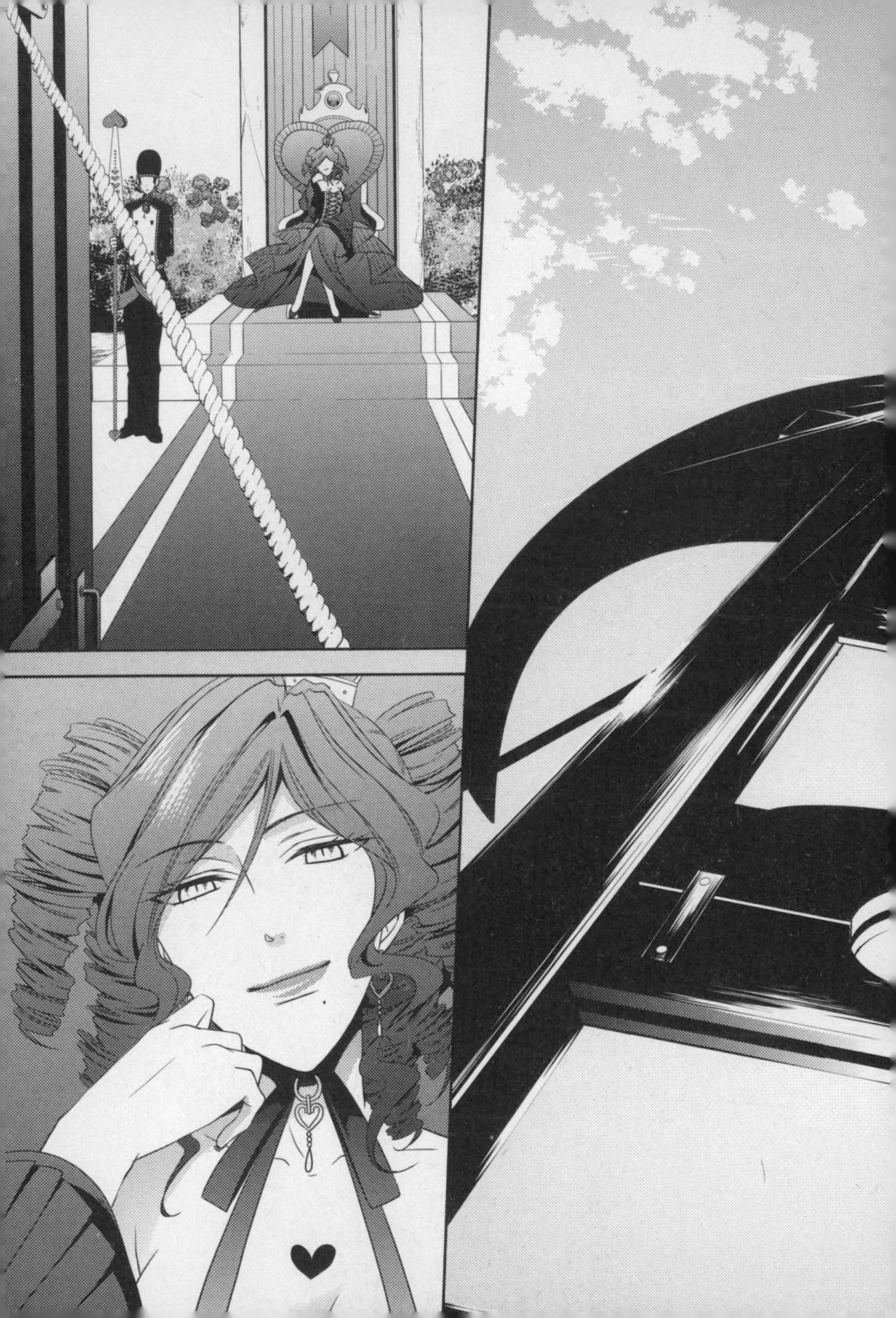

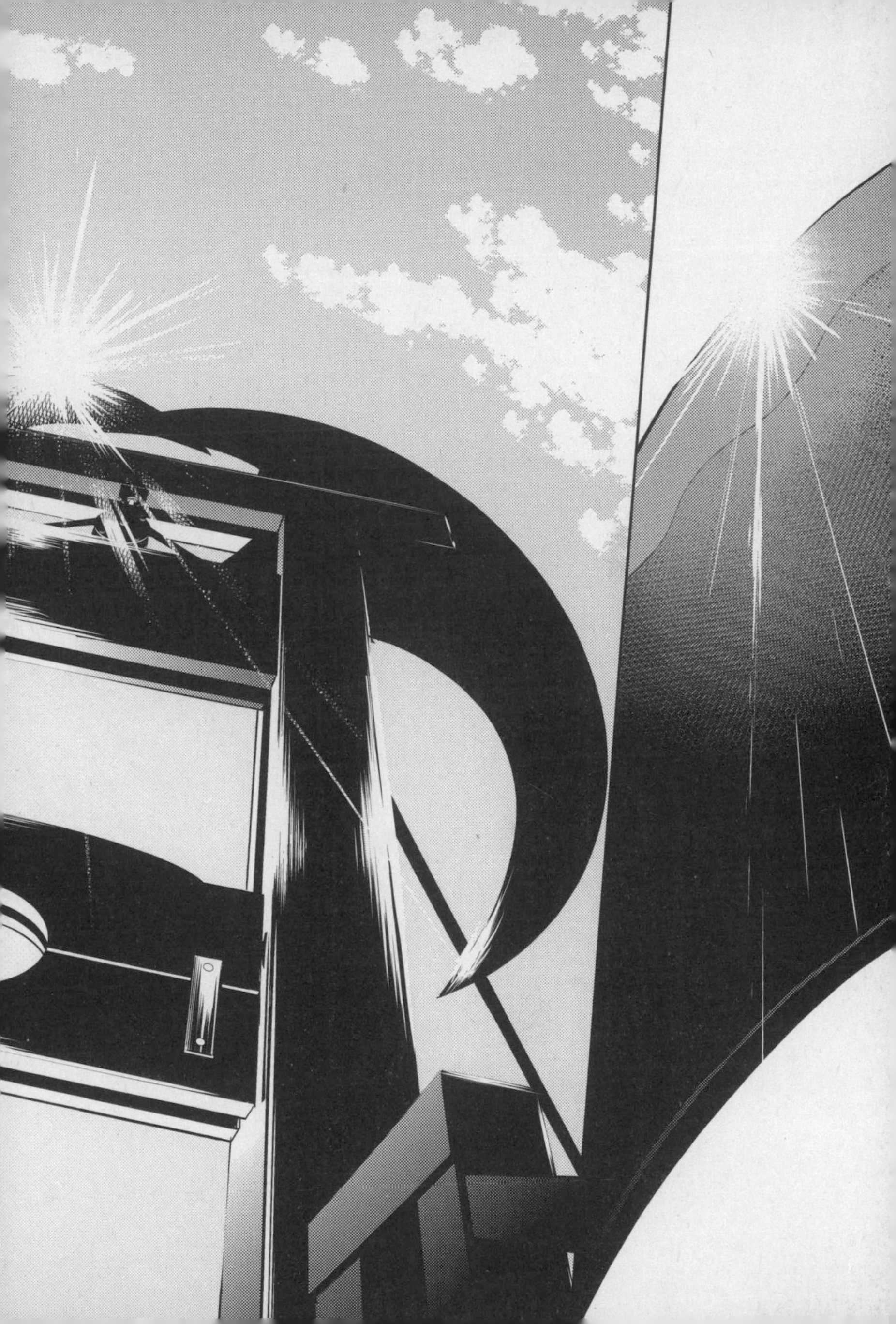

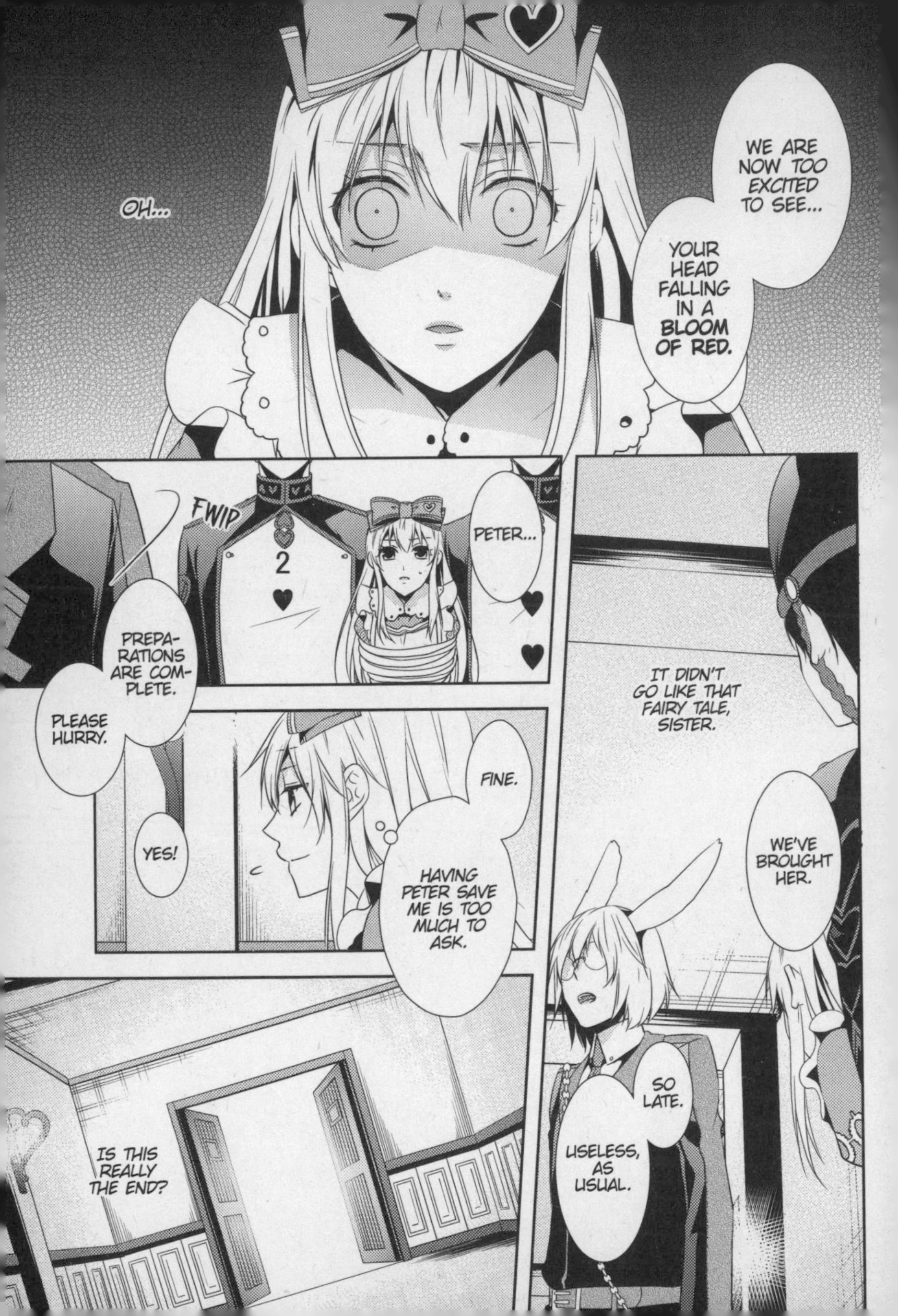
WE ARE NOW TOO EXCITED TO SEE...
YOUR HEAD FALLING IN A BLOOM OF RED.
OH...
IT DIDN'T GO LIKE THAT FAIRY TALE, SISTER.
WE'VE BROUGHT HER.
SO LATE.
USELESS, AS USUAL.
PETER...
FWIP
2
PREPARATIONS ARE COMPLETE.
PLEASE HURRY.
FINE.
HAVING PETER SAVE ME IS TOO MUCH TO ASK.
YES!
IS THIS REALLY THE END?

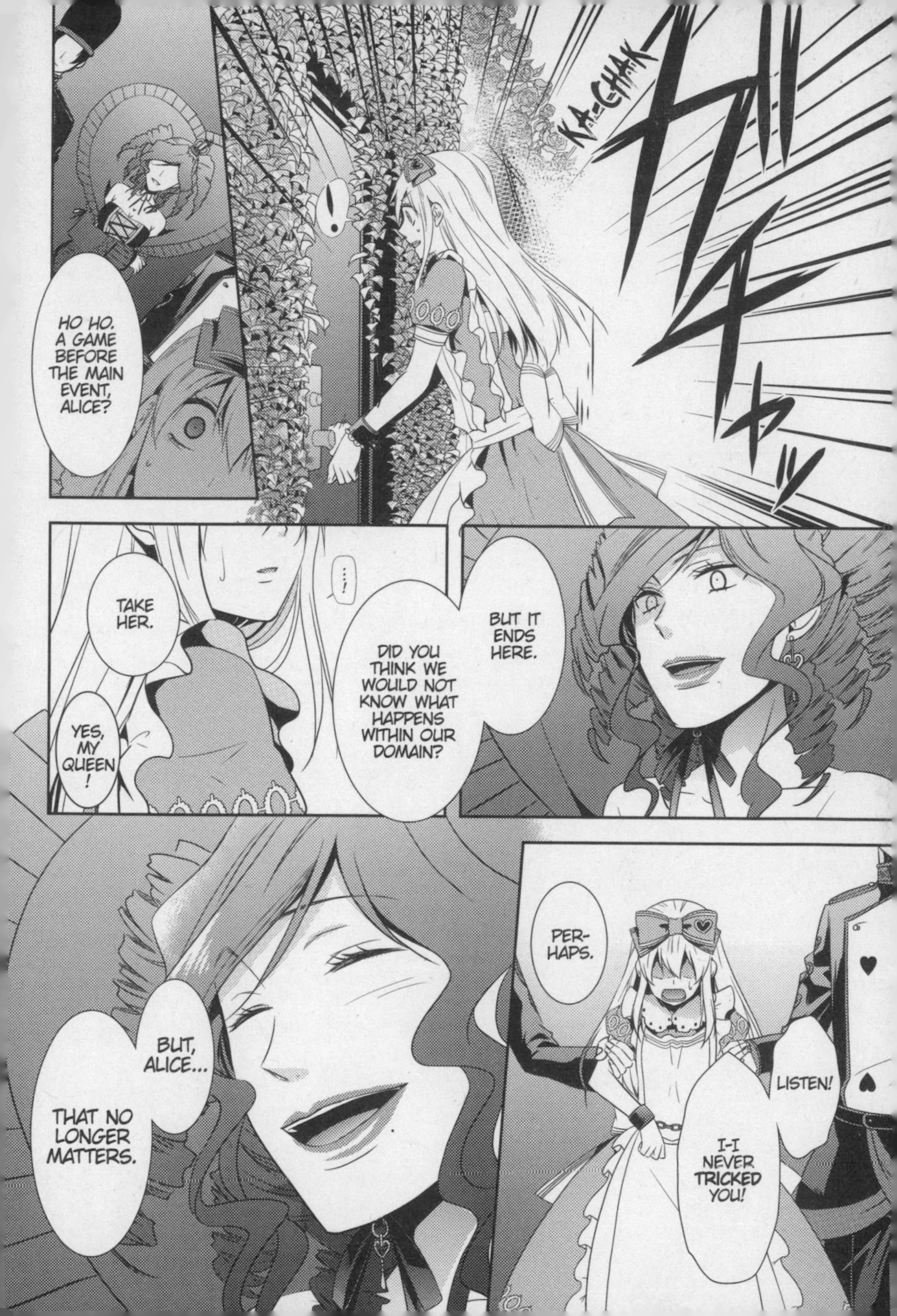

KA-CHAK
ガチャッ
!
HO HO. A GAME BEFORE THE MAIN EVENT, ALICE?
BUT IT ENDS HERE.
DID YOU THINK WE WOULD NOT KNOW WHAT HAPPENS WITHIN OUR DOMAIN?
...!
TAKE HER.
YES, MY QUEEN!
LISTEN!
I-I NEVER TRICKED YOU!
PER-HAPS.
BUT, ALICE...
THAT NO LONGER MATTERS.

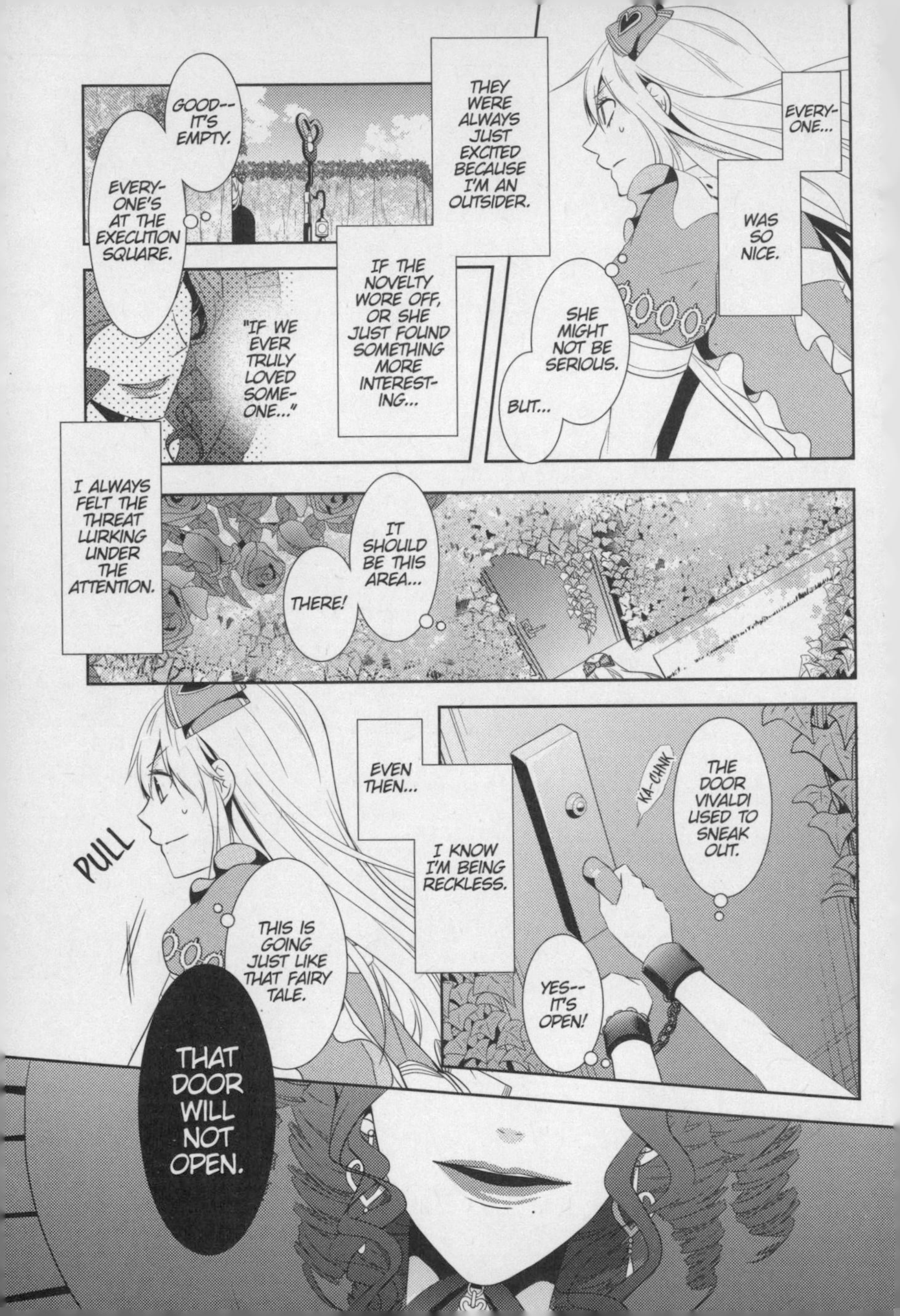
EVERY-ONE...
WAS SO NICE.
THEY WERE ALWAYS JUST EXCITED BECAUSE I'M AN OUTSIDER.
GOOD-- IT'S EMPTY.
EVERY-ONE'S AT THE EXECUTION SQUARE.
IF THE NOVELTY WORE OFF, OR SHE JUST FOUND SOMETHING MORE INTEREST-ING...
SHE MIGHT NOT BE SERIOUS.
BUT...
"IF WE EVER TRULY LOVED SOME-ONE..."
IT SHOULD BE THIS AREA...
THERE!
I ALWAYS FELT THE THREAT LURKING UNDER THE ATTENTION.
THE DOOR VIVALDI USED TO SNEAK OUT.
KA-CHINK
YES-- IT'S OPEN!
EVEN THEN...
I KNOW I'M BEING RECKLESS.
PULL
THIS IS GOING JUST LIKE THAT FAIRY TALE.
THAT DOOR WILL NOT OPEN.

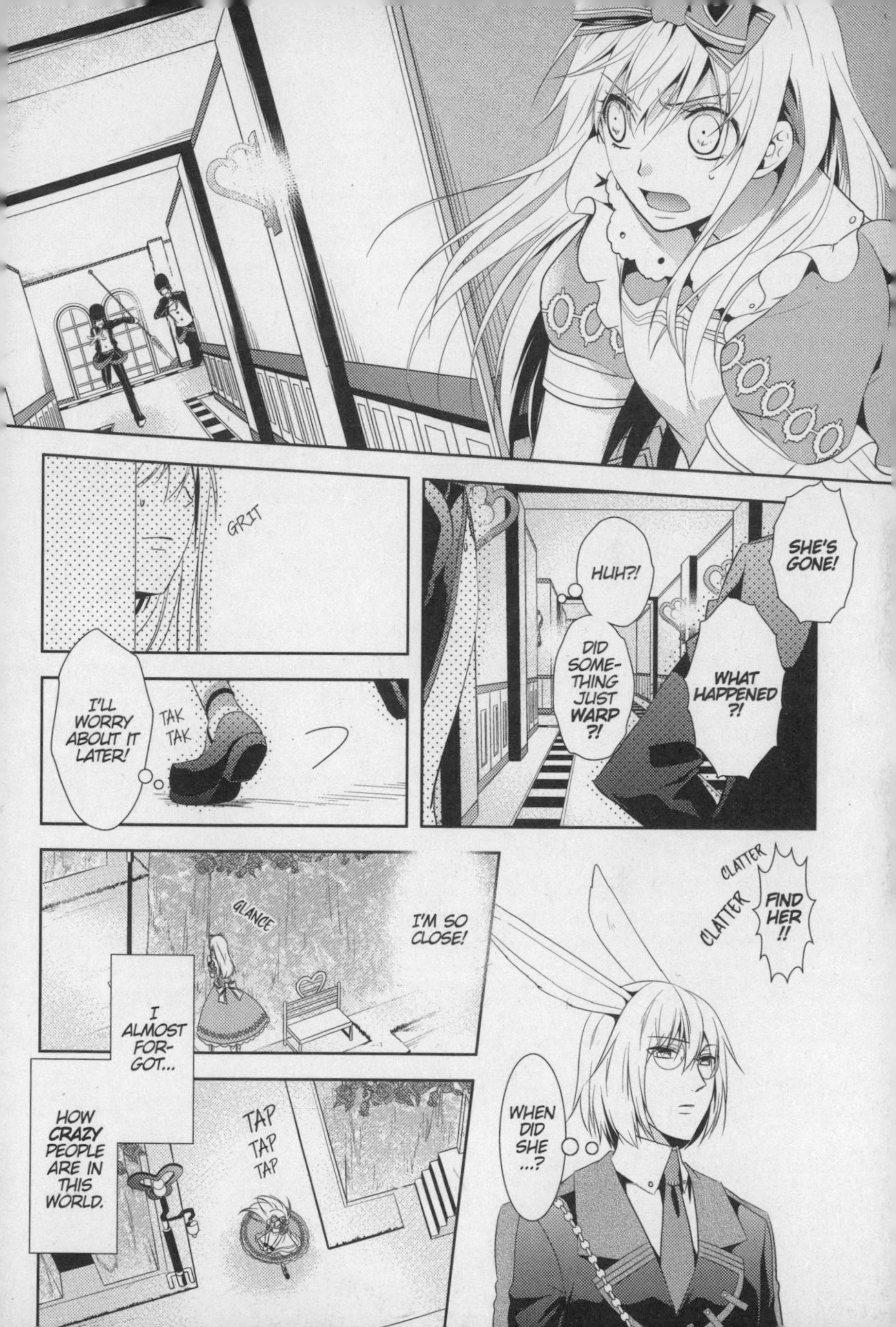
SHE'S GONE!
WHAT HAPPENED ?!
HUH?!
DID SOME-THING JUST WARP ?!
GRIT
TAK TAK
I'LL WORRY ABOUT IT LATER!
CLATTER CLATTER
FIND HER!!
WHEN DID SHE ...?
I'M SO CLOSE!
GLANCE
I ALMOST FOR-GOT...
HOW CRAZY PEOPLE ARE IN THIS WORLD.
TAP TAP TAP

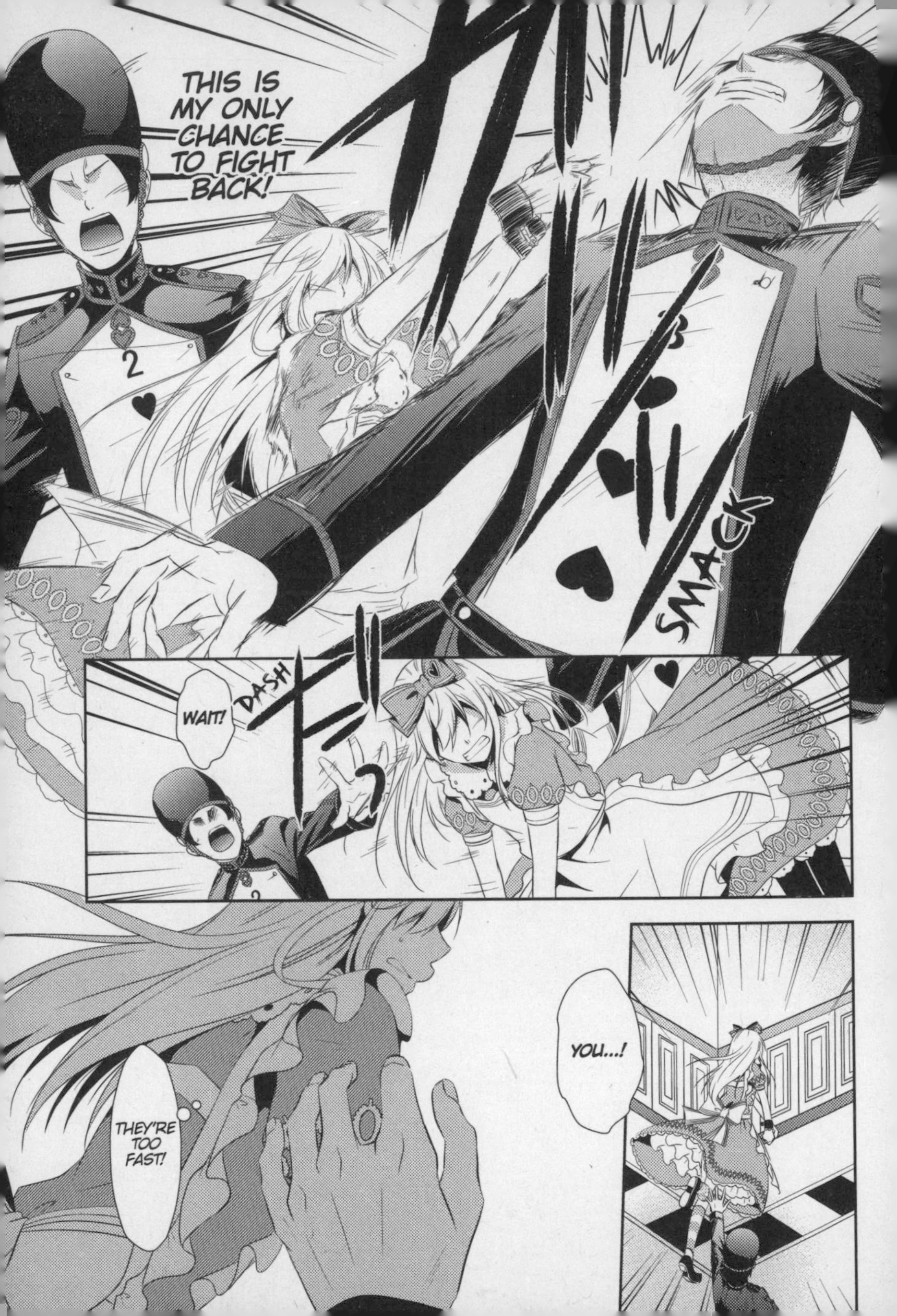
SMACK
THIS IS MY ONLY CHANCE TO FIGHT BACK!
DASH
WAIT!
YOU...!
THEY'RE TOO FAST!

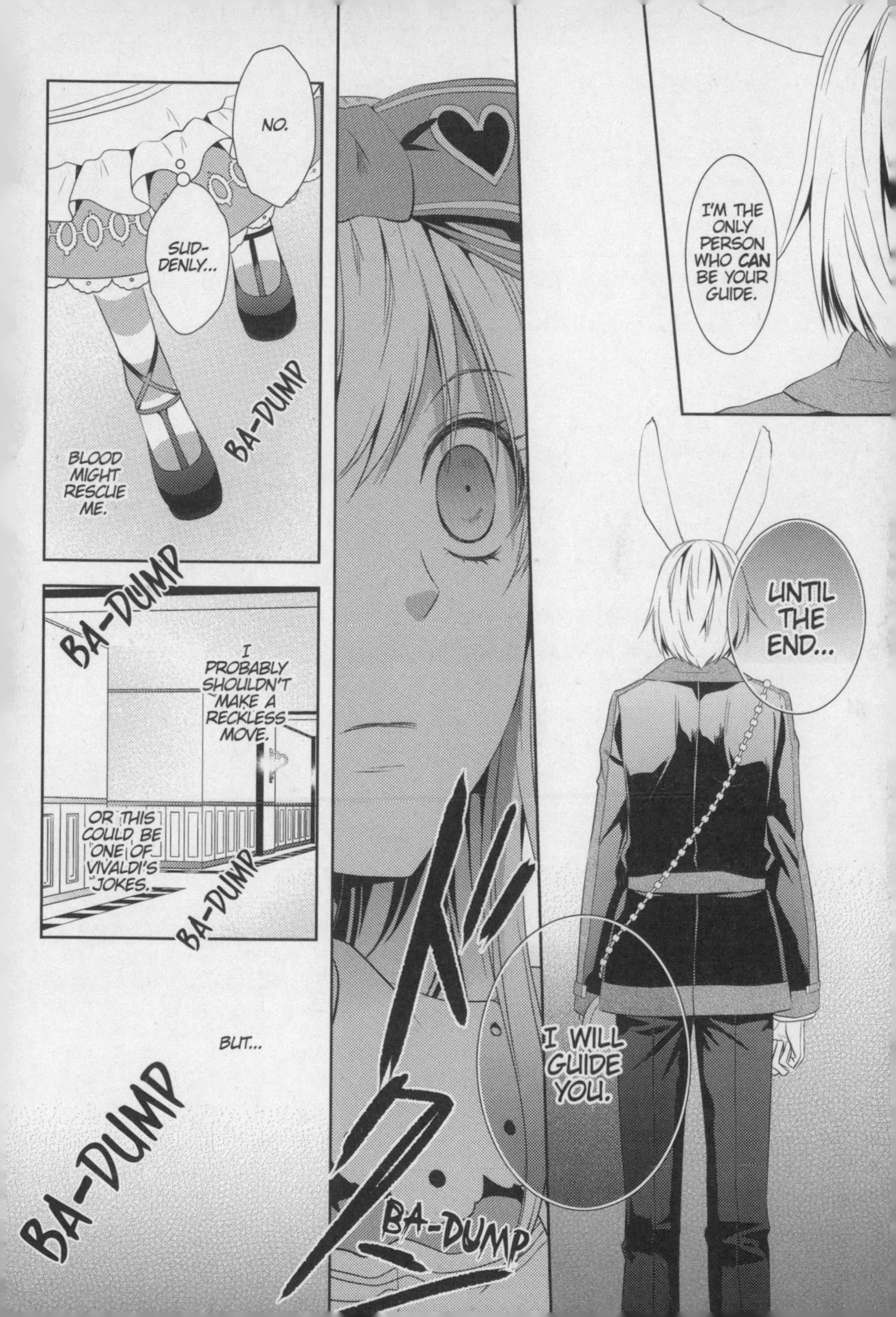
I'M THE ONLY PERSON WHO CAN BE YOUR GUIDE.
UNTIL THE END...
I WILL GUIDE YOU.
BA-DUMP
NO.
SUD-DENLY...
BA-DUMP
BLOOD MIGHT RESCUE ME.
BA-DUMP
BA-DUMP
I PROBABLY SHOULDN'T MAKE A RECKLESS MOVE.
OR THIS COULD BE ONE OF VIVALDI'S JOKES.
BA-DUMP
BUT...
BA-DUMP

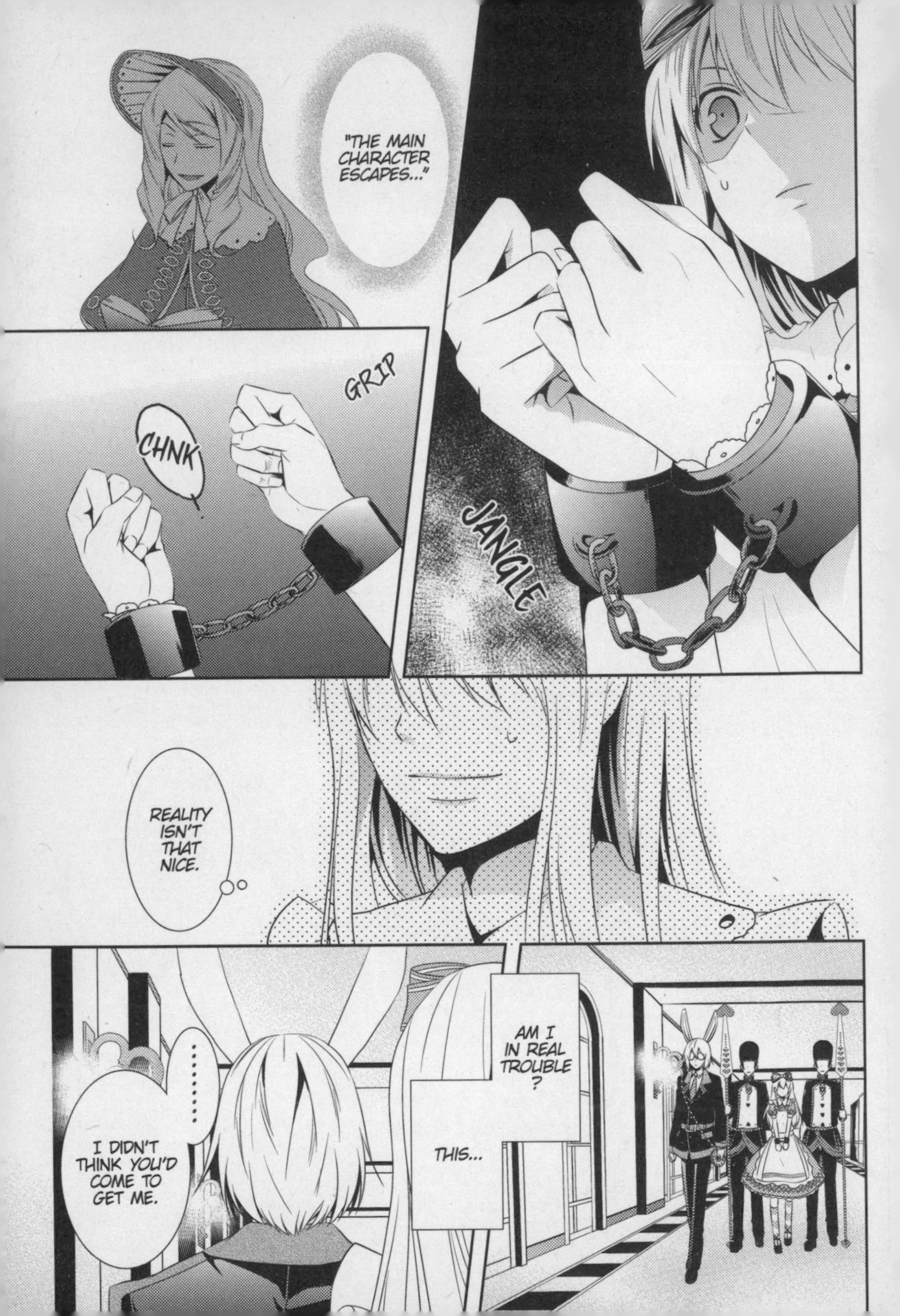
JANGLE
"THE MAIN CHARACTER ESCAPES..."
GRIP
CHNK
REALITY ISN'T THAT NICE.
AM I IN REAL TROUBLE?
THIS...
......
I DIDN'T THINK YOU'D COME TO GET ME.

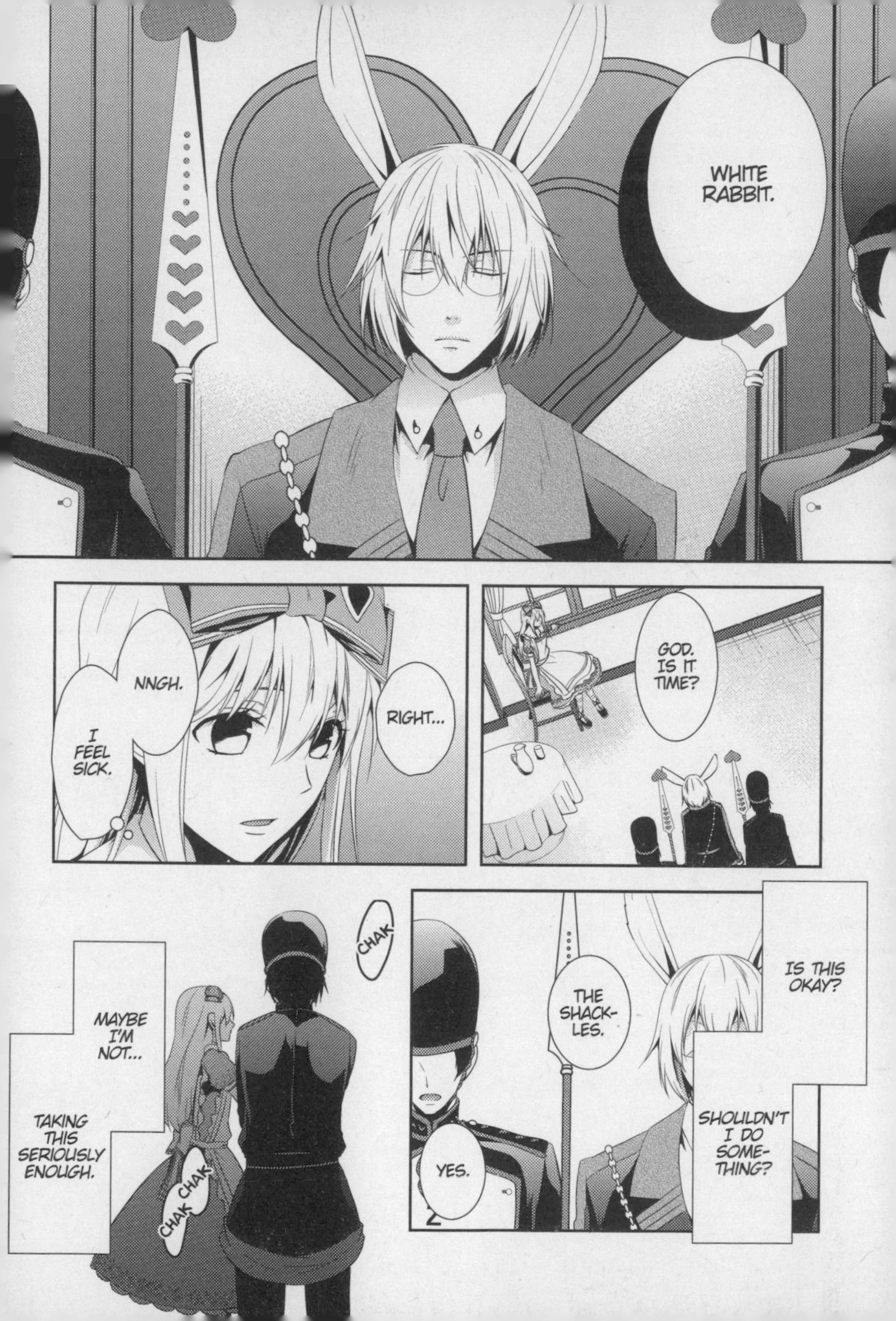
WHITE RABBIT.
GOD. IS IT TIME?
RIGHT...
NNGH.
I FEEL SICK.
IS THIS OKAY?
THE SHACK-LES.
SHOULDN'T I DO SOME-THING?
YES.
CHAK
MAYBE I'M NOT...
TAKING THIS SERIOUSLY ENOUGH.
CHAK CHAK

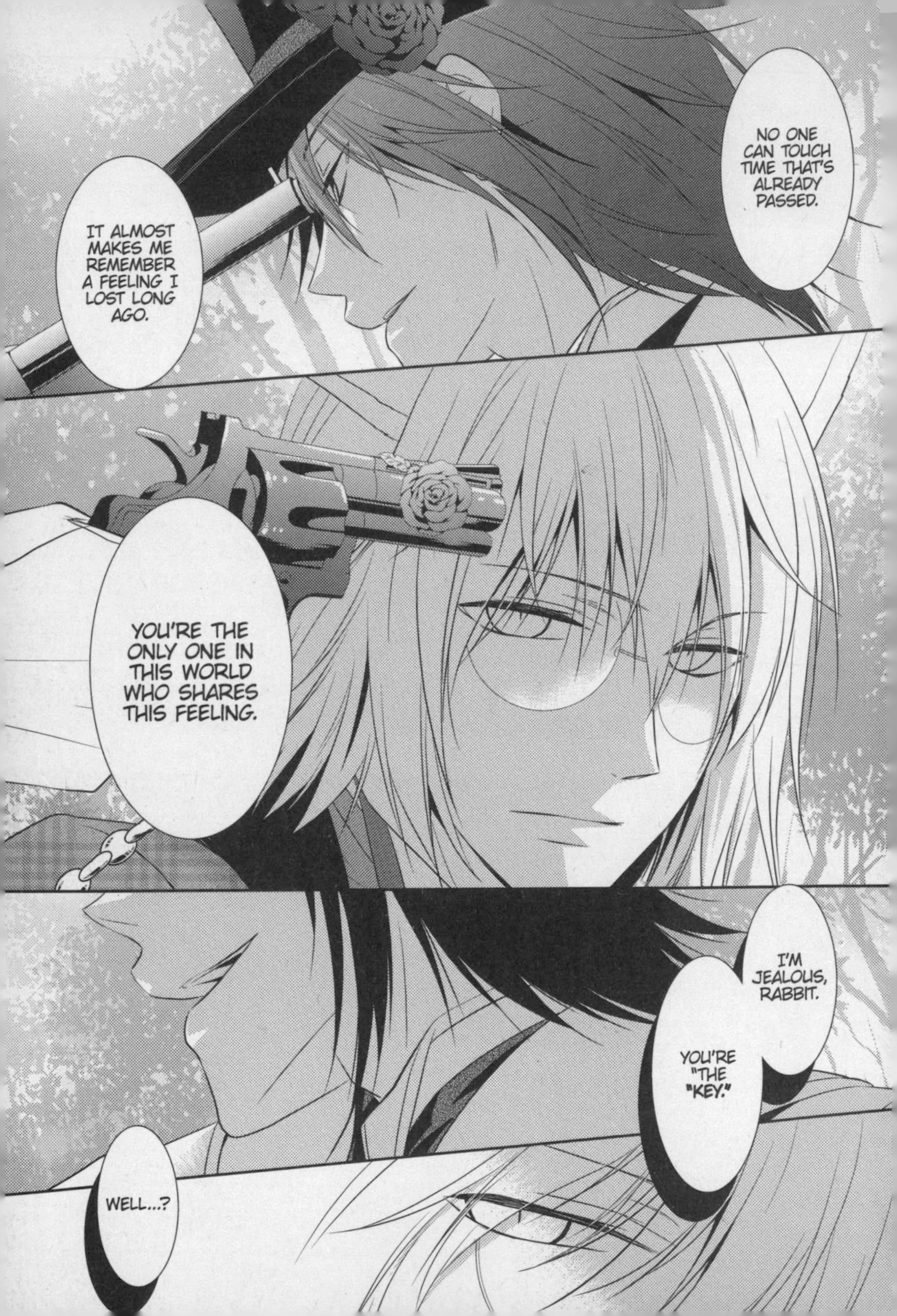
NO ONE CAN TOUCH TIME THAT'S ALREADY PASSED.
IT ALMOST MAKES ME REMEMBER A FEELING I LOST LONG AGO.
YOU'RE THE ONLY ONE IN THIS WORLD WHO SHARES THIS FEELING.
I'M JEALOUS, RABBIT.
YOU'RE "THE "KEY."
WELL...?

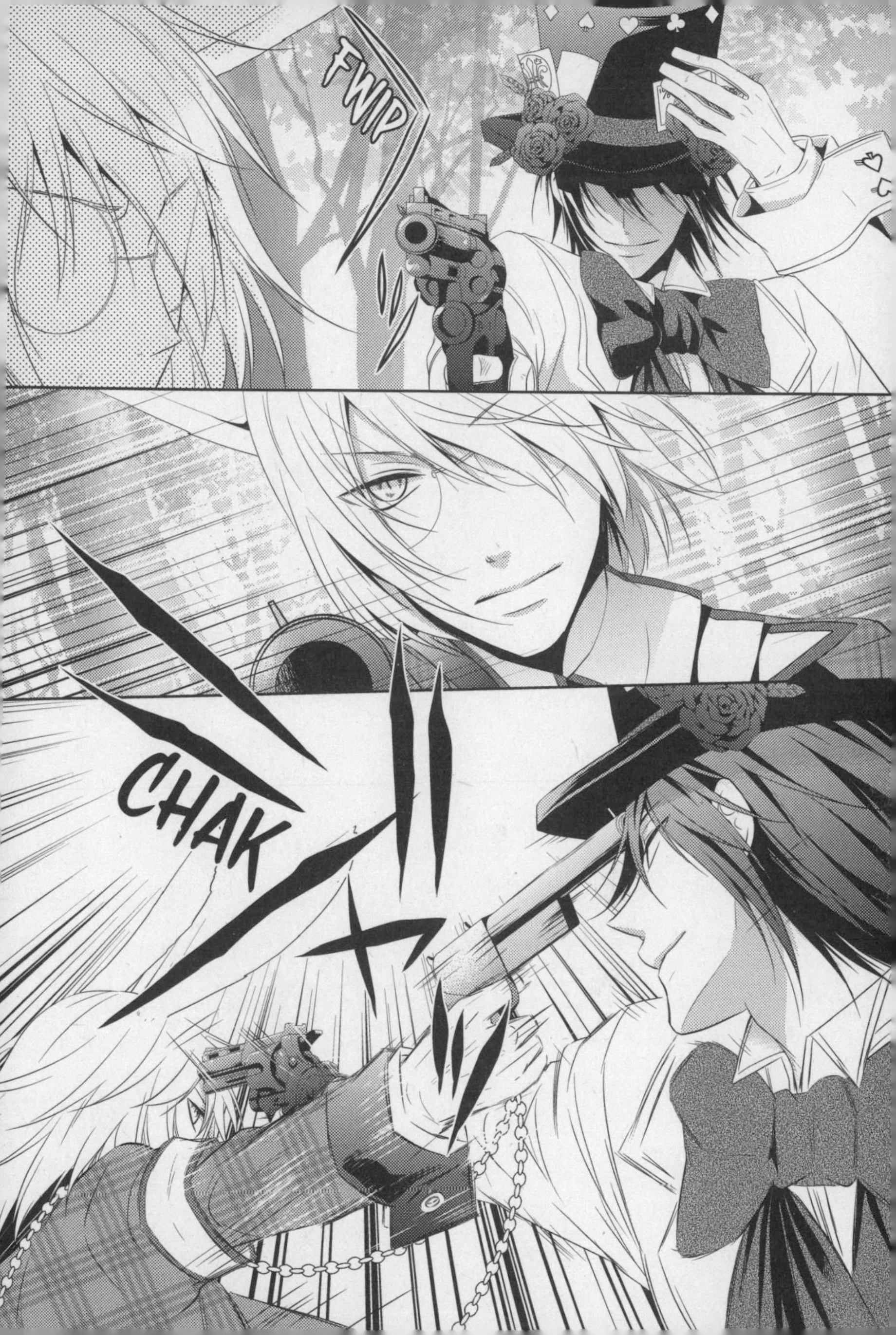
FWIP
CHAK

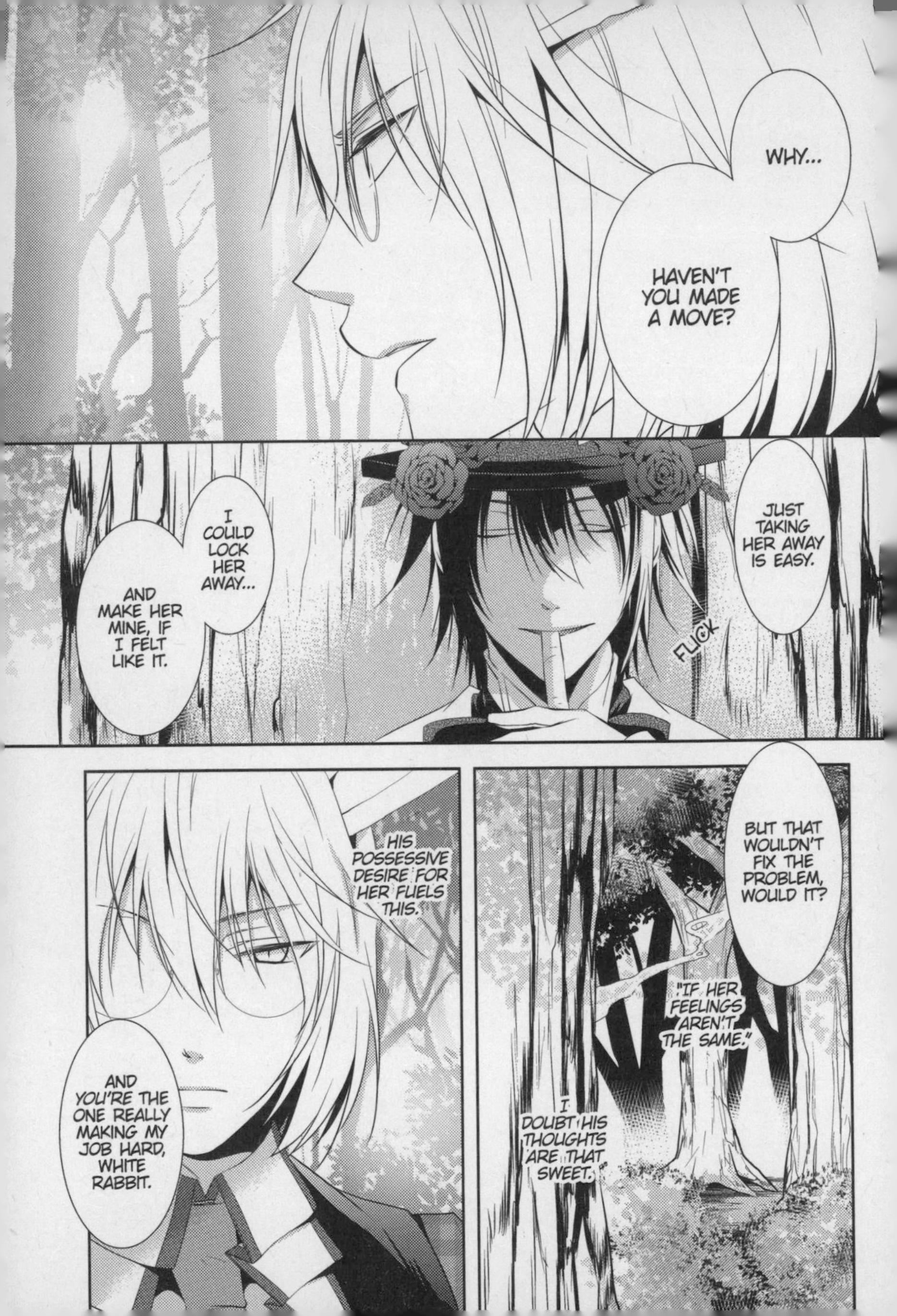
WHY...
HAVEN'T YOU MADE A MOVE?
JUST TAKING HER AWAY IS EASY.
FLICK
I COULD LOCK HER AWAY...
AND MAKE HER MINE, IF I FELT LIKE IT.
BUT THAT WOULDN'T FIX THE PROBLEM, WOULD IT?
"IF HER FEELINGS AREN'T THE SAME."
I DOUBT HIS THOUGHTS ARE THAT SWEET.
HIS POSSESSIVE DESIRE FOR HER FUELS THIS.
AND YOU'RE THE ONE REALLY MAKING MY JOB HARD, WHITE RABBIT.

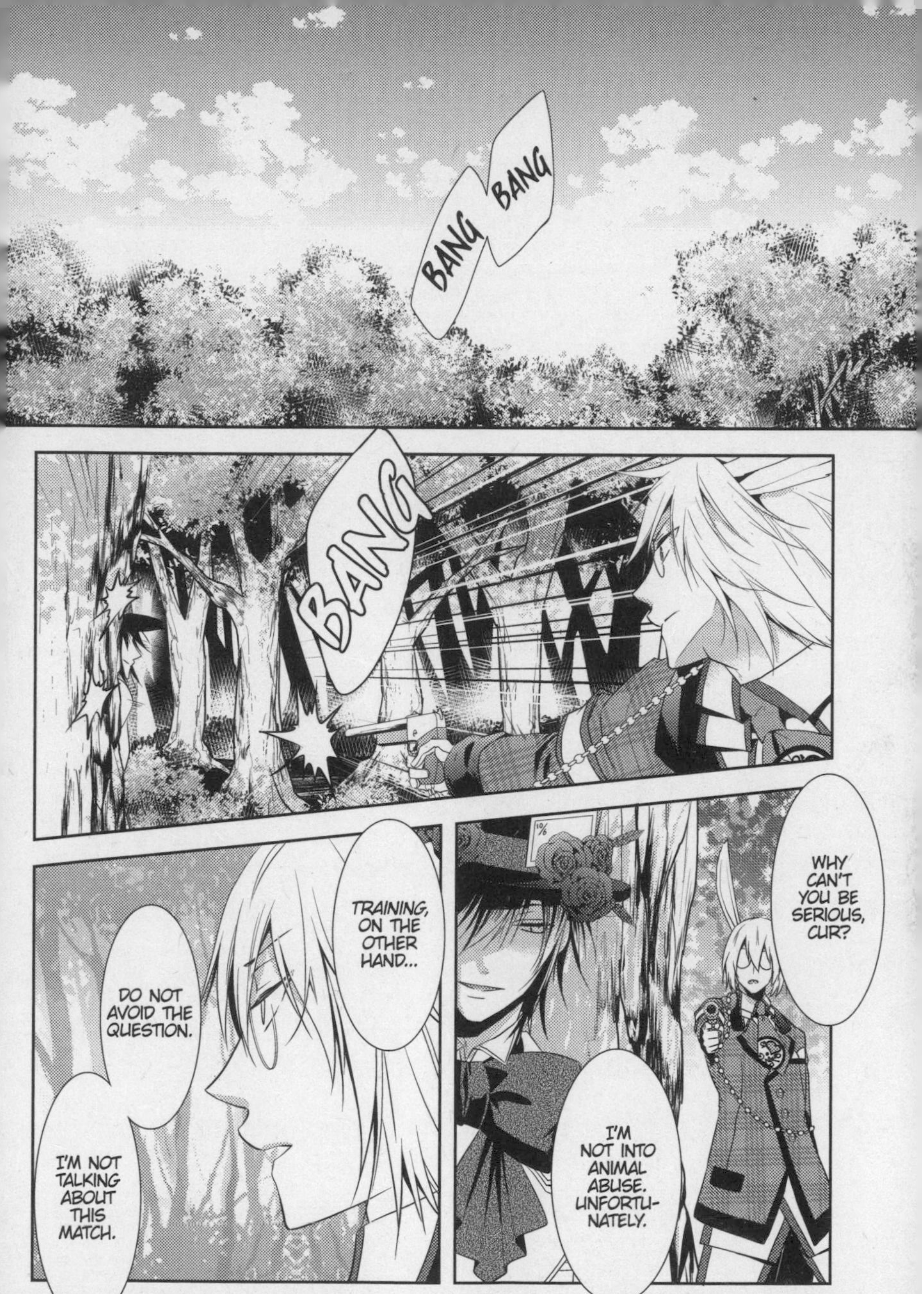

BANG
BANG
BANG
WHY CAN'T YOU BE SERIOUS, CUR?
I'M NOT INTO ANIMAL ABUSE. UNFORTUNATELY.
TRAINING, ON THE OTHER HAND...
DO NOT AVOID THE QUESTION.
I'M NOT TALKING ABOUT THIS MATCH.

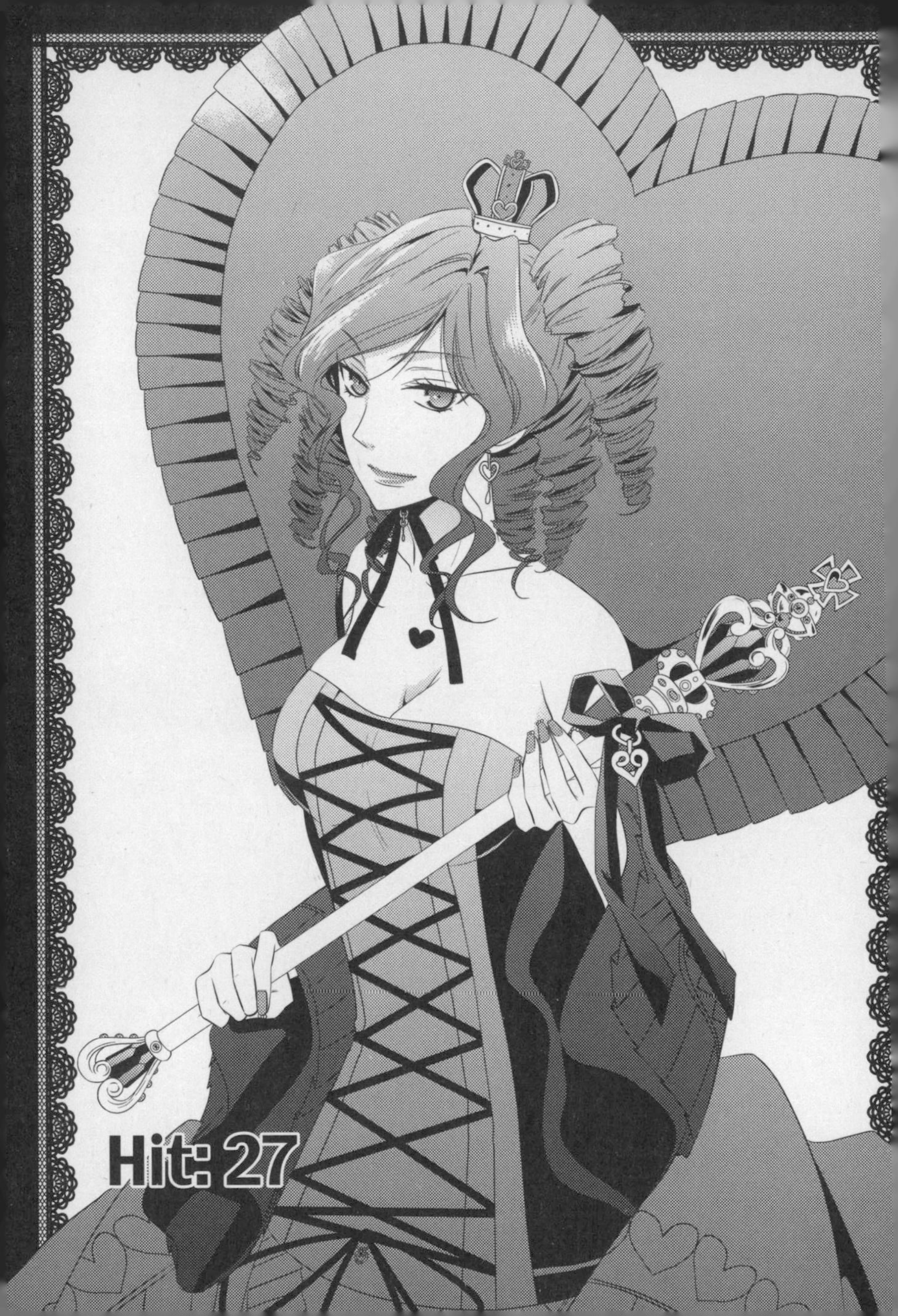
Hit: 27

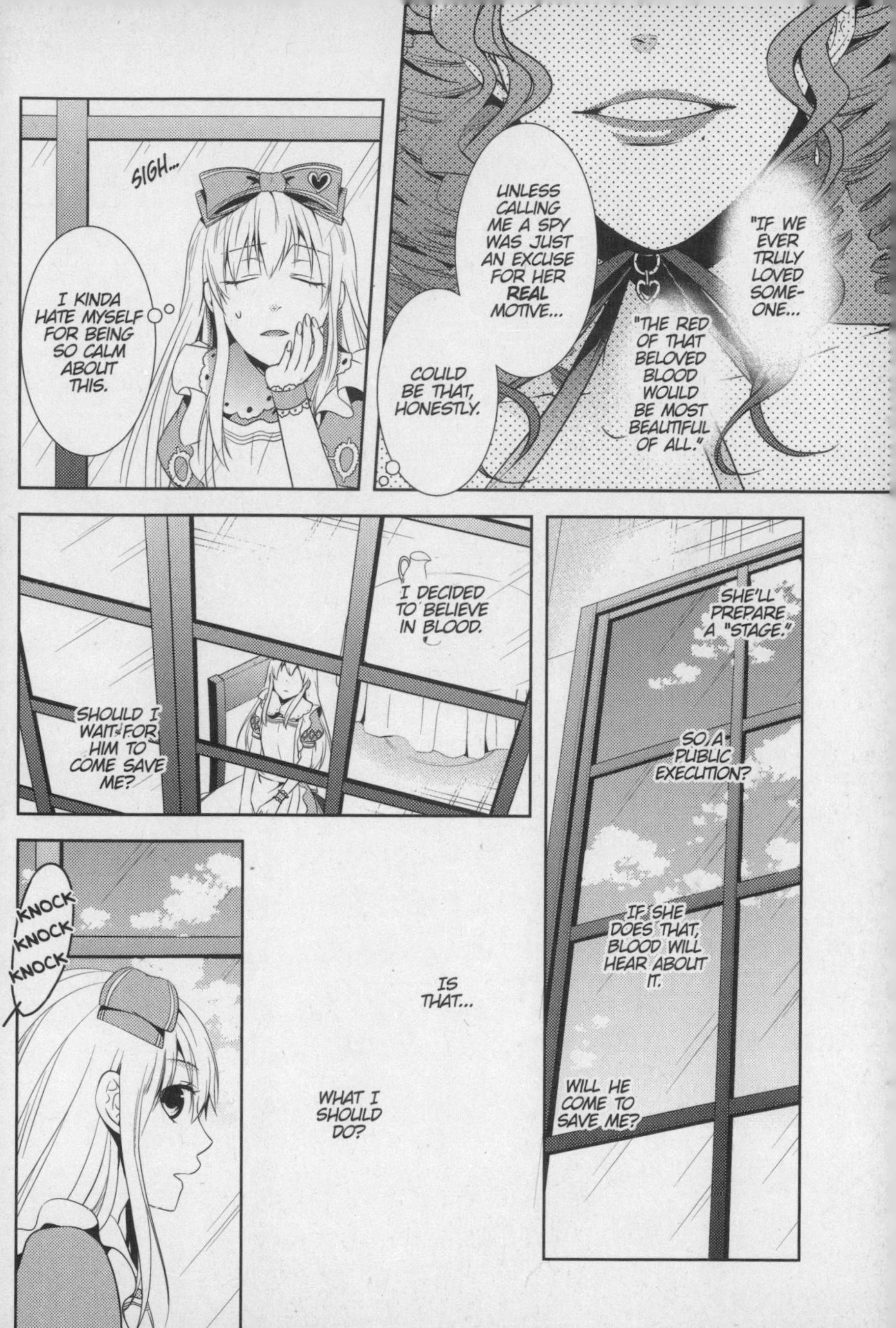
"IF WE EVER TRULY LOVED SOME-ONE...
"THE RED OF THAT BELOVED BLOOD WOULD BE MOST BEAUTIFUL OF ALL."
UNLESS CALLING ME A SPY WAS JUST AN EXCUSE FOR HER REAL MOTIVE...
COULD BE THAT, HONESTLY.
SIGH...
I KINDA HATE MYSELF FOR BEING SO CALM ABOUT THIS.
SHE'LL PREPARE A "STAGE."
SO A PUBLIC EXECUTION?
IF SHE DOES THAT, BLOOD WILL HEAR ABOUT IT.
WILL HE COME TO SAVE ME?
I DECIDED TO BELIEVE IN BLOOD.
SHOULD I WAIT FOR HIM TO COME SAVE ME?
IS THAT...
WHAT I SHOULD DO?
KNOCK KNOCK KNOCK

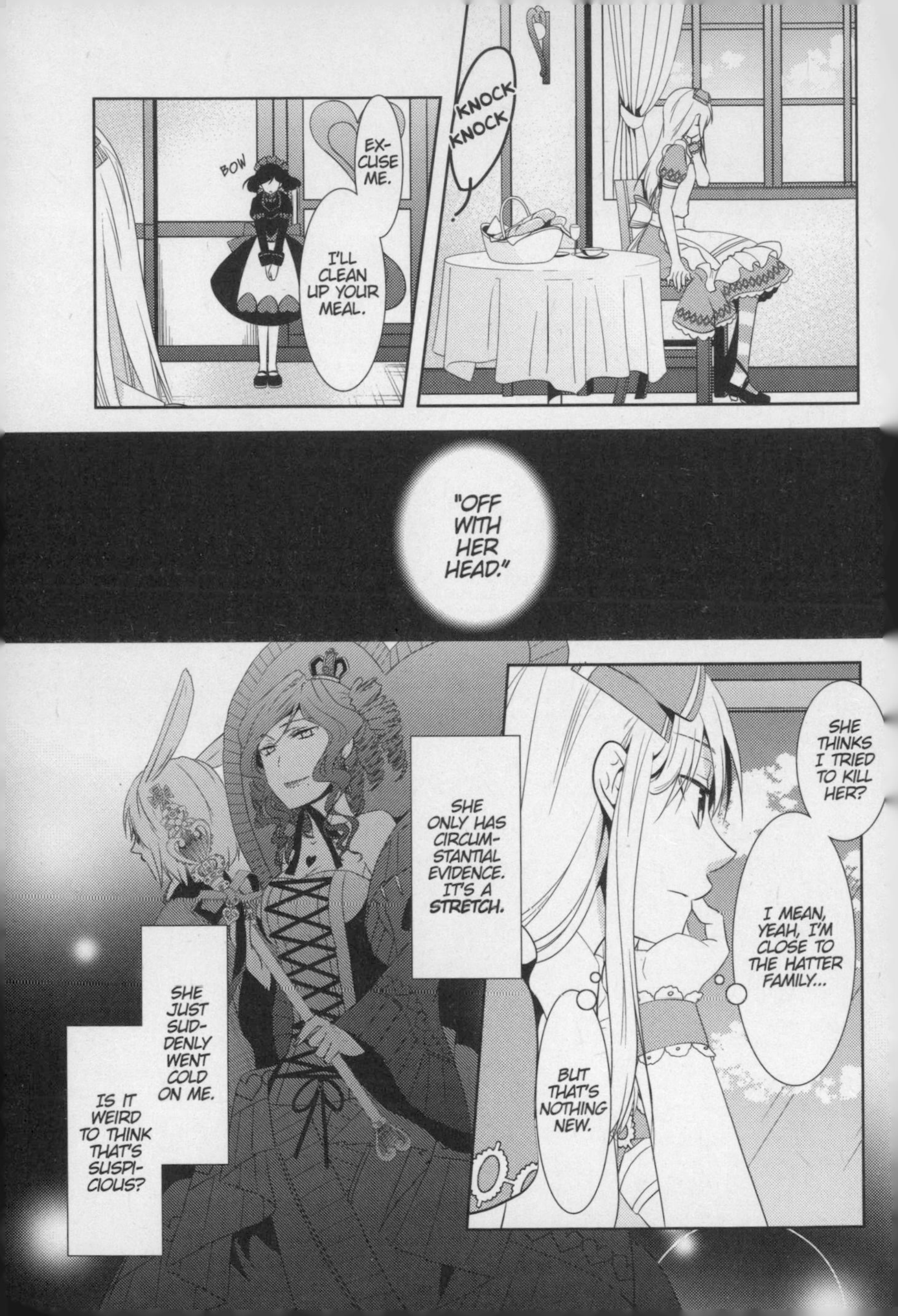
KNOCK KNOCK
BOW
EX-CUSE ME.
I'LL CLEAN UP YOUR MEAL.
"OFF WITH HER HEAD."
SHE THINKS I TRIED TO KILL HER?
I MEAN, YEAH, I'M CLOSE TO THE HATTER FAMILY...
SHE ONLY HAS CIRCUM-STANTIAL EVIDENCE. IT'S A STRETCH.
BUT THAT'S NOTHING NEW.
SHE JUST SUD-DENLY WENT COLD ON ME.
IS IT WEIRD TO THINK THAT'S SUSPI-CIOUS?

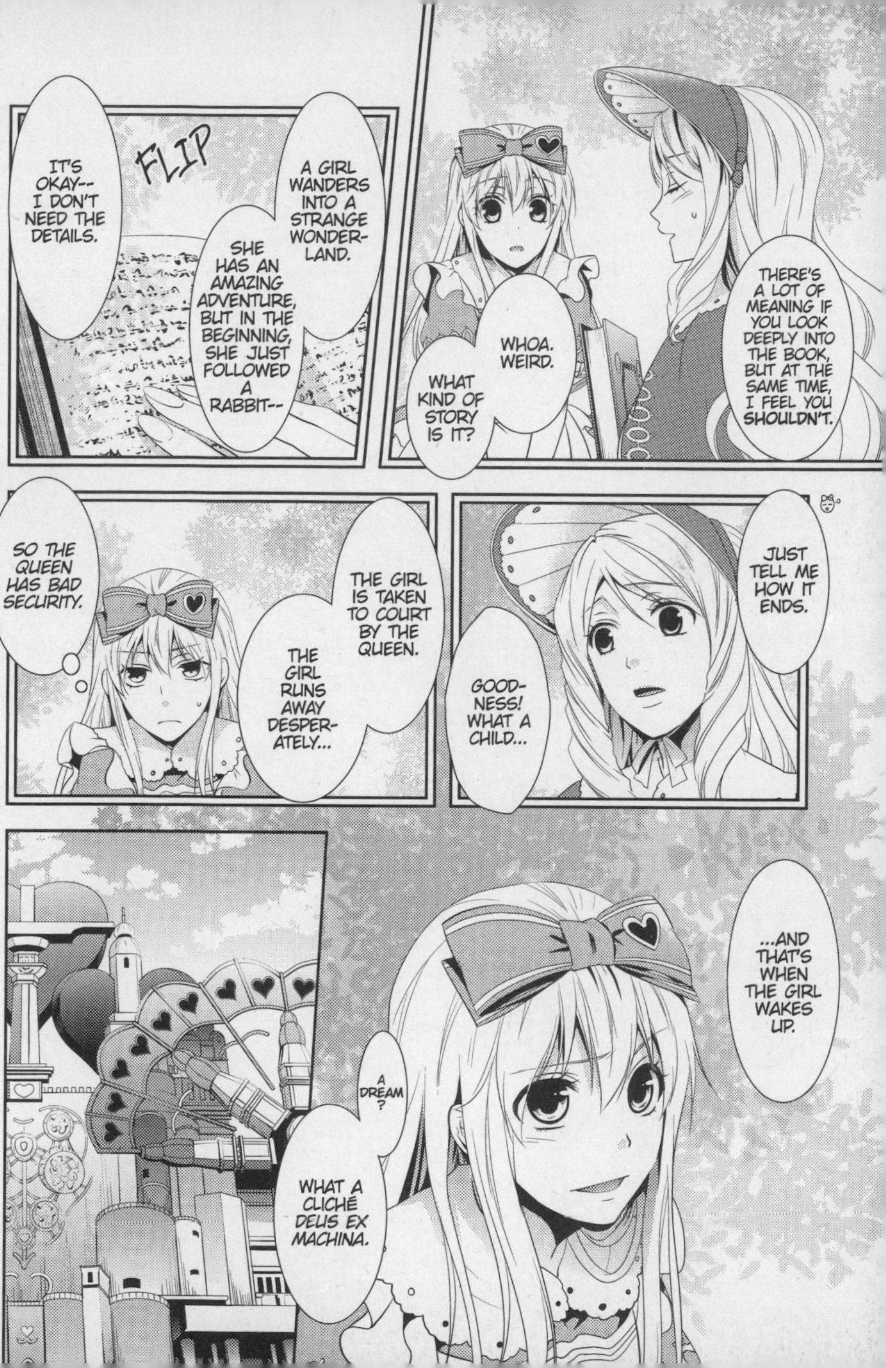
THERE'S A LOT OF MEANING IF YOU LOOK DEEPLY INTO THE BOOK, BUT AT THE SAME TIME, I FEEL YOU SHOULDN'T.
WHOA. WEIRD.
WHAT KIND OF STORY IS IT?
A GIRL WANDERS INTO A STRANGE WONDER-LAND.
SHE HAS AN AMAZING ADVENTURE, BUT IN THE BEGINNING, SHE JUST FOLLOWED A RABBIT--
FLIP
IT'S OKAY-- I DON'T NEED THE DETAILS.
JUST TELL ME HOW IT ENDS.
GOOD-NESS! WHAT A CHILD...
THE GIRL IS TAKEN TO COURT BY THE QUEEN.
THE GIRL RUNS AWAY DESPER-ATELY...
SO THE QUEEN HAS BAD SECURITY.
...AND THAT'S WHEN THE GIRL WAKES UP.
A DREAM?
WHAT A CLICHÉ DEUS EX MACHINA.

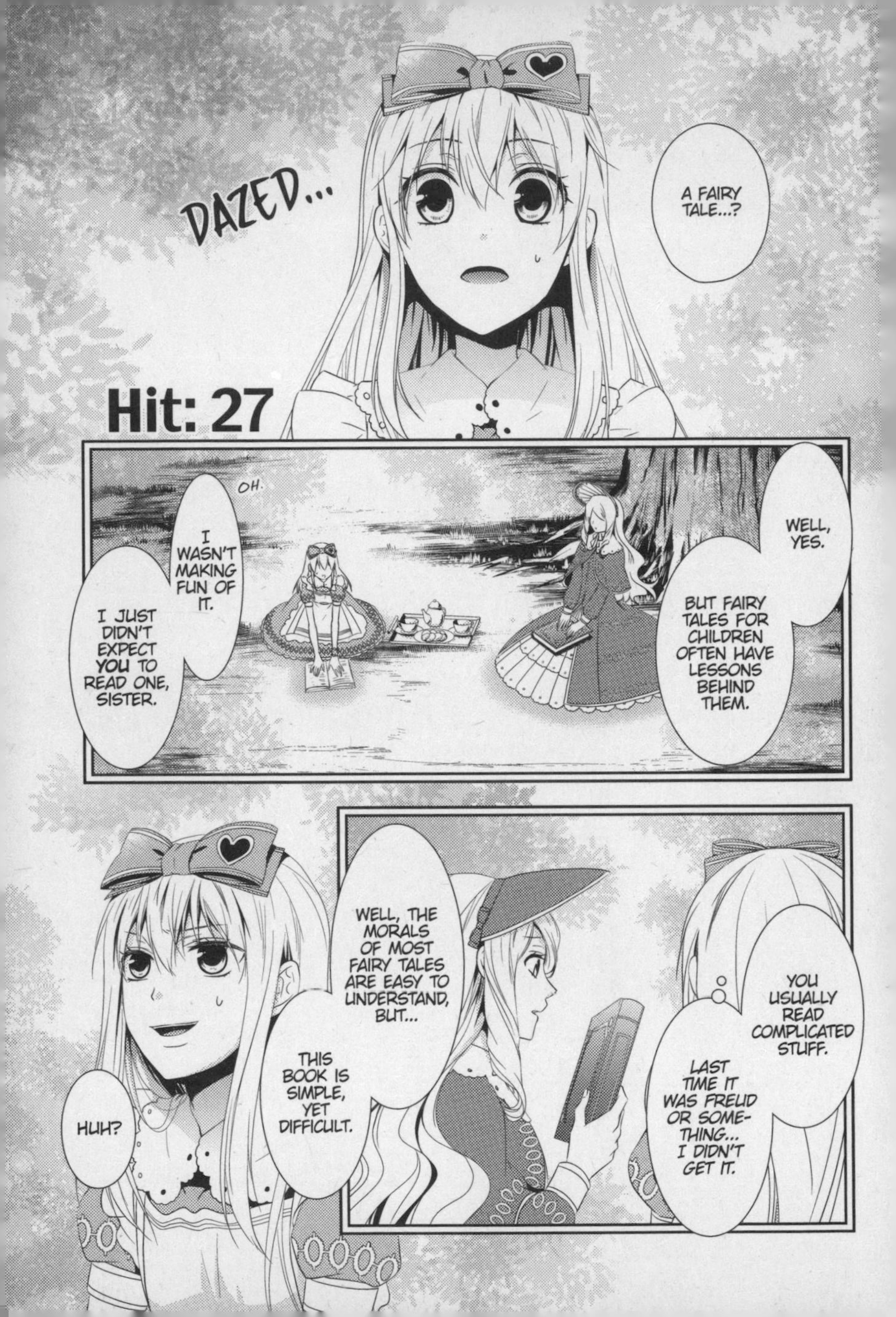
A FAIRY TALE...?
DAZED...
Hit: 27
WELL, YES.
BUT FAIRY TALES FOR CHILDREN OFTEN HAVE LESSONS BEHIND THEM.
OH.
I WASN'T MAKING FUN OF IT.
I JUST DIDN'T EXPECT YOU TO READ ONE, SISTER.
YOU USUALLY READ COMPLICATED STUFF.
LAST TIME IT WAS FREUD OR SOME-THING... I DIDN'T GET IT.
WELL, THE MORALS OF MOST FAIRY TALES ARE EASY TO UNDERSTAND, BUT...
THIS BOOK IS SIMPLE, YET DIFFICULT.
HUH?

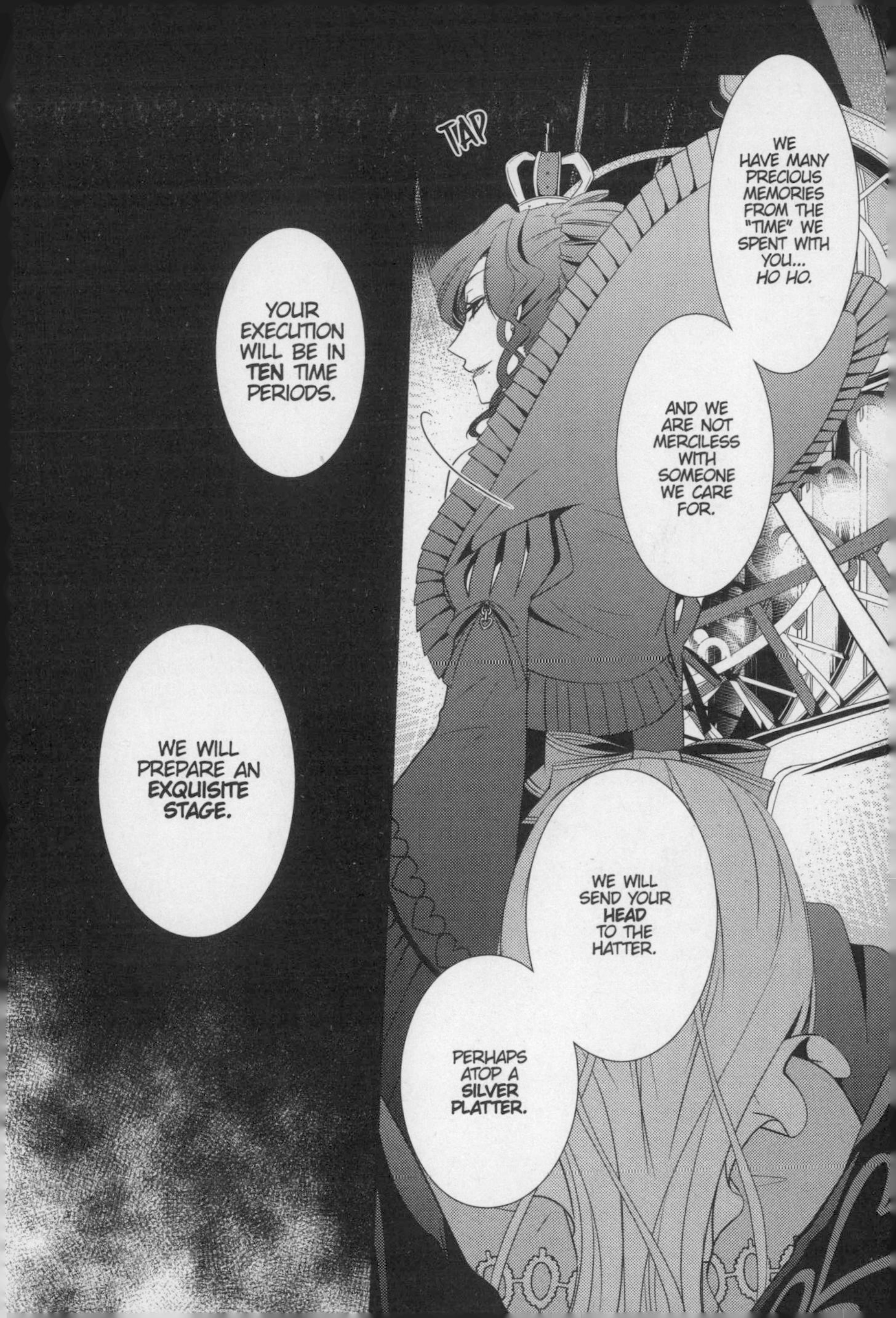
WE HAVE MANY PRECIOUS MEMORIES FROM THE "TIME" WE SPENT WITH YOU... HO HO.
AND WE ARE NOT MERCILESS WITH SOMEONE WE CARE FOR.
TAP
YOUR EXECUTION WILL BE IN TEN TIME PERIODS.
WE WILL PREPARE AN EXQUISITE STAGE.
WE WILL SEND YOUR HEAD TO THE HATTER.
PERHAPS ATOP A SILVER PLATTER.

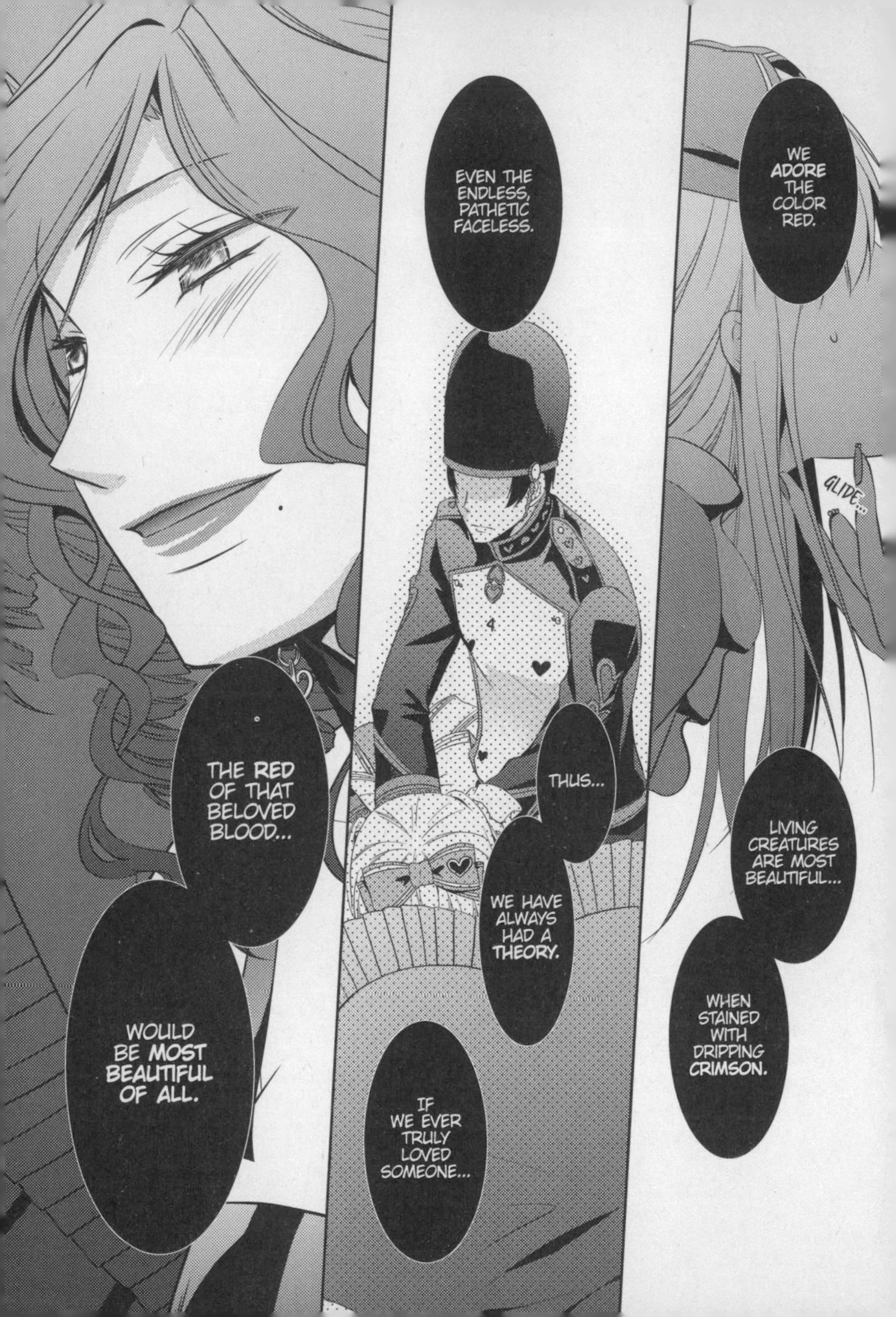
WE ADORE THE COLOR RED.
GLIDE...
LIVING CREATURES ARE MOST BEAUTIFUL...
WHEN STAINED WITH DRIPPING CRIMSON.
EVEN THE ENDLESS, PATHETIC FACELESS.
THUS...
WE HAVE ALWAYS HAD A THEORY.
IF WE EVER TRULY LOVED SOMEONE...
THE RED OF THAT BELOVED BLOOD...
WOULD BE MOST BEAUTIFUL OF ALL.

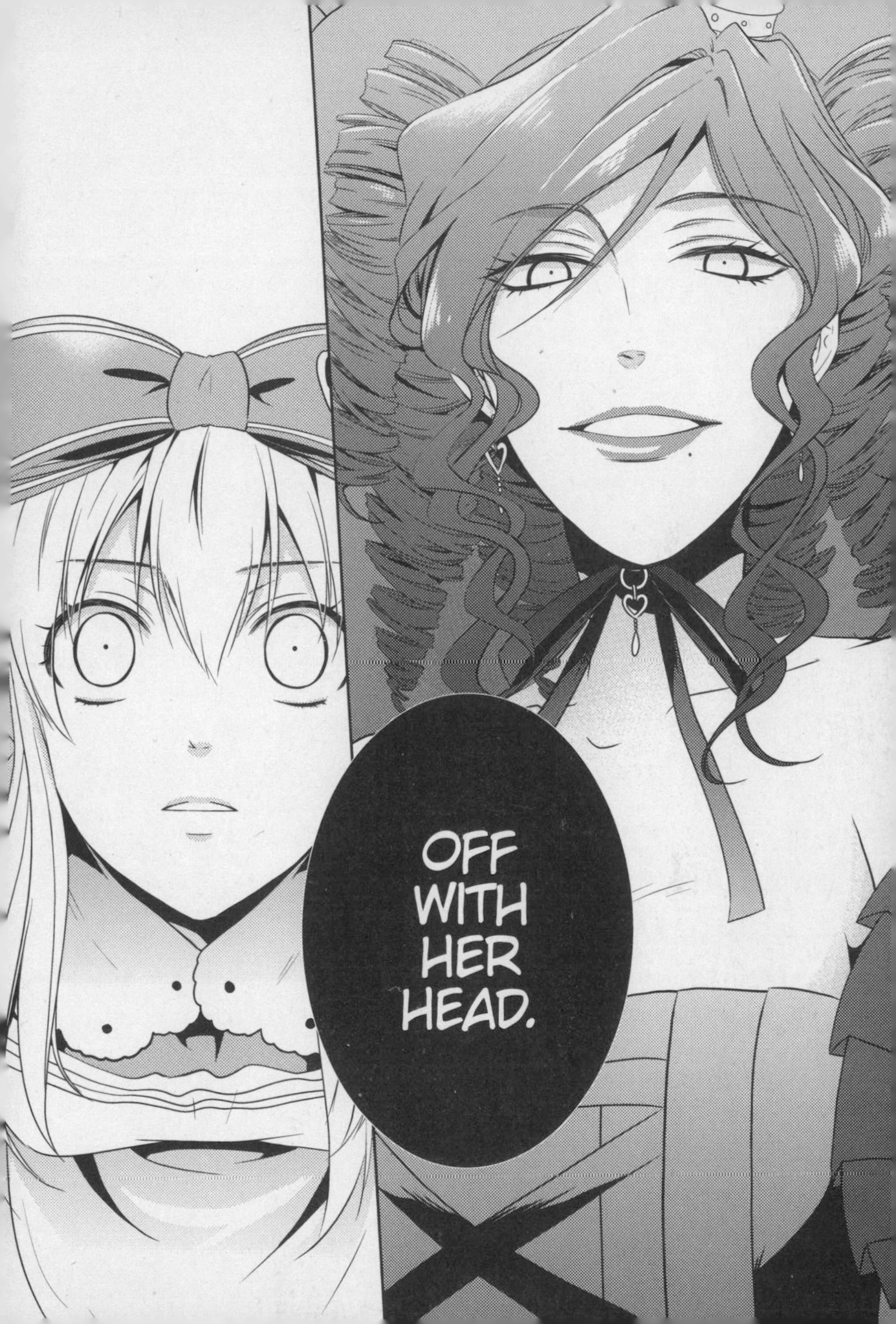
OFF WITH HER HEAD.

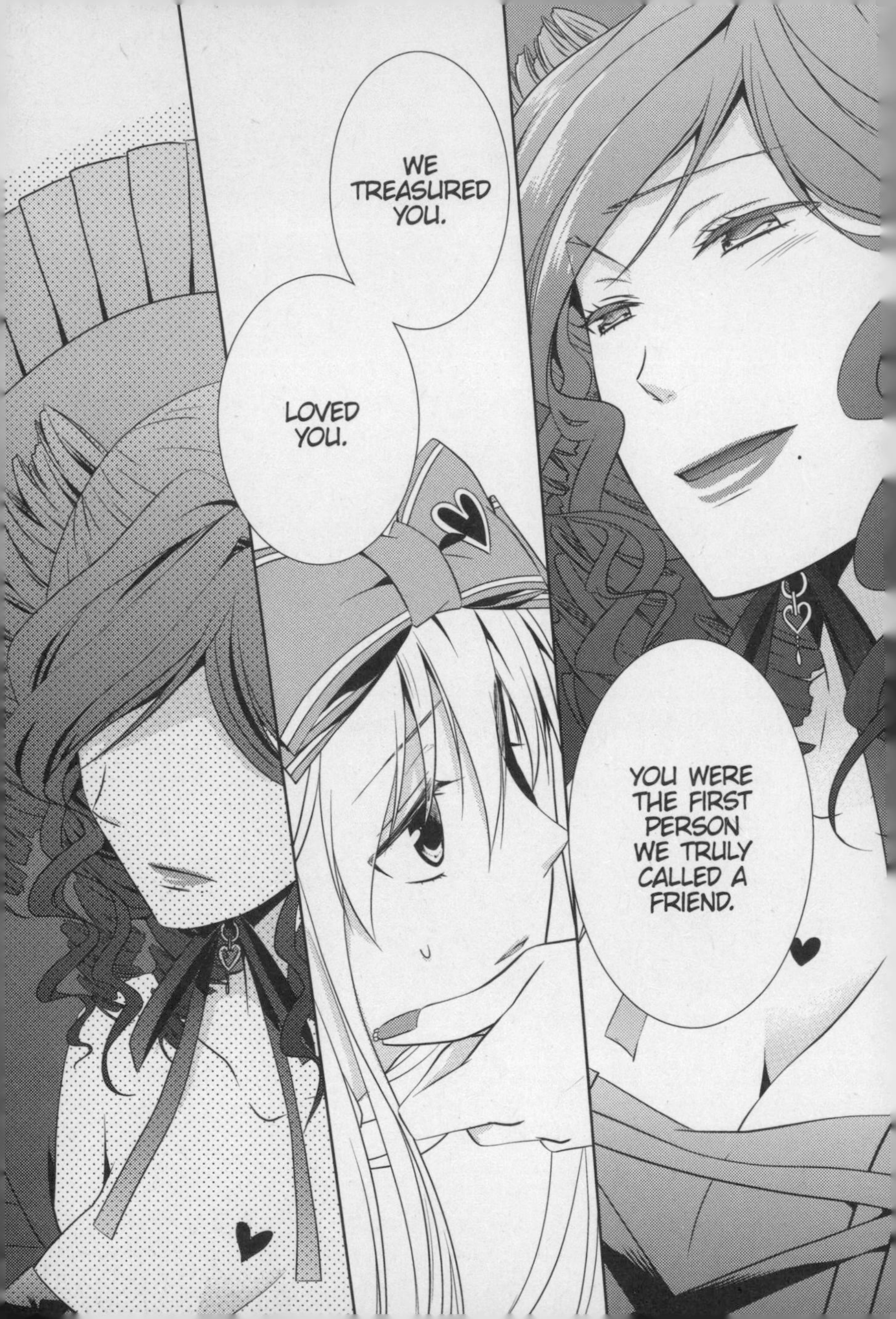
WE TREASURED YOU.
LOVED YOU.
YOU WERE THE FIRST PERSON WE TRULY CALLED A FRIEND.

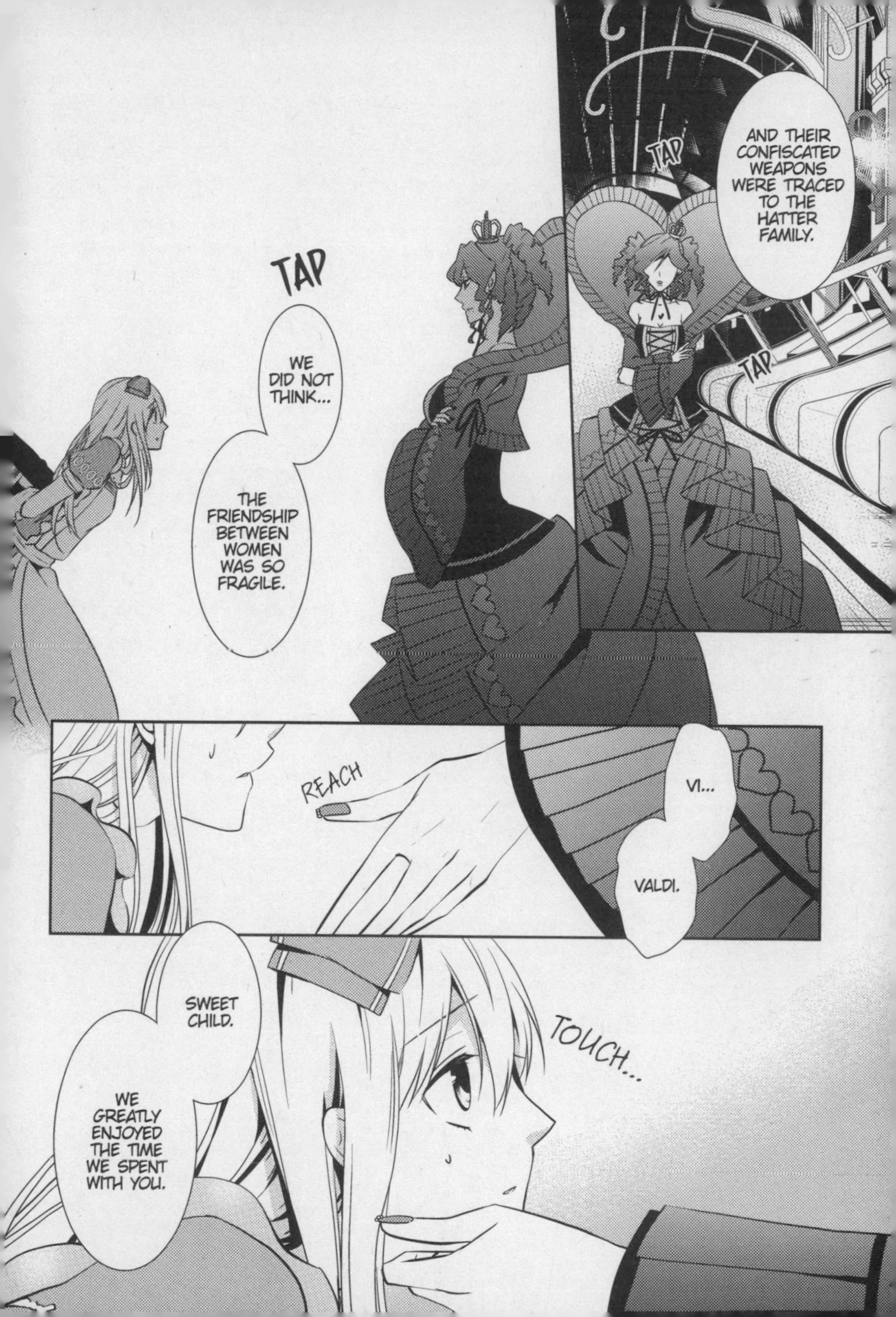
AND THEIR CONFISCATED WEAPONS WERE TRACED TO THE HATTER FAMILY.
TAP
TAP
TAP
WE DID NOT THINK...
THE FRIENDSHIP BETWEEN WOMEN WAS SO FRAGILE.
VI...
VALDI.
REACH
TOUCH...
SWEET CHILD.
WE GREATLY ENJOYED THE TIME WE SPENT WITH YOU.

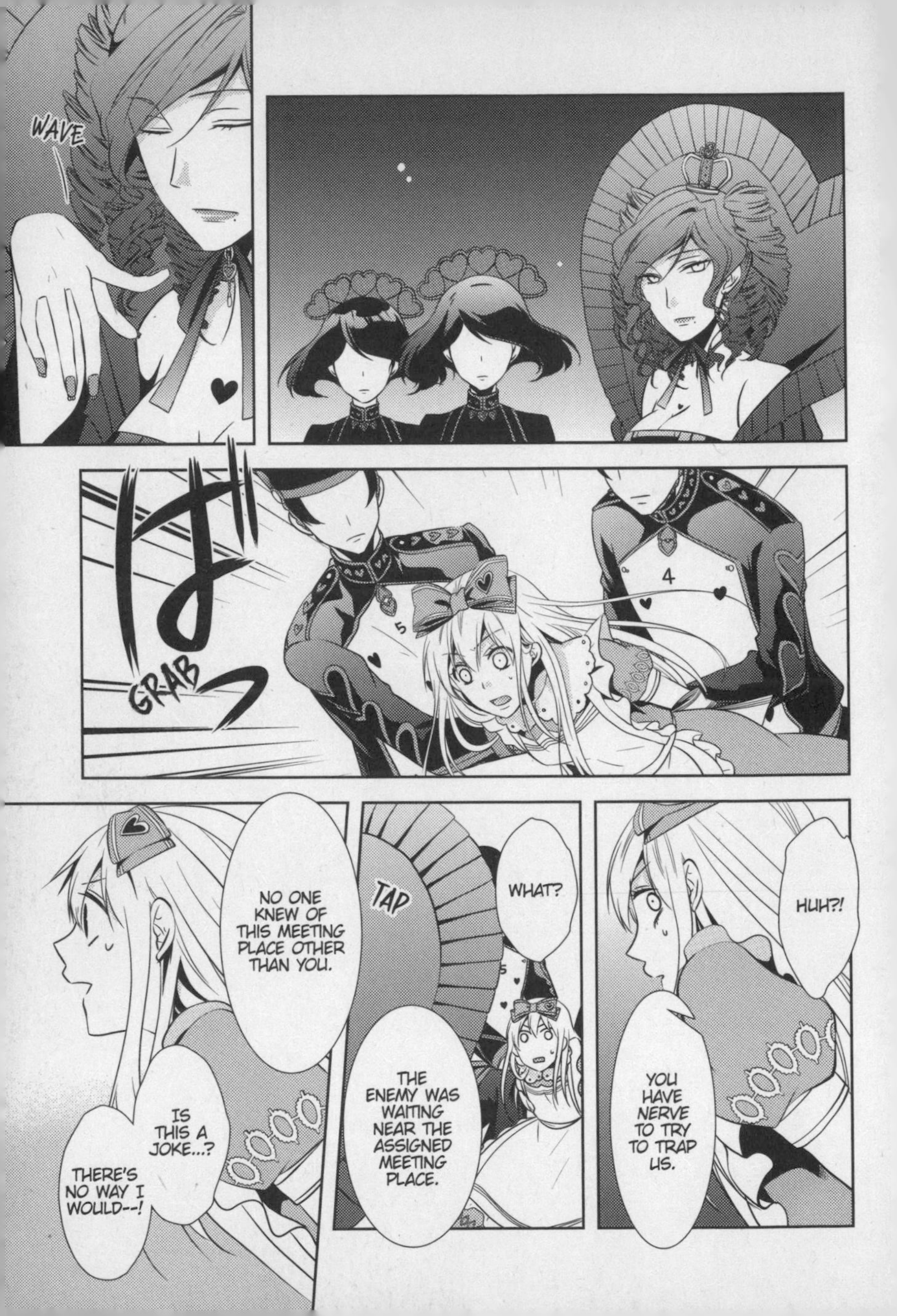
WAVE
GRAB
HUH?!
YOU HAVE NERVE TO TRY TO TRAP US.
WHAT?
TAP
THE ENEMY WAS WAITING NEAR THE ASSIGNED MEETING PLACE.
NO ONE KNEW OF THIS MEETING PLACE OTHER THAN YOU.
IS THIS A JOKE...?
THERE'S NO WAY I WOULD--!

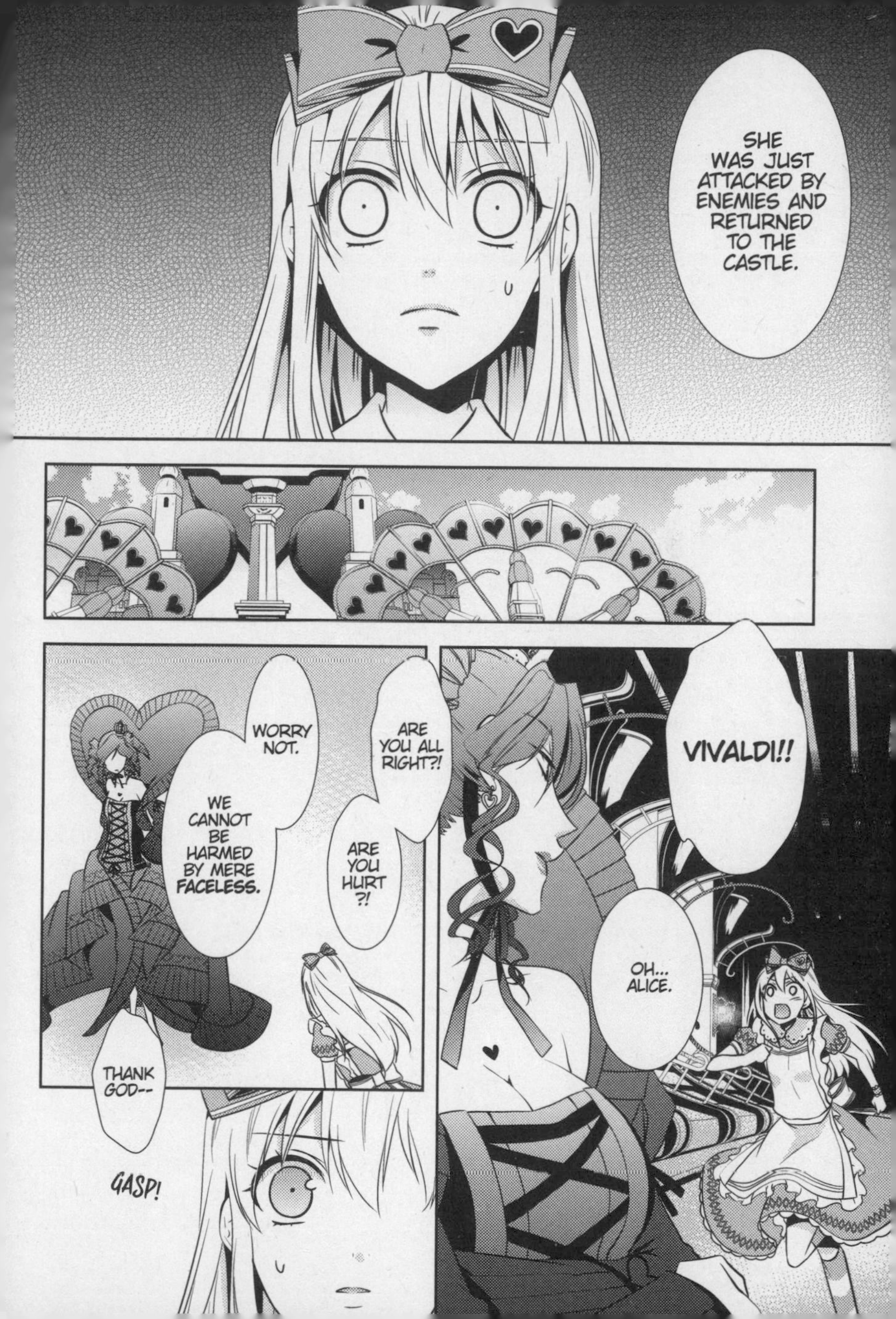
SHE WAS JUST ATTACKED BY ENEMIES AND RETURNED TO THE CASTLE.
VIVALDI!!
OH... ALICE.
ARE YOU ALL RIGHT?!
ARE YOU HURT ?!
WORRY NOT.
WE CANNOT BE HARMED BY MERE FACELESS.
THANK GOD--
GASP!

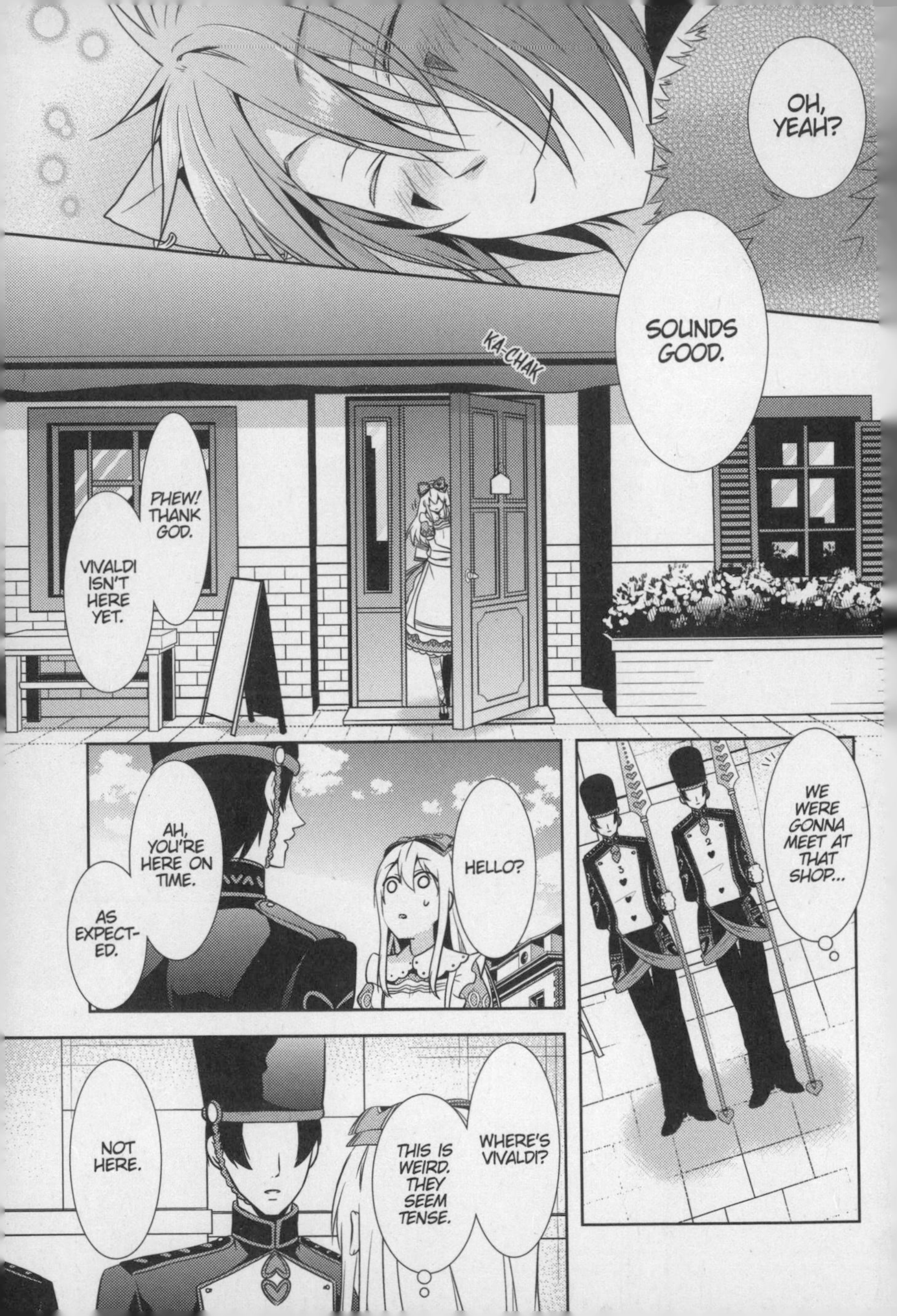

OH, YEAH?
SOUNDS GOOD.
KA-CHAK
PHEW! THANK GOD.
VIVALDI ISN'T HERE YET.
WE WERE GONNA MEET AT THAT SHOP...
HELLO?
AH, YOU'RE HERE ON TIME.
AS EXPECT-ED.
WHERE'S VIVALDI?
THIS IS WEIRD. THEY SEEM TENSE.
NOT HERE.

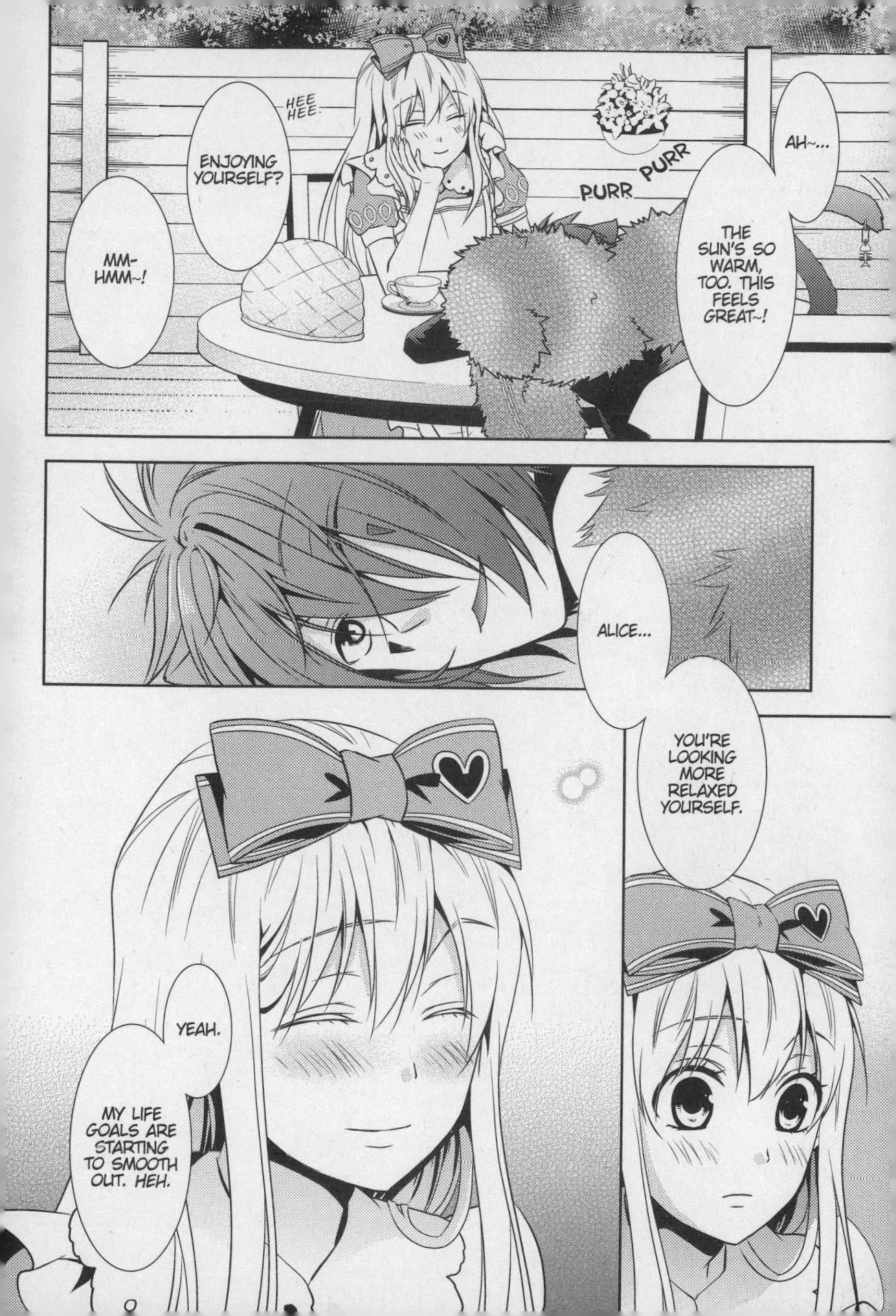
AH~... THE SUN'S SO WARM, TOO. THIS FEELS GREAT~!
PURR PURR
HEE HEE.
ENJOYING YOURSELF?
MM-HMM~!
ALICE... YOU'RE LOOKING MORE RELAXED YOURSELF.
YEAH.
MY LIFE GOALS ARE STARTING TO SMOOTH OUT. HEH.

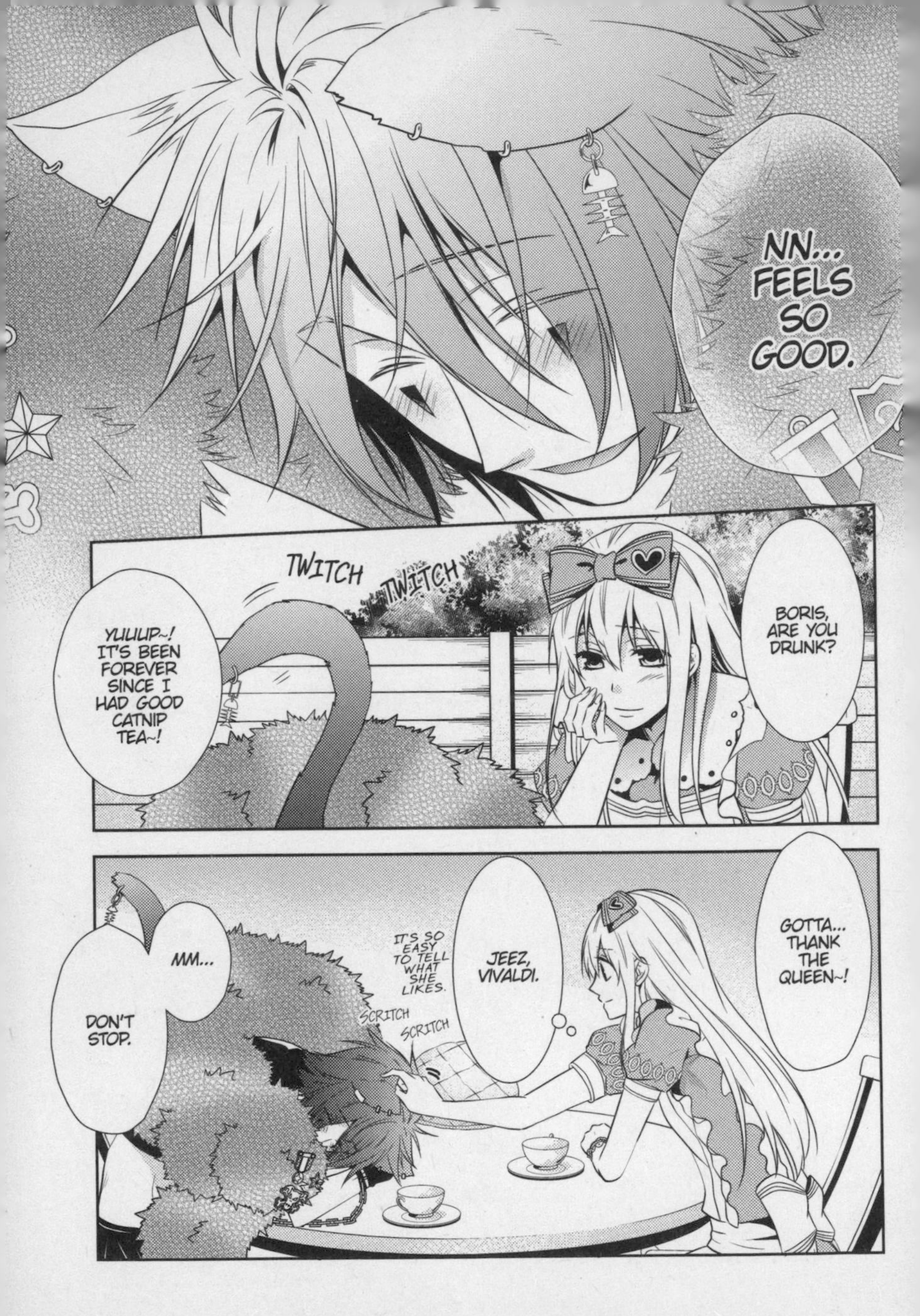
NN... FEELS SO GOOD.
BORIS, ARE YOU DRUNK?
TWITCH
TWITCH
YUULUP~! IT'S BEEN FOREVER SINCE I HAD GOOD CATNIP TEA~!
GOTTA... THANK THE QUEEN~!
JEEZ, VIVALDI.
IT'S SO EASY TO TELL WHAT SHE LIKES.
SCRITCH
SCRITCH
MM...
DON'T STOP.

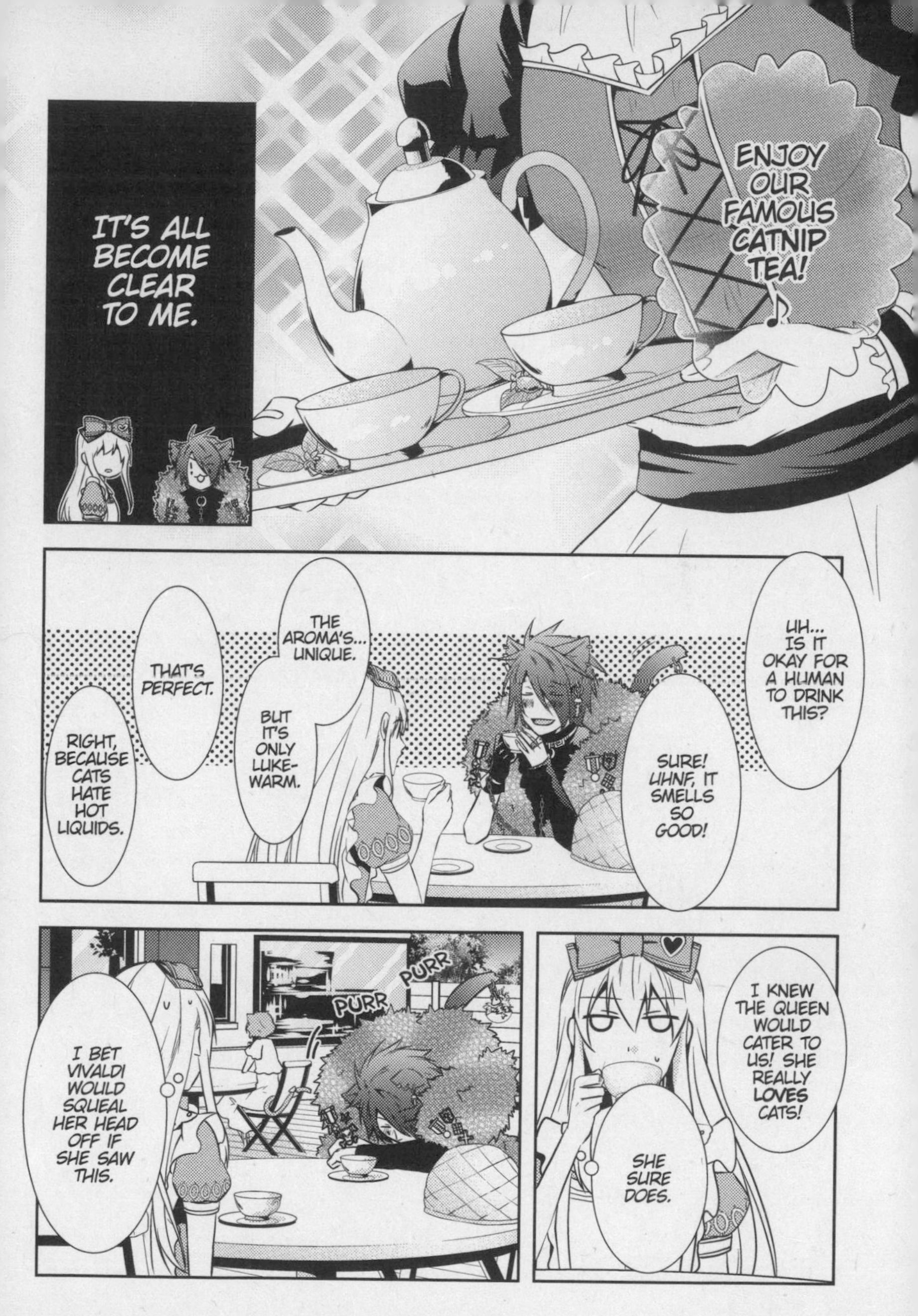
ENJOY OUR FAMOUS CATNIP TEA! ♪
IT'S ALL BECOME CLEAR TO ME.
UH... IS IT OKAY FOR A HUMAN TO DRINK THIS?
SURE! UHNF, IT SMELLS SO GOOD!
THE AROMA'S... UNIQUE.
BUT IT'S ONLY LUKE-WARM.
THAT'S PERFECT.
RIGHT, BECAUSE CATS HATE HOT LIQUIDS.
I KNEW THE QUEEN WOULD CATER TO US! SHE REALLY **LOVES** CATS!
SHE SURE DOES.
PURR
PURR
I BET VIVALDI WOULD SQUEAL HER HEAD OFF IF SHE SAW THIS.

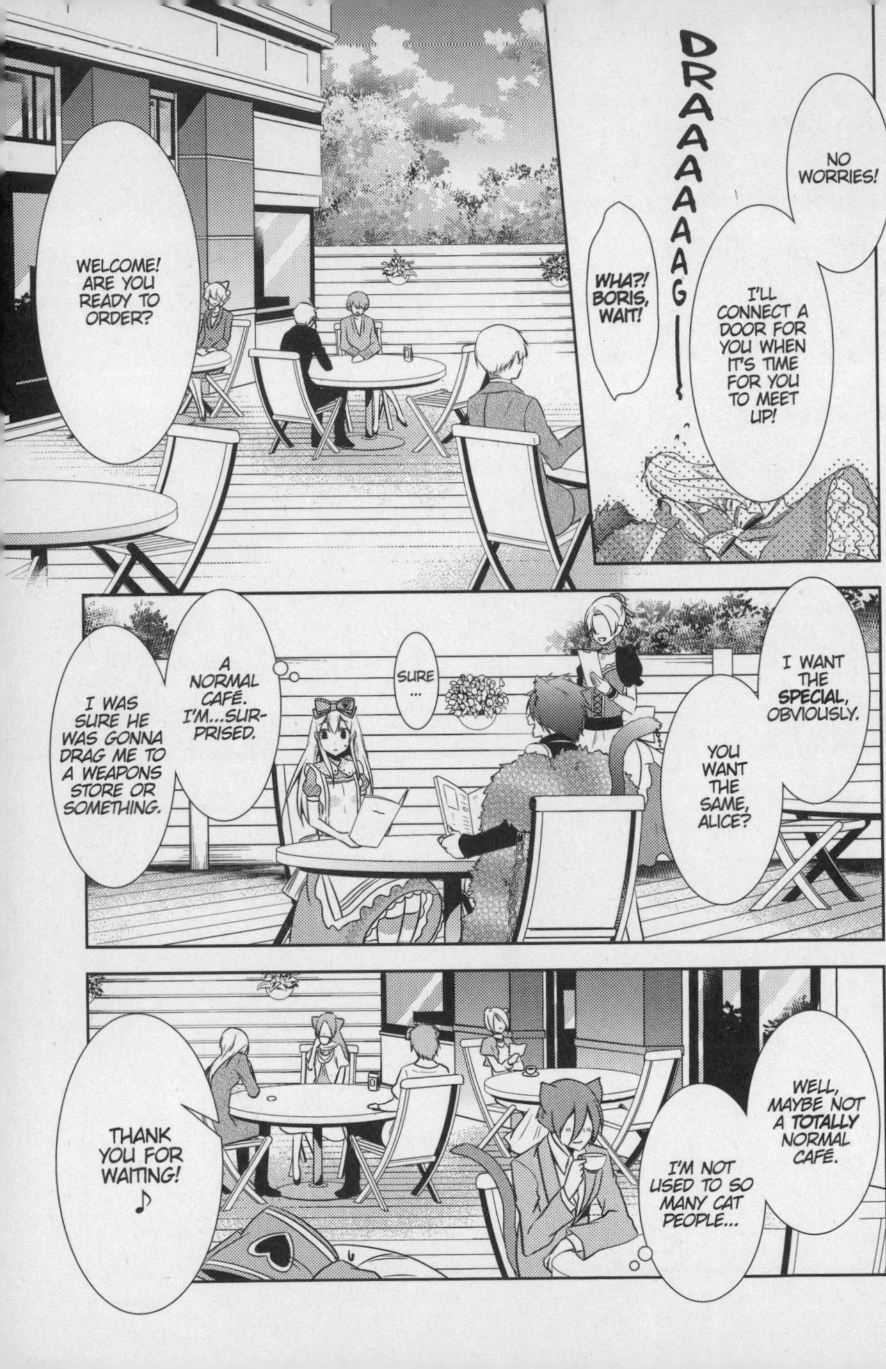
NO WORRIES!
I'LL CONNECT A DOOR FOR YOU WHEN IT'S TIME FOR YOU TO MEET UP!
WHA?! BORIS, WAIT!
DRAAAAAAG
WELCOME! ARE YOU READY TO ORDER?
I WANT THE SPECIAL, OBVIOUSLY.
YOU WANT THE SAME, ALICE?
SURE...
A NORMAL CAFÉ. I'M...SURPRISED.
I WAS SURE HE WAS GONNA DRAG ME TO A WEAPONS STORE OR SOMETHING.
WELL, MAYBE NOT A TOTALLY NORMAL CAFÉ.
I'M NOT USED TO SO MANY CAT PEOPLE...
THANK YOU FOR WAITING! ♪

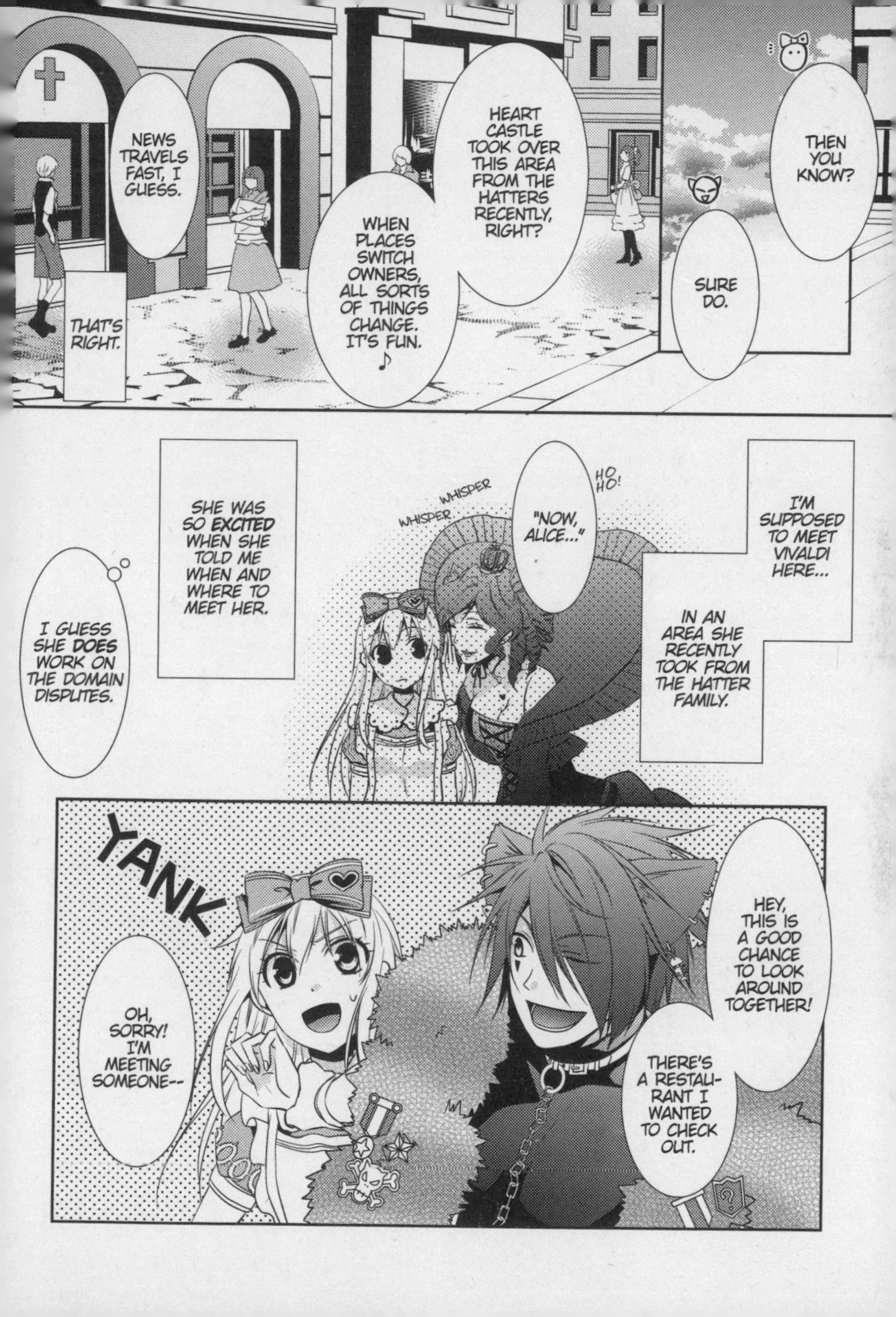
THEN YOU KNOW?
SURE DO.
HEART CASTLE TOOK OVER THIS AREA FROM THE HATTERS RECENTLY, RIGHT?
WHEN PLACES SWITCH OWNERS, ALL SORTS OF THINGS CHANGE. IT'S FUN. ♪
NEWS TRAVELS FAST, I GUESS.
THAT'S RIGHT.
I'M SUPPOSED TO MEET VIVALDI HERE...
IN AN AREA SHE RECENTLY TOOK FROM THE HATTER FAMILY.
HO HO!
"NOW, ALICE..."
WHISPER WHISPER
SHE WAS SO EXCITED WHEN SHE TOLD ME WHEN AND WHERE TO MEET HER.
I GUESS SHE DOES WORK ON THE DOMAIN DISPUTES.
HEY, THIS IS A GOOD CHANCE TO LOOK AROUND TOGETHER!
THERE'S A RESTAURANT I WANTED TO CHECK OUT.
YANK
OH, SORRY! I'M MEETING SOMEONE--

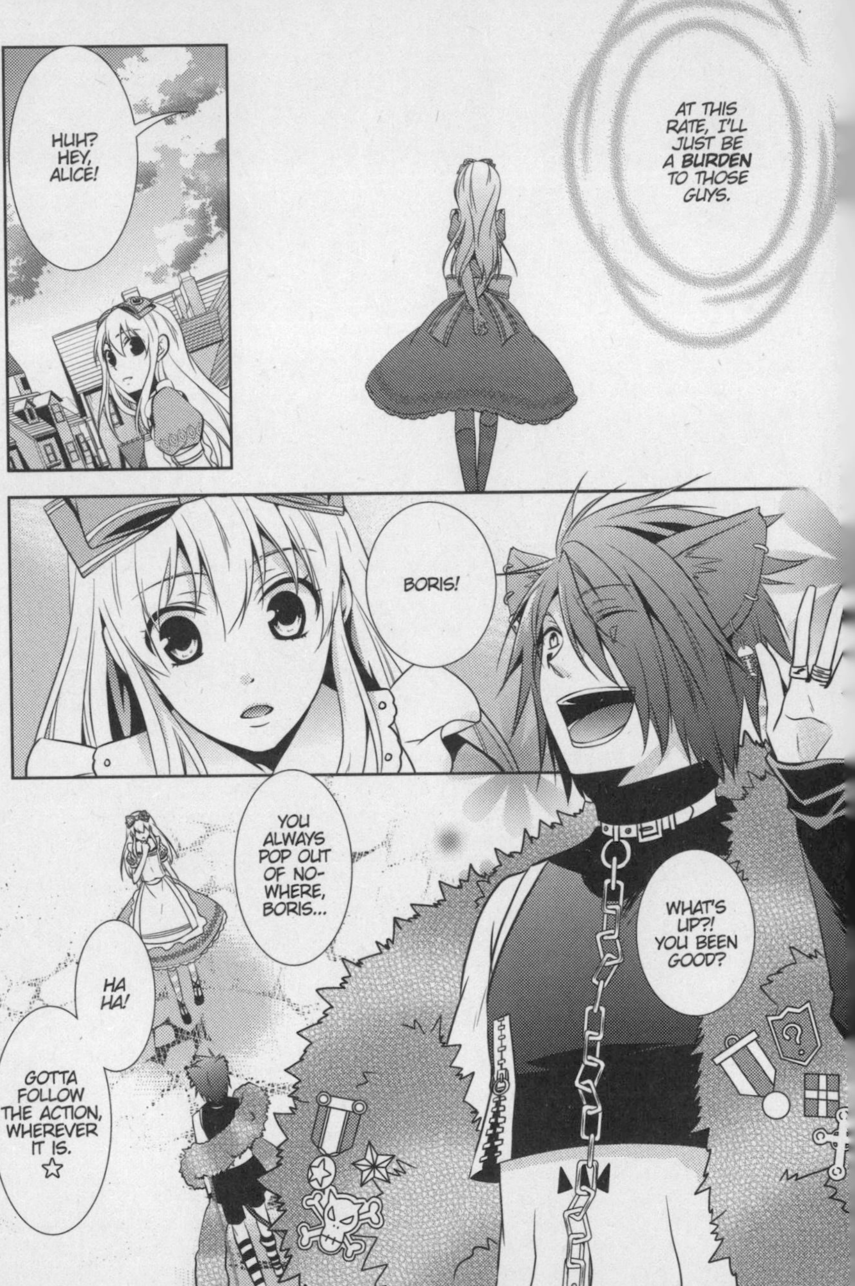
AT THIS RATE, I'LL JUST BE A **BURDEN** TO THOSE GUYS.
HUH? HEY, ALICE!
BORIS!
WHAT'S UP?! YOU BEEN GOOD?
YOU ALWAYS POP OUT OF NO-WHERE, BORIS...
HA HA!
GOTTA FOLLOW THE ACTION, WHEREVER IT IS. ☆

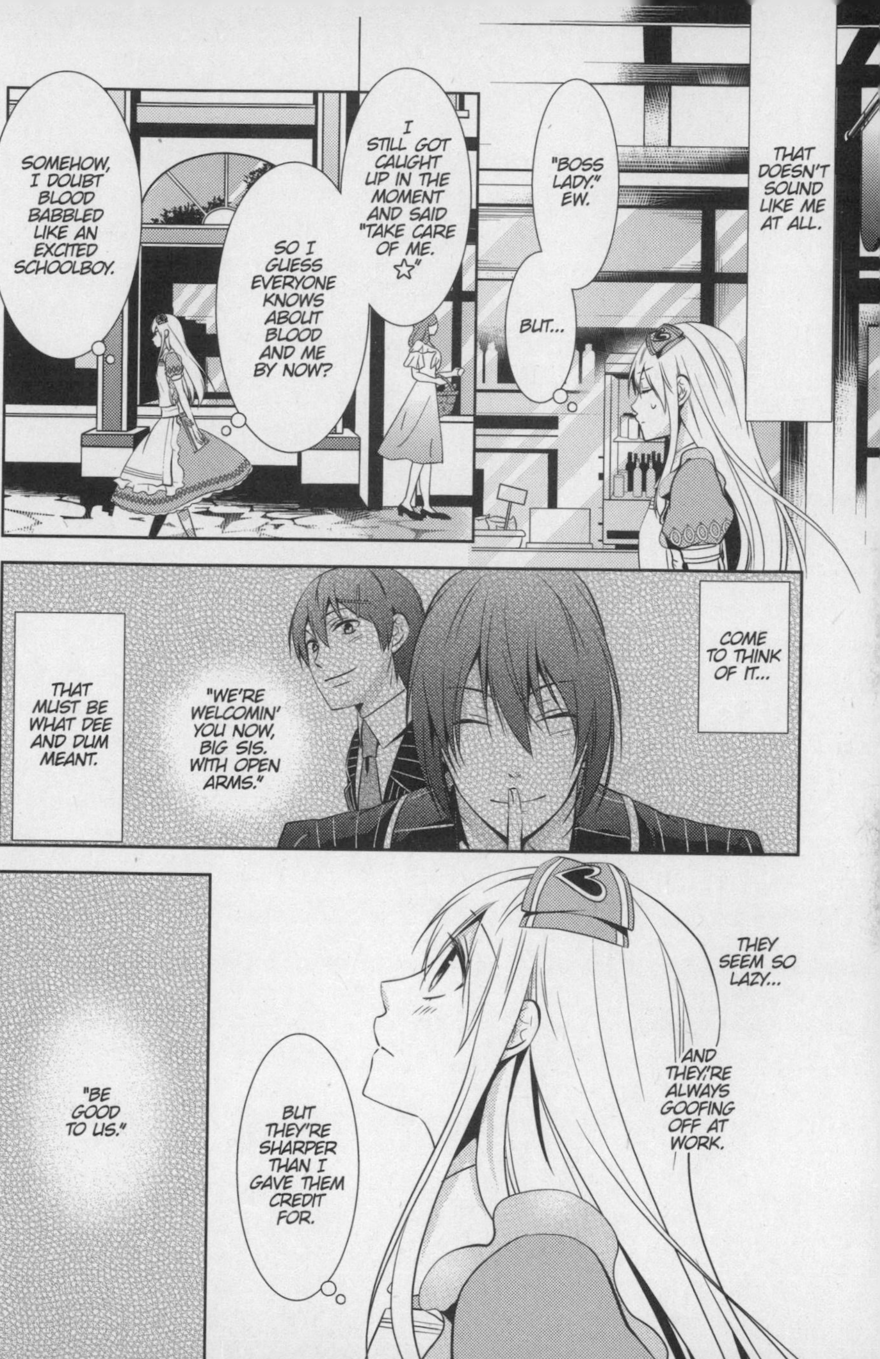
THAT DOESN'T SOUND LIKE ME AT ALL.
"BOSS LADY." EW.
BUT...
I STILL GOT CAUGHT UP IN THE MOMENT AND SAID "TAKE CARE OF ME. ☆"
SO I GUESS EVERYONE KNOWS ABOUT BLOOD AND ME BY NOW?
SOMEHOW, I DOUBT BLOOD BABBLED LIKE AN EXCITED SCHOOLBOY.
COME TO THINK OF IT...
"WE'RE WELCOMIN' YOU NOW, BIG SIS. WITH OPEN ARMS."
THAT MUST BE WHAT DEE AND DUM MEANT.
THEY SEEM SO LAZY...
AND THEY'RE ALWAYS GOOFING OFF AT WORK.
BUT THEY'RE SHARPER THAN I GAVE THEM CREDIT FOR.
"BE GOOD TO US."

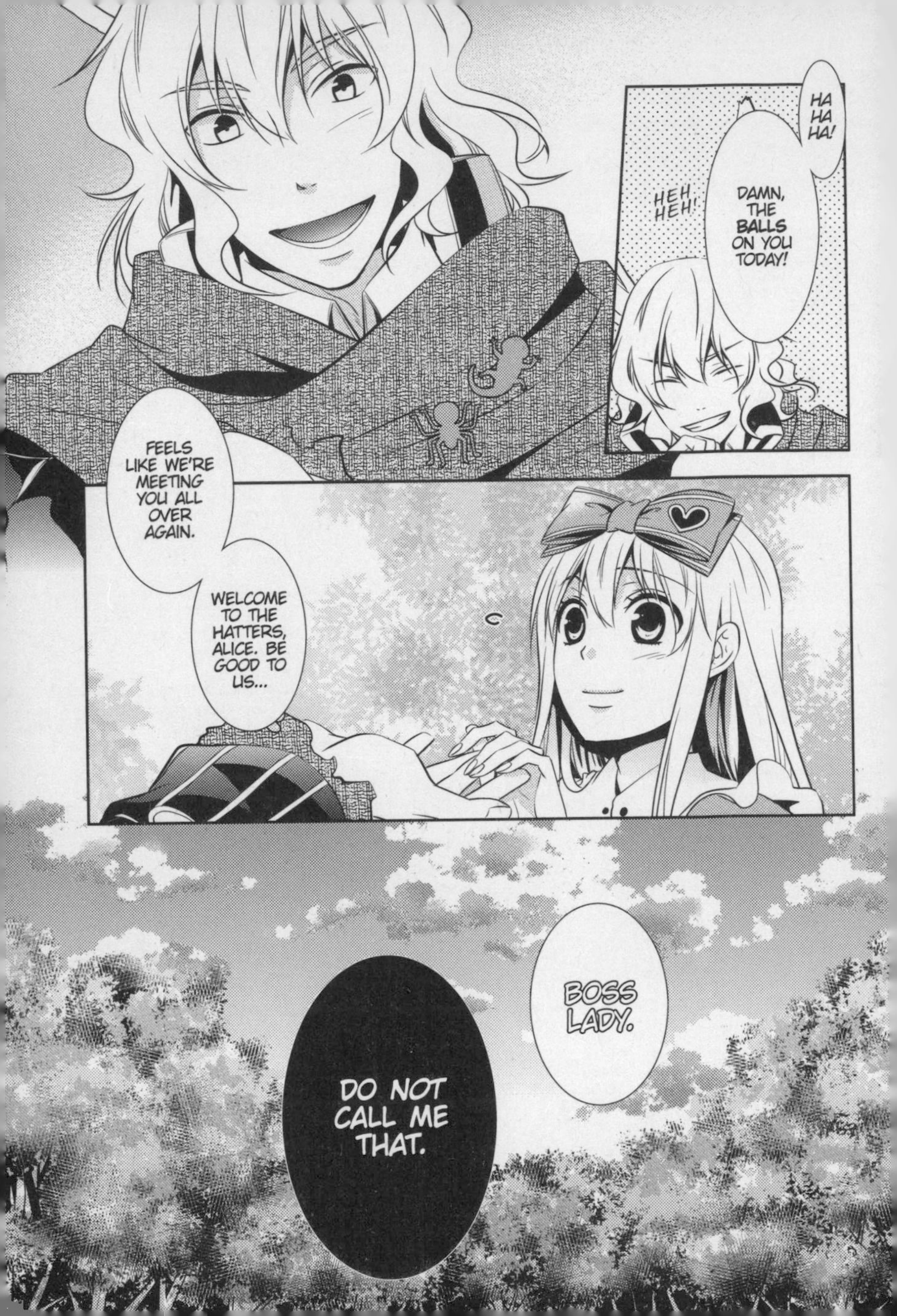
HA HA HA!
DAMN, THE BALLS ON YOU TODAY!
HEH HEH!
FEELS LIKE WE'RE MEETING YOU ALL OVER AGAIN.
WELCOME TO THE HATTERS, ALICE. BE GOOD TO US...
BOSS LADY.
DO NOT CALL ME THAT.

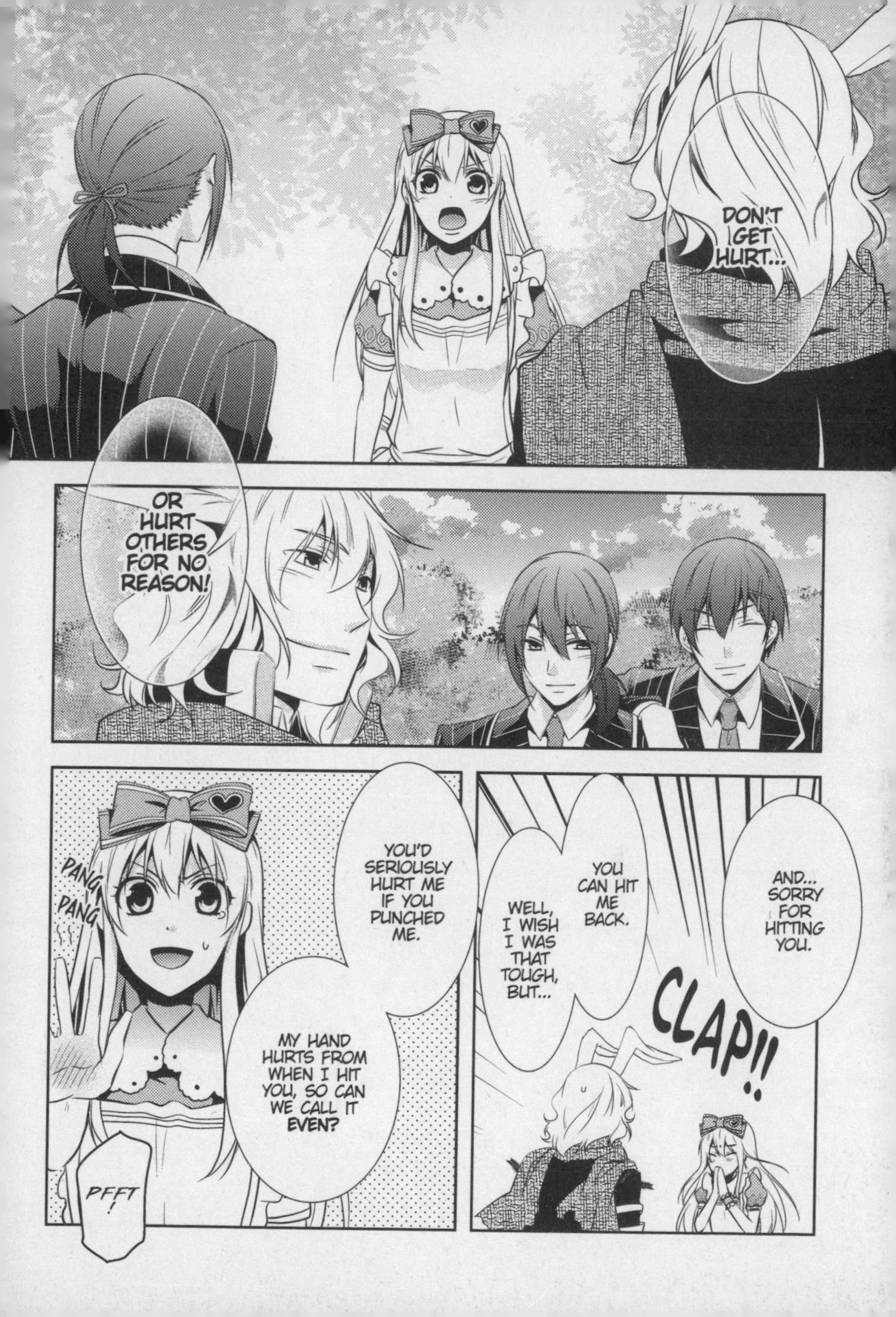
DON'T GET HURT...
OR HURT OTHERS FOR NO REASON!
AND... SORRY FOR HITTING YOU.
YOU CAN HIT ME BACK.
WELL, I WISH I WAS THAT TOUGH, BUT...
CLAP!!
YOU'D SERIOUSLY HURT ME IF YOU PUNCHED ME.
PANG PANG
MY HAND HURTS FROM WHEN I HIT YOU, SO CAN WE CALL IT EVEN?
PFFT!

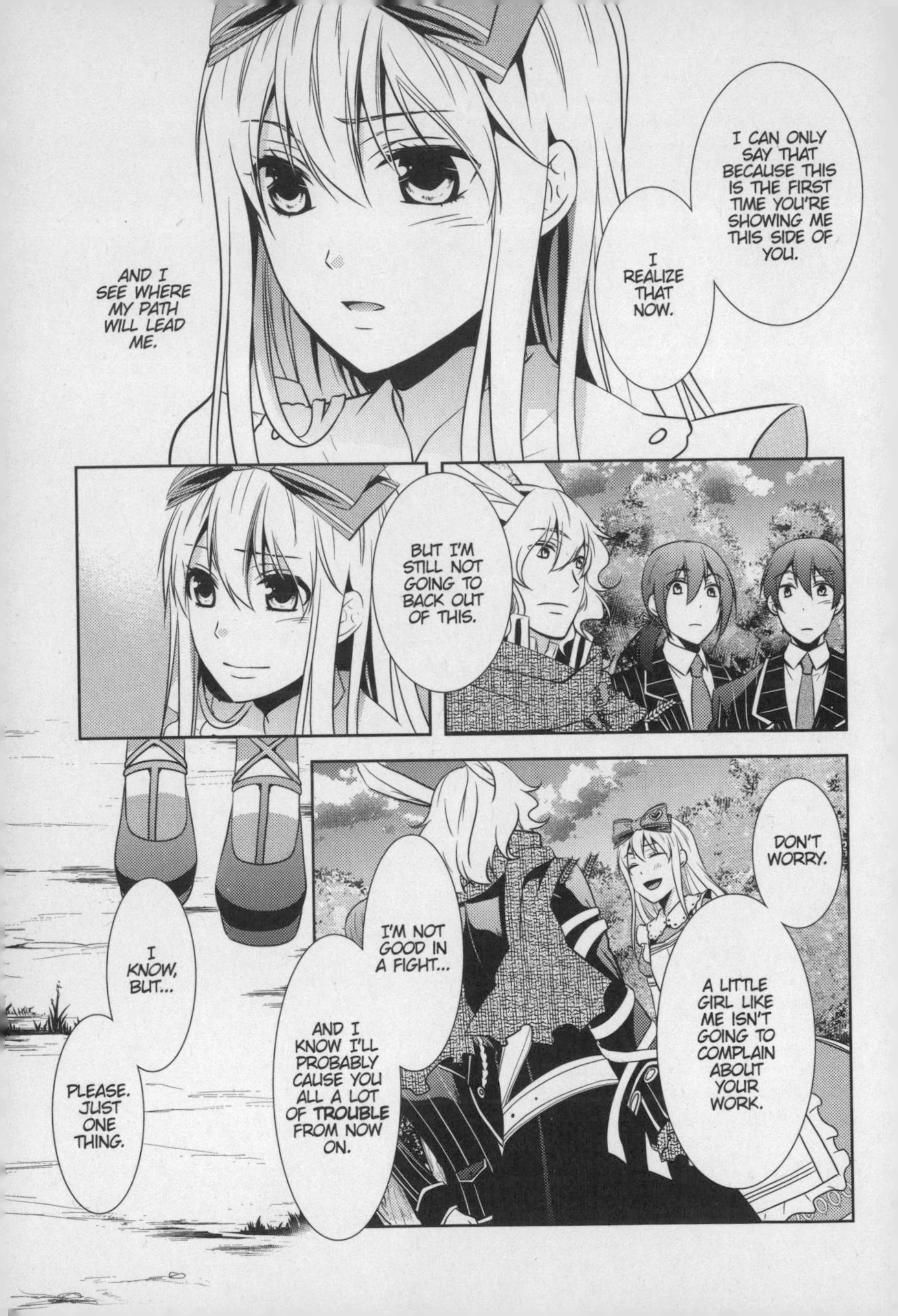
I CAN ONLY SAY THAT BECAUSE THIS IS THE FIRST TIME YOU'RE SHOWING ME THIS SIDE OF YOU.
I REALIZE THAT NOW.
AND I SEE WHERE MY PATH WILL LEAD ME.
BUT I'M STILL NOT GOING TO BACK OUT OF THIS.
DON'T WORRY.
A LITTLE GIRL LIKE ME ISN'T GOING TO COMPLAIN ABOUT YOUR WORK.
I'M NOT GOOD IN A FIGHT...
AND I KNOW I'LL PROBABLY CAUSE YOU ALL A LOT OF **TROUBLE** FROM NOW ON.
I KNOW, BUT...
PLEASE. JUST ONE THING.

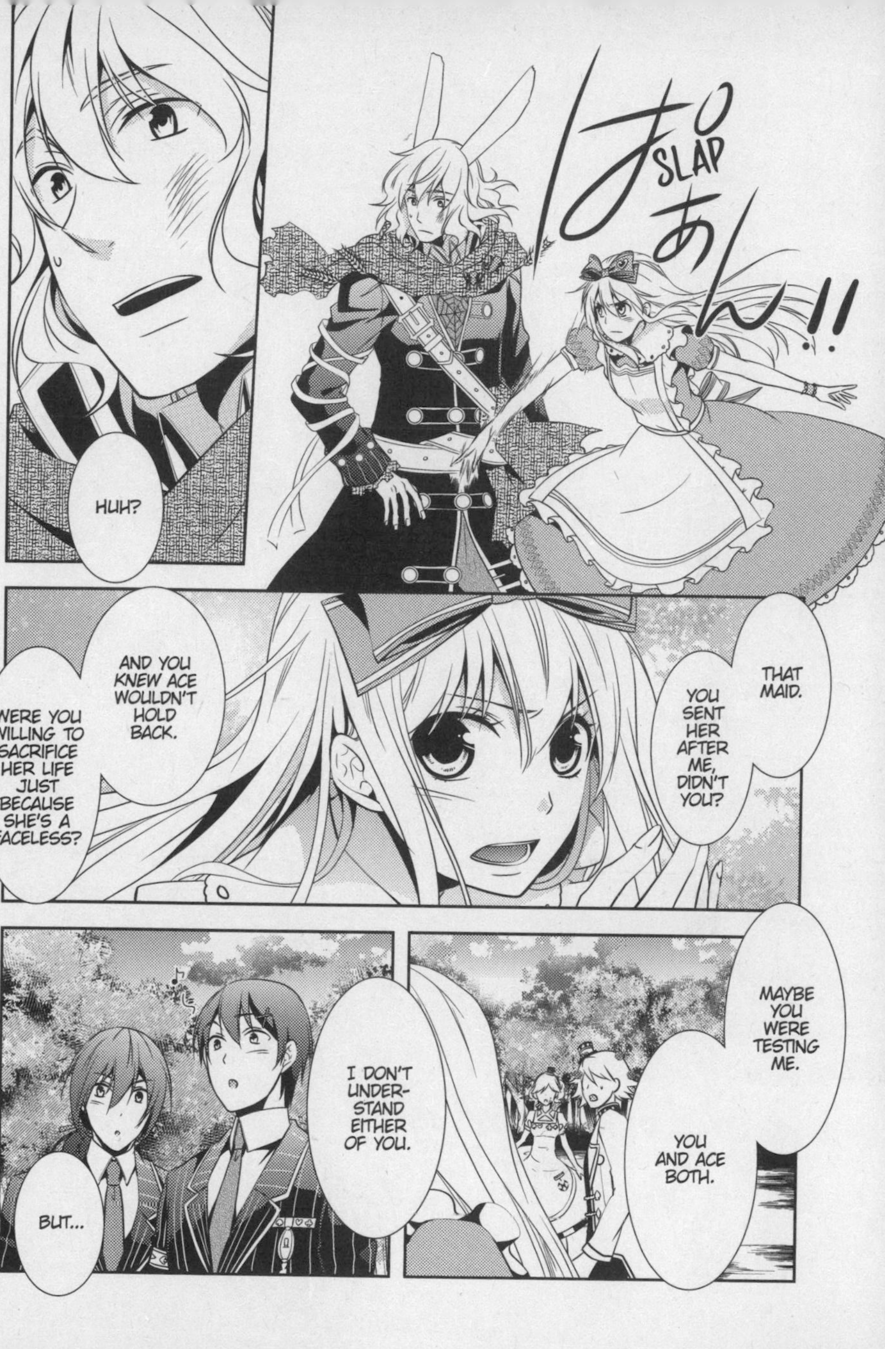
ぱぁん!!
SLAP
HUH?
THAT MAID.
YOU SENT HER AFTER ME, DIDN'T YOU?
AND YOU KNEW ACE WOULDN'T HOLD BACK.
WERE YOU WILLING TO SACRIFICE HER LIFE JUST BECAUSE SHE'S A FACELESS?
MAYBE YOU WERE TESTING ME.
YOU AND ACE BOTH.
I DON'T UNDER-STAND EITHER OF YOU.
BUT...

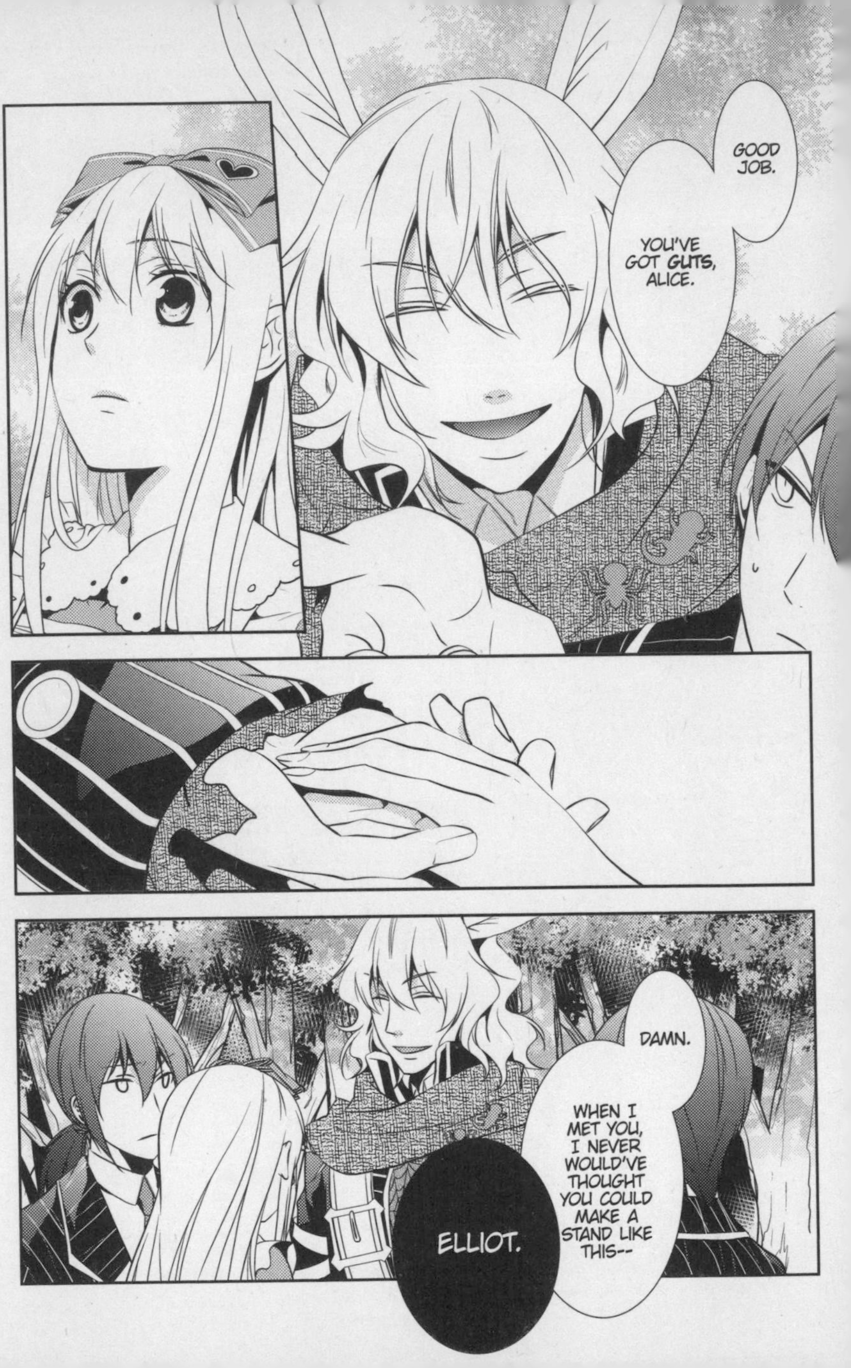
GOOD JOB.
YOU'VE GOT GUTS, ALICE.
DAMN.
WHEN I MET YOU, I NEVER WOULD'VE THOUGHT YOU COULD MAKE A STAND LIKE THIS--
ELLIOT.

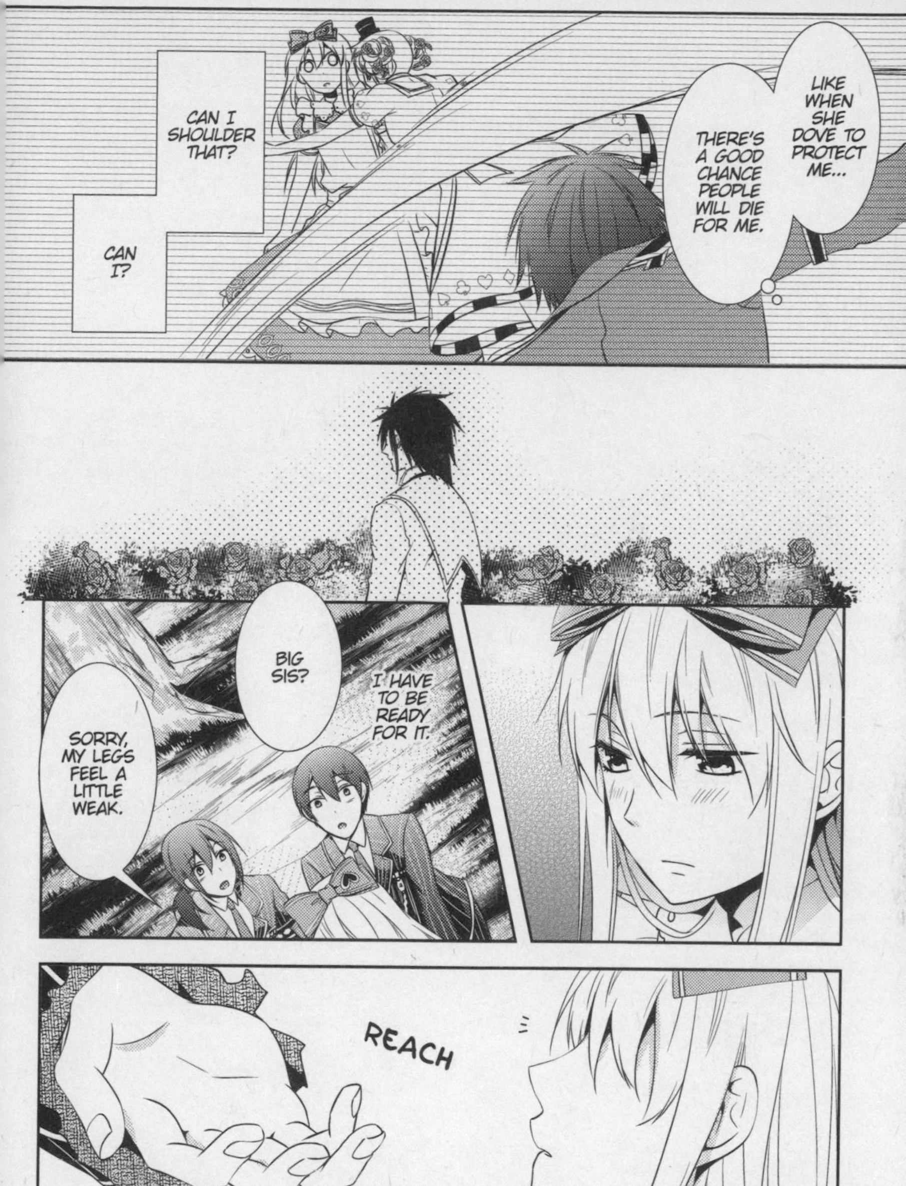
LIKE WHEN SHE DOVE TO PROTECT ME...
THERE'S A GOOD CHANCE PEOPLE WILL DIE FOR ME.
CAN I SHOULDER THAT?
CAN I?
I HAVE TO BE READY FOR IT.
BIG SIS?
SORRY, MY LEGS FEEL A LITTLE WEAK.
REACH

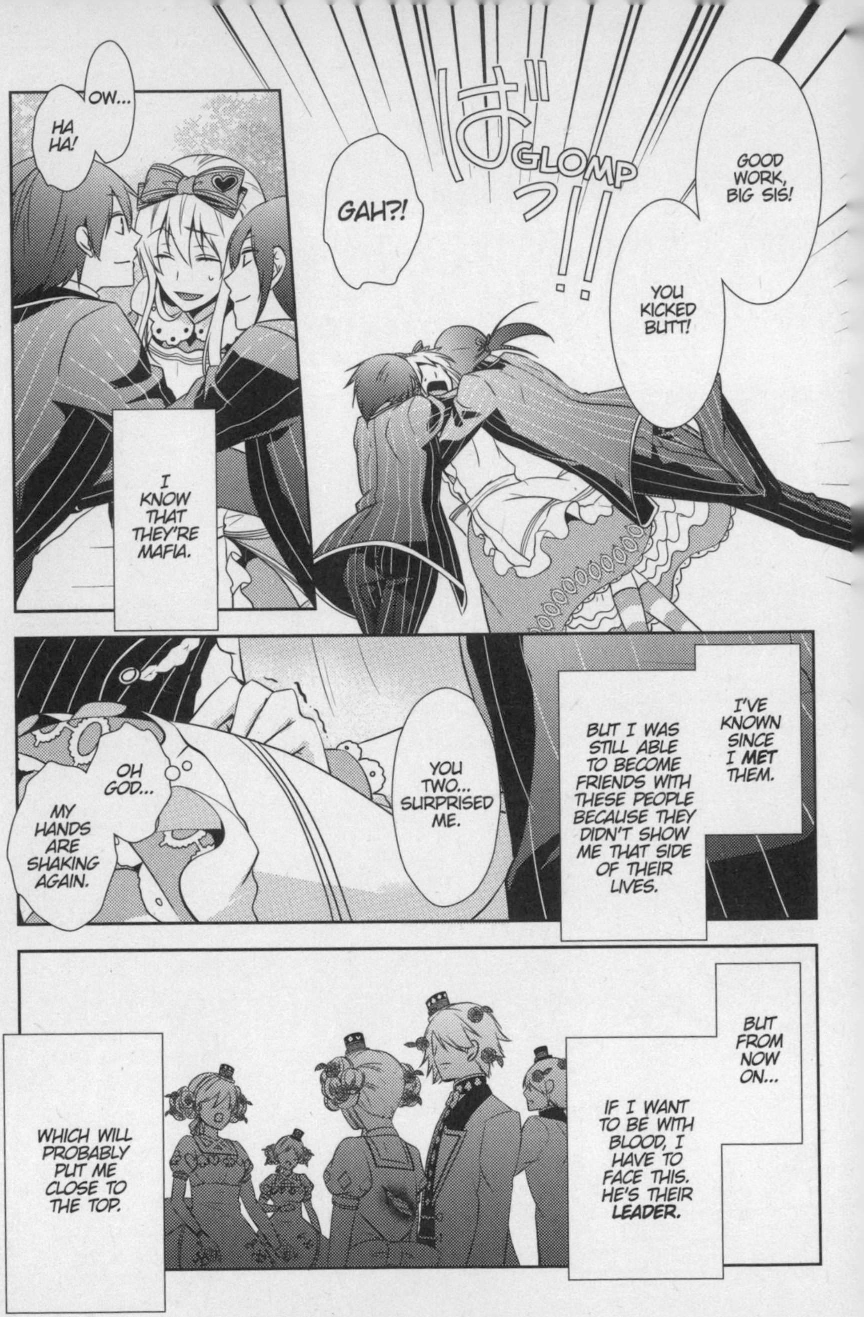
GOOD WORK, BIG SIS!
YOU KICKED BUTT!
ばっ!!
GLOMP
GAH?!
OW... HA HA!
I KNOW THAT THEY'RE MAFIA.
I'VE KNOWN SINCE I **MET** THEM.
BUT I WAS STILL ABLE TO BECOME FRIENDS WITH THESE PEOPLE BECAUSE THEY DIDN'T SHOW ME THAT SIDE OF THEIR LIVES.
YOU TWO... SURPRISED ME.
OH GOD...
MY HANDS ARE SHAKING AGAIN.
BUT FROM NOW ON...
IF I WANT TO BE WITH BLOOD, I HAVE TO FACE THIS. HE'S THEIR **LEADER**.
WHICH WILL PROBABLY PUT ME CLOSE TO THE TOP.

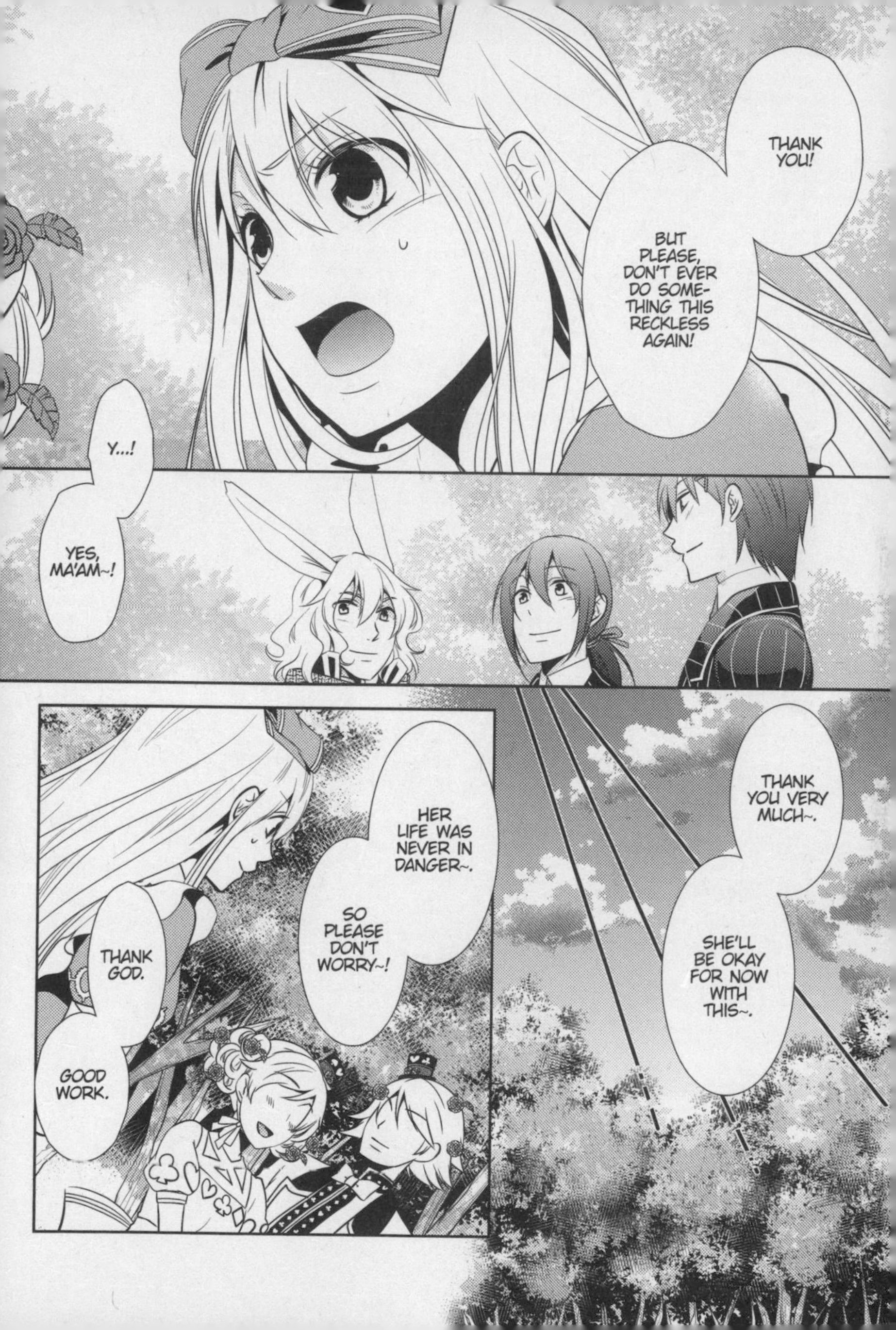
THANK YOU!
BUT PLEASE, DON'T EVER DO SOMETHING THIS RECKLESS AGAIN!
Y...!
YES, MA'AM~!
THANK YOU VERY MUCH~.
SHE'LL BE OKAY FOR NOW WITH THIS~.
HER LIFE WAS NEVER IN DANGER~.
SO PLEASE DON'T WORRY~!
THANK GOD.
GOOD WORK.

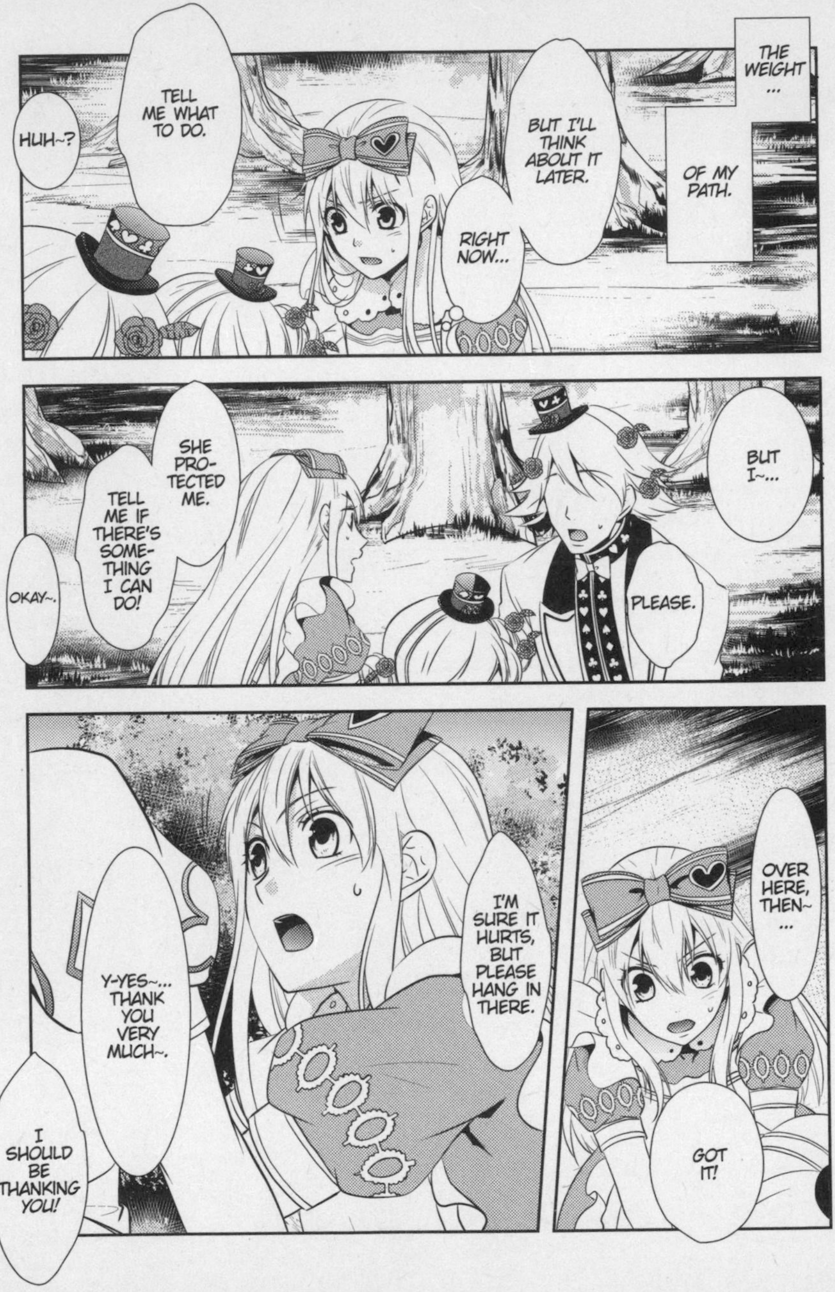
THE WEIGHT ...
OF MY PATH.
BUT I'LL THINK ABOUT IT LATER.
RIGHT NOW...
TELL ME WHAT TO DO.
HUH~?
BUT I~...
PLEASE.
SHE PROTECTED ME.
TELL ME IF THERE'S SOMETHING I CAN DO!
OKAY~.
OVER HERE, THEN~ ...
GOT IT!
I'M SURE IT HURTS, BUT PLEASE HANG IN THERE.
Y-YES~... THANK YOU VERY MUCH~.
I SHOULD BE THANKING YOU!

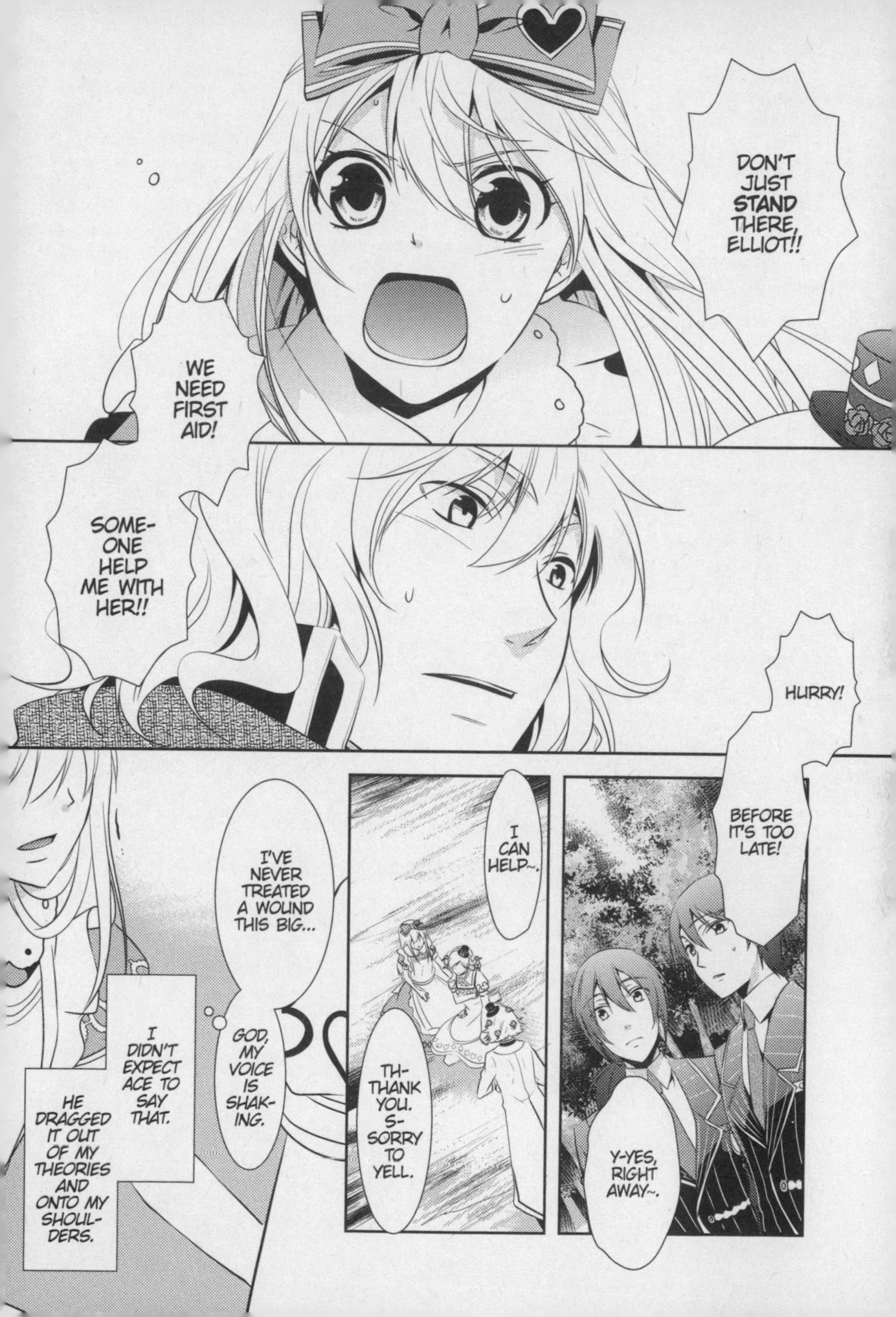
DON'T JUST STAND THERE, ELLIOT!!
WE NEED FIRST AID!
SOME-ONE HELP ME WITH HER!!
HURRY!
BEFORE IT'S TOO LATE!
Y-YES, RIGHT AWAY~.
I CAN HELP~.
TH-THANK YOU. S-SORRY TO YELL.
I'VE NEVER TREATED A WOUND THIS BIG...
GOD, MY VOICE IS SHAK-ING.
I DIDN'T EXPECT ACE TO SAY THAT.
HE DRAGGED IT OUT OF MY THEORIES AND ONTO MY SHOUL-DERS.

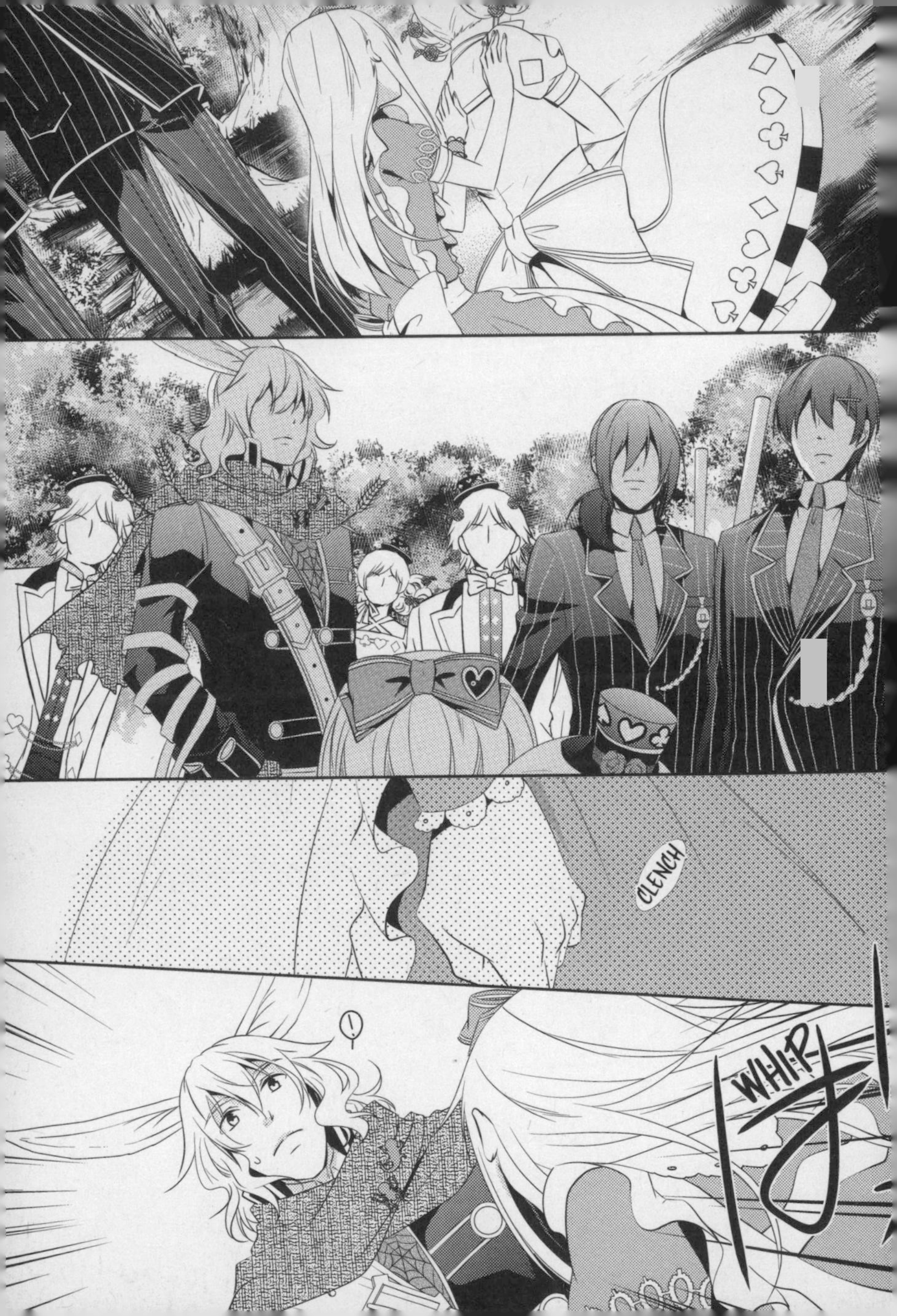
CLENCH
!
WHIP

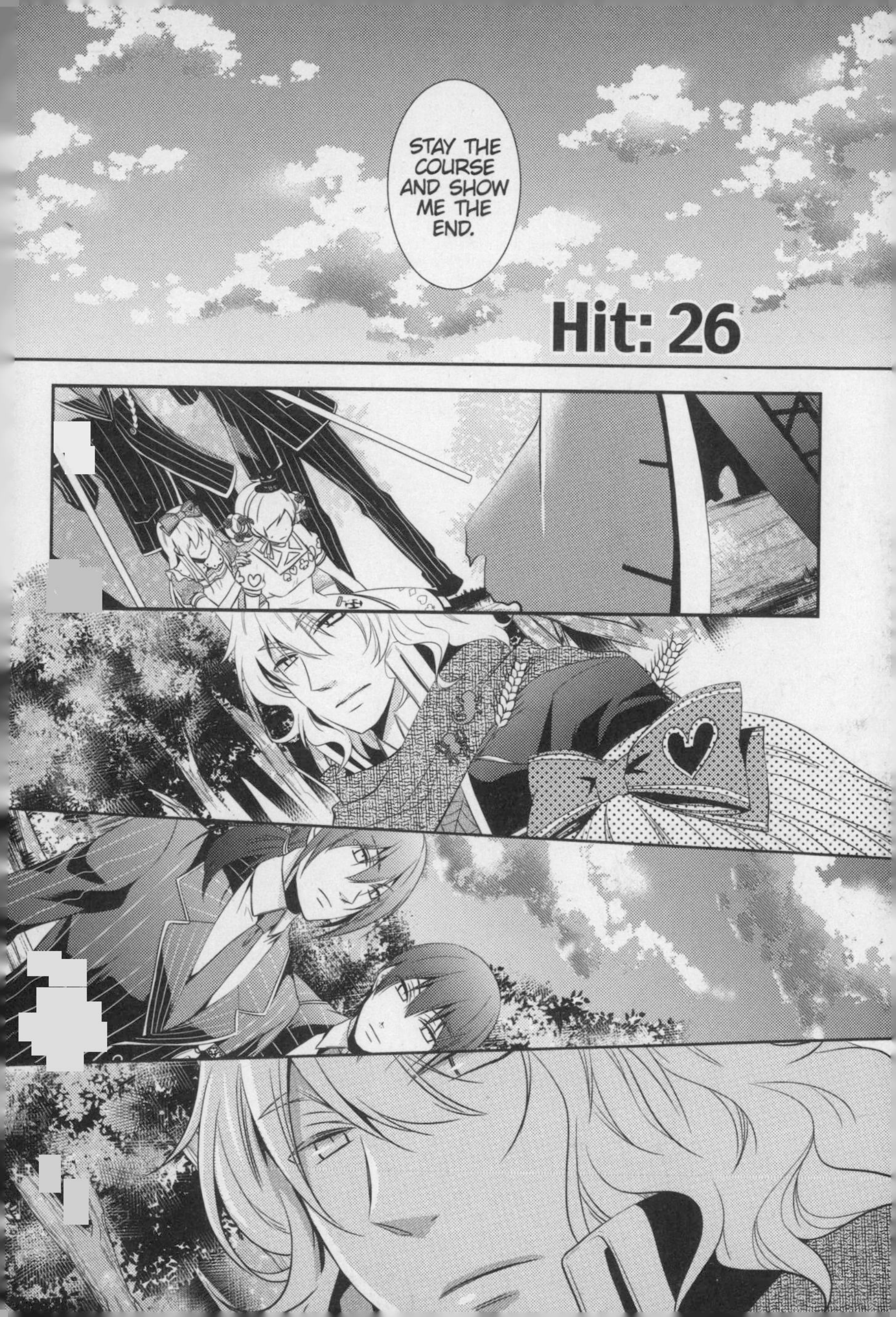
STAY THE COURSE AND SHOW ME THE END.
Hit: 26

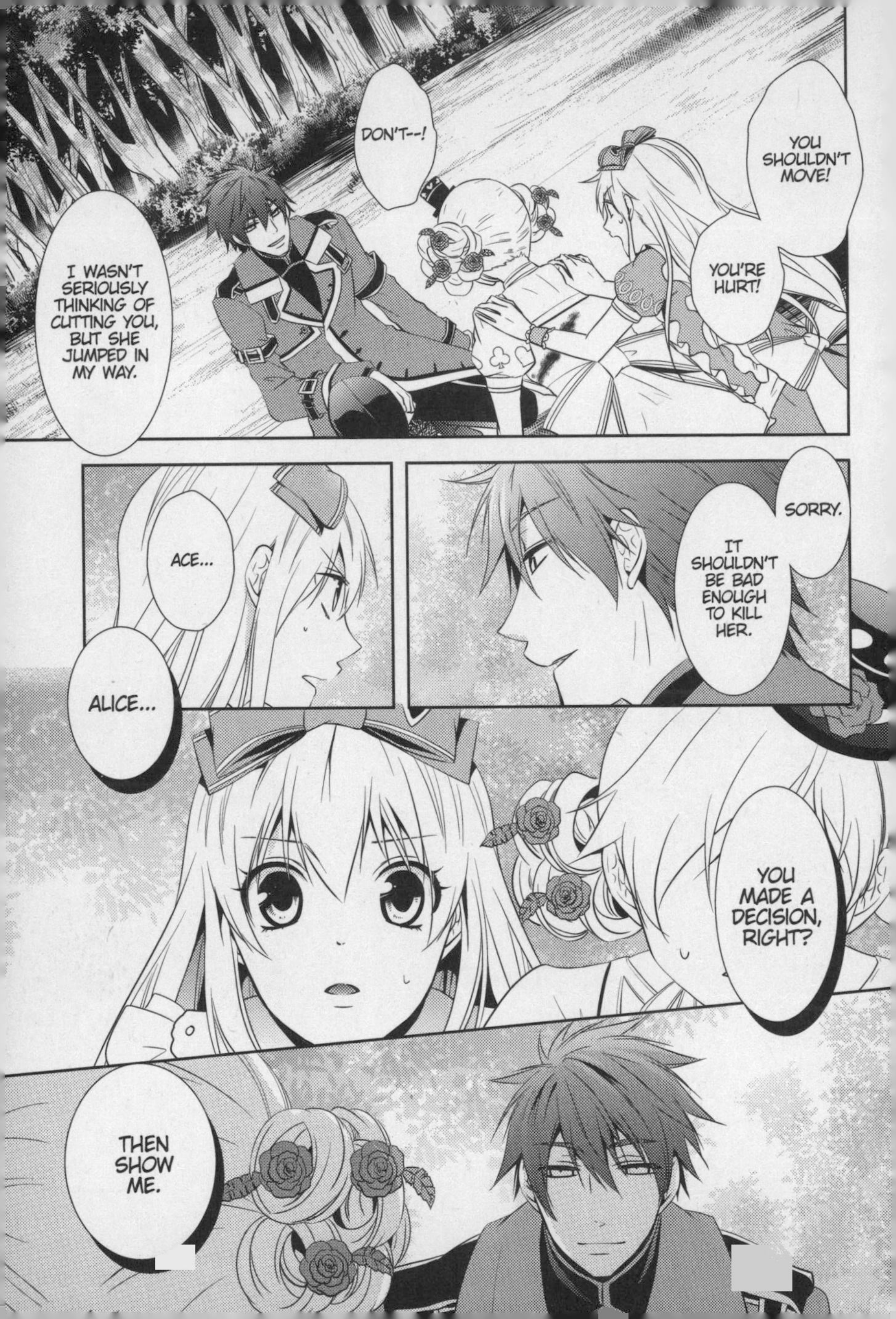
YOU SHOULDN'T MOVE!
YOU'RE HURT!
DON'T--!
I WASN'T SERIOUSLY THINKING OF CUTTING YOU, BUT SHE JUMPED IN MY WAY.
SORRY.
IT SHOULDN'T BE BAD ENOUGH TO KILL HER.
ACE...
ALICE...
YOU MADE A DECISION, RIGHT?
THEN SHOW ME.

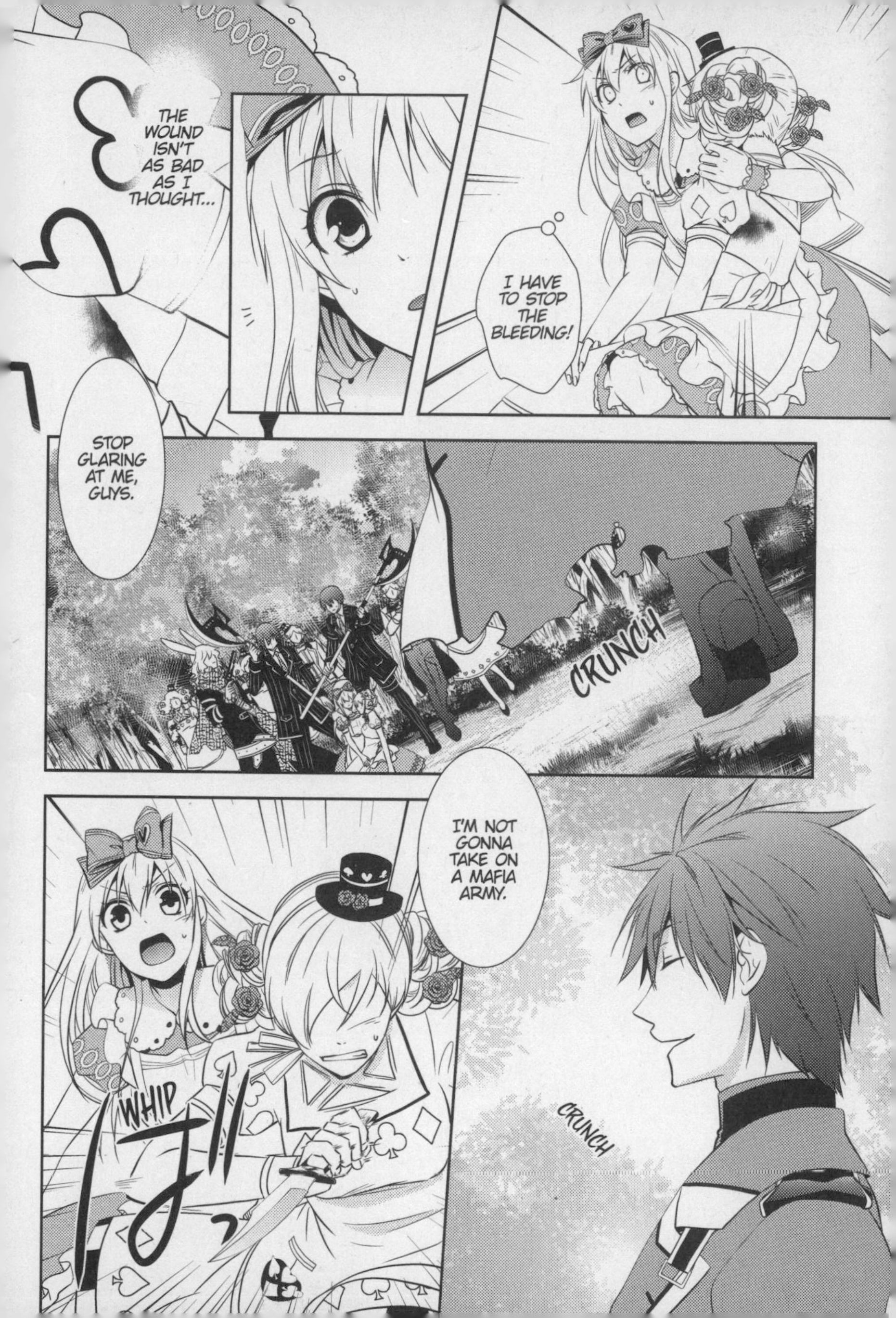
I HAVE TO STOP THE BLEEDING!
THE WOUND ISN'T AS BAD AS I THOUGHT...
STOP GLARING AT ME, GUYS.
CRUNCH
I'M NOT GONNA TAKE ON A MAFIA ARMY.
CRUNCH
WHIP

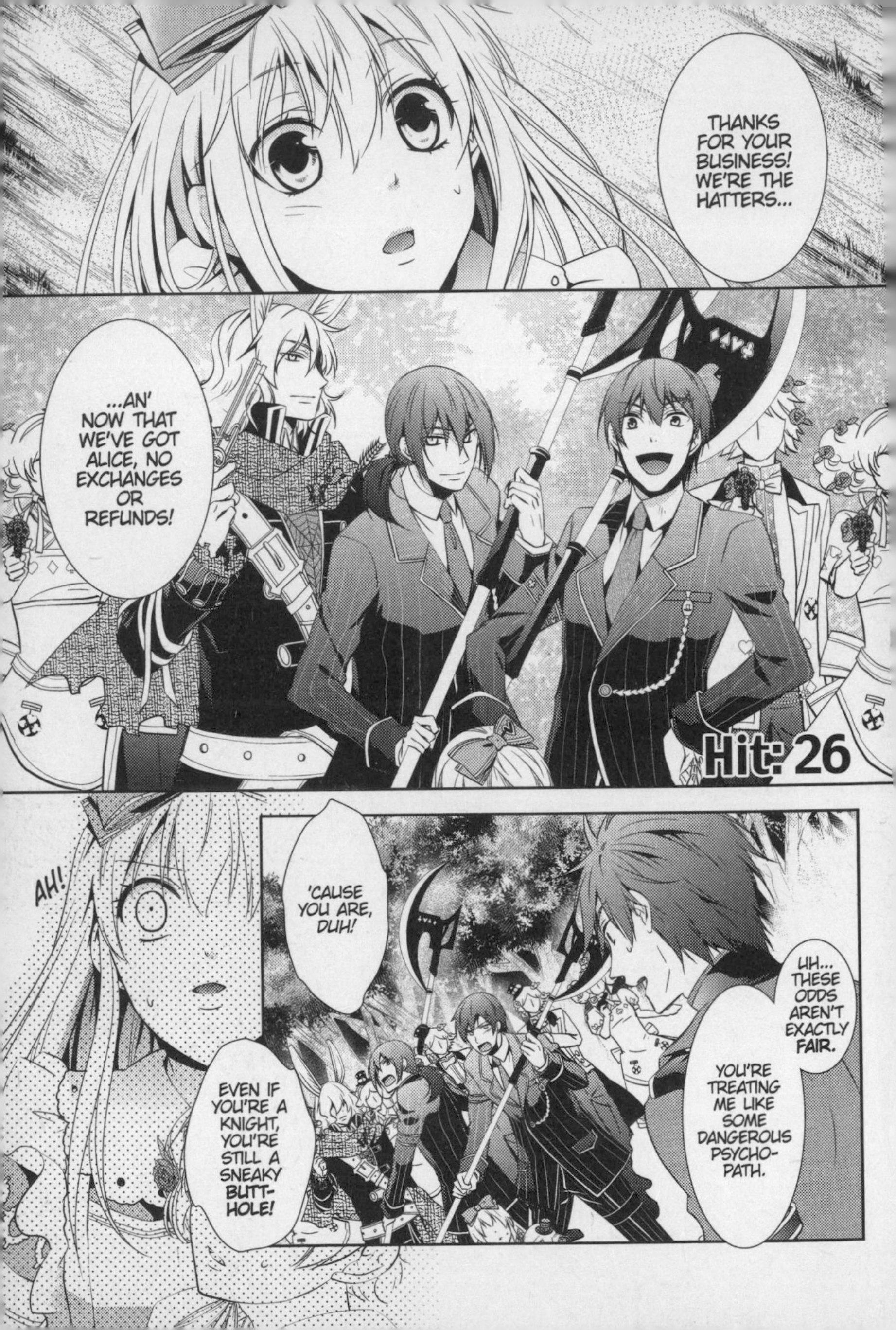

THANKS FOR YOUR BUSINESS! WE'RE THE HATTERS...
...AN' NOW THAT WE'VE GOT ALICE, NO EXCHANGES OR REFUNDS!
Hit: 26
UH... THESE ODDS AREN'T EXACTLY FAIR.
YOU'RE TREATING ME LIKE SOME DANGEROUS PSYCHO-PATH.
'CAUSE YOU ARE, DUH!
EVEN IF YOU'RE A KNIGHT, YOU'RE STILL A SNEAKY BUTT-HOLE!
AH!

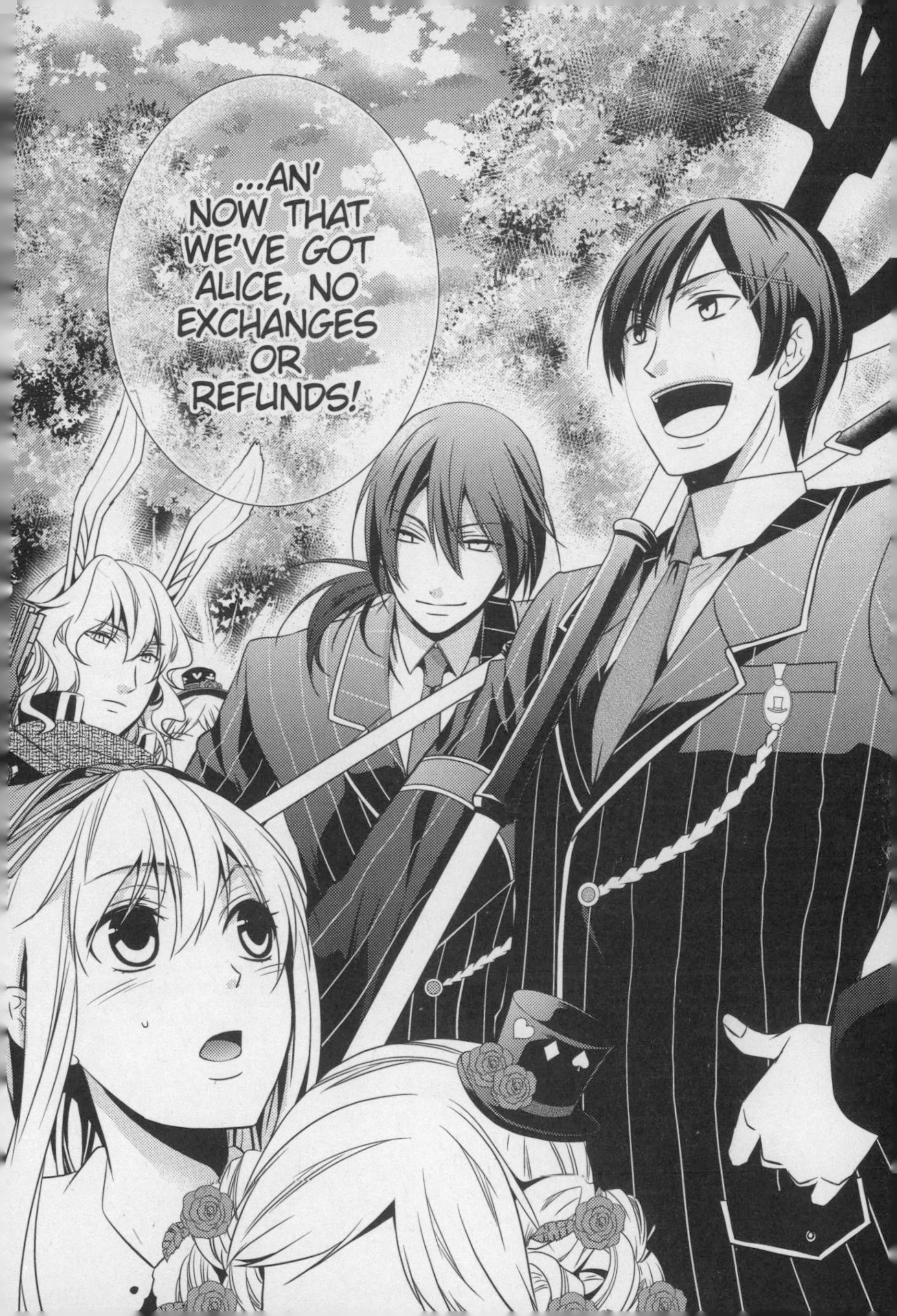
...AN' NOW THAT WE'VE GOT ALICE, NO EXCHANGES OR REFUNDS!

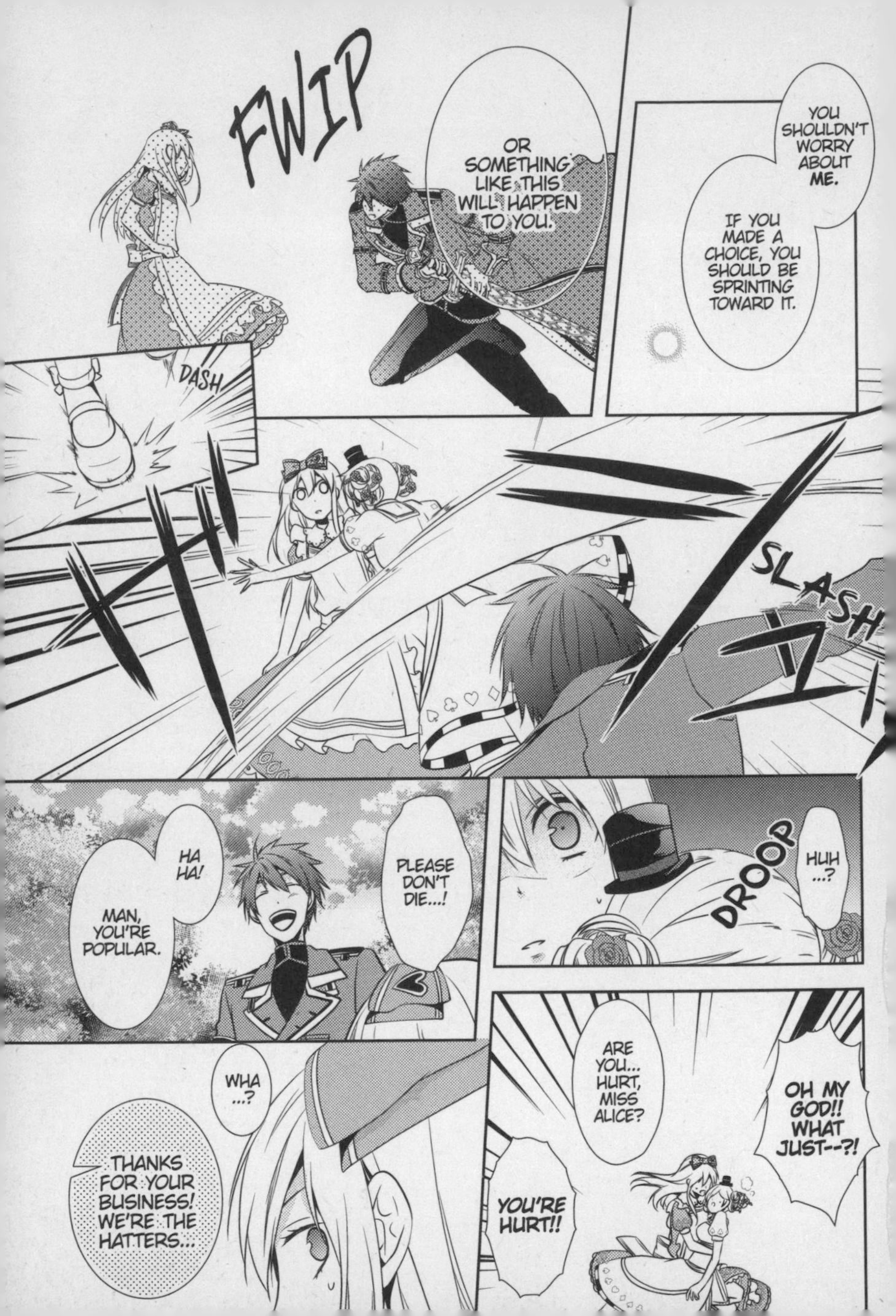
YOU SHOULDN'T WORRY ABOUT ME.
IF YOU MADE A CHOICE, YOU SHOULD BE SPRINTING TOWARD IT.
OR SOMETHING LIKE THIS WILL HAPPEN TO YOU.
FWIP
DASH
SLASH
HUH ...?
DROOP
PLEASE DON'T DIE...!
HA HA!
MAN, YOU'RE POPULAR.
OH MY GOD!! WHAT JUST--?!
ARE YOU... HURT, MISS ALICE?
YOU'RE HURT!!
WHA ...?
THANKS FOR YOUR BUSINESS! WE'RE THE HATTERS...

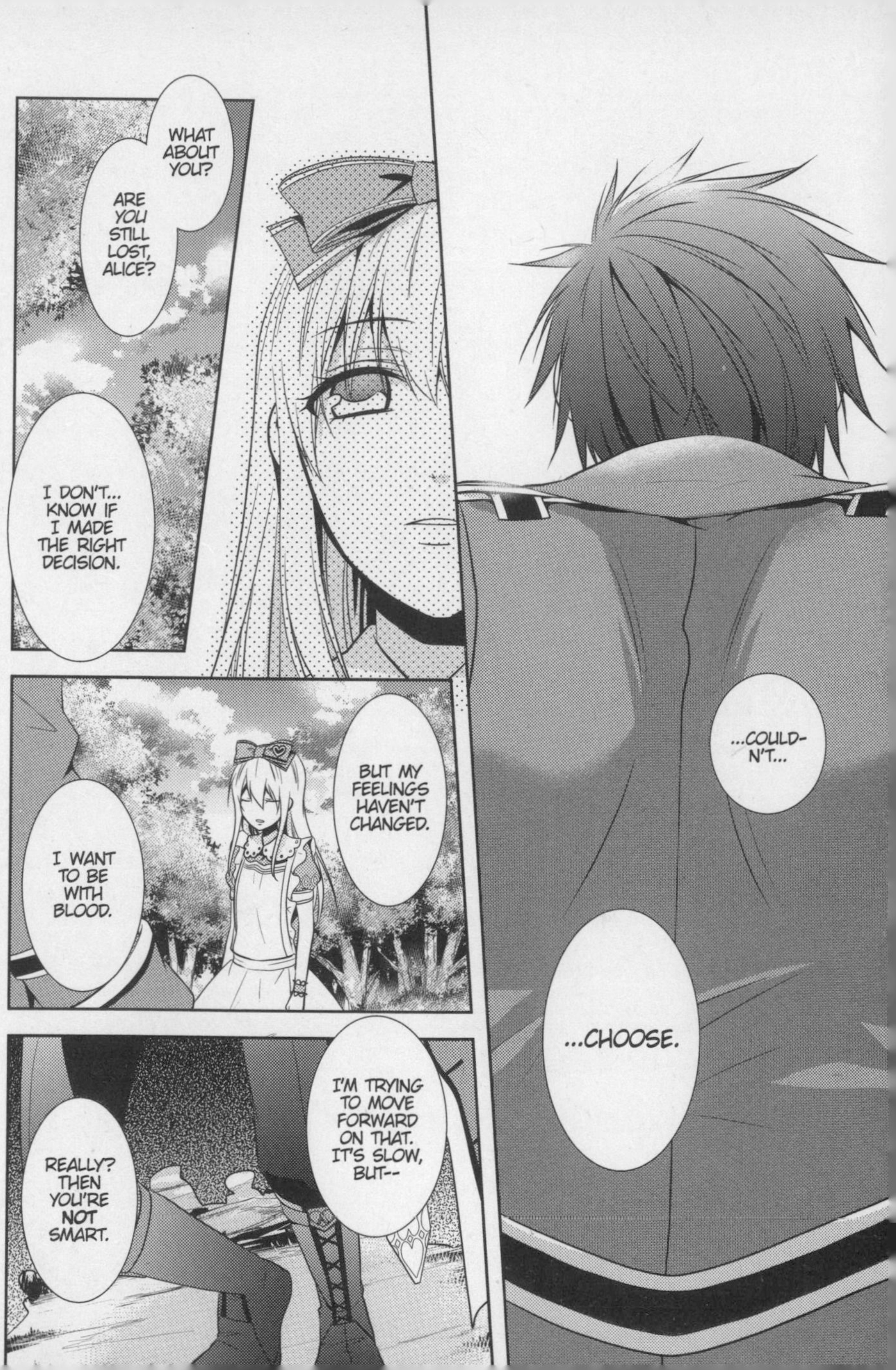
...COULD-N'T...
...CHOOSE.
WHAT ABOUT YOU?
ARE YOU STILL LOST, ALICE?
I DON'T... KNOW IF I MADE THE RIGHT DECISION.
BUT MY FEELINGS HAVEN'T CHANGED.
I WANT TO BE WITH BLOOD.
I'M TRYING TO MOVE FORWARD ON THAT. IT'S SLOW, BUT--
REALLY? THEN YOU'RE NOT SMART.

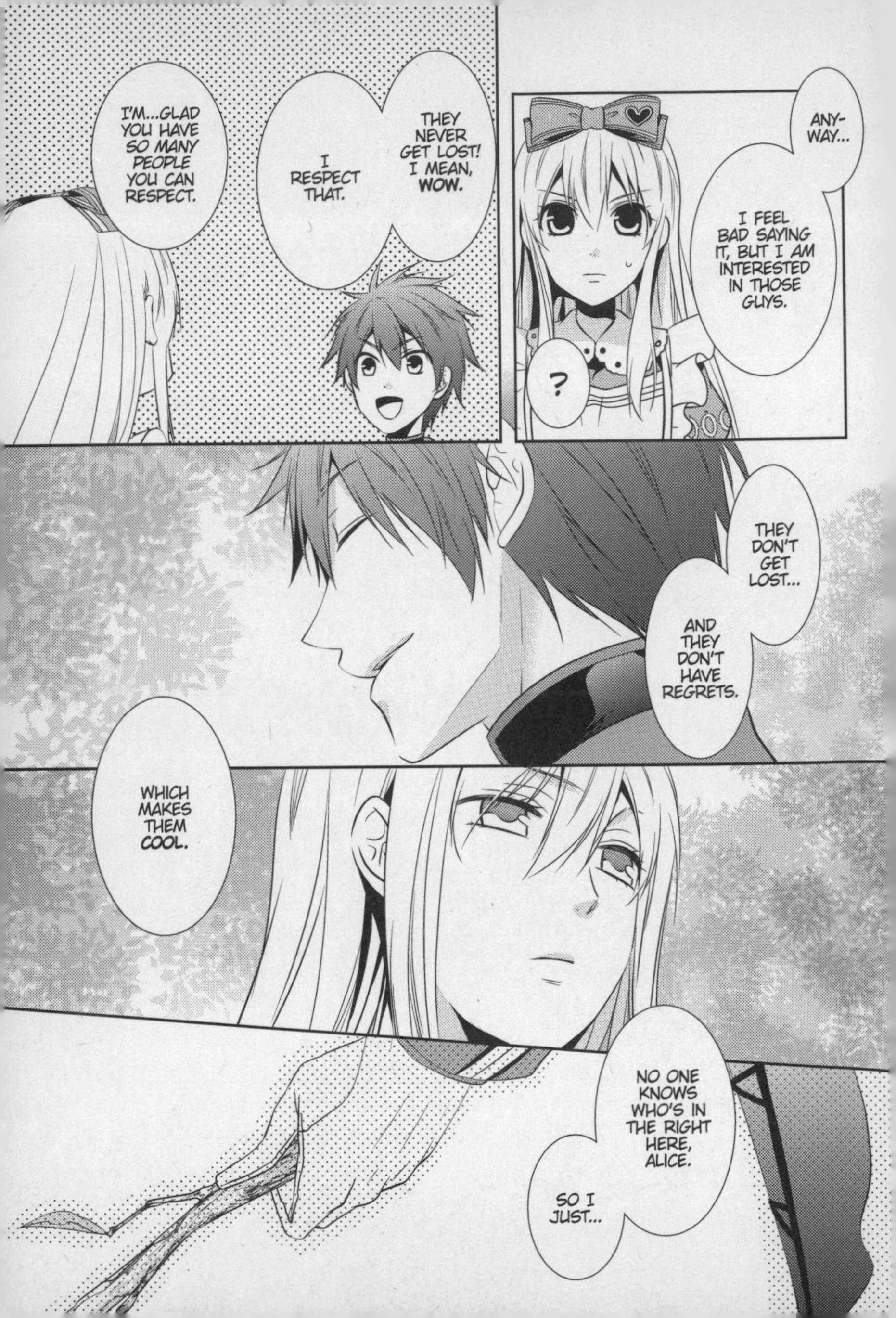
ANY-WAY...
I FEEL BAD SAYING IT, BUT I AM INTERESTED IN THOSE GUYS.
?
THEY NEVER GET LOST! I MEAN, WOW.
I RESPECT THAT.
I'M...GLAD YOU HAVE SO MANY PEOPLE YOU CAN RESPECT.
THEY DON'T GET LOST...
AND THEY DON'T HAVE REGRETS.
WHICH MAKES THEM COOL.
NO ONE KNOWS WHO'S IN THE RIGHT HERE, ALICE.
SO I JUST...

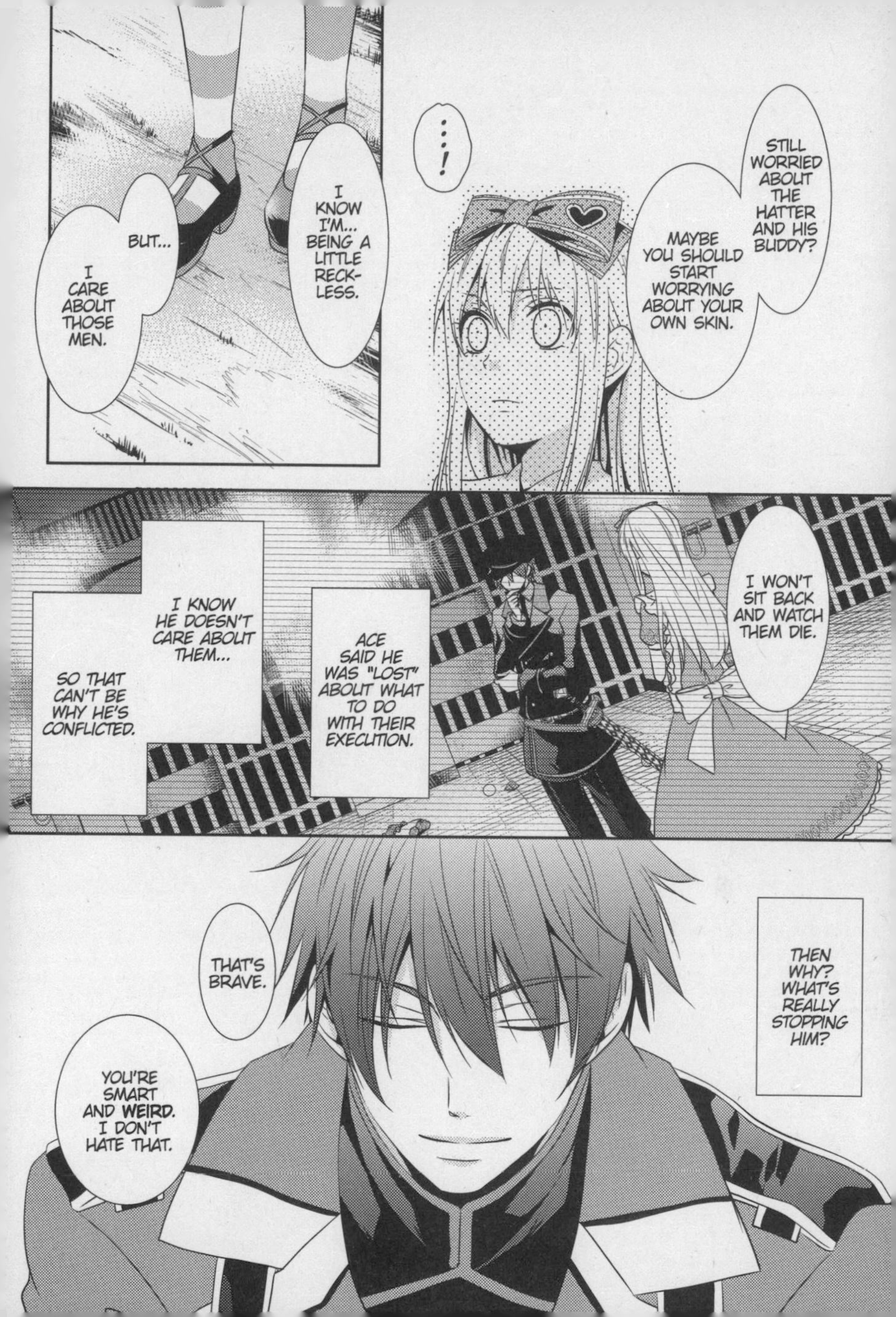
STILL WORRIED ABOUT THE HATTER AND HIS BUDDY?
MAYBE YOU SHOULD START WORRYING ABOUT YOUR OWN SKIN.
...!
I KNOW I'M... BEING A LITTLE RECK-LESS.
BUT...
I CARE ABOUT THOSE MEN.
I WON'T SIT BACK AND WATCH THEM DIE.
ACE SAID HE WAS "LOST" ABOUT WHAT TO DO WITH THEIR EXECUTION.
I KNOW HE DOESN'T CARE ABOUT THEM...
SO THAT CAN'T BE WHY HE'S CONFLICTED.
THEN WHY? WHAT'S REALLY STOPPING HIM?
THAT'S BRAVE.
YOU'RE SMART AND WEIRD. I DON'T HATE THAT.

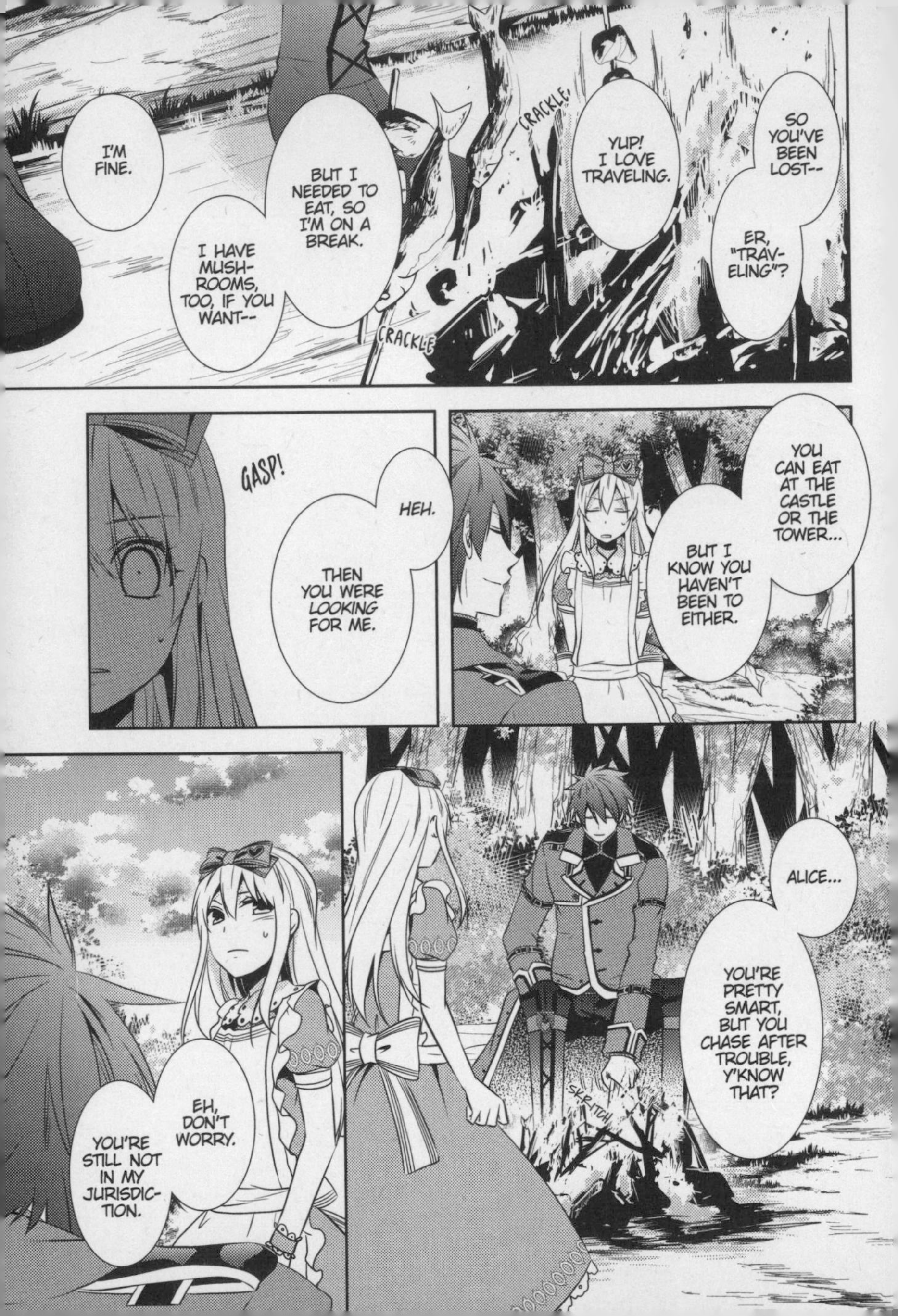
SO YOU'VE BEEN LOST--
ER, "TRAVELING"?
YUP! I LOVE TRAVELING.
CRACKLE
BUT I NEEDED TO EAT, SO I'M ON A BREAK.
I HAVE MUSH-ROOMS, TOO, IF YOU WANT--
CRACKLE
I'M FINE.
YOU CAN EAT AT THE CASTLE OR THE TOWER...
BUT I KNOW YOU HAVEN'T BEEN TO EITHER.
HEH.
THEN YOU WERE LOOKING FOR ME.
GASP!
ALICE...
YOU'RE PRETTY SMART, BUT YOU CHASE AFTER TROUBLE, Y'KNOW THAT?
SKRITCH
EH, DON'T WORRY.
YOU'RE STILL NOT IN MY JURISDIC-TION.

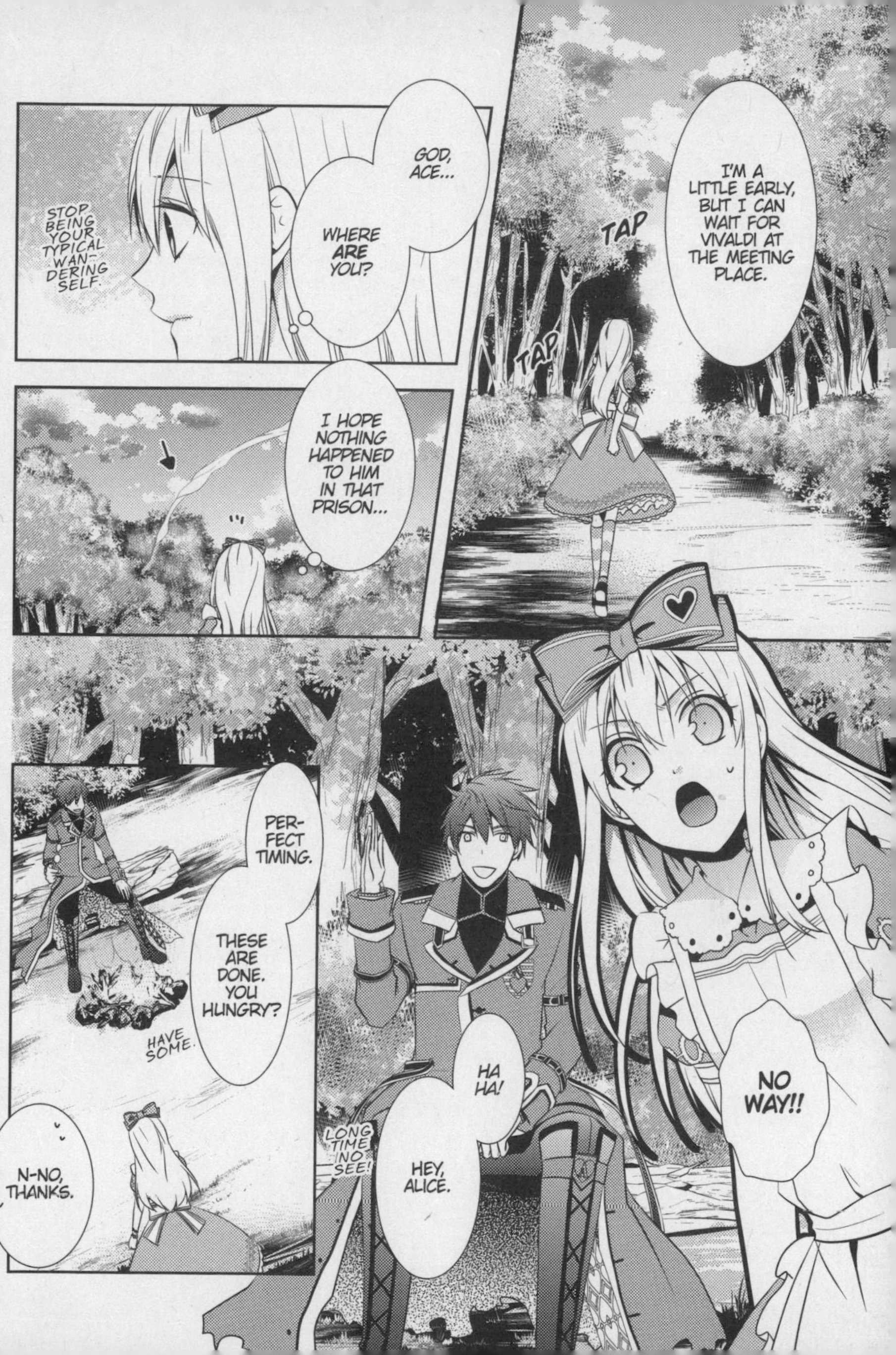
I'M A LITTLE EARLY, BUT I CAN WAIT FOR VIVALDI AT THE MEETING PLACE.
TAP
TAP
GOD, ACE...
WHERE ARE YOU?
STOP BEING YOUR TYPICAL WAN-DERING SELF.
I HOPE NOTHING HAPPENED TO HIM IN THAT PRISON...
NO WAY!!
HA HA!
HEY, ALICE.
LONG TIME NO SEE!
PER-FECT TIMING.
THESE ARE DONE. YOU HUNGRY?
HAVE SOME.
N-NO, THANKS.

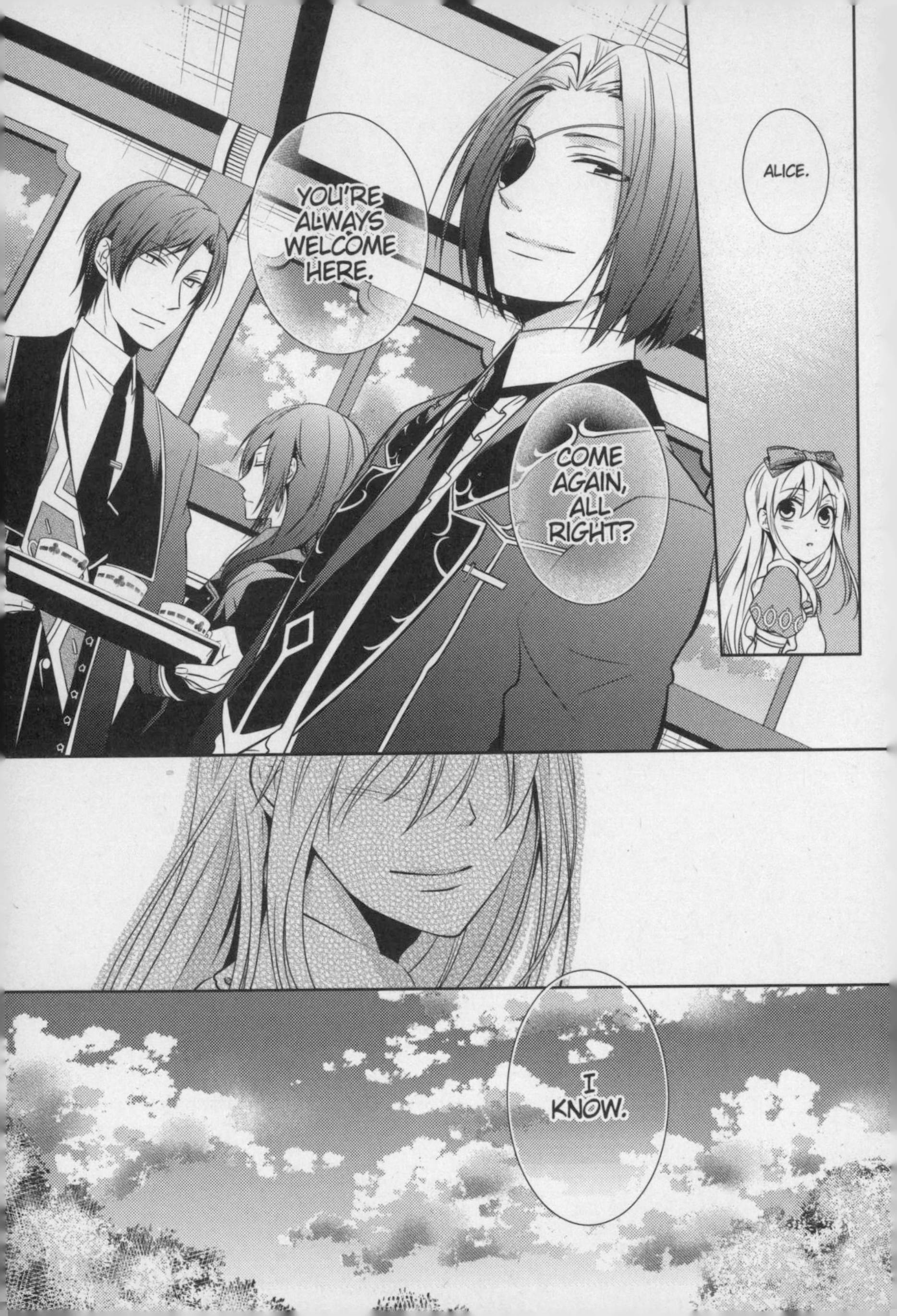
ALICE.
YOU'RE ALWAYS WELCOME HERE.
COME AGAIN, ALL RIGHT?
I KNOW.

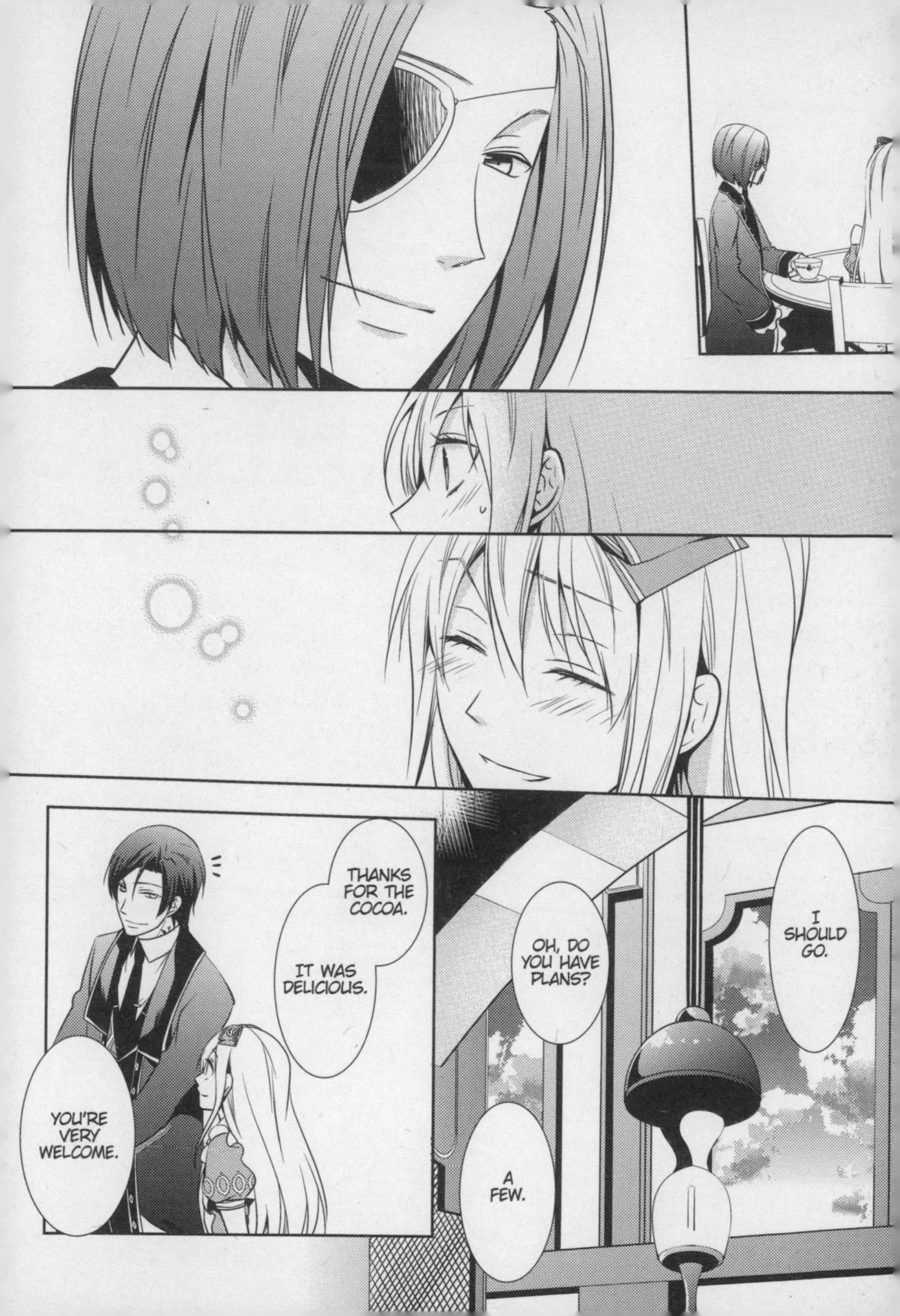
I SHOULD GO.
OH, DO YOU HAVE PLANS?
A FEW.
THANKS FOR THE COCOA.
IT WAS DELICIOUS.
YOU'RE VERY WELCOME.

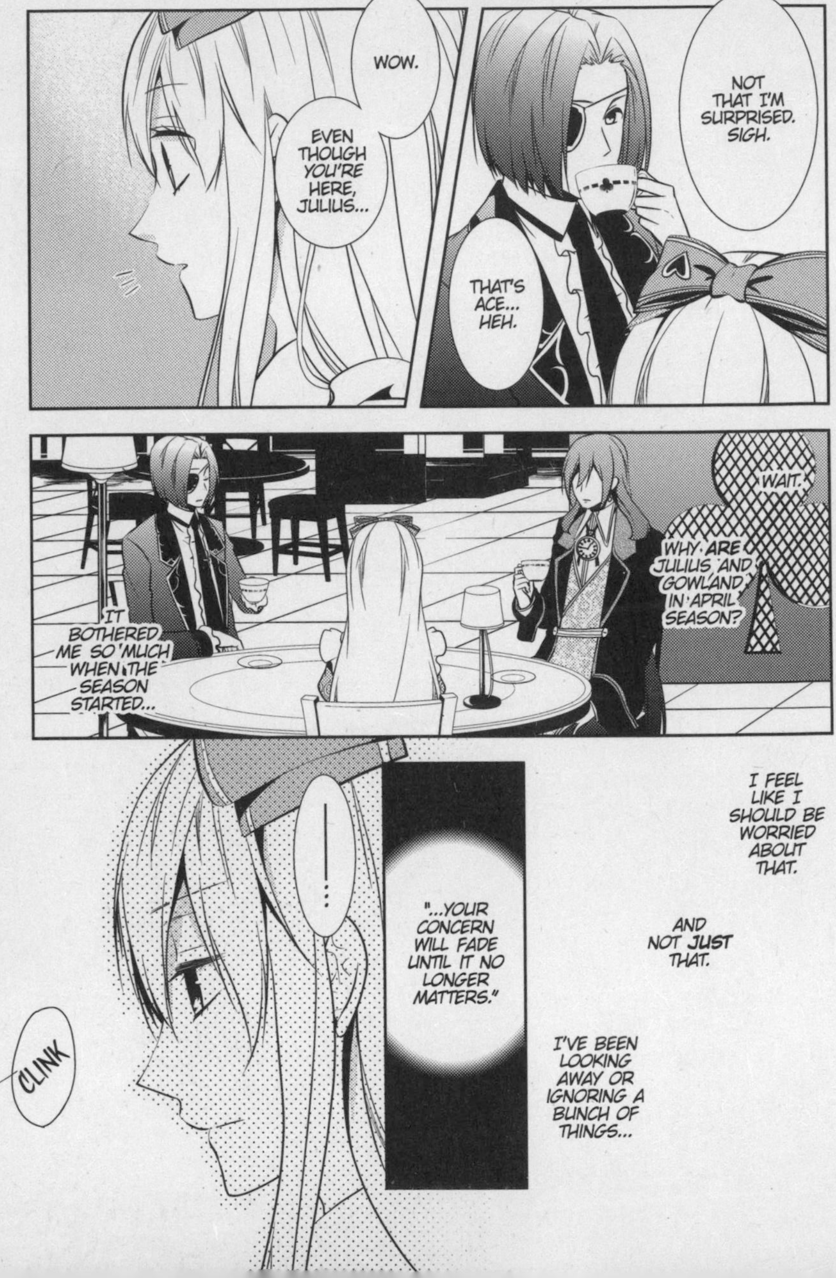
NOT THAT I'M SURPRISED. SIGH.
THAT'S ACE... HEH.
WOW.
EVEN THOUGH YOU'RE HERE, JULIUS...
WAIT.
WHY ARE JULIUS AND GOWLAND IN APRIL SEASON?
IT BOTHERED ME SO MUCH WHEN THE SEASON STARTED...
I FEEL LIKE I SHOULD BE WORRIED ABOUT THAT.
AND NOT JUST THAT.
I'VE BEEN LOOKING AWAY OR IGNORING A BUNCH OF THINGS...
"...YOUR CONCERN WILL FADE UNTIL IT NO LONGER MATTERS."
!...
CLINK

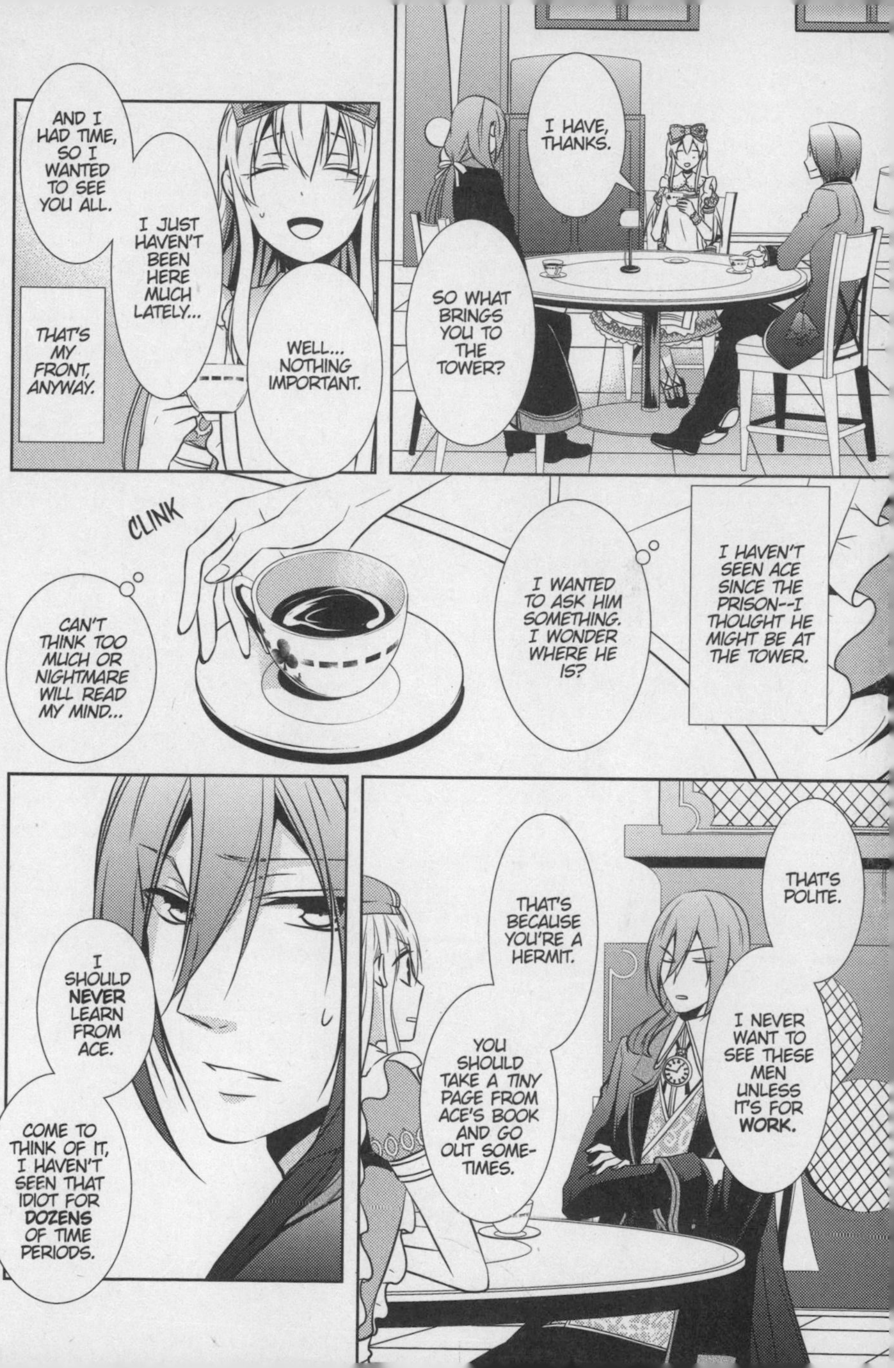
I HAVE, THANKS.
SO WHAT BRINGS YOU TO THE TOWER?
WELL... NOTHING IMPORTANT.
I JUST HAVEN'T BEEN HERE MUCH LATELY...
AND I HAD TIME, SO I WANTED TO SEE YOU ALL.
THAT'S MY FRONT, ANYWAY.
I HAVEN'T SEEN ACE SINCE THE PRISON--I THOUGHT HE MIGHT BE AT THE TOWER.
I WANTED TO ASK HIM SOMETHING. I WONDER WHERE HE IS?
CLINK
CAN'T THINK TOO MUCH OR NIGHTMARE WILL READ MY MIND...
THAT'S POLITE.
I NEVER WANT TO SEE THESE MEN UNLESS IT'S FOR **WORK.**
THAT'S BECAUSE YOU'RE A HERMIT.
YOU SHOULD TAKE A TINY PAGE FROM ACE'S BOOK AND GO OUT SOME-TIMES.
I SHOULD **NEVER** LEARN FROM ACE.
COME TO THINK OF IT, I HAVEN'T SEEN THAT IDIOT FOR **DOZENS** OF TIME PERIODS.

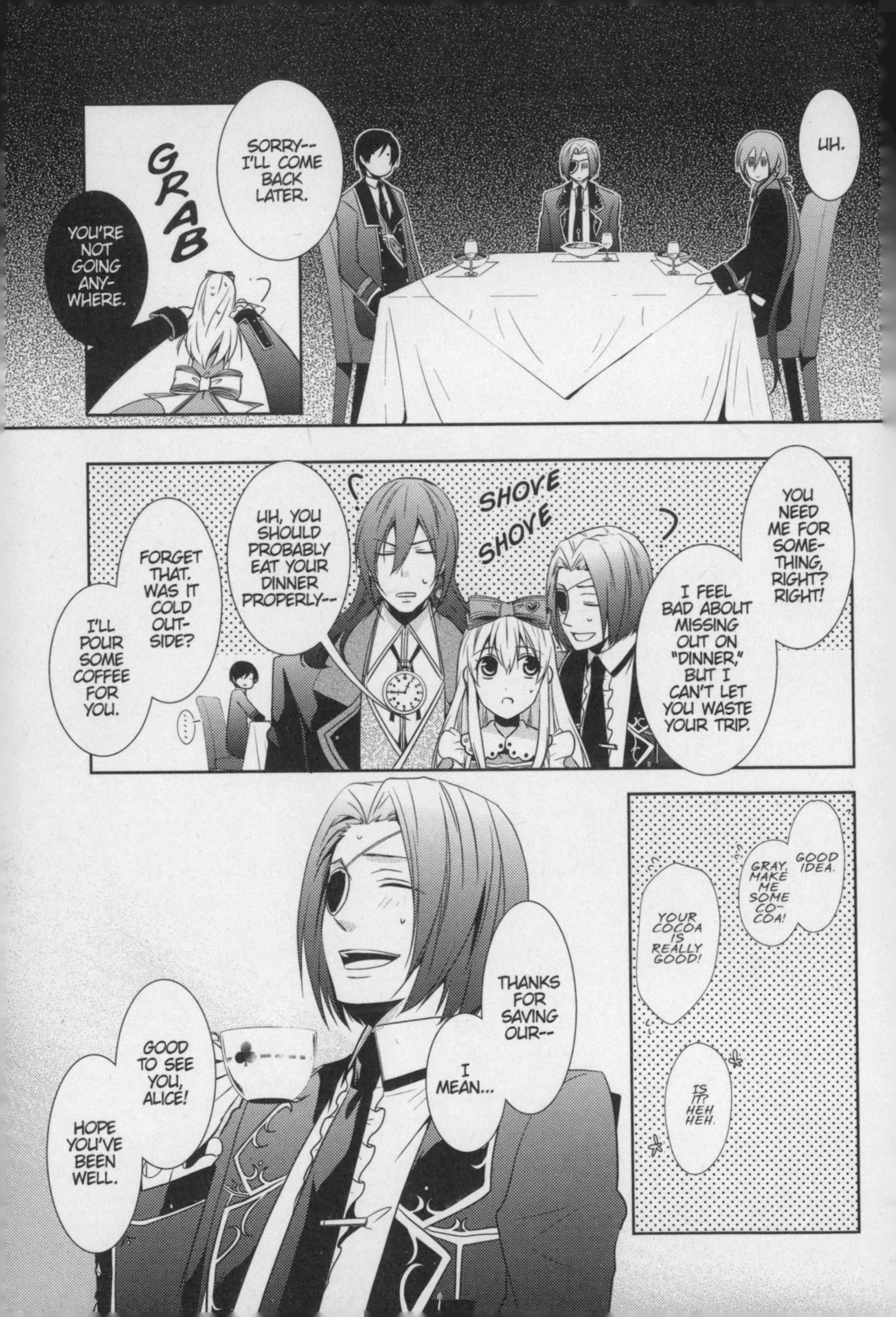
UH.
SORRY-- I'LL COME BACK LATER.
GRAB
YOU'RE NOT GOING ANY-WHERE.
YOU NEED ME FOR SOME-THING, RIGHT? RIGHT!
I FEEL BAD ABOUT MISSING OUT ON "DINNER," BUT I CAN'T LET YOU WASTE YOUR TRIP.
SHOVE SHOVE
UH, YOU SHOULD PROBABLY EAT YOUR DINNER PROPERLY--
FORGET THAT. WAS IT COLD OUT-SIDE?
I'LL POUR SOME COFFEE FOR YOU.
...
GOOD IDEA.
GRAY, MAKE ME SOME CO-COA!
YOUR COCOA IS REALLY GOOD!
IS IT? HEH HEH.
THANKS FOR SAVING OUR--
I MEAN...
GOOD TO SEE YOU, ALICE!
HOPE YOU'VE BEEN WELL.

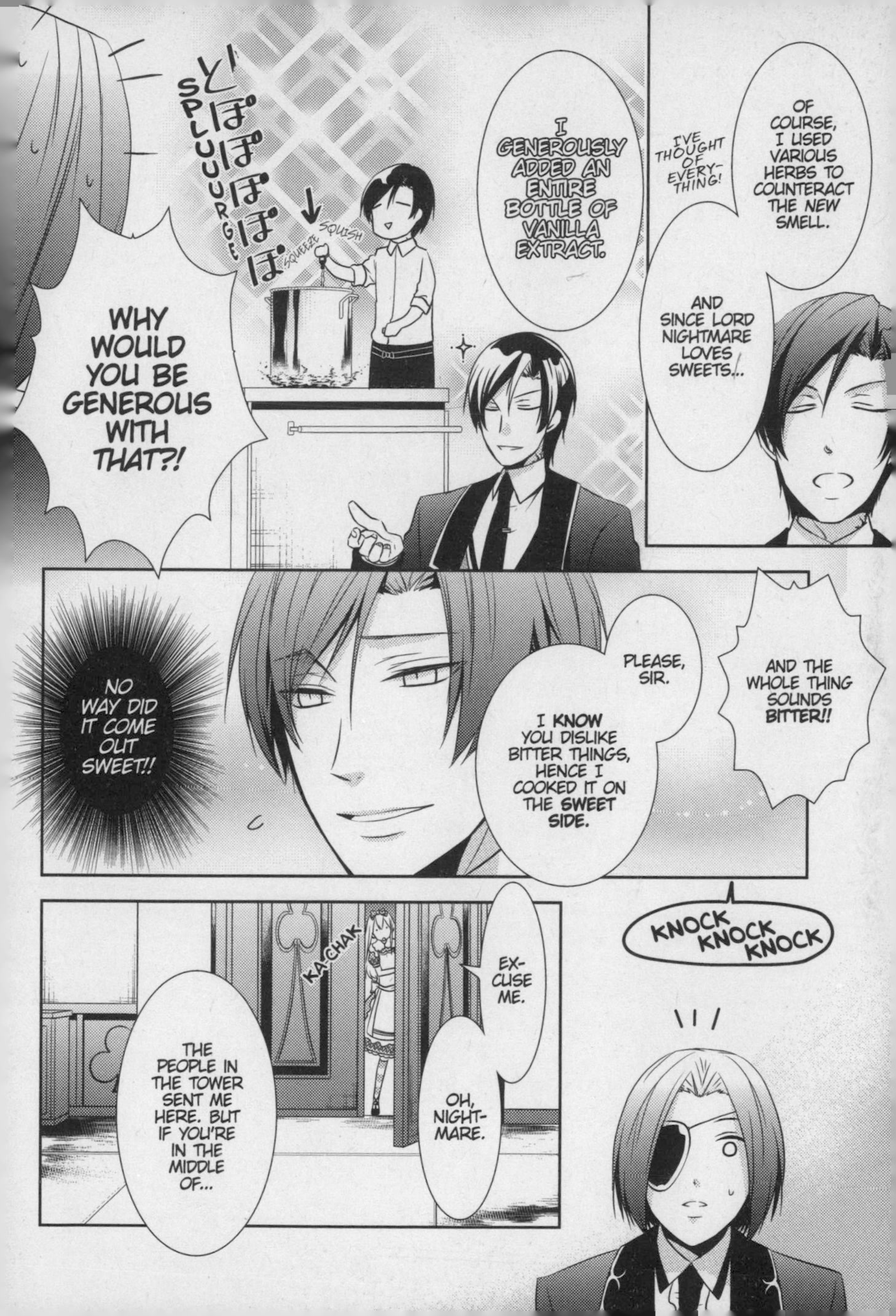
OF COURSE, I USED VARIOUS HERBS TO COUNTERACT THE NEW SMELL.
I'VE THOUGHT OF EVERY-THING!
AND SINCE LORD NIGHTMARE LOVES SWEETS...
I GENEROUSLY ADDED AN ENTIRE BOTTLE OF VANILLA EXTRACT.
SQUISH
SQUEEZE
とぽぽぽぽぽ
SPLUUURGE
WHY WOULD YOU BE GENEROUS WITH THAT?!
AND THE WHOLE THING SOUNDS BITTER!!
PLEASE, SIR.
I KNOW YOU DISLIKE BITTER THINGS, HENCE I COOKED IT ON THE SWEET SIDE.
NO WAY DID IT COME OUT SWEET!!
KNOCK KNOCK KNOCK
EX-CUSE ME.
KA-CHAK
OH, NIGHT-MARE.
THE PEOPLE IN THE TOWER SENT ME HERE. BUT IF YOU'RE IN THE MIDDLE OF...

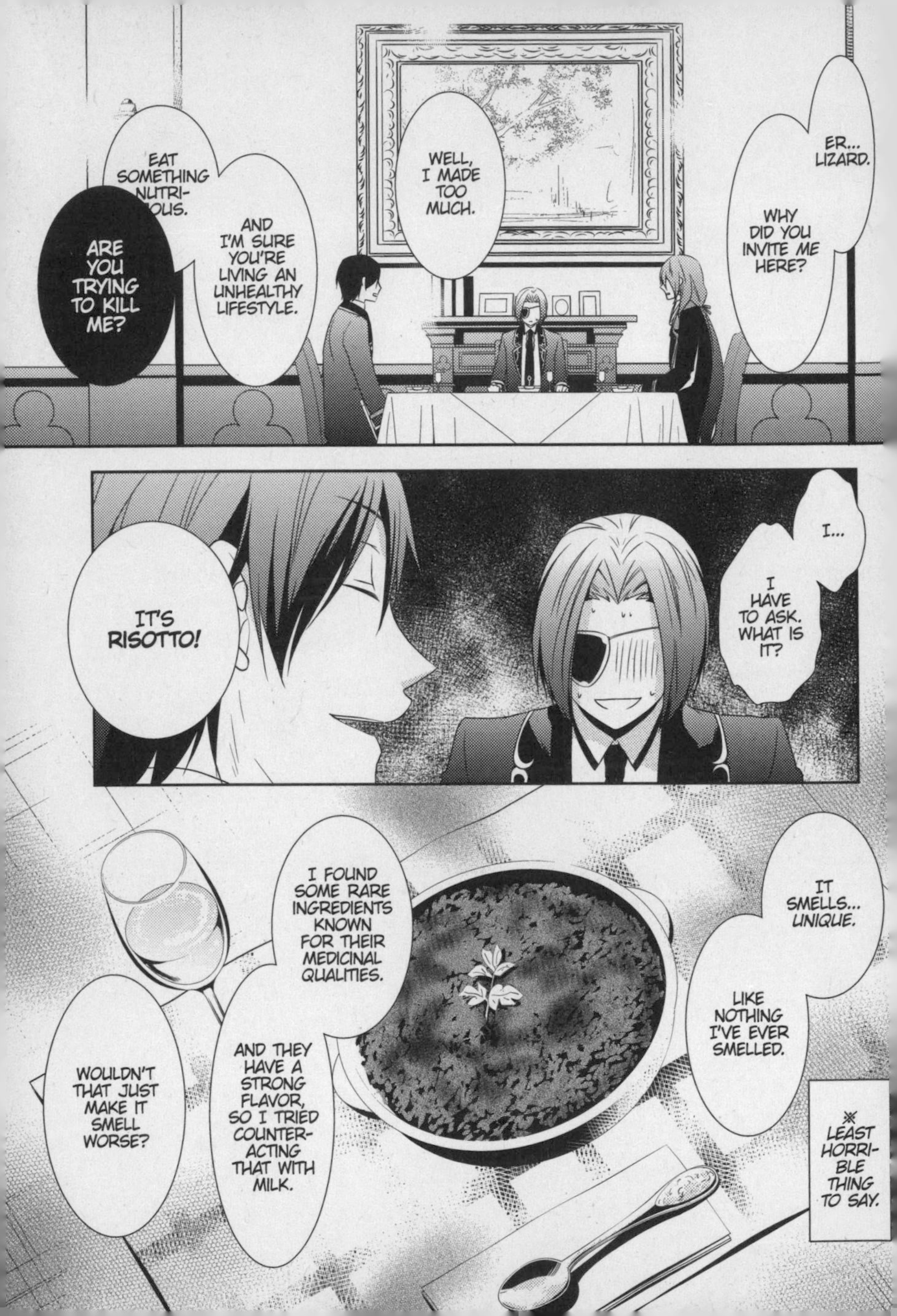
ER... LIZARD.
WHY DID YOU INVITE ME HERE?
WELL, I MADE TOO MUCH.
EAT SOMETHING NUTRI- IOUS.
AND I'M SURE YOU'RE LIVING AN UNHEALTHY LIFESTYLE.
ARE YOU TRYING TO KILL ME?
I... I HAVE TO ASK. WHAT IS IT?
IT'S RISOTTO!
IT SMELLS... UNIQUE.
LIKE NOTHING I'VE EVER SMELLED.
※ LEAST HORRIBLE THING TO SAY.
I FOUND SOME RARE INGREDIENTS KNOWN FOR THEIR MEDICINAL QUALITIES.
AND THEY HAVE A STRONG FLAVOR, SO I TRIED COUNTER-ACTING THAT WITH MILK.
WOULDN'T THAT JUST MAKE IT SMELL WORSE?

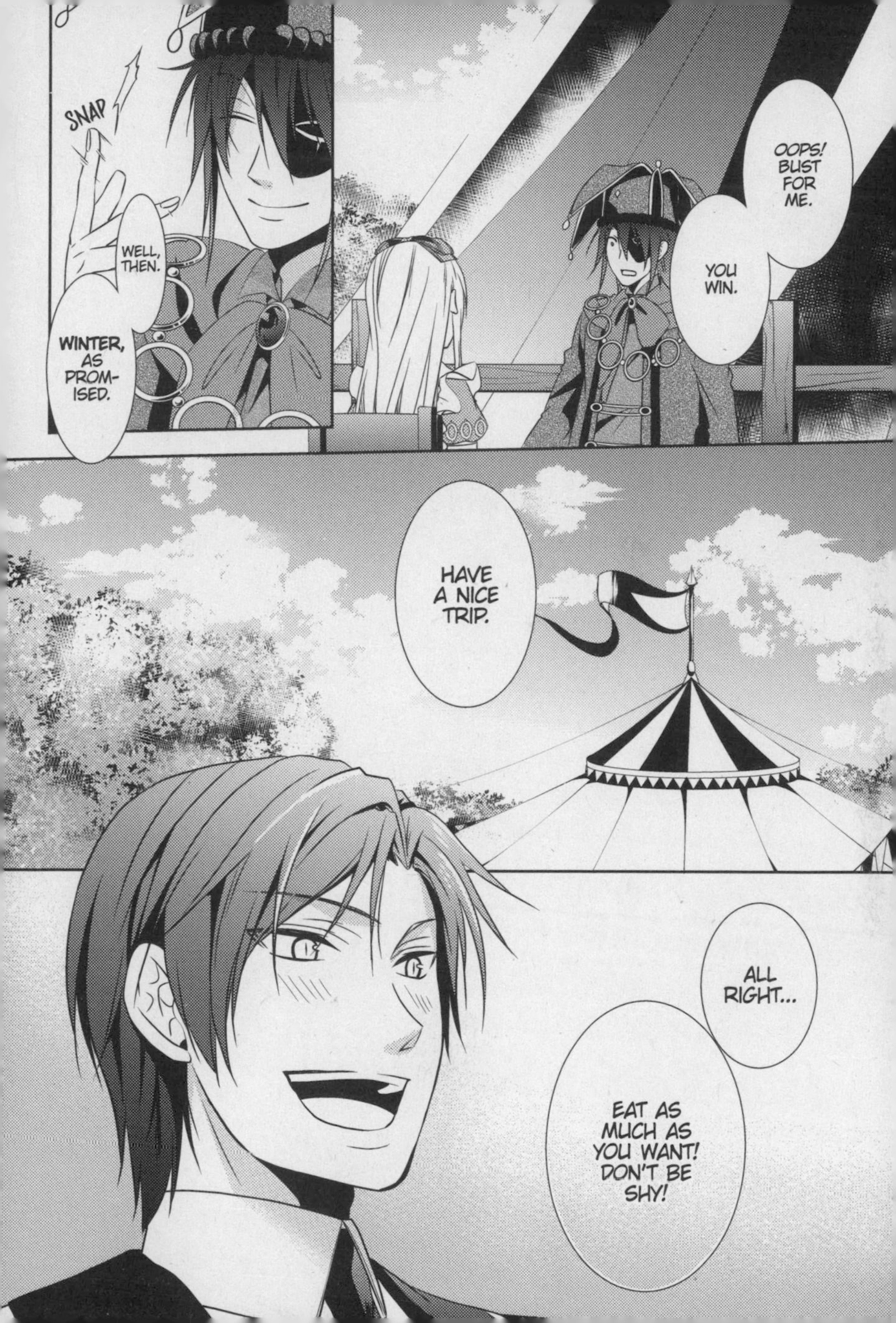
OOPS! BUST FOR ME.
YOU WIN.
SNAP
WELL, THEN.
WINTER, AS PROM-ISED.
HAVE A NICE TRIP.
ALL RIGHT...
EAT AS MUCH AS YOU WANT! DON'T BE SHY!

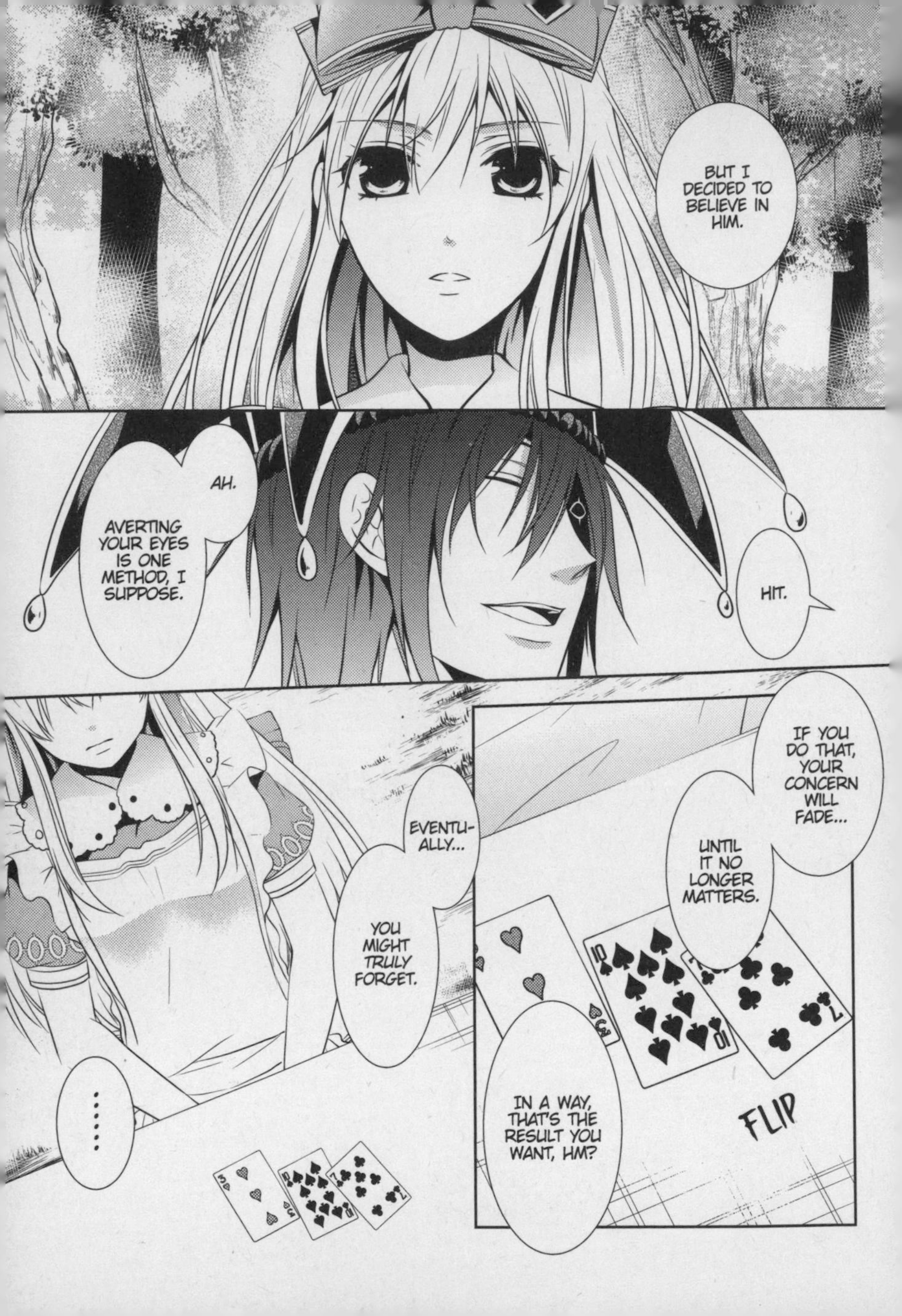
BUT I DECIDED TO BELIEVE IN HIM.
AH.
AVERTING YOUR EYES IS ONE METHOD, I SUPPOSE.
HIT.
IF YOU DO THAT, YOUR CONCERN WILL FADE...
UNTIL IT NO LONGER MATTERS.
IN A WAY, THAT'S THE RESULT YOU WANT, HM?
FLIP
EVENTU-ALLY...
YOU MIGHT TRULY FORGET.
......

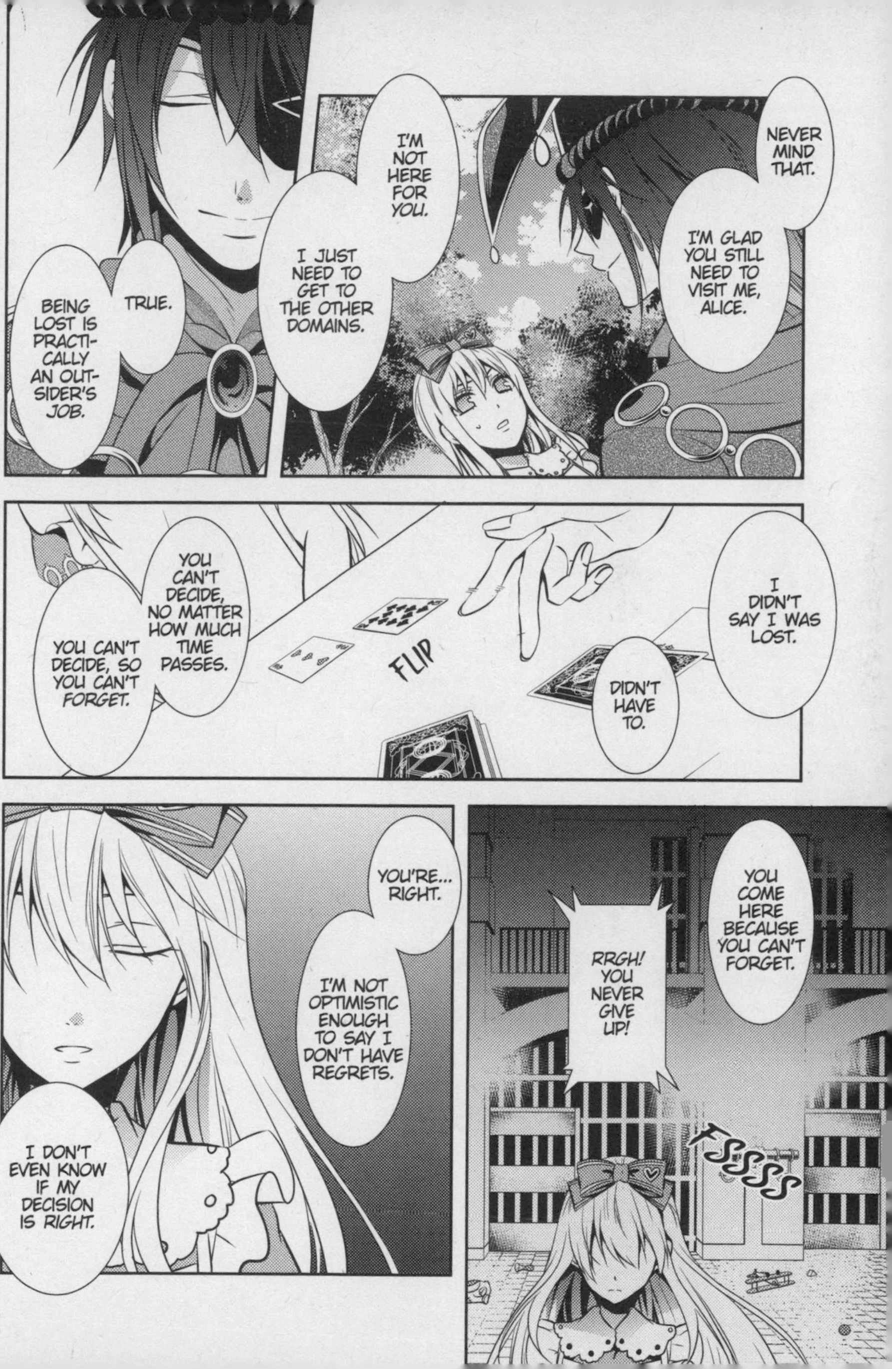
NEVER MIND THAT.
I'M GLAD YOU STILL NEED TO VISIT ME, ALICE.
I'M NOT HERE FOR YOU.
I JUST NEED TO GET TO THE OTHER DOMAINS.
TRUE.
BEING LOST IS PRACTICALLY AN OUTSIDER'S JOB.
I DIDN'T SAY I WAS LOST.
DIDN'T HAVE TO.
FLIP
YOU CAN'T DECIDE, NO MATTER HOW MUCH TIME PASSES.
YOU CAN'T DECIDE, SO YOU CAN'T FORGET.
YOU COME HERE BECAUSE YOU CAN'T FORGET.
RRGH! YOU NEVER GIVE UP!
FSSSS
YOU'RE... RIGHT.
I'M NOT OPTIMISTIC ENOUGH TO SAY I DON'T HAVE REGRETS.
I DON'T EVEN KNOW IF MY DECISION IS RIGHT.

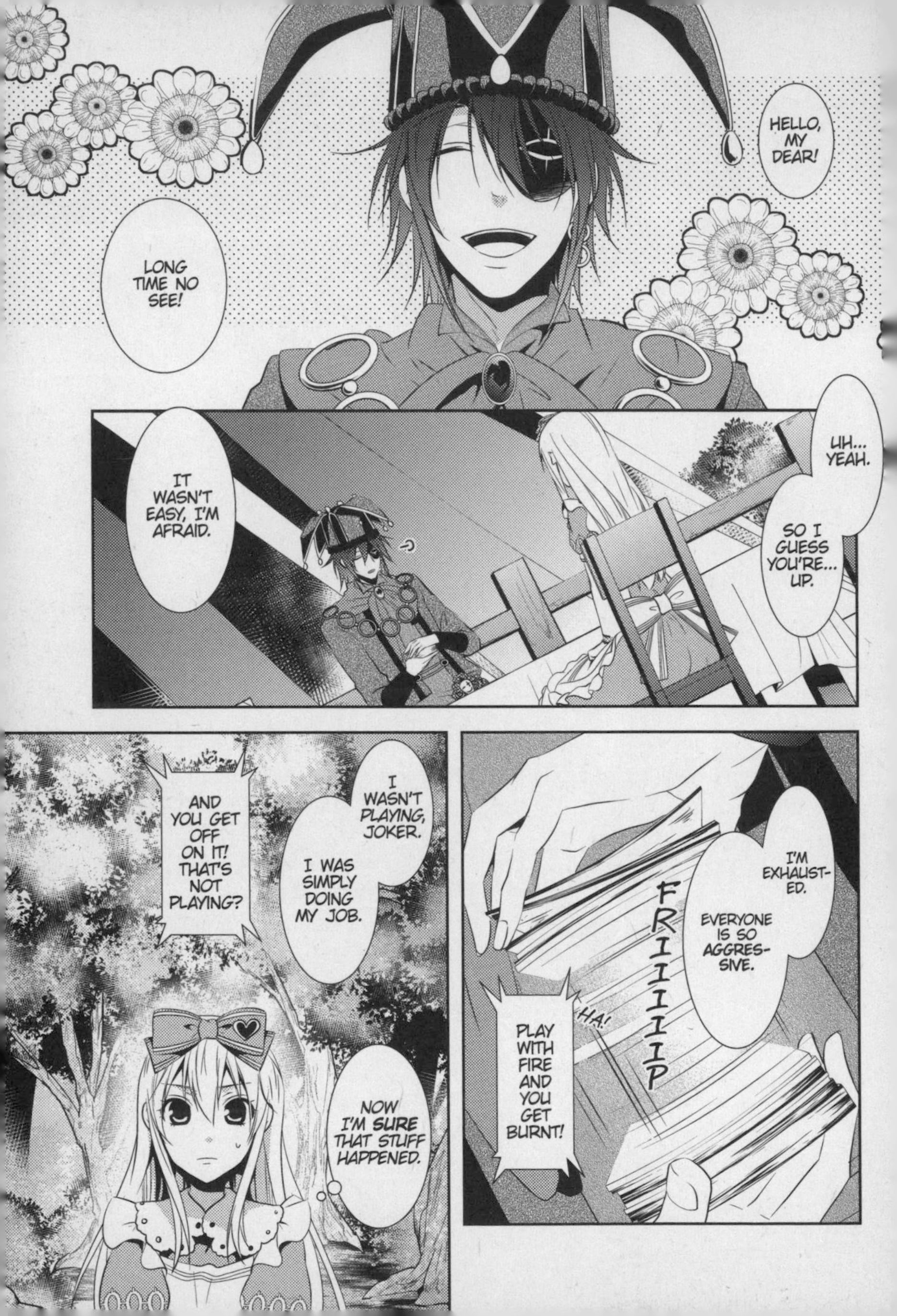
HELLO, MY DEAR!
LONG TIME NO SEE!
UH... YEAH.
SO I GUESS YOU'RE... UP.
IT WASN'T EASY, I'M AFRAID.
I'M EXHAUST-ED.
EVERYONE IS SO AGGRES-SIVE.
FRIIIIIP
HA!
PLAY WITH FIRE AND YOU GET BURNT!
I WASN'T PLAYING, JOKER.
I WAS SIMPLY DOING MY JOB.
AND YOU GET OFF ON IT! THAT'S NOT PLAYING?
NOW I'M SURE THAT STUFF HAPPENED.

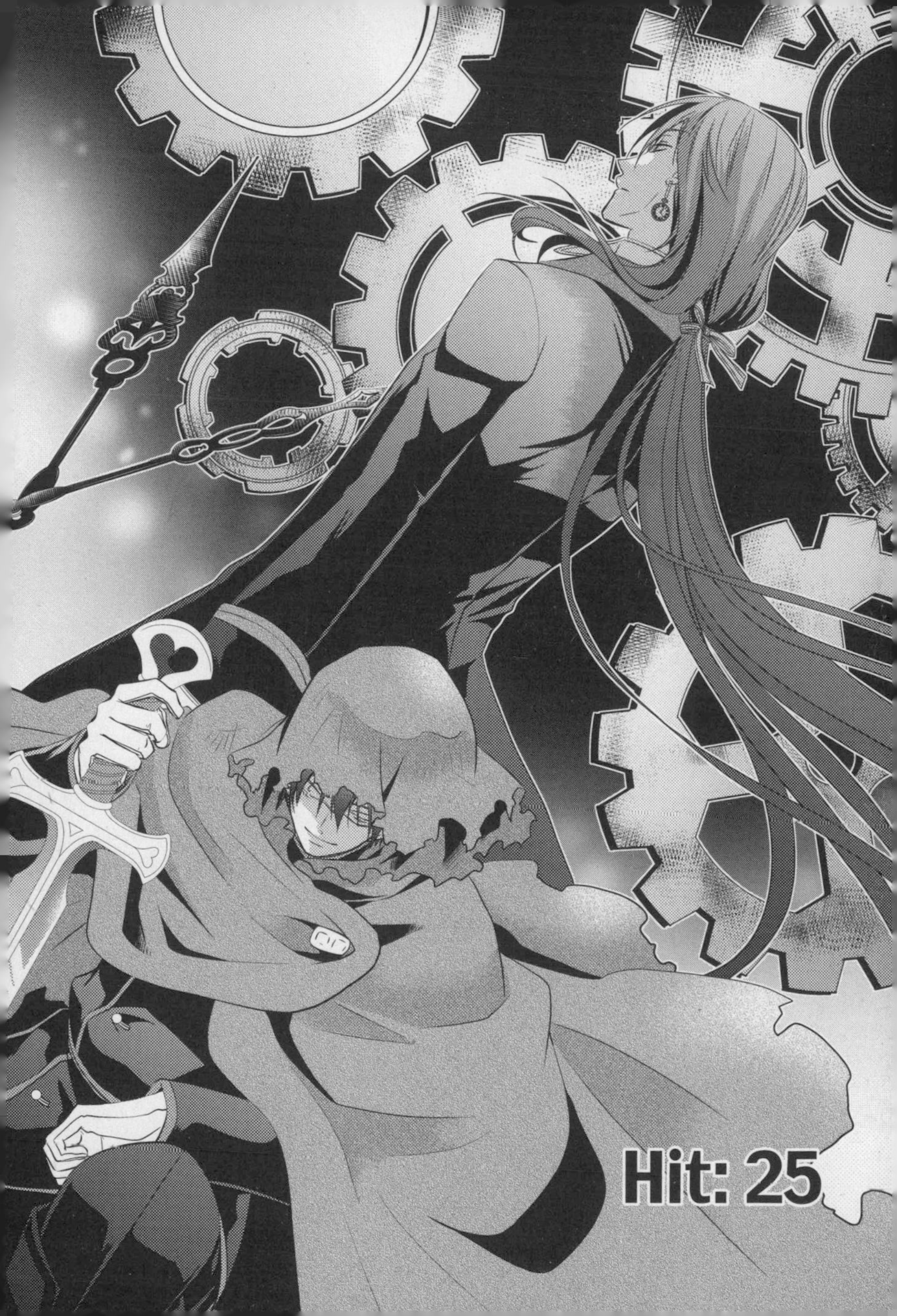
Hit: 25

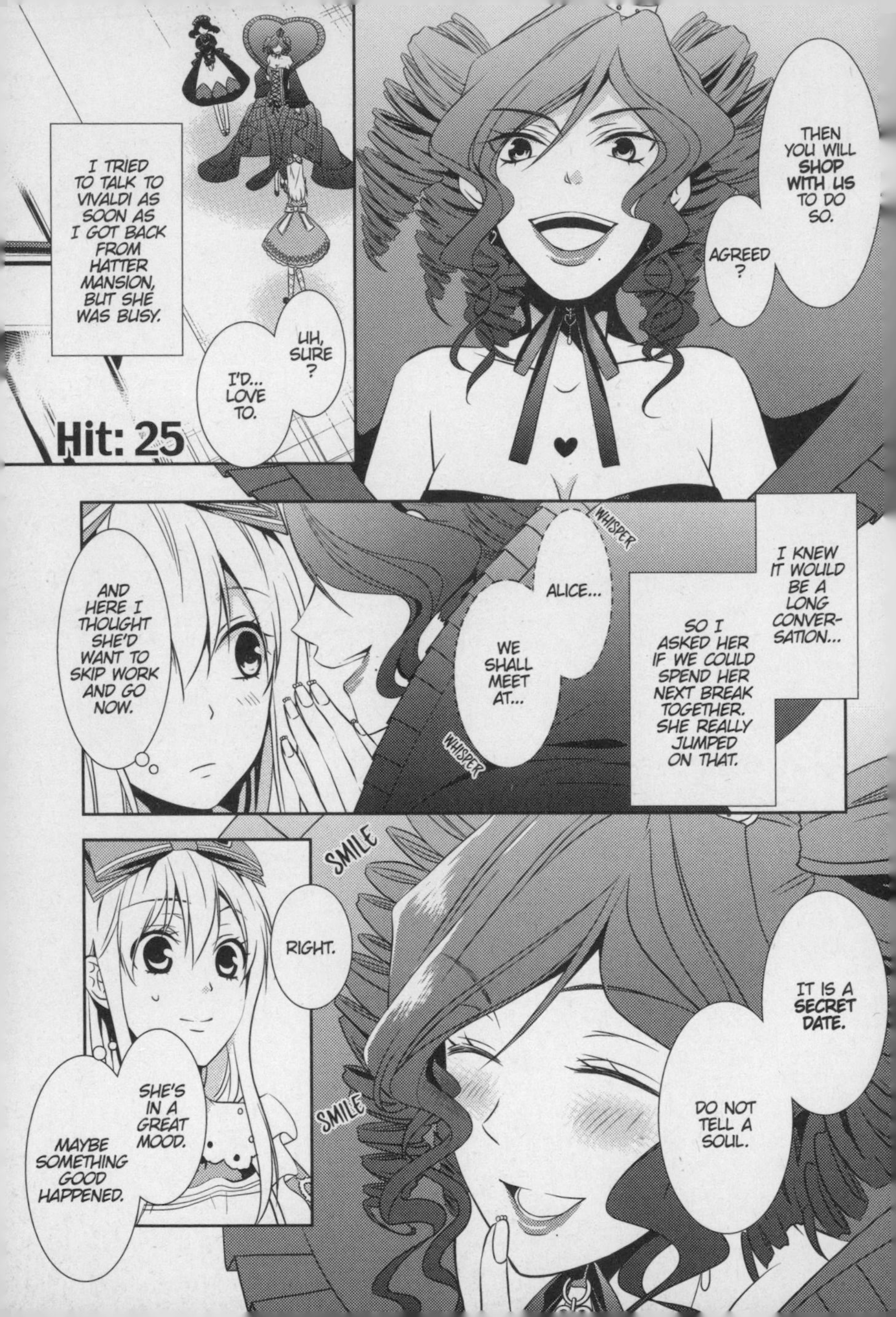
THEN YOU WILL SHOP WITH US TO DO SO.
AGREED?
I TRIED TO TALK TO VIVALDI AS SOON AS I GOT BACK FROM HATTER MANSION, BUT SHE WAS BUSY.
UH, SURE? I'D... LOVE TO.
Hit: 25
I KNEW IT WOULD BE A LONG CONVERSATION...
SO I ASKED HER IF WE COULD SPEND HER NEXT BREAK TOGETHER. SHE REALLY JUMPED ON THAT.
WHISPER
ALICE... WE SHALL MEET AT...
WHISPER
AND HERE I THOUGHT SHE'D WANT TO SKIP WORK AND GO NOW.
SMILE
IT IS A SECRET DATE.
DO NOT TELL A SOUL.
SMILE
RIGHT.
SHE'S IN A GREAT MOOD.
MAYBE SOMETHING GOOD HAPPENED.

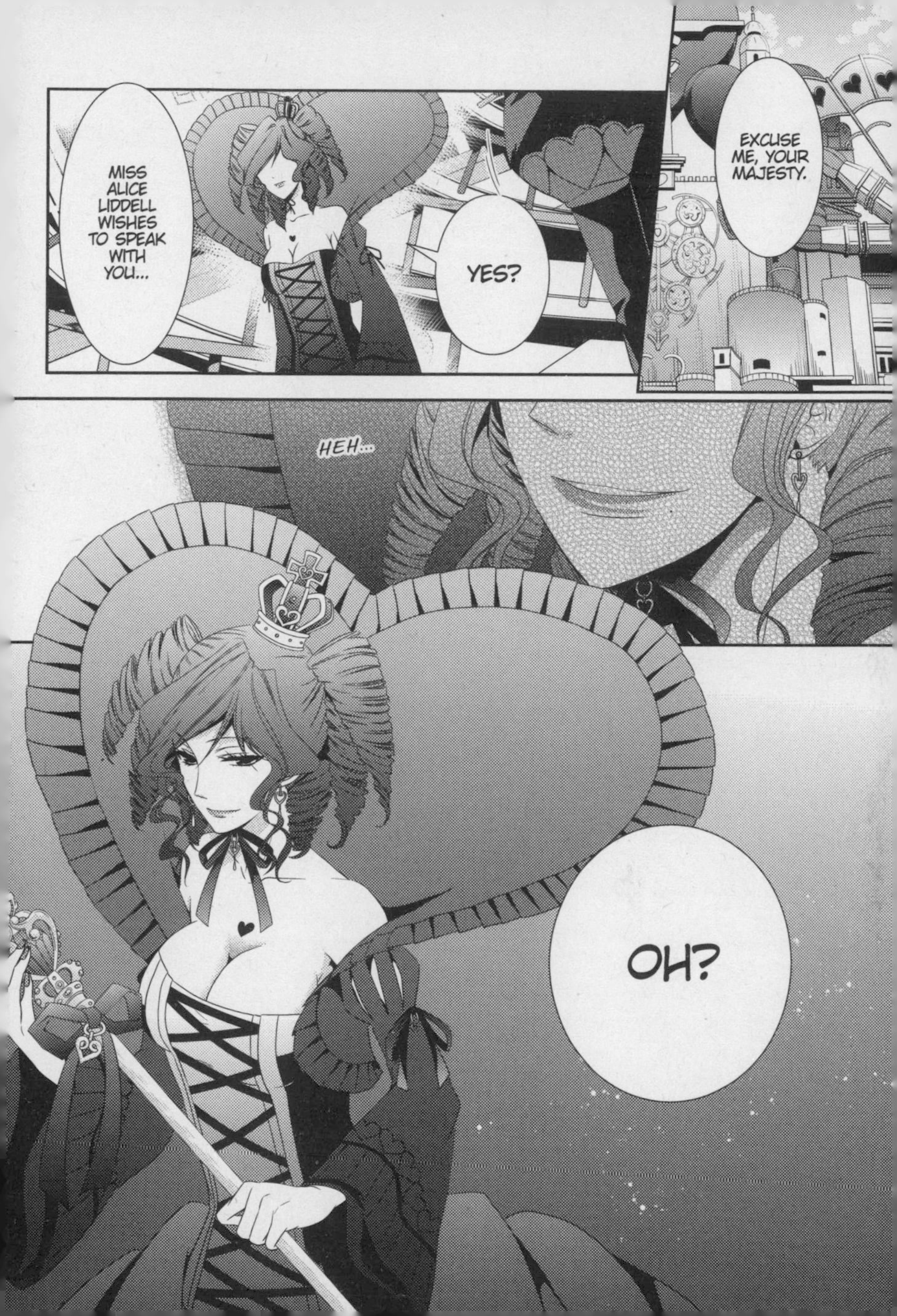
EXCUSE ME, YOUR MAJESTY.
YES?
MISS ALICE LIDDELL WISHES TO SPEAK WITH YOU...
HEH...
OH?

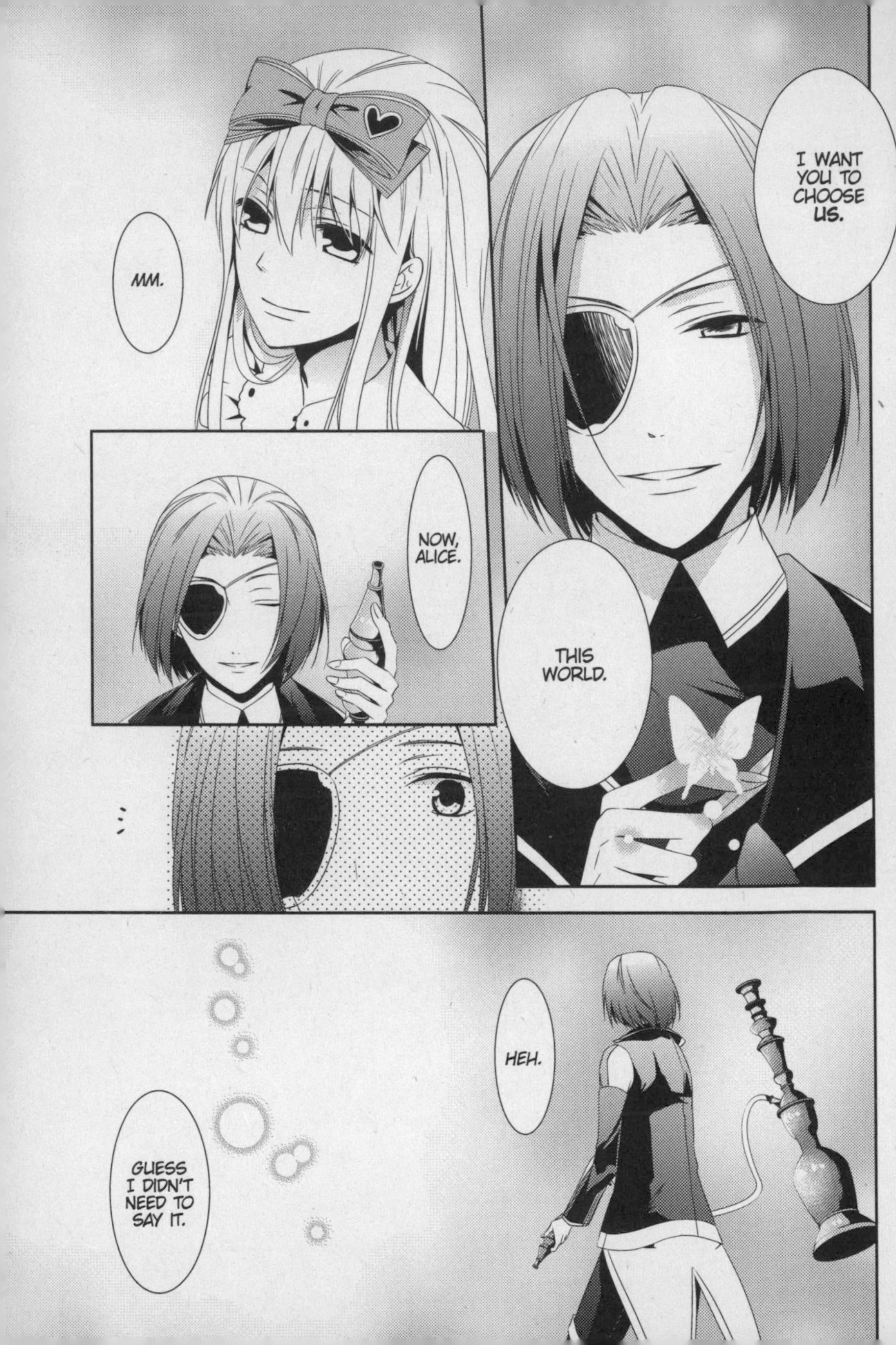
I WANT YOU TO CHOOSE US.
THIS WORLD.
MM.
NOW, ALICE.
...
HEH.
GUESS I DIDN'T NEED TO SAY IT.

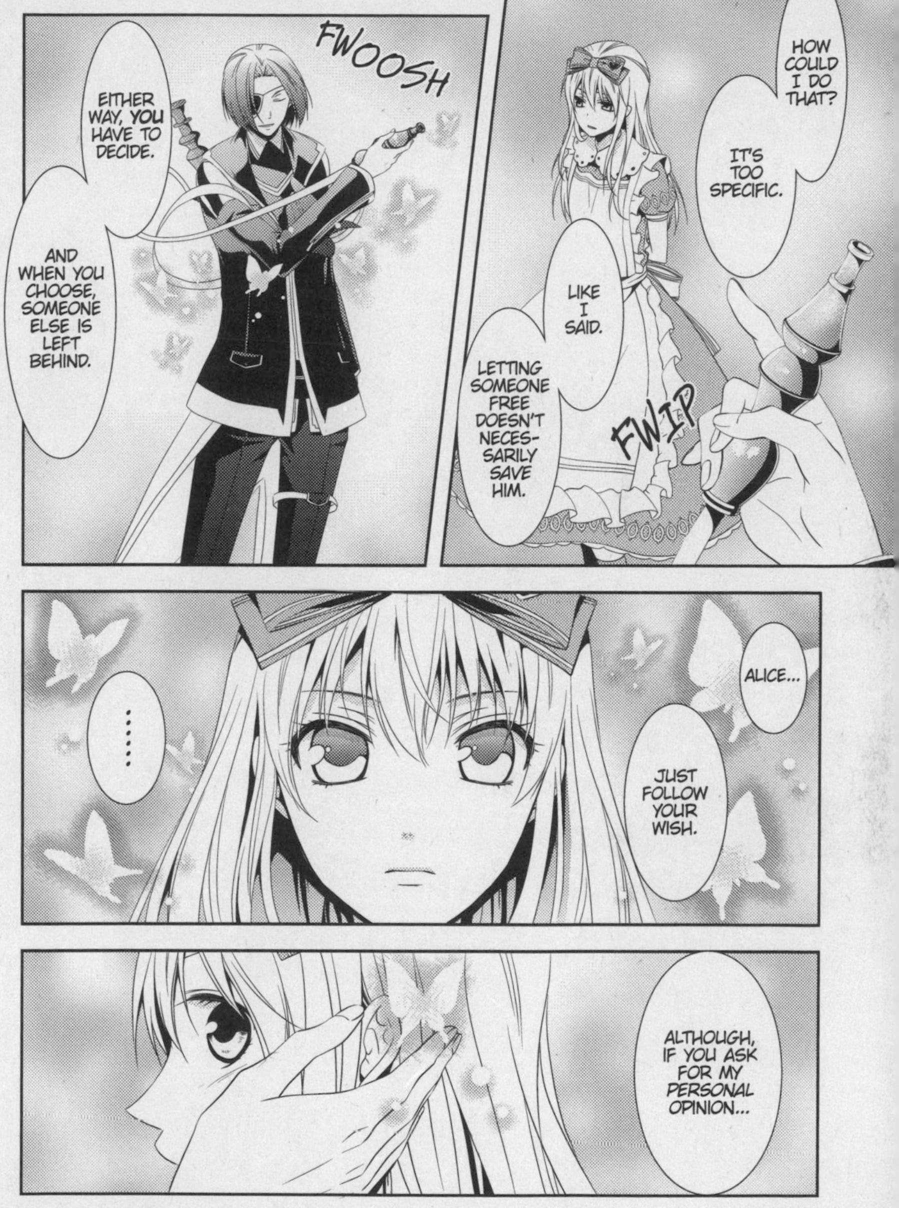
HOW COULD I DO THAT?
IT'S TOO SPECIFIC.
LIKE I SAID.
LETTING SOMEONE FREE DOESN'T NECES-SARILY SAVE HIM.
FWIP
FWOOSH
EITHER WAY, YOU HAVE TO DECIDE.
AND WHEN YOU CHOOSE, SOMEONE ELSE IS LEFT BEHIND.
ALICE...
JUST FOLLOW YOUR WISH.
......
ALTHOUGH, IF YOU ASK FOR MY PERSONAL OPINION...

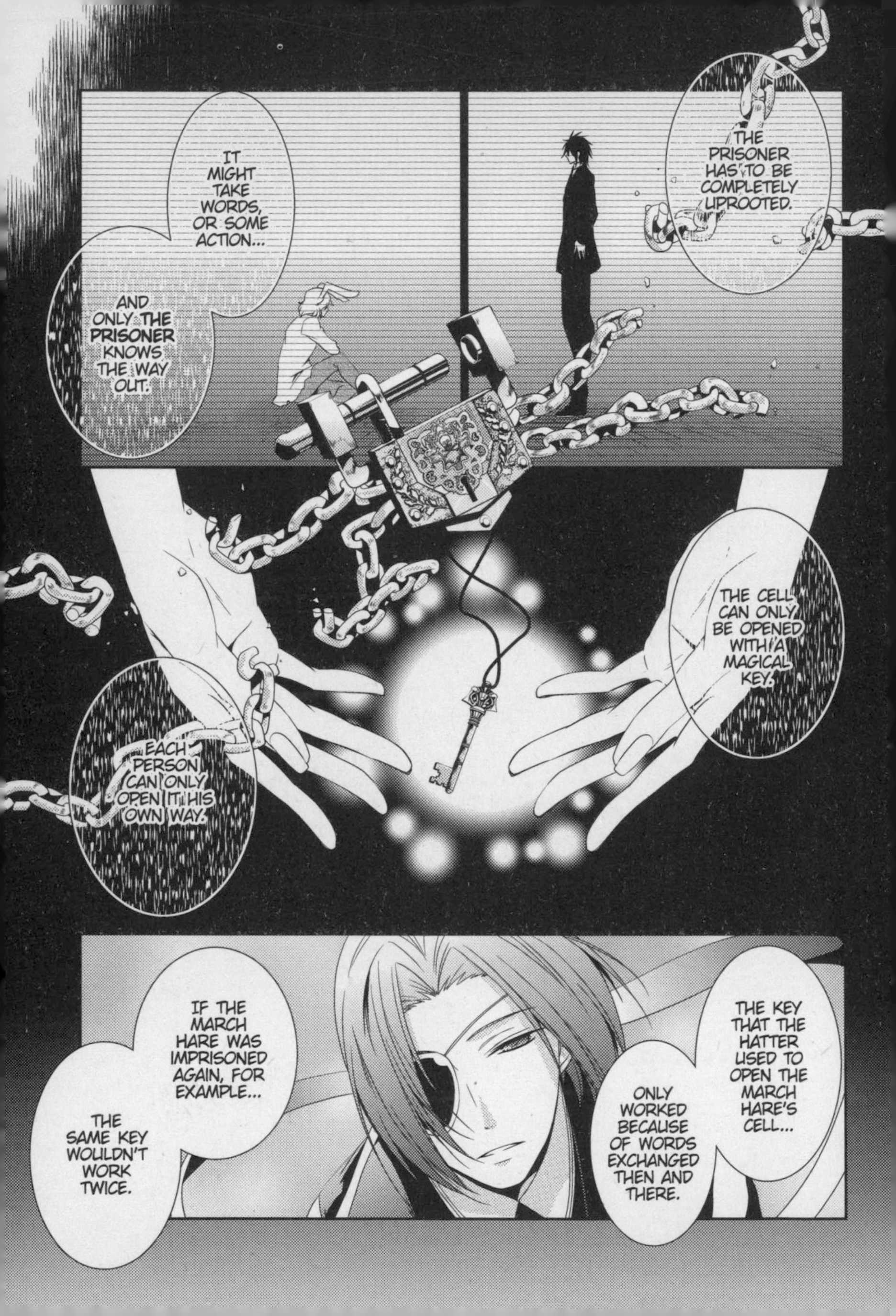
THE PRISONER HAS TO BE COMPLETELY UPROOTED.
IT MIGHT TAKE WORDS, OR SOME ACTION...
AND ONLY THE PRISONER KNOWS THE WAY OUT.
THE CELL CAN ONLY BE OPENED WITH A MAGICAL KEY.
EACH PERSON CAN ONLY OPEN IT HIS OWN WAY.
THE KEY THAT THE HATTER USED TO OPEN THE MARCH HARE'S CELL...
ONLY WORKED BECAUSE OF WORDS EXCHANGED THEN AND THERE.
IF THE MARCH HARE WAS IMPRISONED AGAIN, FOR EXAMPLE...
THE SAME KEY WOULDN'T WORK TWICE.

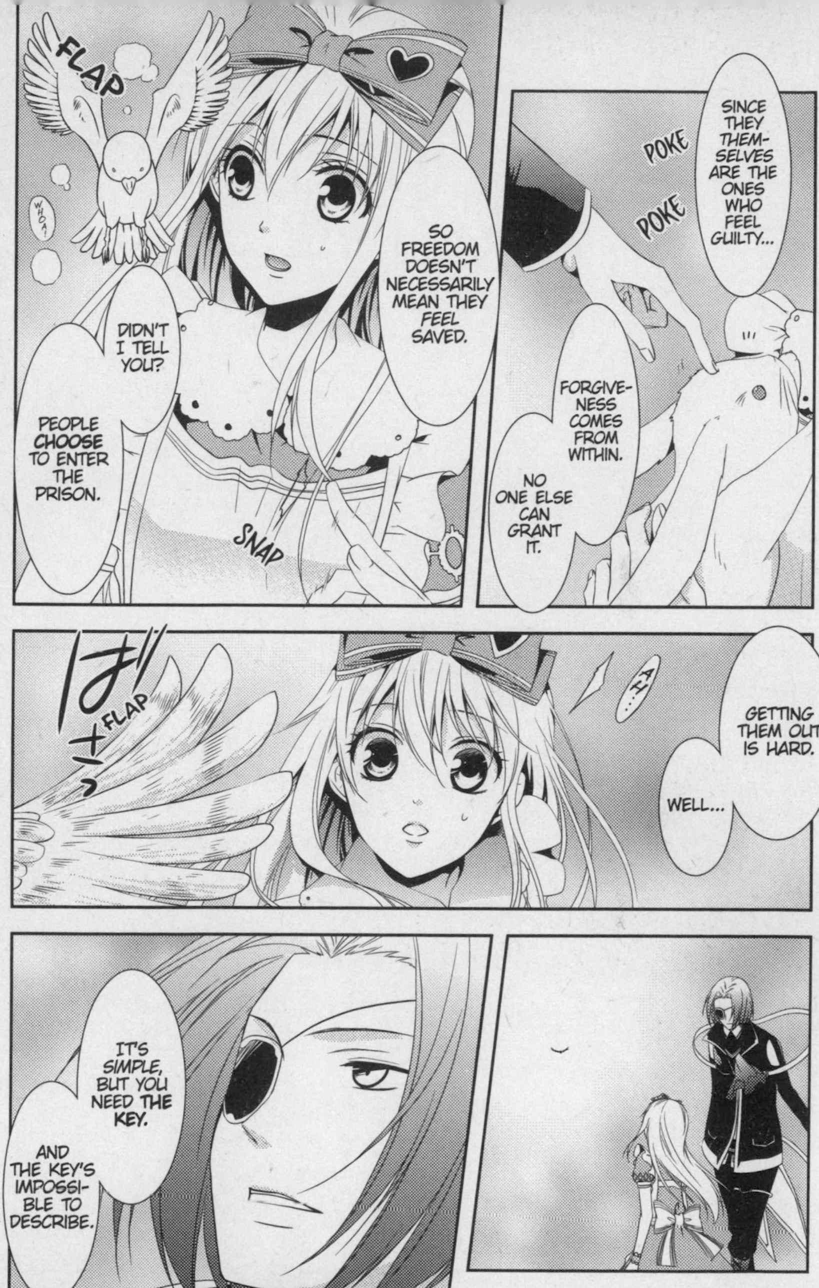
POKE
POKE
SINCE THEY THEM-SELVES ARE THE ONES WHO FEEL GUILTY...
FORGIVE-NESS COMES FROM WITHIN.
NO ONE ELSE CAN GRANT IT.
SO FREEDOM DOESN'T NECESSARILY MEAN THEY FEEL SAVED.
FLAP
WHOA!
DIDN'T I TELL YOU?
PEOPLE CHOOSE TO ENTER THE PRISON.
SNAP
GETTING THEM OUT IS HARD.
WELL...
AH...
FLAP
IT'S SIMPLE, BUT YOU NEED THE KEY.
AND THE KEY'S IMPOSSI-BLE TO DESCRIBE.

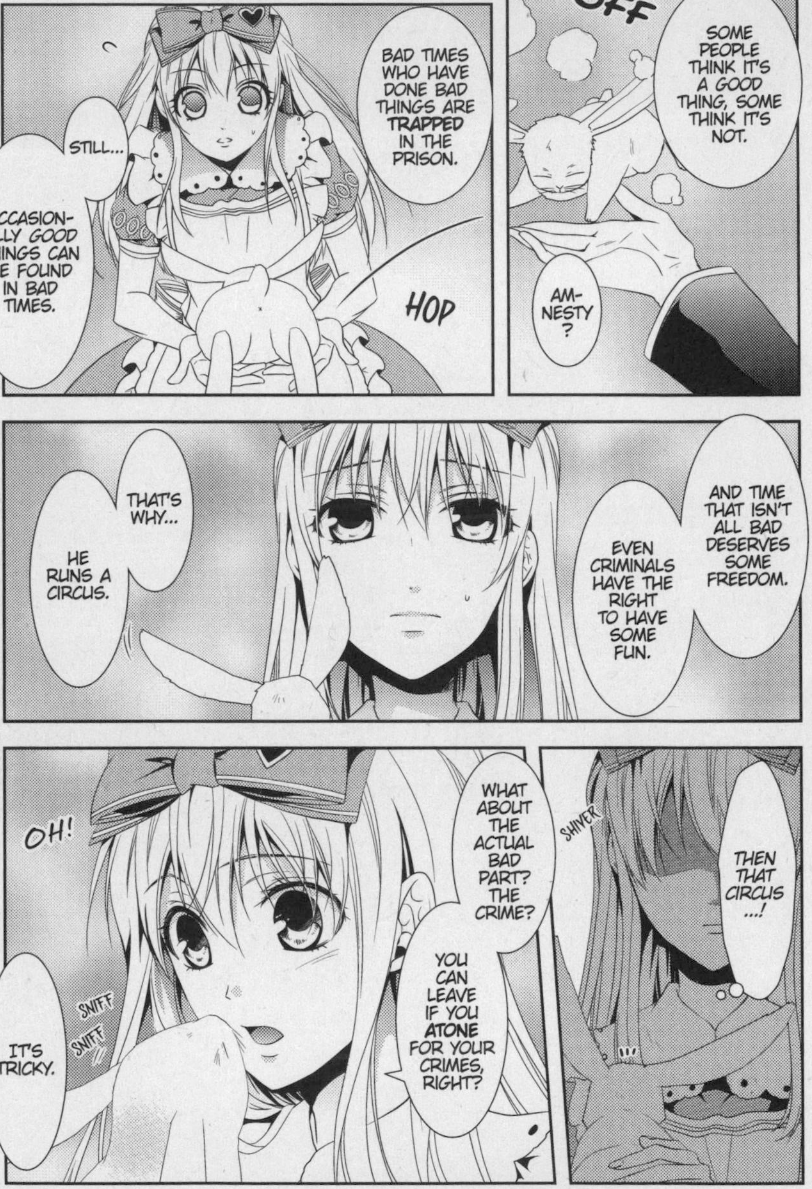
POFF
SOME PEOPLE THINK IT'S A GOOD THING, SOME THINK IT'S NOT.
AM-NESTY?
BAD TIMES WHO HAVE DONE BAD THINGS ARE **TRAPPED** IN THE PRISON.
STILL...
OCCASION-ALLY GOOD THINGS CAN BE FOUND IN BAD TIMES.
HOP
AND TIME THAT ISN'T ALL BAD DESERVES SOME FREEDOM.
EVEN CRIMINALS HAVE THE RIGHT TO HAVE SOME FUN.
THAT'S WHY...
HE RUNS A CIRCUS.
THEN THAT CIRCUS ...!
SHIVER
WHAT ABOUT THE ACTUAL BAD PART? THE CRIME?
YOU CAN LEAVE IF YOU **ATONE** FOR YOUR CRIMES, RIGHT?
OH!
SNIFF
SNIFF
IT'S TRICKY.

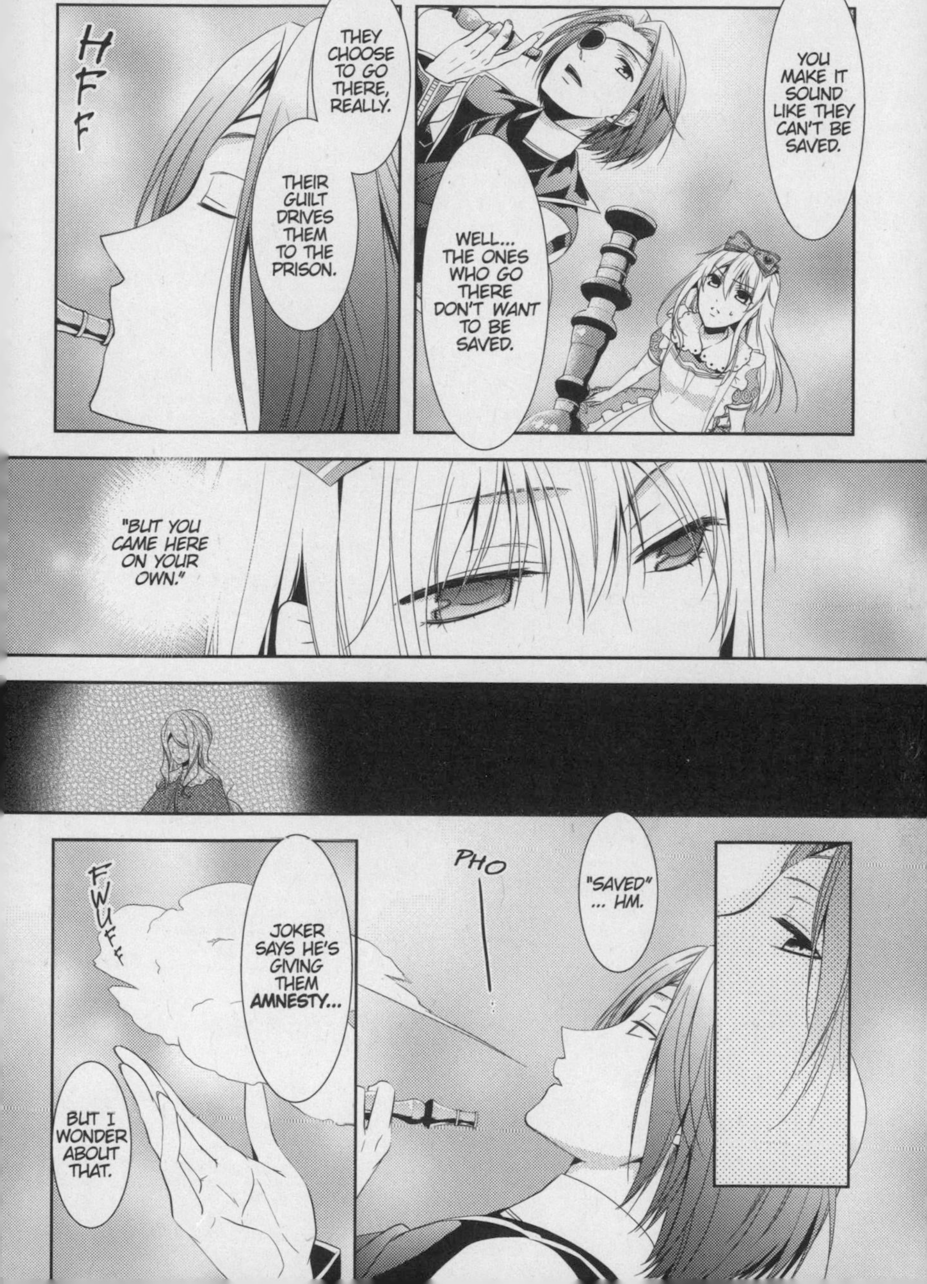
YOU MAKE IT SOUND LIKE THEY CAN'T BE SAVED.
WELL... THE ONES WHO GO THERE DON'T WANT TO BE SAVED.
THEY CHOOSE TO GO THERE, REALLY.
THEIR GUILT DRIVES THEM TO THE PRISON.
HFF
"BUT YOU CAME HERE ON YOUR OWN."
"SAVED" ... HM.
PHO
JOKER SAYS HE'S GIVING THEM **AMNESTY...**
FWUFF
BUT I WONDER ABOUT THAT.

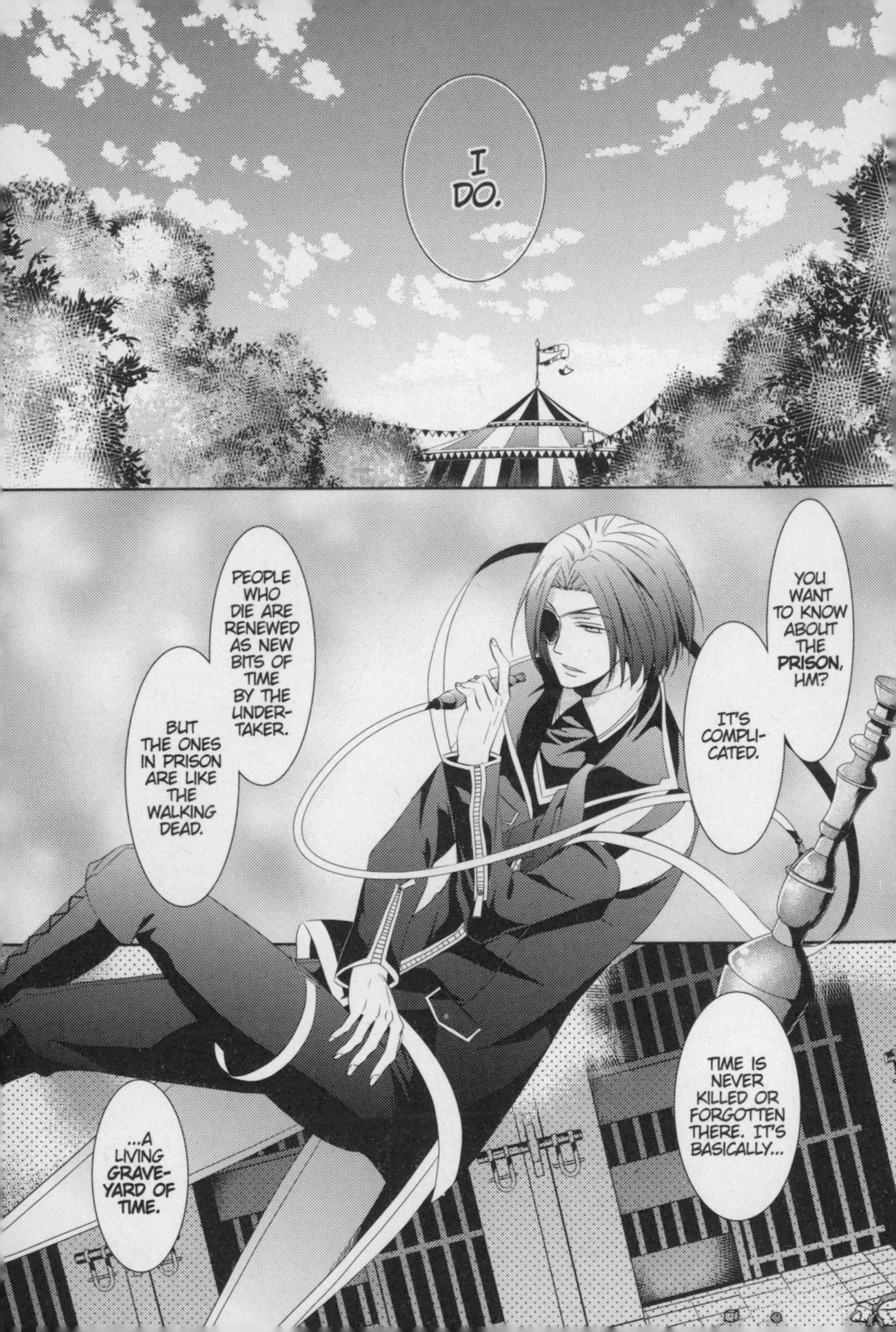
I DO.
YOU WANT TO KNOW ABOUT THE PRISON, HM?
IT'S COMPLICATED.
PEOPLE WHO DIE ARE RENEWED AS NEW BITS OF TIME BY THE UNDER-TAKER.
BUT THE ONES IN PRISON ARE LIKE THE WALKING DEAD.
TIME IS NEVER KILLED OR FORGOTTEN THERE. IT'S BASICALLY...
...A LIVING GRAVE-YARD OF TIME.

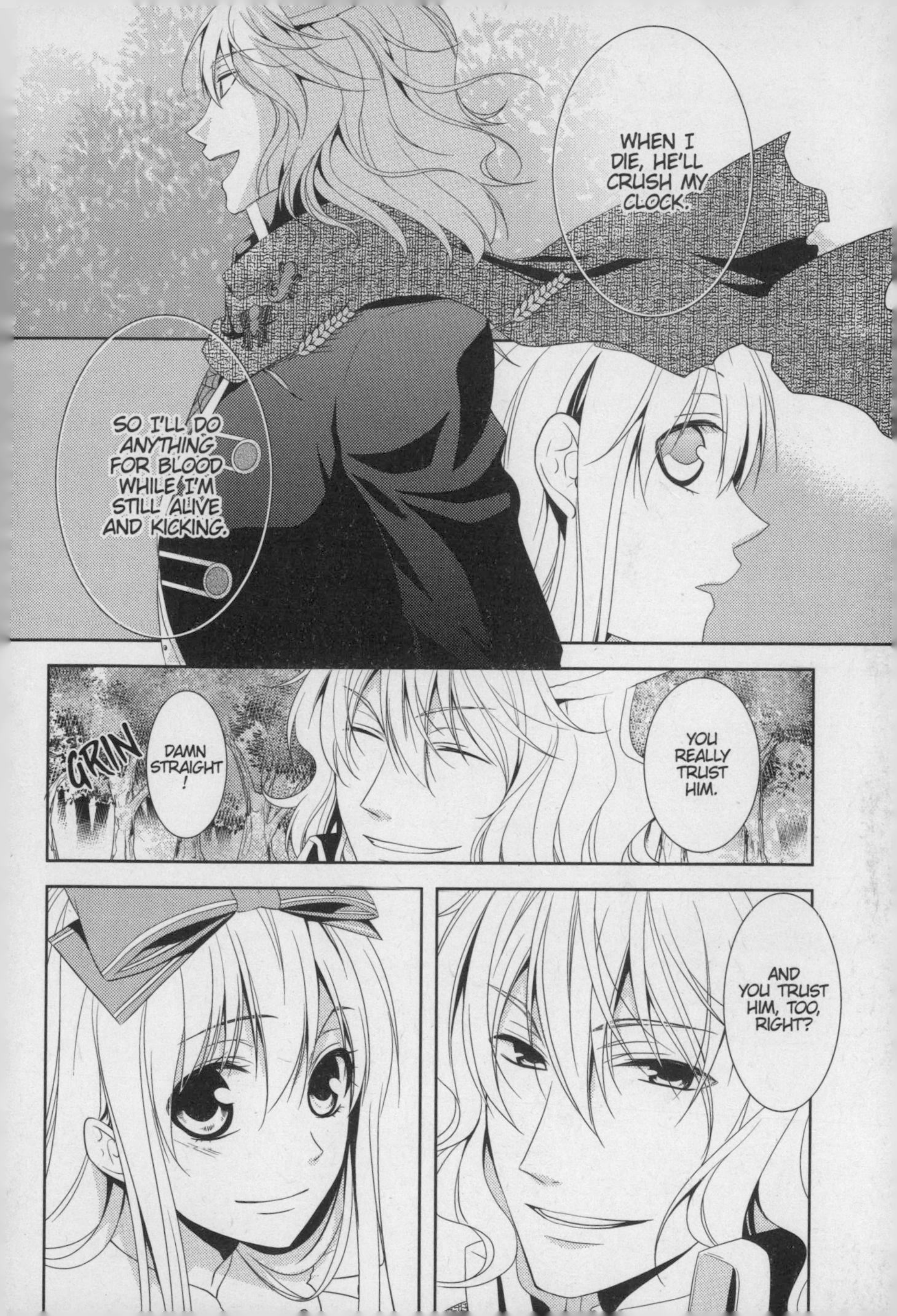
WHEN I DIE, HE'LL CRUSH MY CLOCK.
SO I'LL DO ANYTHING FOR BLOOD WHILE I'M STILL ALIVE AND KICKING.
YOU REALLY TRUST HIM.
DAMN STRAIGHT!
GRIN
AND YOU TRUST HIM, TOO, RIGHT?

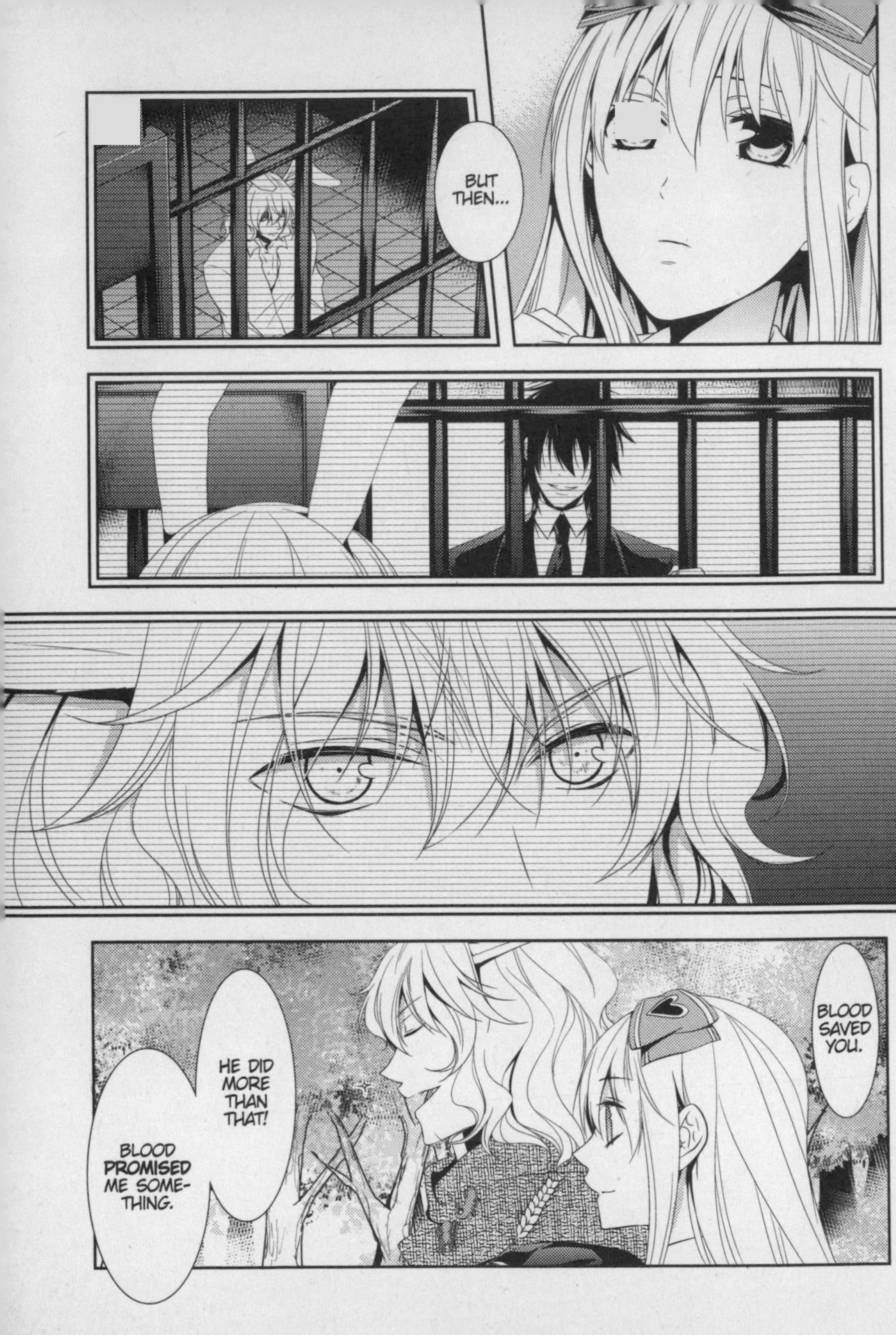
BUT THEN...
BLOOD SAVED YOU.
HE DID MORE THAN THAT!
BLOOD PROMISED ME SOME-THING.

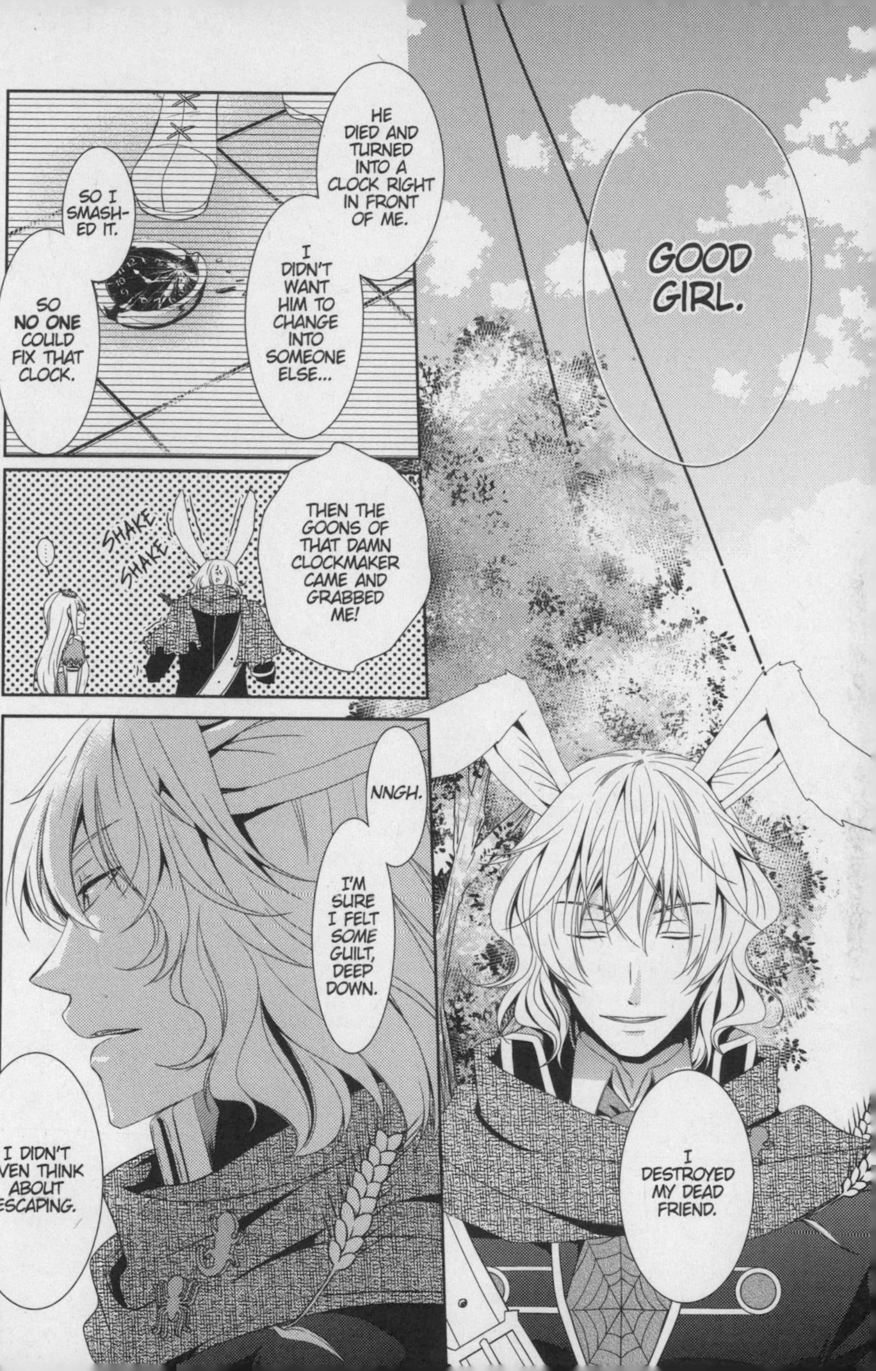
GOOD GIRL.
I DESTROYED MY DEAD FRIEND.
HE DIED AND TURNED INTO A CLOCK RIGHT IN FRONT OF ME.
I DIDN'T WANT HIM TO CHANGE INTO SOMEONE ELSE...
SO I SMASHED IT.
SO NO ONE COULD FIX THAT CLOCK.
THEN THE GOONS OF THAT DAMN CLOCKMAKER CAME AND GRABBED ME!
SHAKE SHAKE
...
NNGH.
I'M SURE I FELT SOME GUILT, DEEP DOWN.
I DIDN'T EVEN THINK ABOUT ESCAPING.

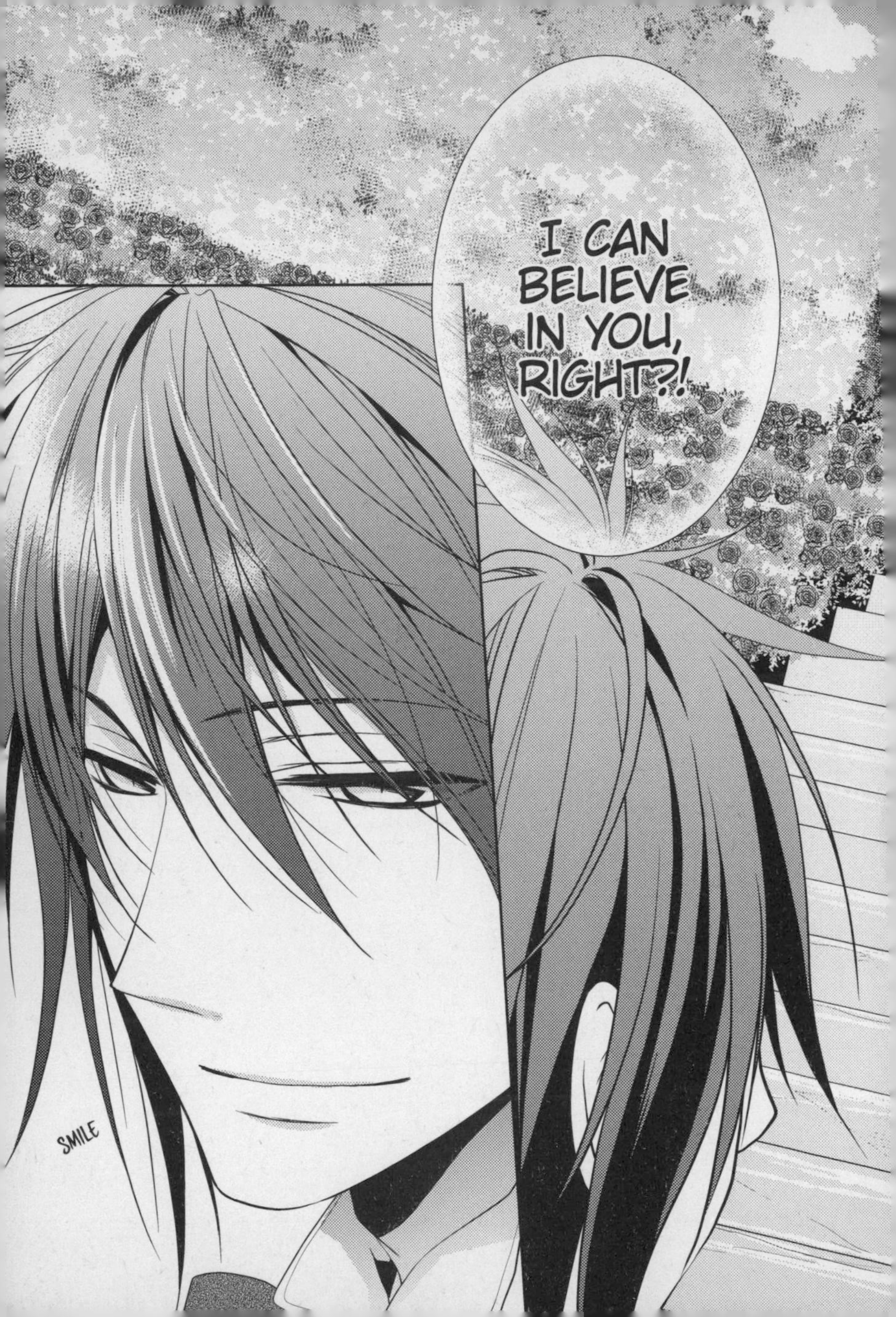
I CAN BELIEVE IN YOU, RIGHT?!
SMILE

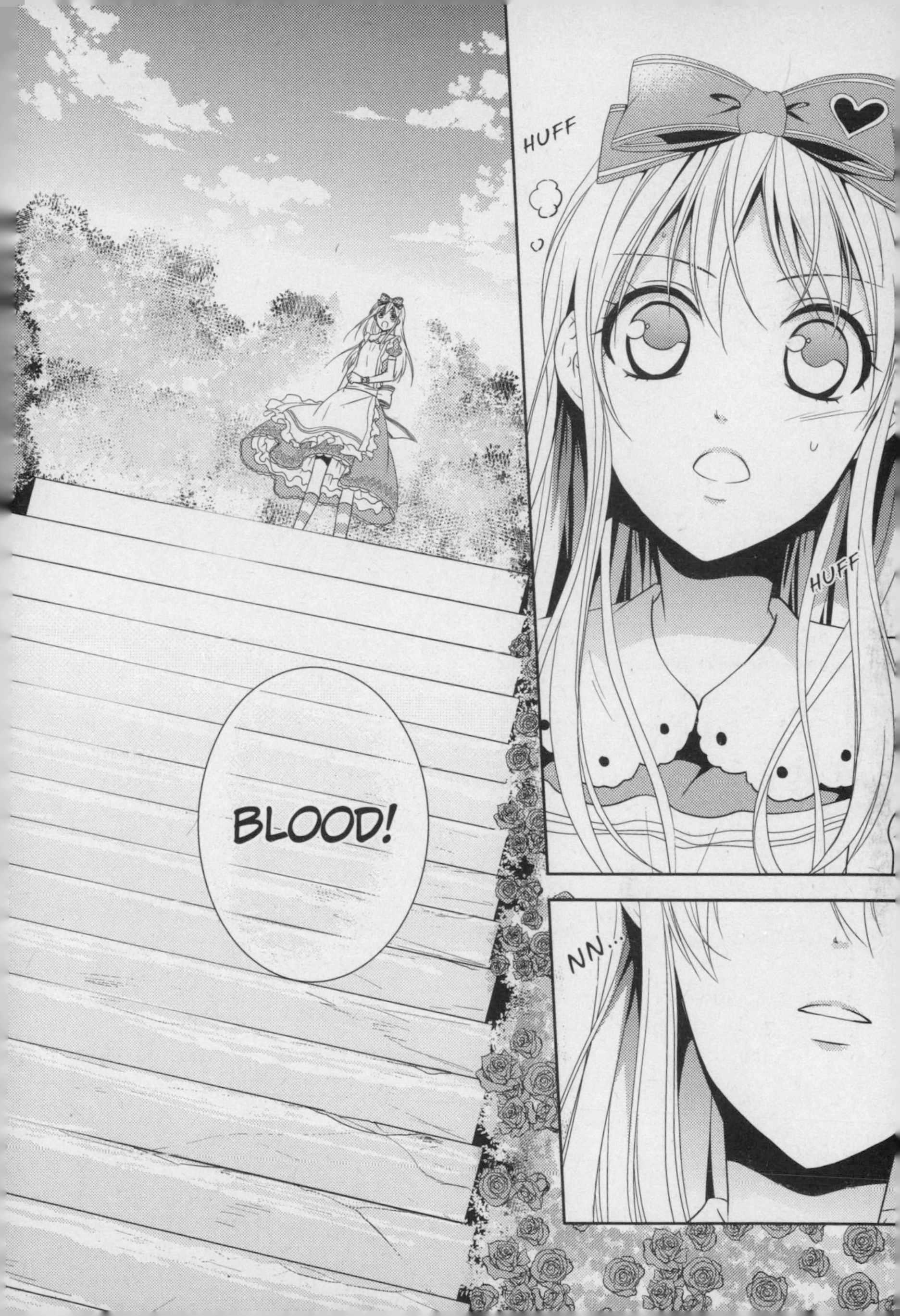
HUFF
HUFF
NN...
BLOOD!

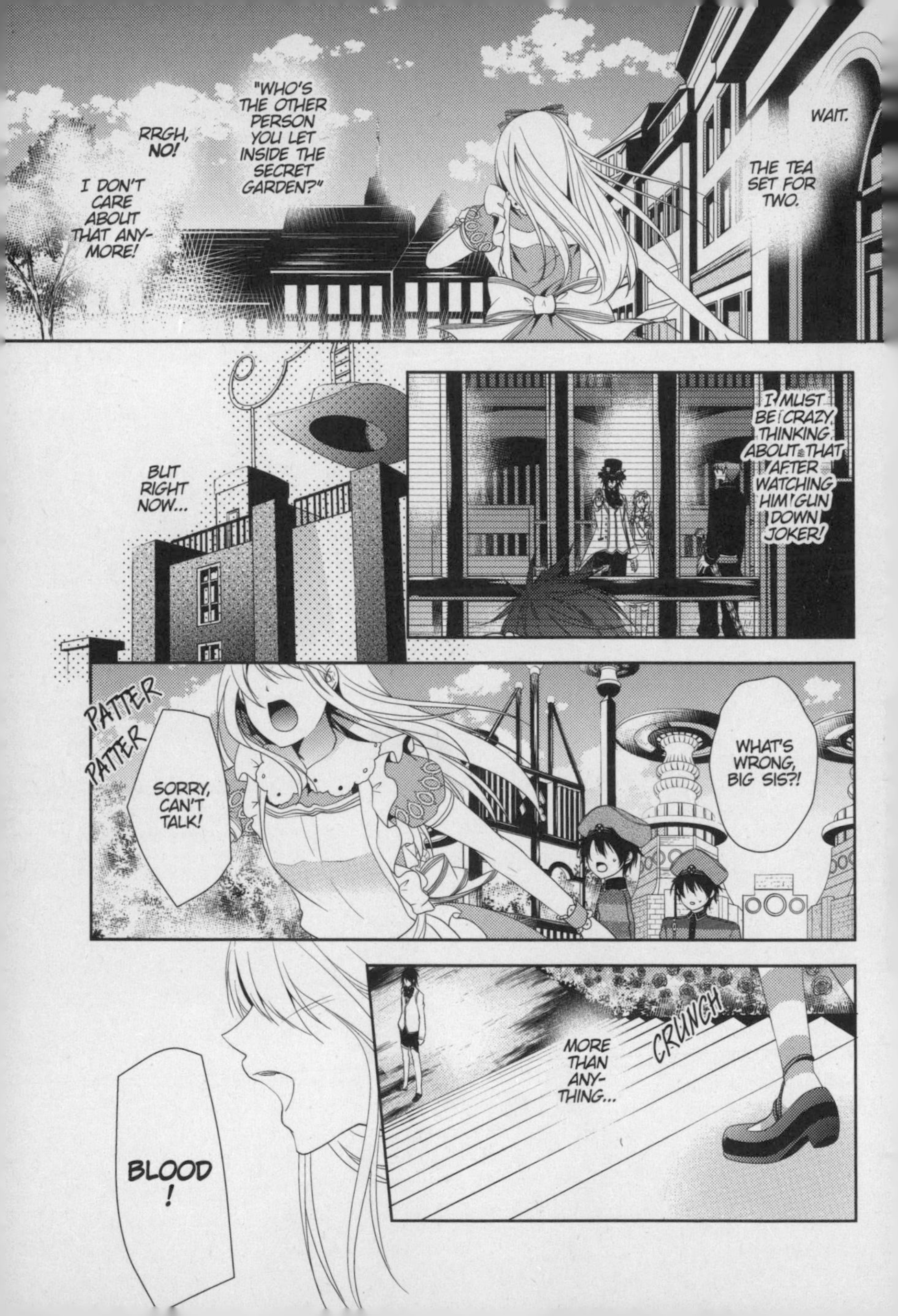
WAIT.
THE TEA SET FOR TWO.
"WHO'S THE OTHER PERSON YOU LET INSIDE THE SECRET GARDEN?"
RRGH, NO!
I DON'T CARE ABOUT THAT ANY-MORE!
I MUST BE CRAZY, THINKING ABOUT THAT AFTER WATCHING HIM GUN DOWN JOKER!
BUT RIGHT NOW...
WHAT'S WRONG, BIG SIS?!
SORRY, CAN'T TALK!
PATTER PATTER
CRUNCH
MORE THAN ANY-THING...
BLOOD!

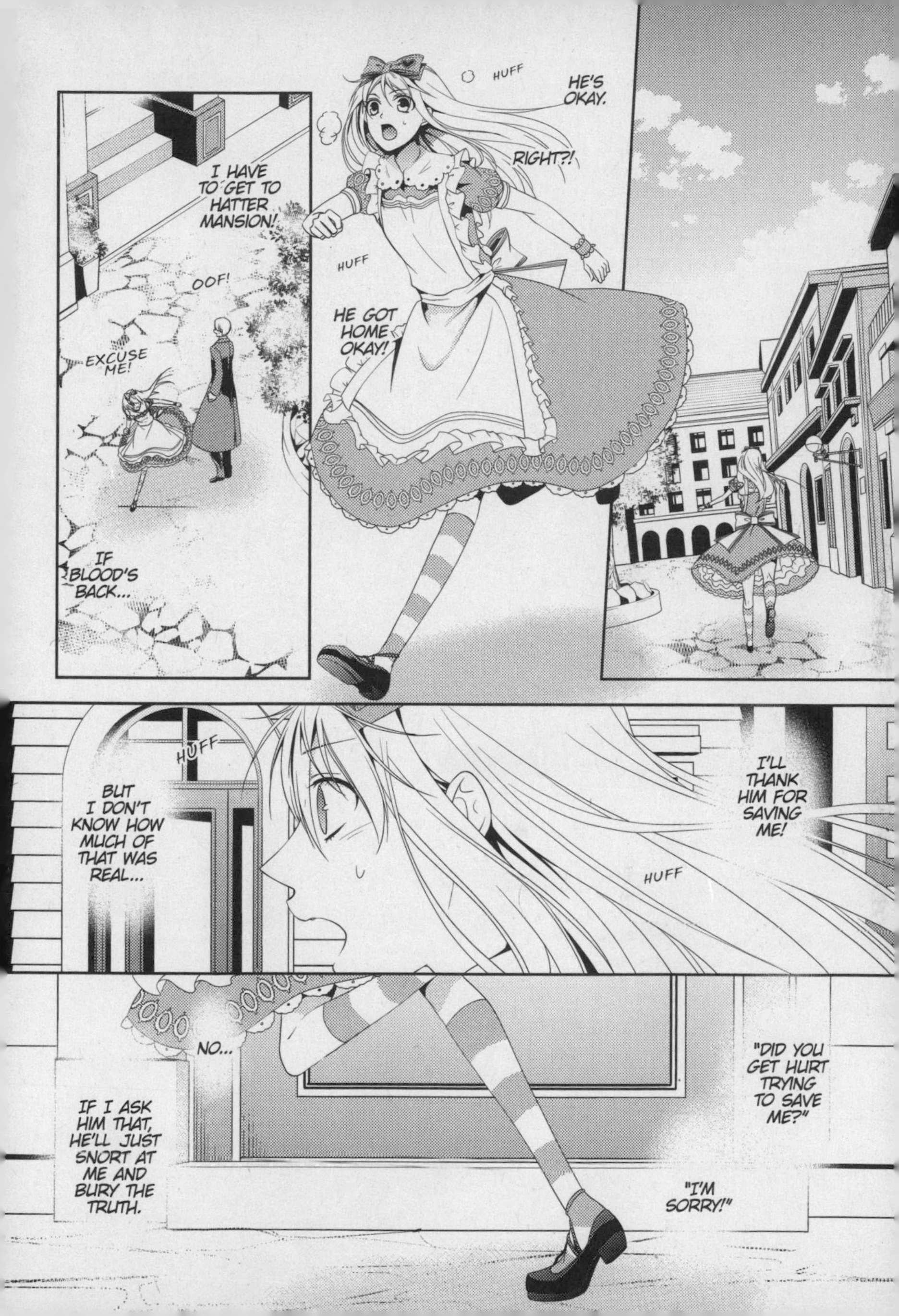
HE'S OKAY.
HUFF
RIGHT?!
HUFF
HE GOT HOME OKAY!
I HAVE TO GET TO HATTER MANSION!
OOF!
EXCUSE ME!
IF BLOOD'S BACK...
I'LL THANK HIM FOR SAVING ME!
HUFF
HUFF
BUT I DON'T KNOW HOW MUCH OF THAT WAS REAL...
"DID YOU GET HURT TRYING TO SAVE ME?"
"I'M SORRY!"
NO...
IF I ASK HIM THAT, HE'LL JUST SNORT AT ME AND BURY THE TRUTH.

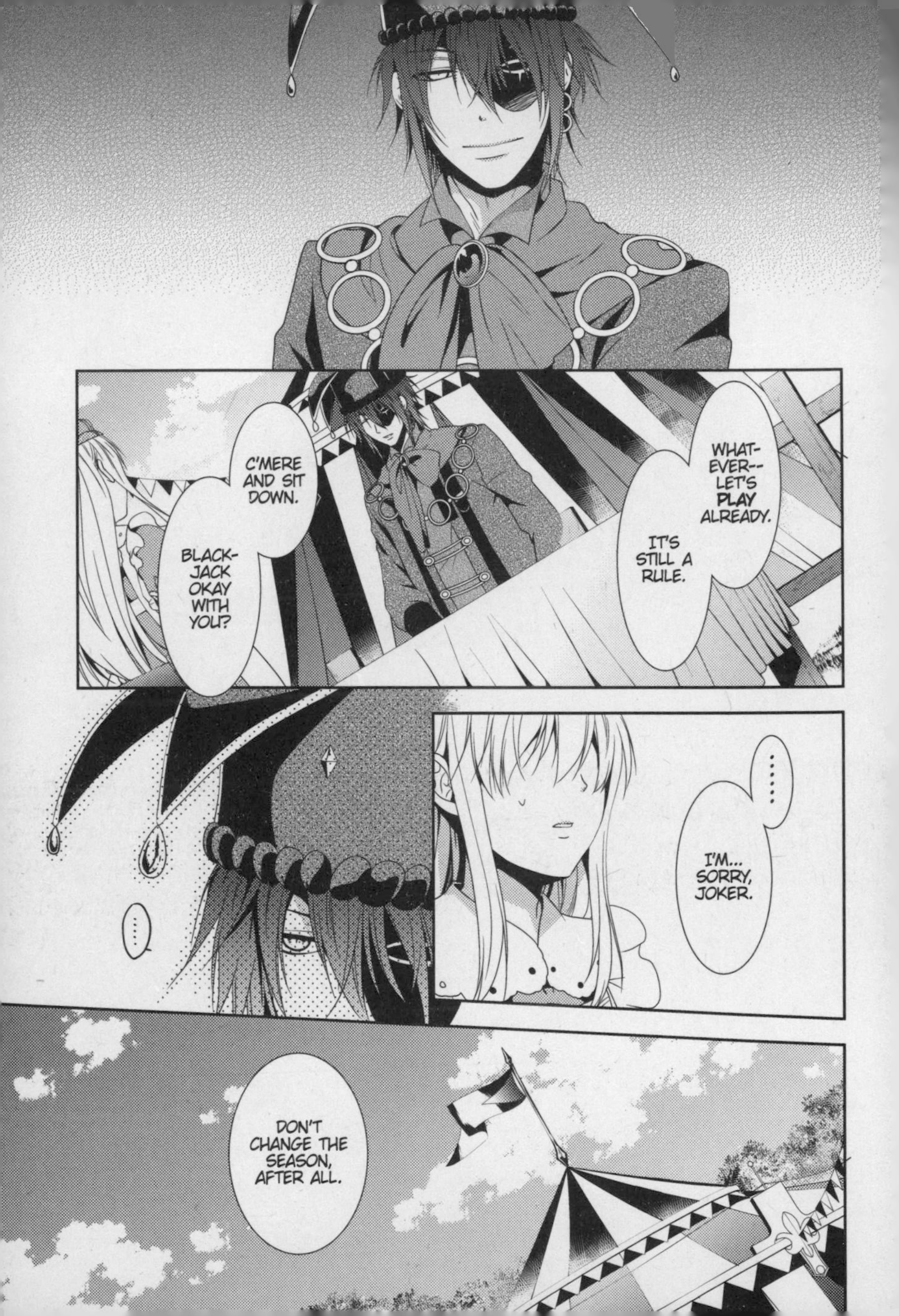
WHAT-EVER--LET'S PLAY ALREADY.
IT'S STILL A RULE.
C'MERE AND SIT DOWN.
BLACK-JACK OKAY WITH YOU?
......
I'M... SORRY, JOKER.
...
DON'T CHANGE THE SEASON, AFTER ALL.

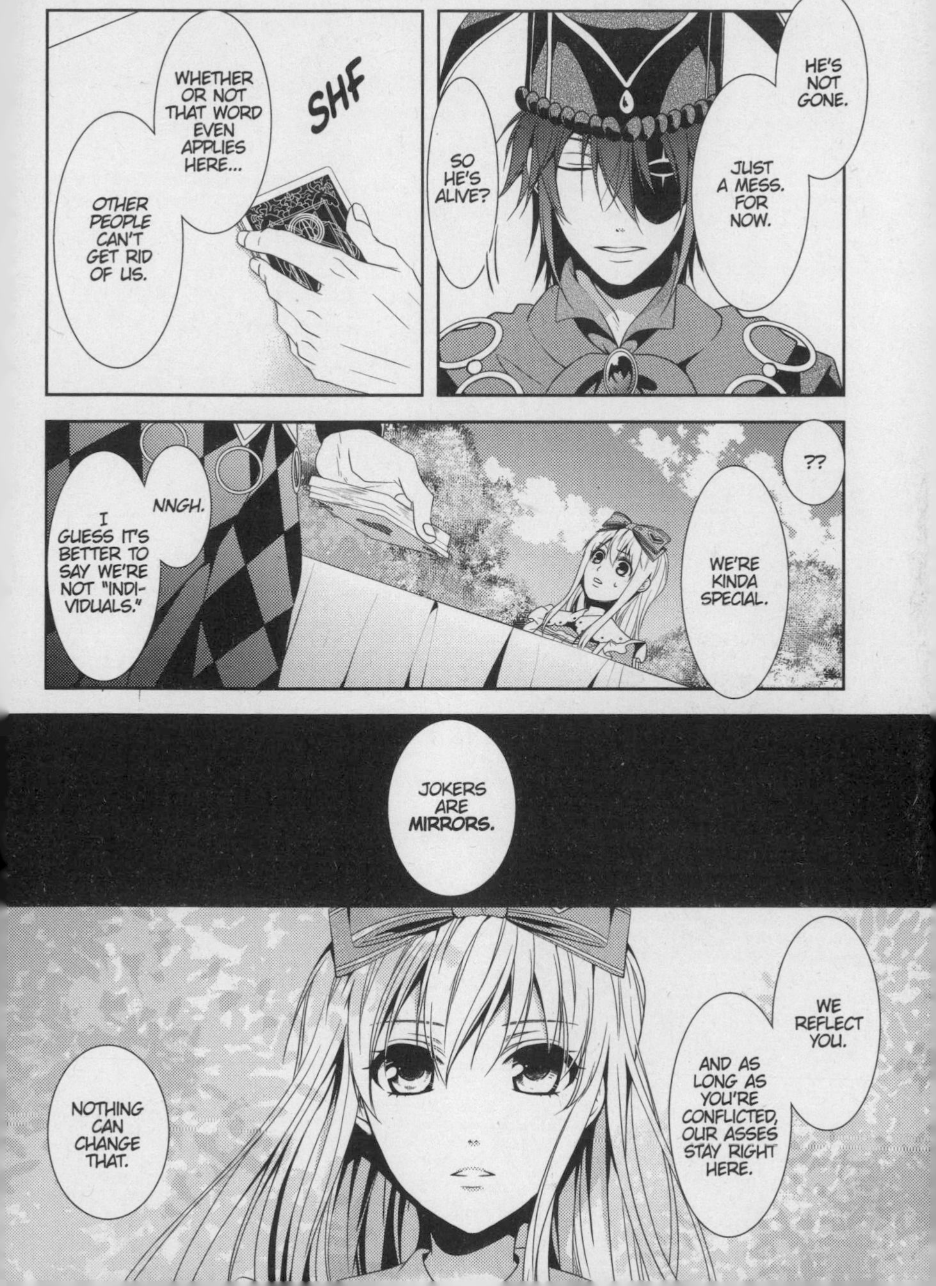
HE'S NOT GONE.
JUST A MESS. FOR NOW.
SO HE'S ALIVE?
WHETHER OR NOT THAT WORD EVEN APPLIES HERE...
SHF
OTHER PEOPLE CAN'T GET RID OF US.
??
WE'RE KINDA SPECIAL.
NNGH.
I GUESS IT'S BETTER TO SAY WE'RE NOT "INDIVIDUALS."
JOKERS ARE MIRRORS.
WE REFLECT YOU.
AND AS LONG AS YOU'RE CONFLICTED, OUR ASSES STAY RIGHT HERE.
NOTHING CAN CHANGE THAT.

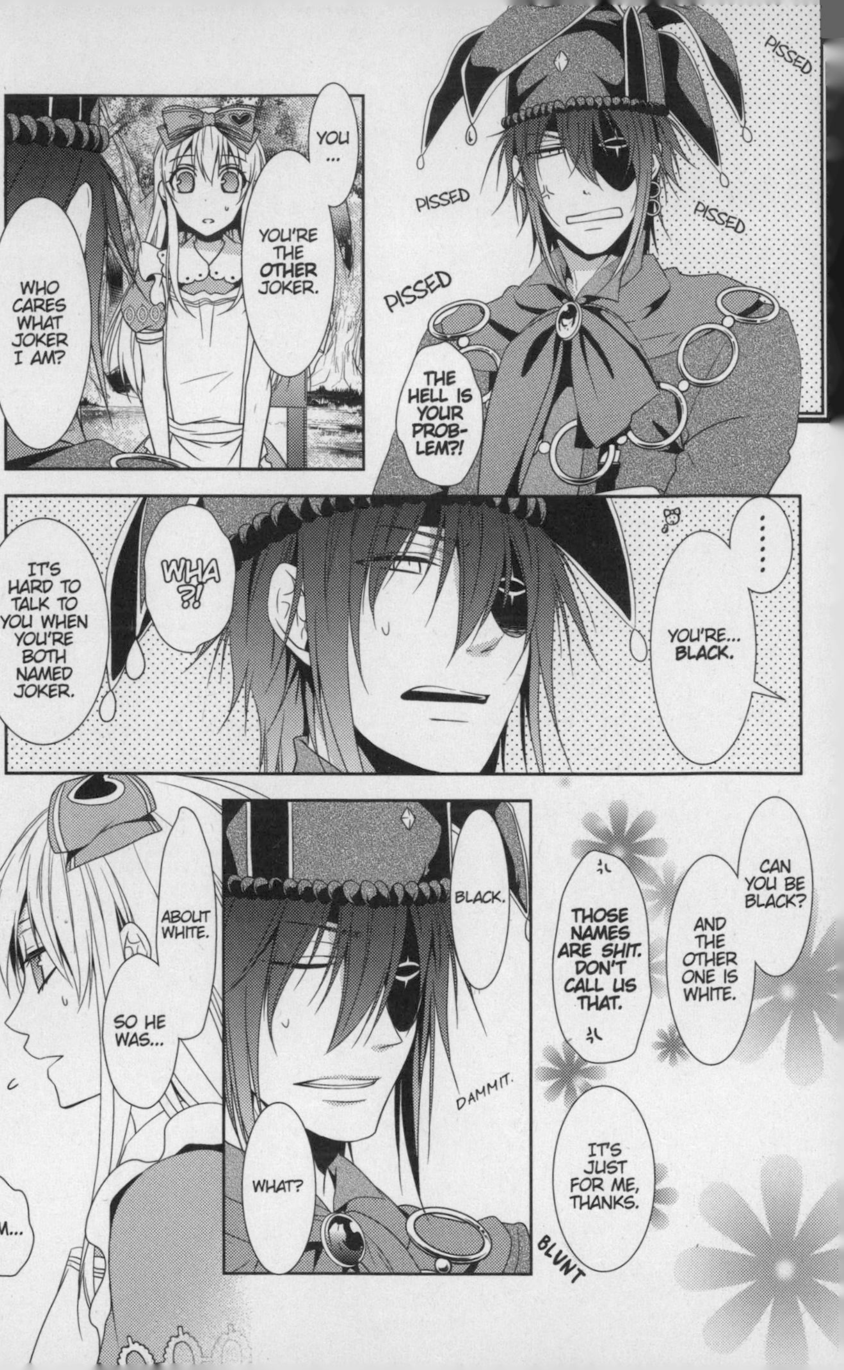
PISSED
PISSED
PISSED
PISSED
THE HELL IS YOUR PROBLEM?!
YOU ...
YOU'RE THE OTHER JOKER.
WHO CARES WHAT JOKER I AM?
......
YOU'RE... BLACK.
WHA ?!
IT'S HARD TO TALK TO YOU WHEN YOU'RE BOTH NAMED JOKER.
CAN YOU BE BLACK?
AND THE OTHER ONE IS WHITE.
THOSE NAMES ARE SHIT. DON'T CALL US THAT.
IT'S JUST FOR ME, THANKS.
BLUNT
BLACK.
DAMMIT.
WHAT?
ABOUT WHITE.
SO HE WAS...
UM...

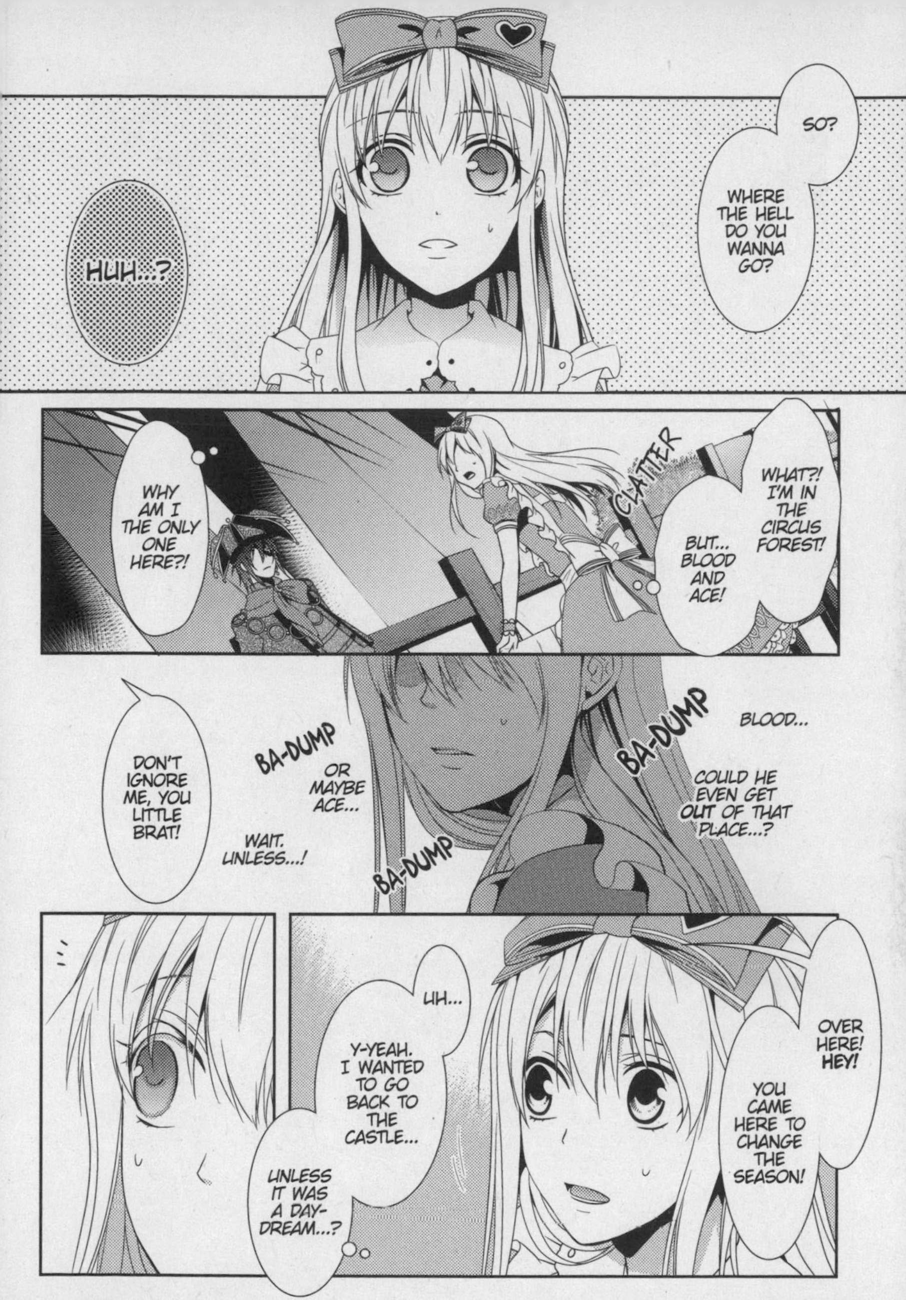
SO?
WHERE THE HELL DO YOU WANNA GO?
HUH...?
WHAT?! I'M IN THE CIRCUS FOREST!
BUT... BLOOD AND ACE!
CLATTER
WHY AM I THE ONLY ONE HERE?!
BLOOD...
COULD HE EVEN GET OUT OF THAT PLACE...?
BA-DUMP
BA-DUMP
OR MAYBE ACE...
WAIT. UNLESS...!
BA-DUMP
DON'T IGNORE ME, YOU LITTLE BRAT!
OVER HERE! HEY!
YOU CAME HERE TO CHANGE THE SEASON!
UH...
Y-YEAH. I WANTED TO GO BACK TO THE CASTLE...
UNLESS IT WAS A DAY-DREAM...?

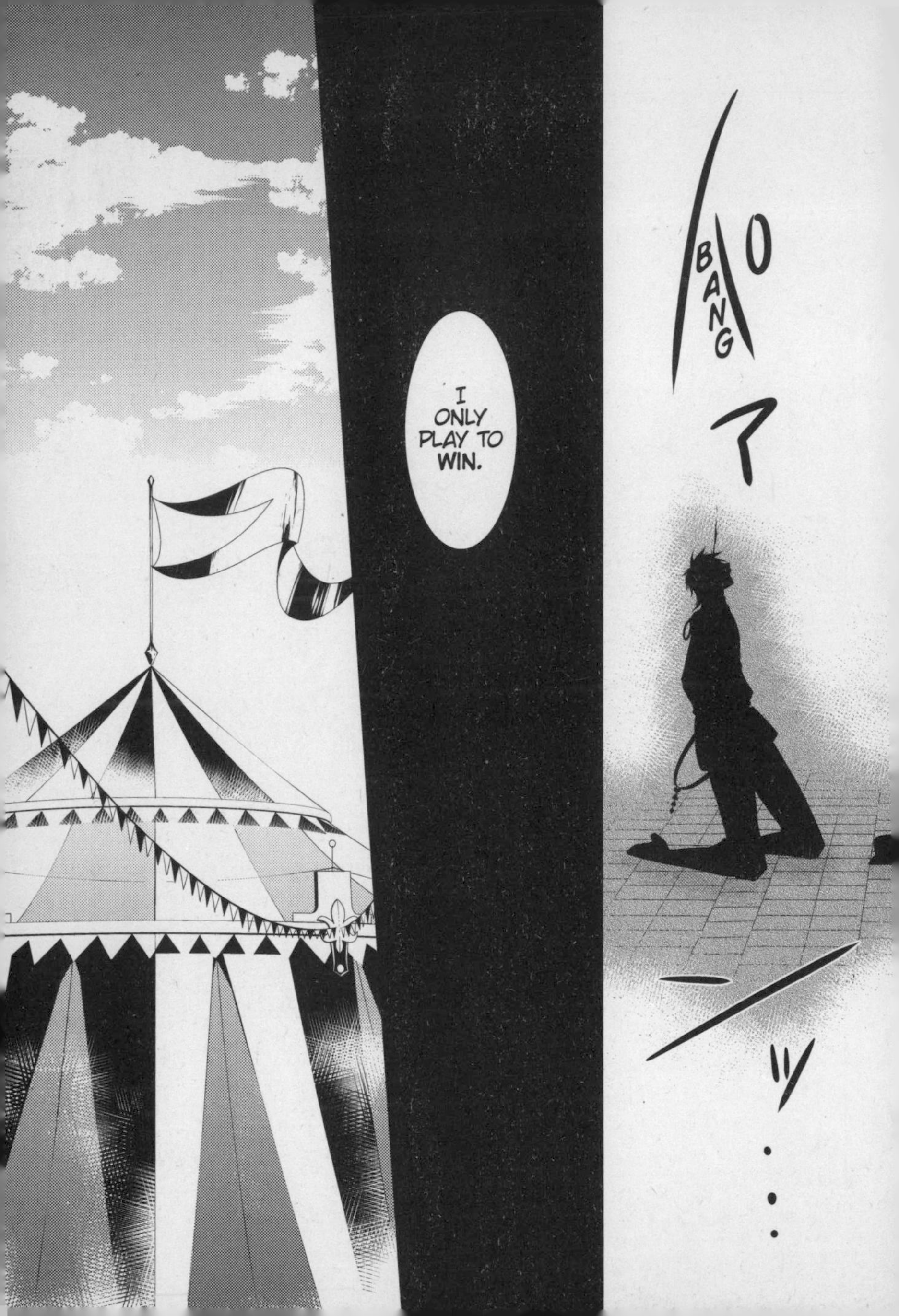
BANG
I ONLY PLAY TO WIN.

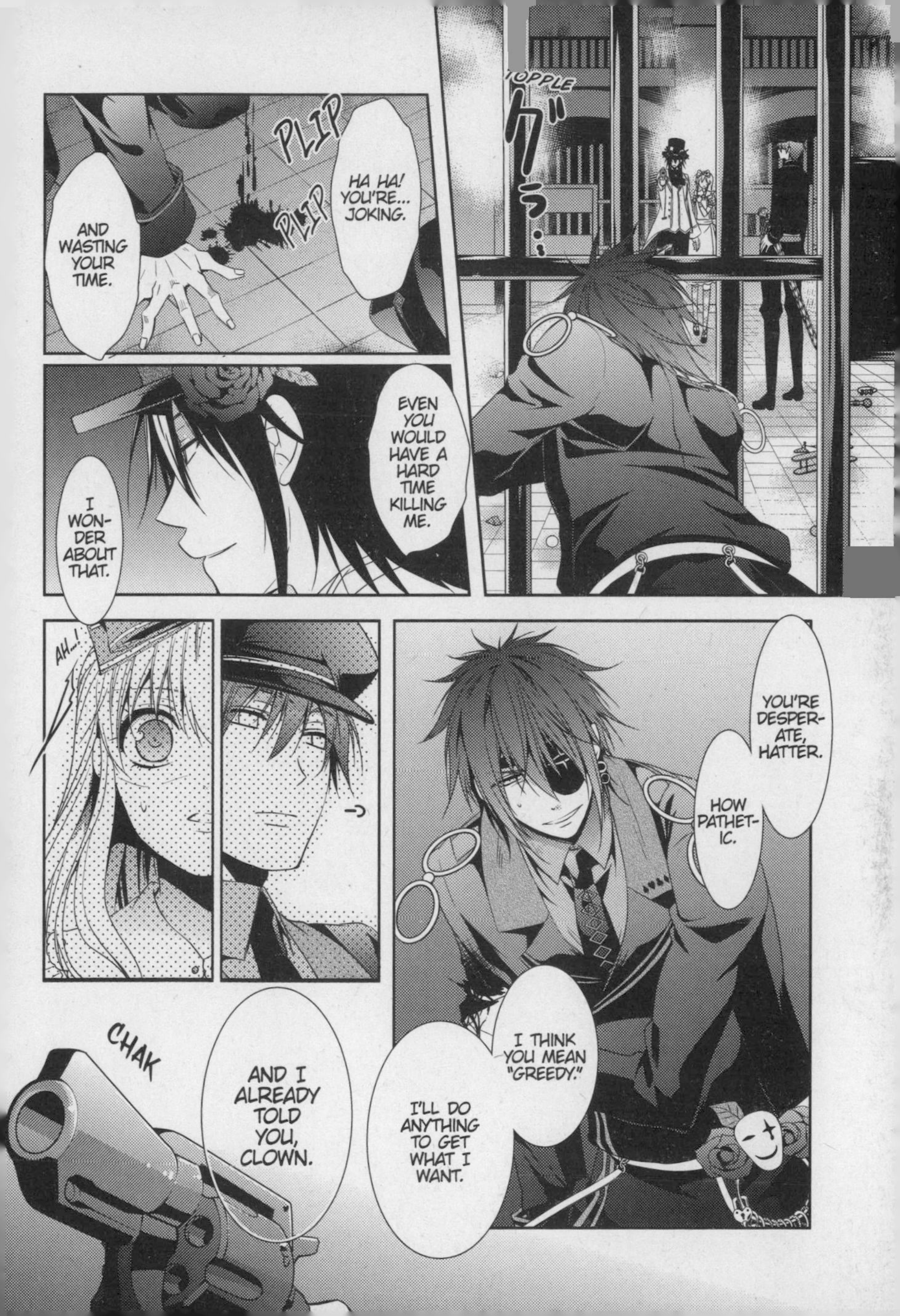
TOPPLE
グら…
PLIP
PLIP
HA HA! YOU'RE... JOKING.
AND WASTING YOUR TIME.
EVEN YOU WOULD HAVE A HARD TIME KILLING ME.
I WONDER ABOUT THAT.
YOU'RE DESPERATE, HATTER.
HOW PATHETIC.
I THINK YOU MEAN "GREEDY."
I'LL DO ANYTHING TO GET WHAT I WANT.
AH...!
CHAK
AND I ALREADY TOLD YOU, CLOWN.

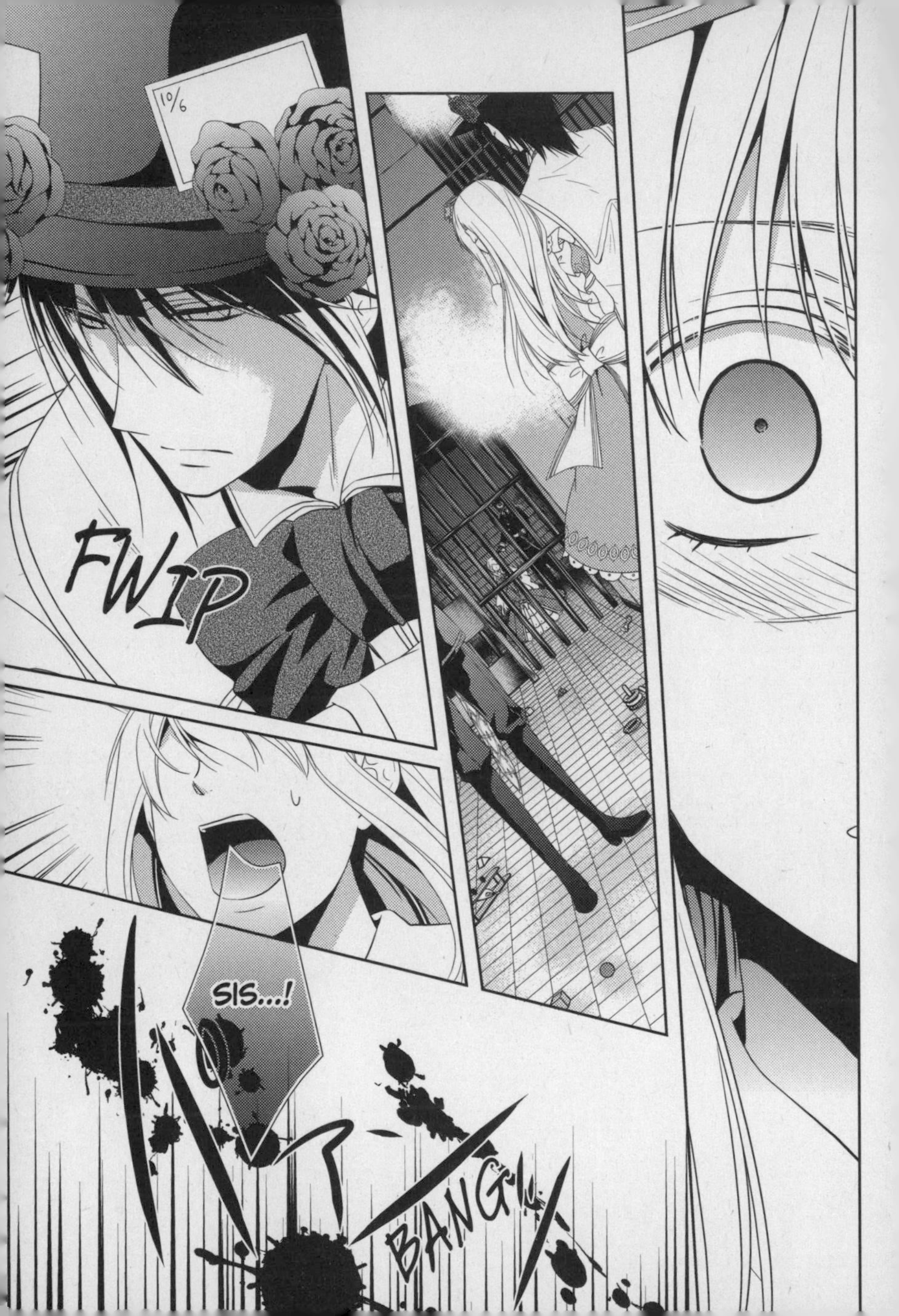
10/6
FWIP
SIS...!
BANG!!

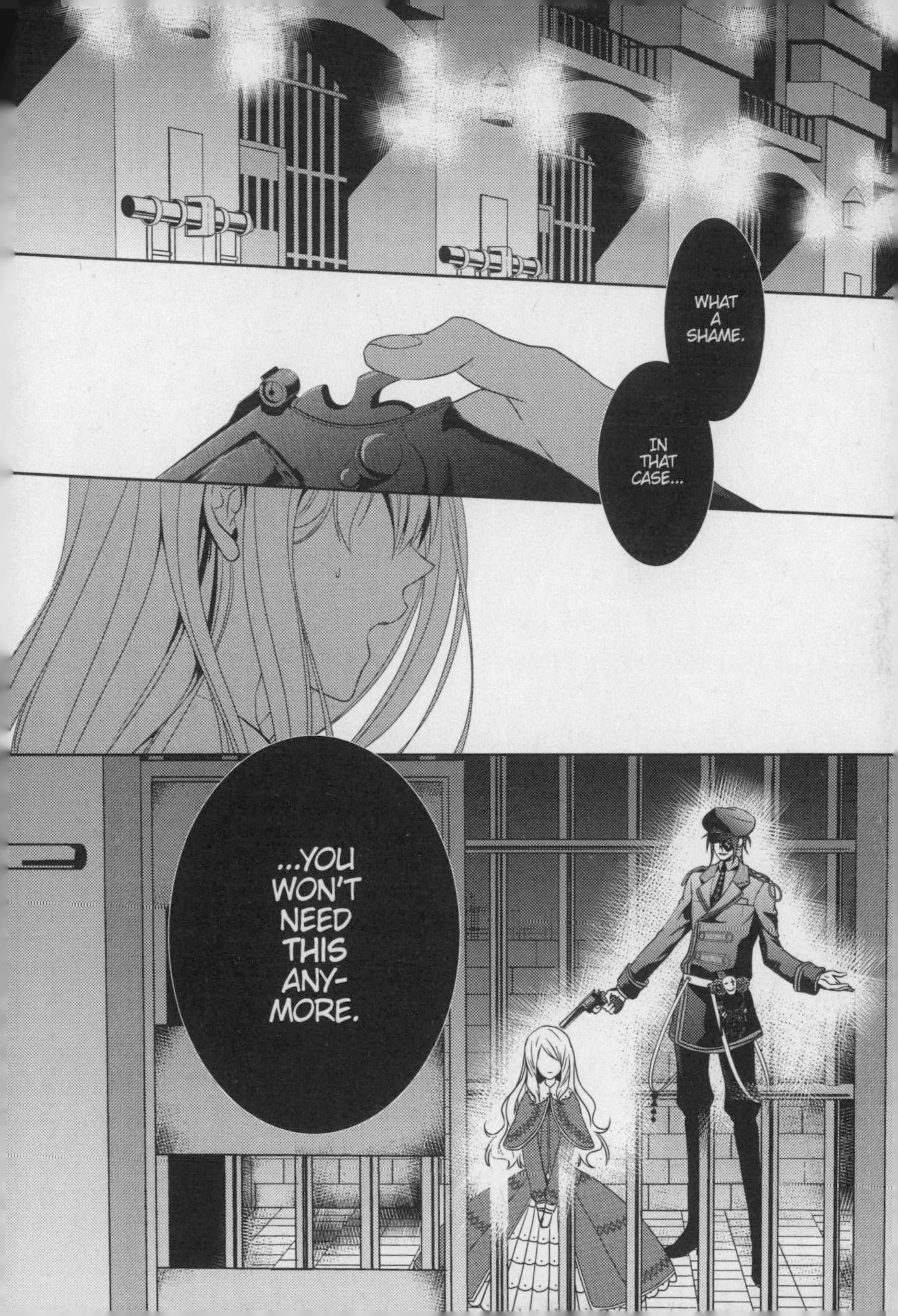
WHAT A SHAME.
IN THAT CASE...
...YOU WON'T NEED THIS ANY-MORE.

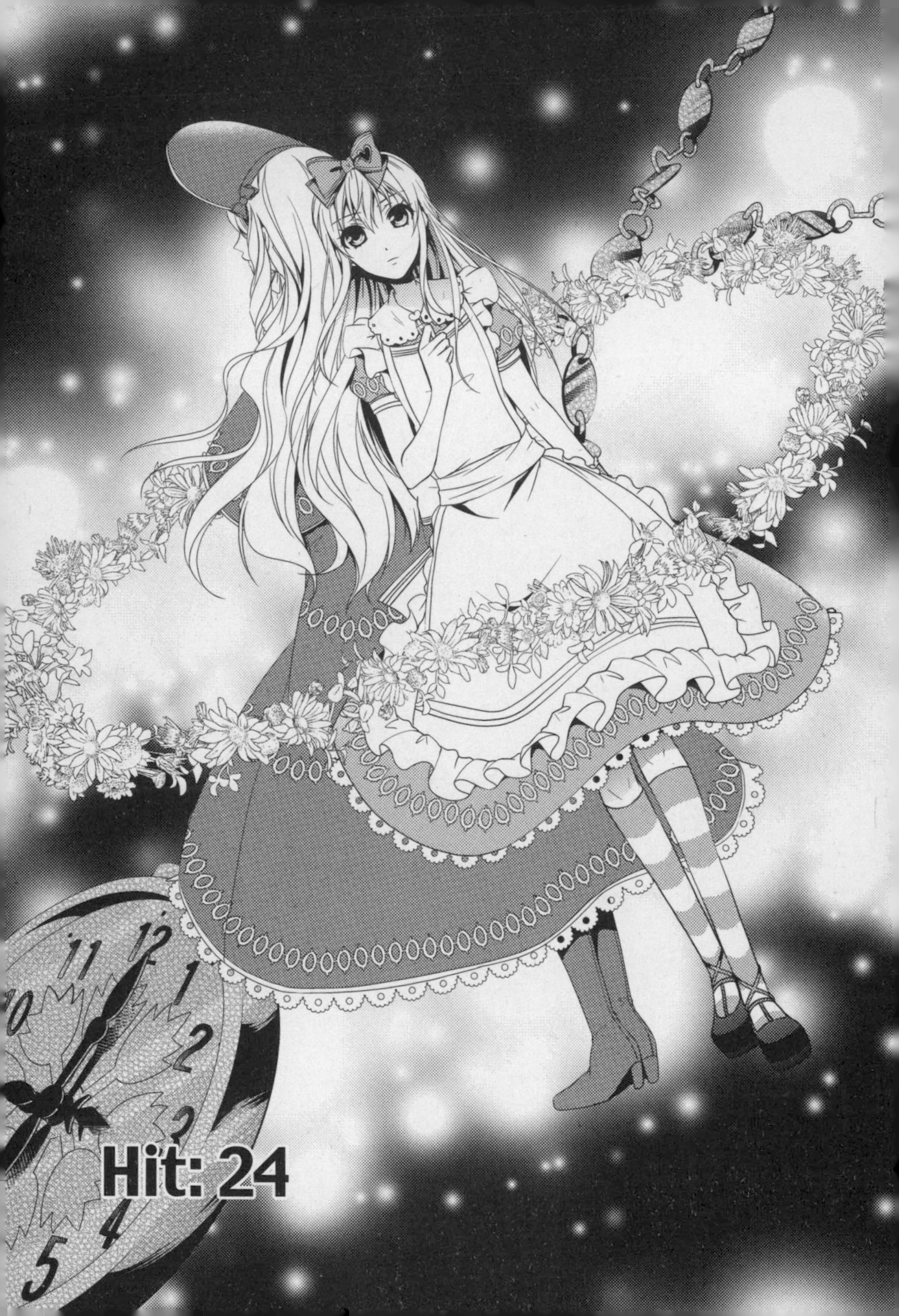
Hit: 24

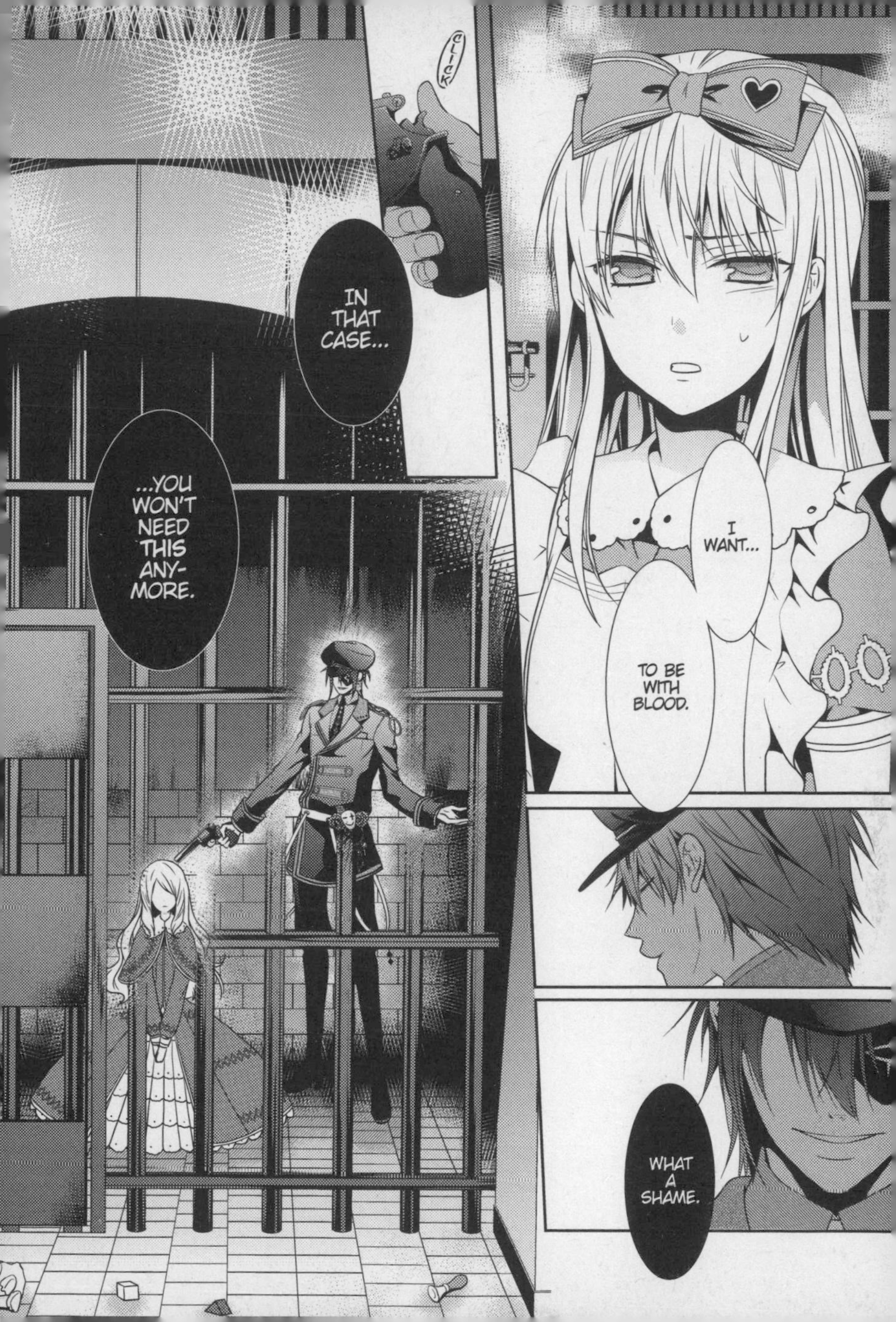
I WANT...
TO BE WITH BLOOD.
WHAT A SHAME.
CLICK
IN THAT CASE...
...YOU WON'T NEED THIS ANYMORE.

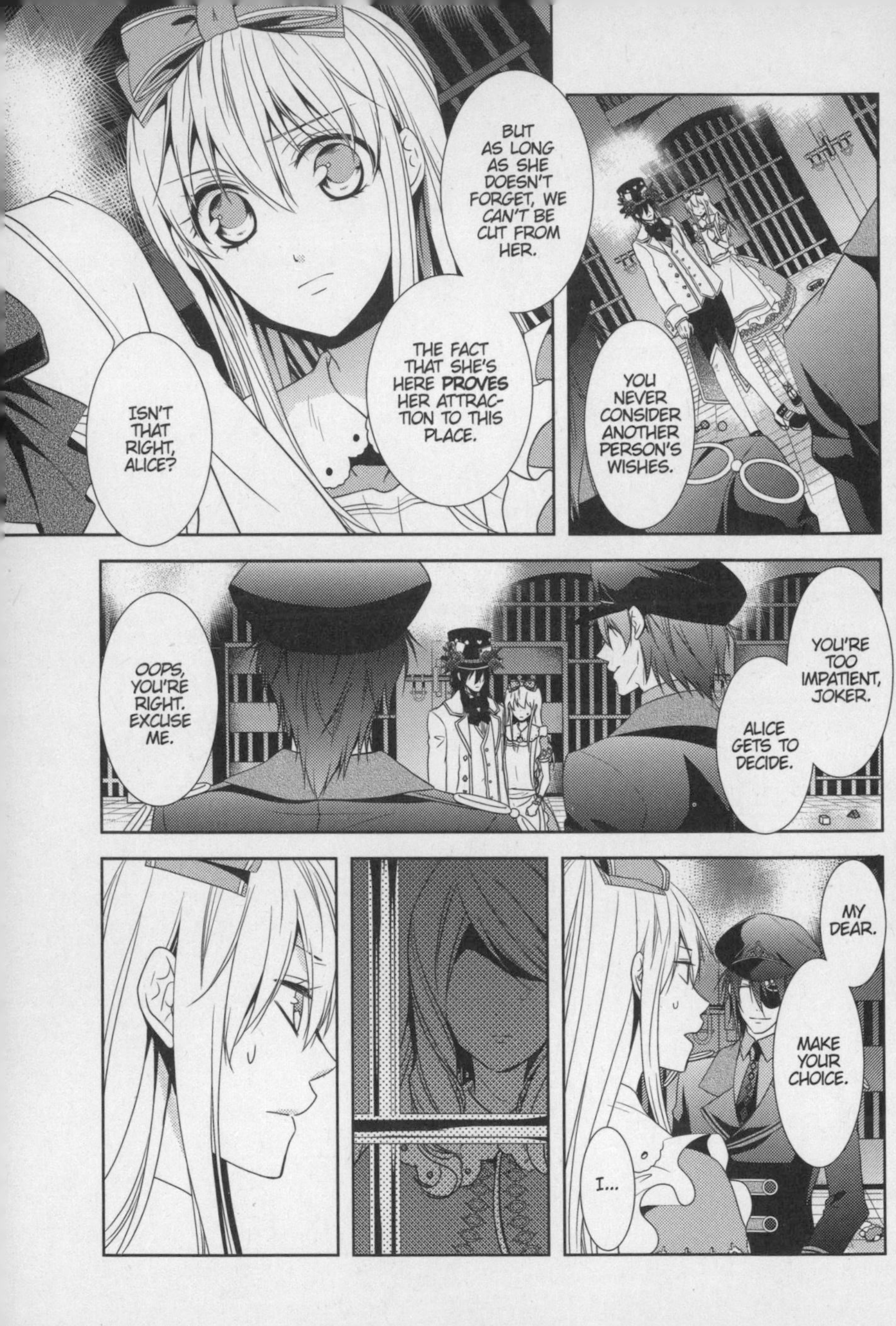
YOU NEVER CONSIDER ANOTHER PERSON'S WISHES.
BUT AS LONG AS SHE DOESN'T FORGET, WE CAN'T BE CUT FROM HER.
THE FACT THAT SHE'S HERE **PROVES** HER ATTRACTION TO THIS PLACE.
ISN'T THAT RIGHT, ALICE?
YOU'RE TOO IMPATIENT, JOKER.
ALICE GETS TO DECIDE.
OOPS, YOU'RE RIGHT. EXCUSE ME.
MY DEAR.
MAKE YOUR CHOICE.
I...

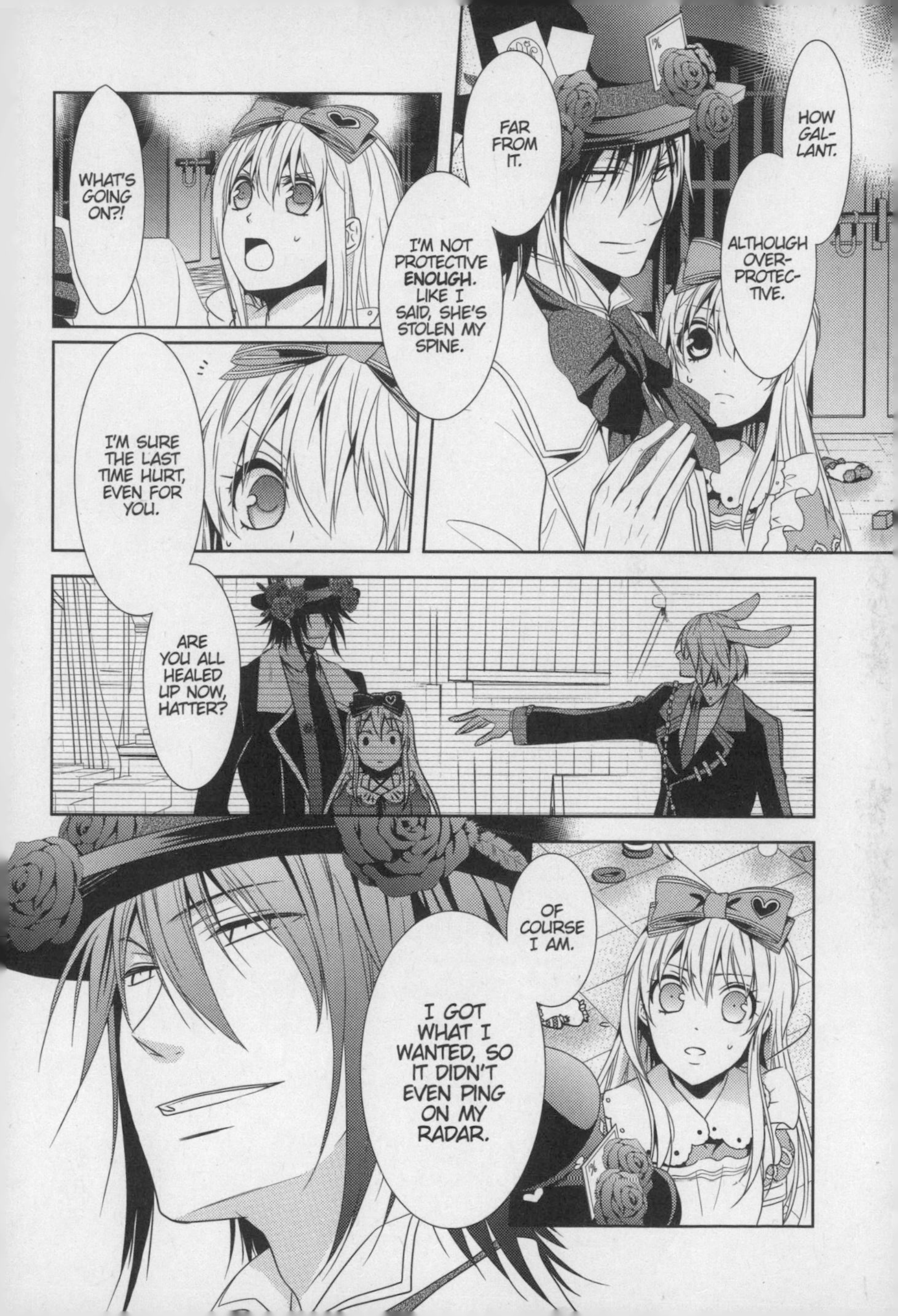
HOW GAL-LANT.
ALTHOUGH OVER-PROTEC-TIVE.
FAR FROM IT.
I'M NOT PROTECTIVE ENOUGH. LIKE I SAID, SHE'S STOLEN MY SPINE.
WHAT'S GOING ON?!
I'M SURE THE LAST TIME HURT, EVEN FOR YOU.
ARE YOU ALL HEALED UP NOW, HATTER?
OF COURSE I AM.
I GOT WHAT I WANTED, SO IT DIDN'T EVEN PING ON MY RADAR.

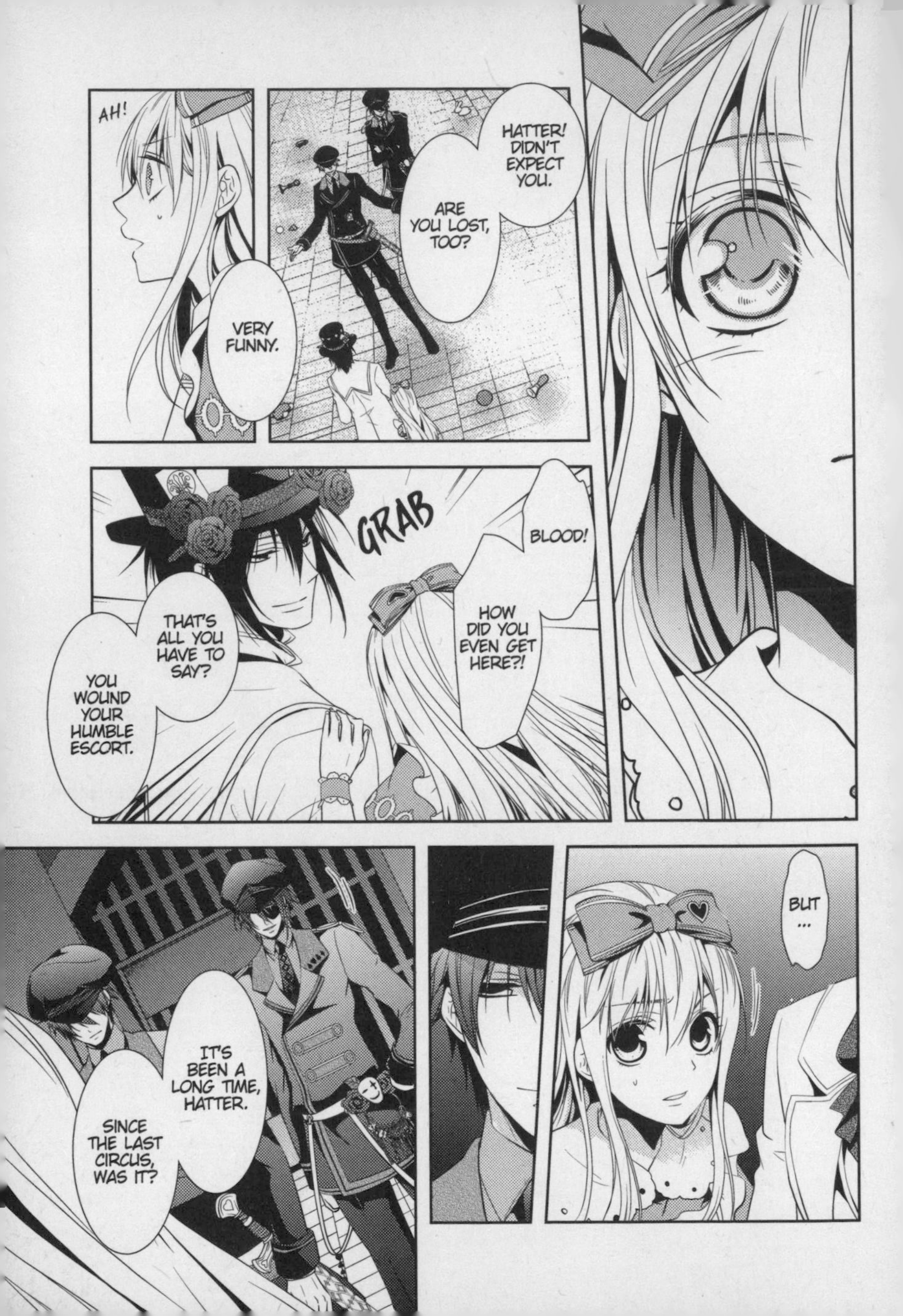
HATTER! DIDN'T EXPECT YOU.
ARE YOU LOST, TOO?
VERY FUNNY.
AH!
GRAB
BLOOD!
HOW DID YOU EVEN GET HERE?!
THAT'S ALL YOU HAVE TO SAY?
YOU WOUND YOUR HUMBLE ESCORT.
BUT ...
IT'S BEEN A LONG TIME, HATTER.
SINCE THE LAST CIRCUS, WAS IT?

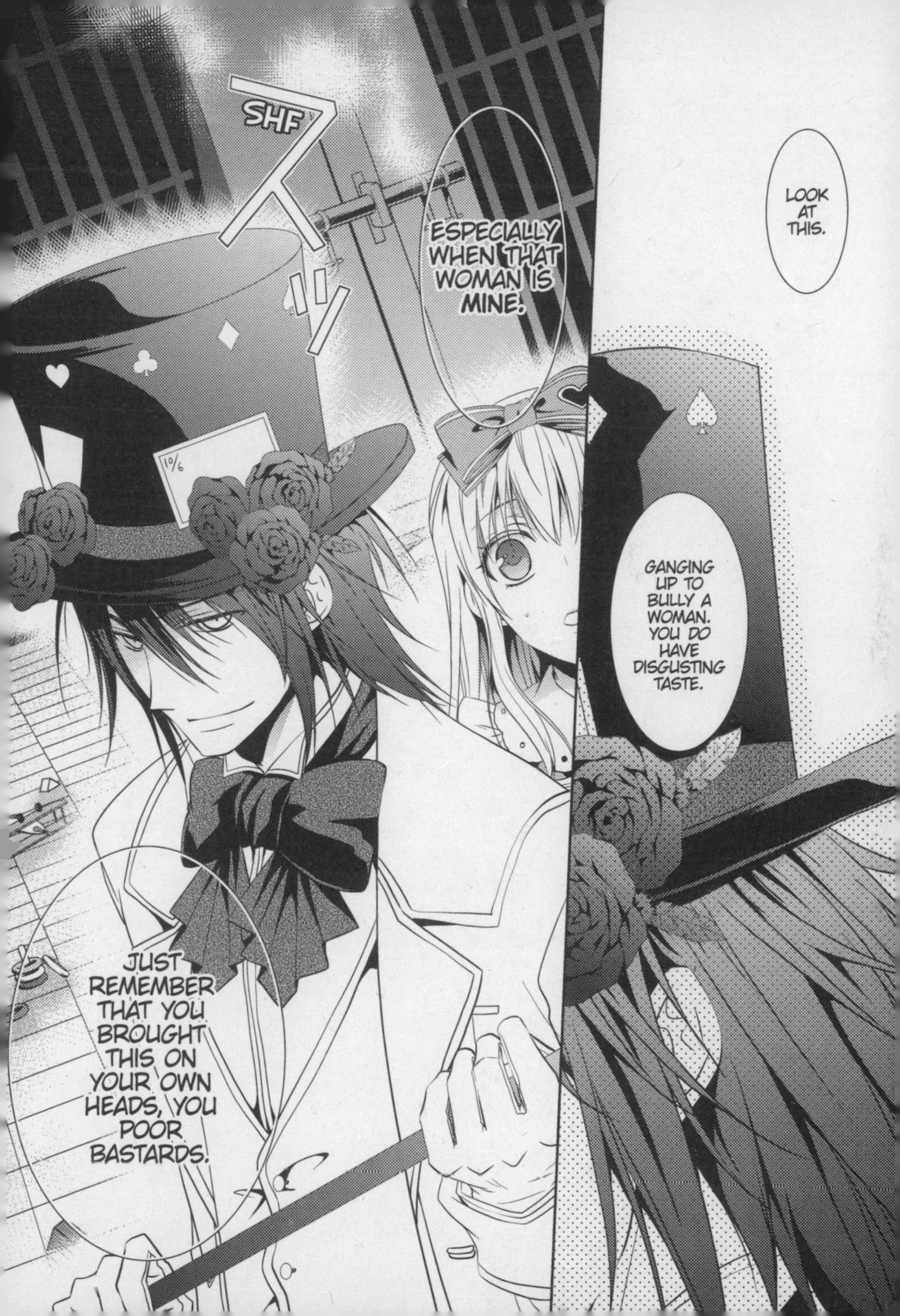
LOOK AT THIS.
GANGING UP TO BULLY A WOMAN. YOU DO HAVE DISGUSTING TASTE.
SHF
ESPECIALLY WHEN THAT WOMAN IS MINE.
JUST REMEMBER THAT YOU BROUGHT THIS ON YOUR OWN HEADS, YOU POOR BASTARDS.

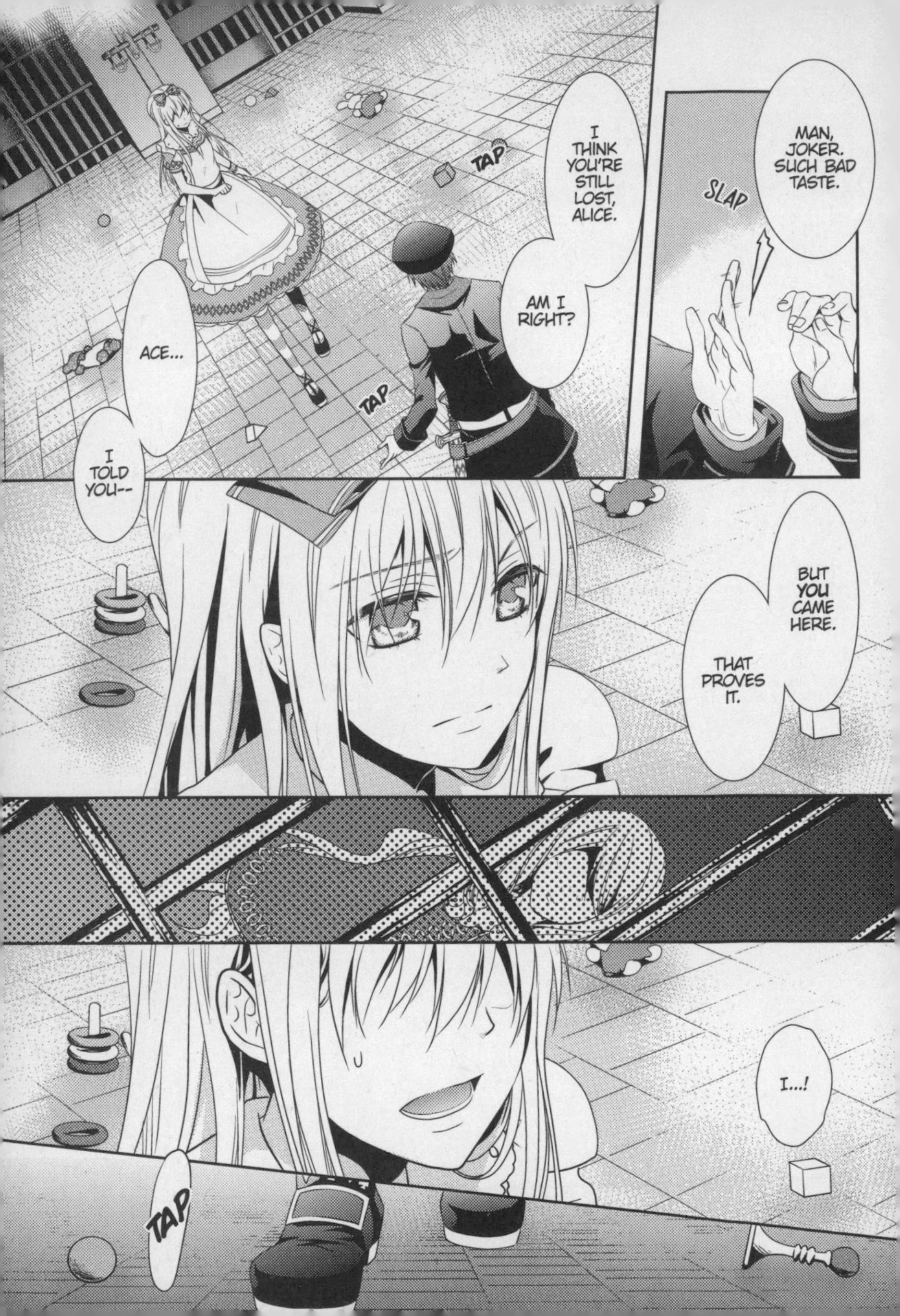
MAN, JOKER. SUCH BAD TASTE.
SLAP
I THINK YOU'RE STILL LOST, ALICE.
TAP
AM I RIGHT?
TAP
ACE...
I TOLD YOU--
BUT YOU CAME HERE.
THAT PROVES IT.
I...!
TAP

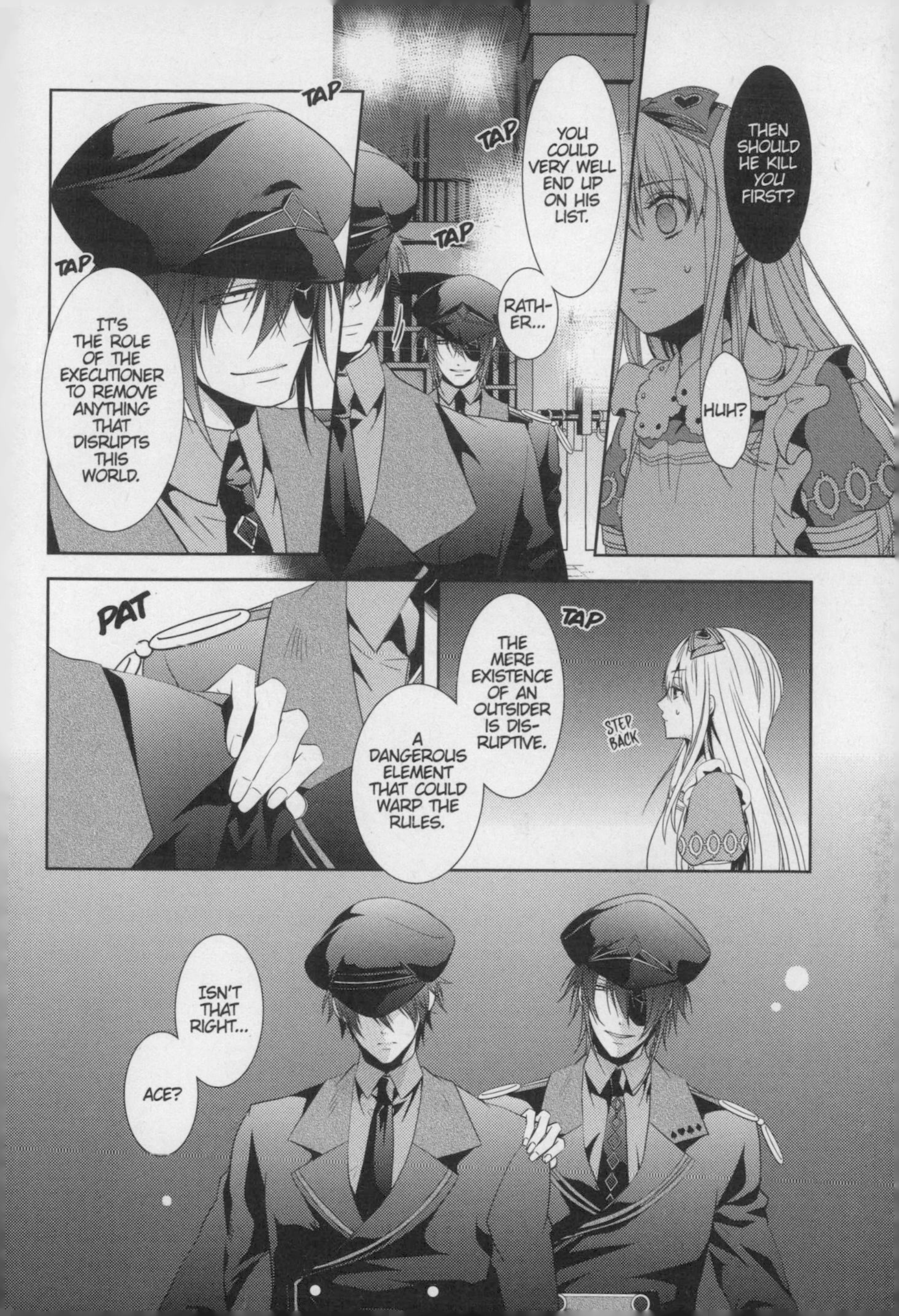
THEN SHOULD HE KILL YOU FIRST?
HUH?
TAP
YOU COULD VERY WELL END UP ON HIS LIST.
TAP
RATHER...
TAP
TAP
IT'S THE ROLE OF THE EXECUTIONER TO REMOVE ANYTHING THAT DISRUPTS THIS WORLD.
TAP
THE MERE EXISTENCE OF AN OUTSIDER IS DISRUPTIVE.
STEP BACK
A DANGEROUS ELEMENT THAT COULD WARP THE RULES.
PAT
ISN'T THAT RIGHT...
ACE?

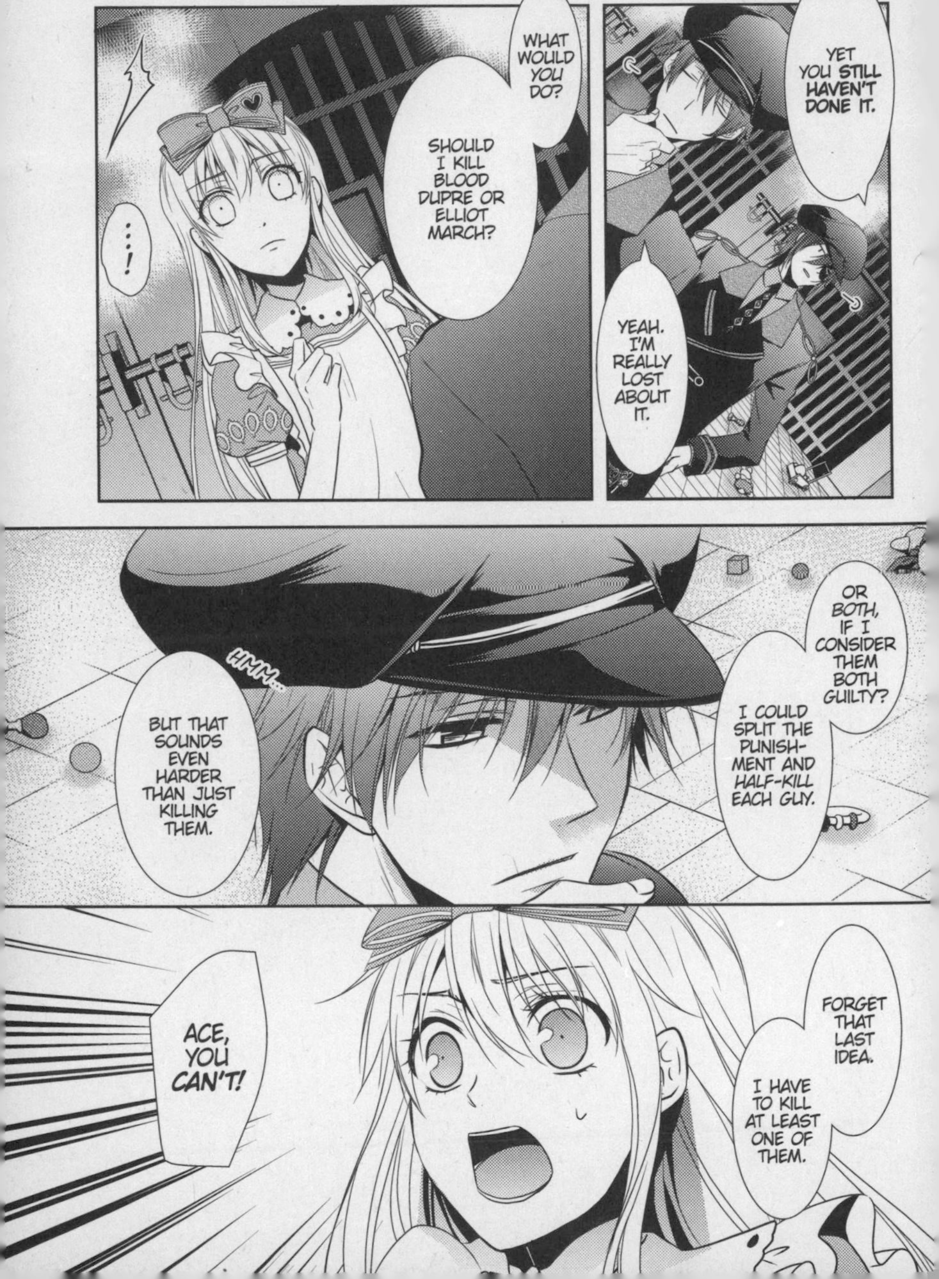
YET YOU STILL HAVEN'T DONE IT.
YEAH. I'M REALLY LOST ABOUT IT.
WHAT WOULD YOU DO?
SHOULD I KILL BLOOD DUPRE OR ELLIOT MARCH?
...!
OR BOTH, IF I CONSIDER THEM BOTH GUILTY?
I COULD SPLIT THE PUNISH-MENT AND HALF-KILL EACH GUY.
HMM...
BUT THAT SOUNDS EVEN HARDER THAN JUST KILLING THEM.
FORGET THAT LAST IDEA.
I HAVE TO KILL AT LEAST ONE OF THEM.
ACE, YOU CAN'T!

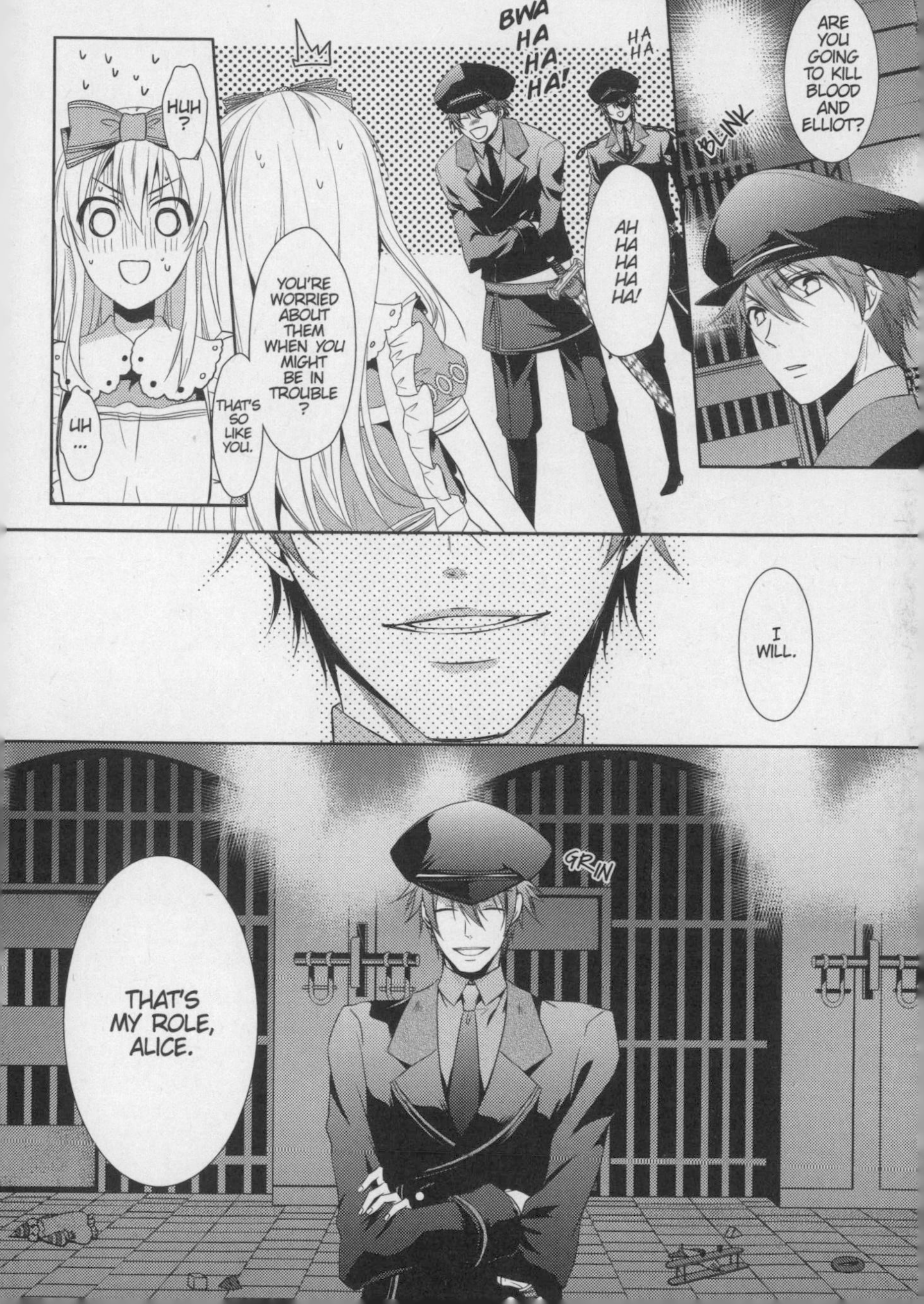
ARE YOU GOING TO KILL BLOOD AND ELLIOT?
BLINK
BWA HA HA HA!
HA HA
AH HA HA HA HA HA!
YOU'RE WORRIED ABOUT THEM WHEN YOU MIGHT BE IN TROUBLE?
THAT'S SO LIKE YOU.
HUH?
UH ...
I WILL.
GR-IN
THAT'S MY ROLE, ALICE.

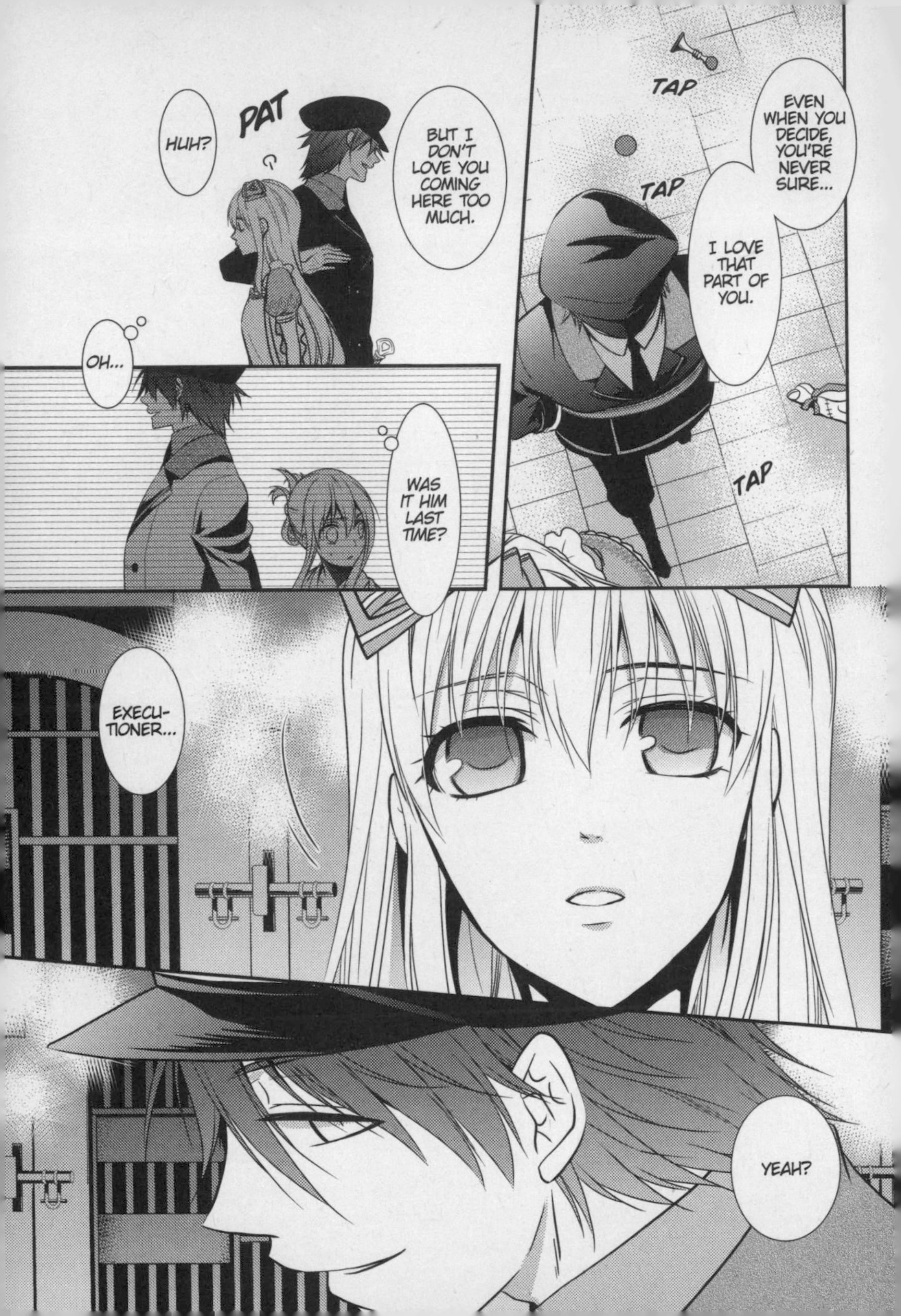
TAP
EVEN WHEN YOU DECIDE, YOU'RE NEVER SURE...
TAP
I LOVE THAT PART OF YOU.
TAP
BUT I DON'T LOVE YOU COMING HERE TOO MUCH.
PAT
HUH?
WAS IT HIM LAST TIME?
OH...
EXECUTIONER...
YEAH?

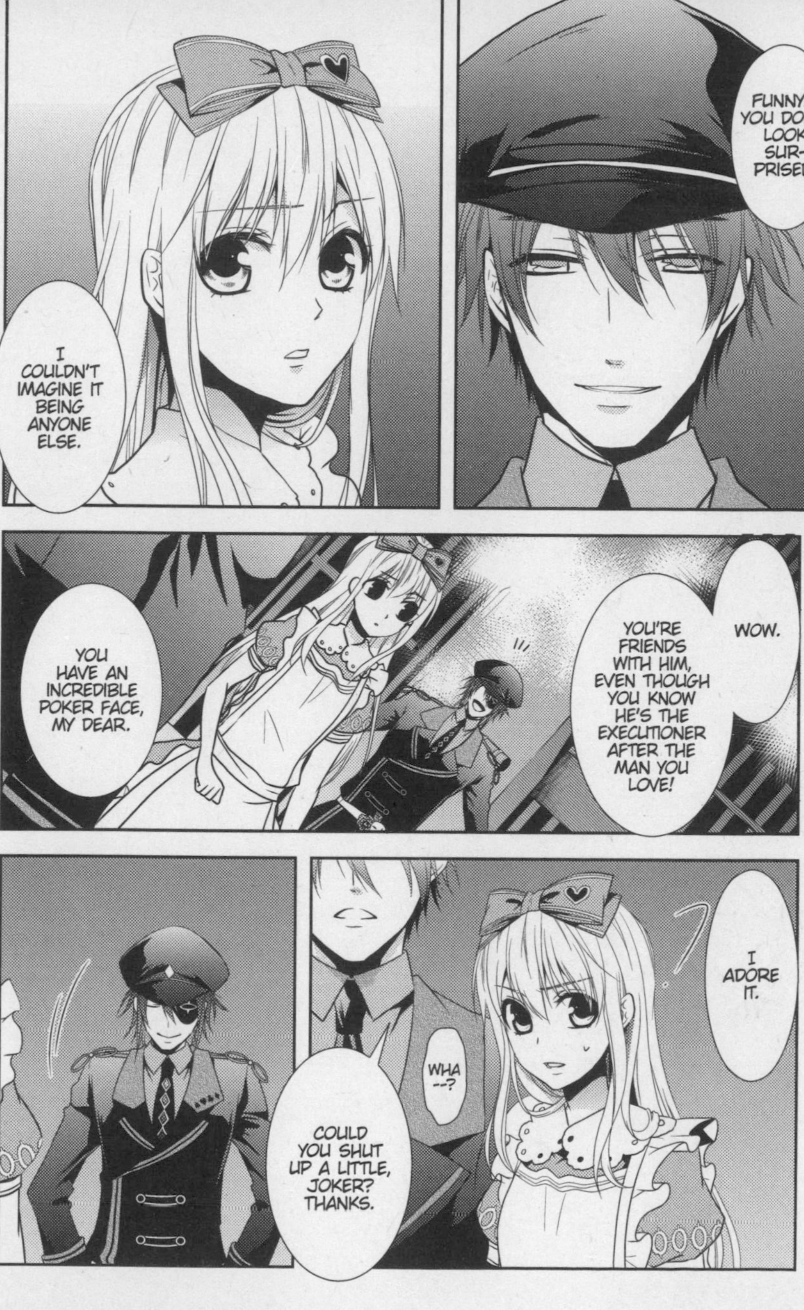
FUNNY... YOU DON'T LOOK SUR-PRISED.
I COULDN'T IMAGINE IT BEING ANYONE ELSE.
WOW.
YOU'RE FRIENDS WITH HIM, EVEN THOUGH YOU KNOW HE'S THE EXECUTIONER AFTER THE MAN YOU LOVE!
YOU HAVE AN INCREDIBLE POKER FACE, MY DEAR.
I ADORE IT.
WHA--?
COULD YOU SHUT UP A LITTLE, JOKER? THANKS.

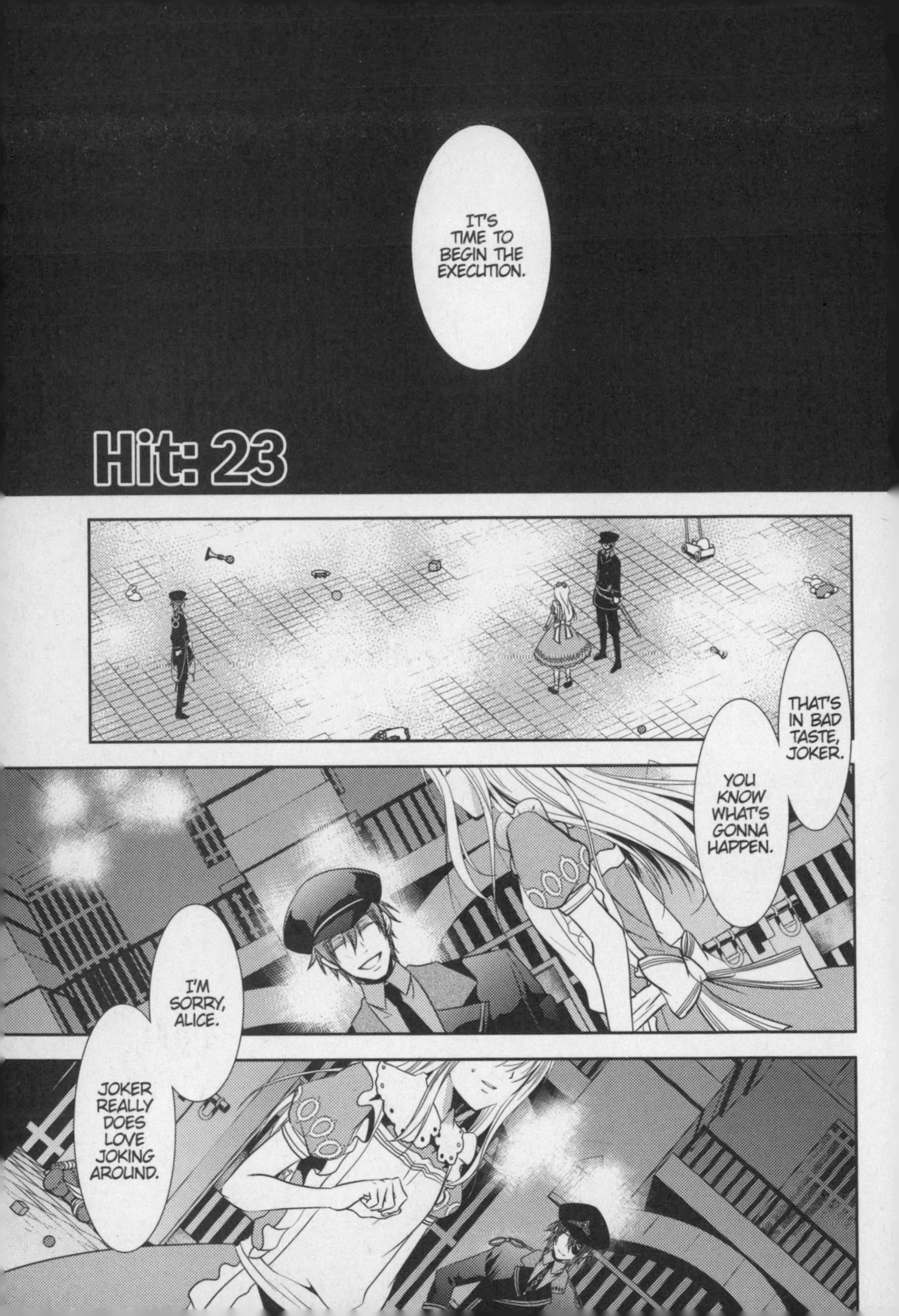
IT'S TIME TO BEGIN THE EXECUTION.
Hit: 23
THAT'S IN BAD TASTE, JOKER.
YOU KNOW WHAT'S GONNA HAPPEN.
I'M SORRY, ALICE.
JOKER REALLY DOES LOVE JOKING AROUND.

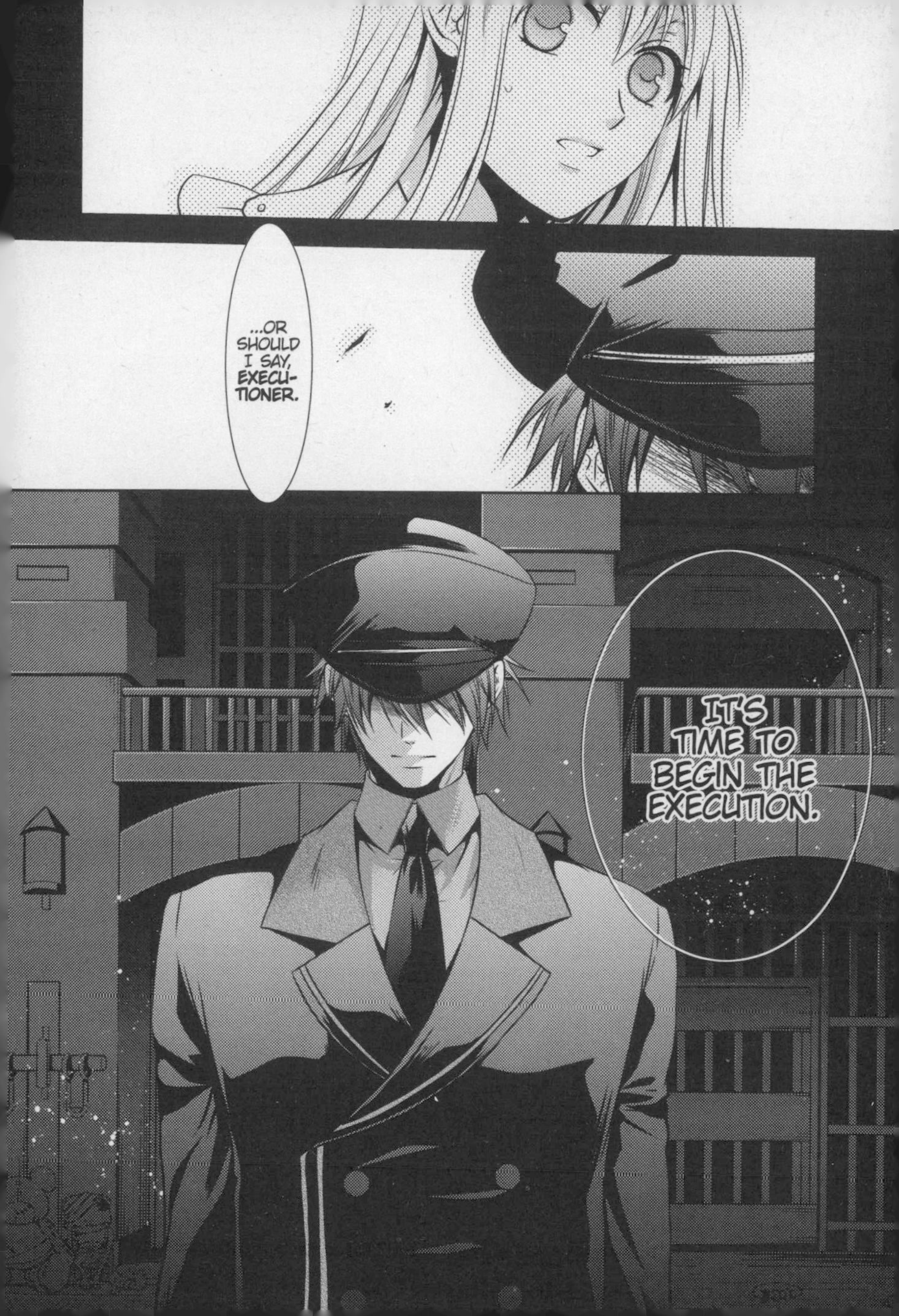
...OR SHOULD I SAY, EXECU-TIONER.
IT'S TIME TO BEGIN THE EXECUTION.

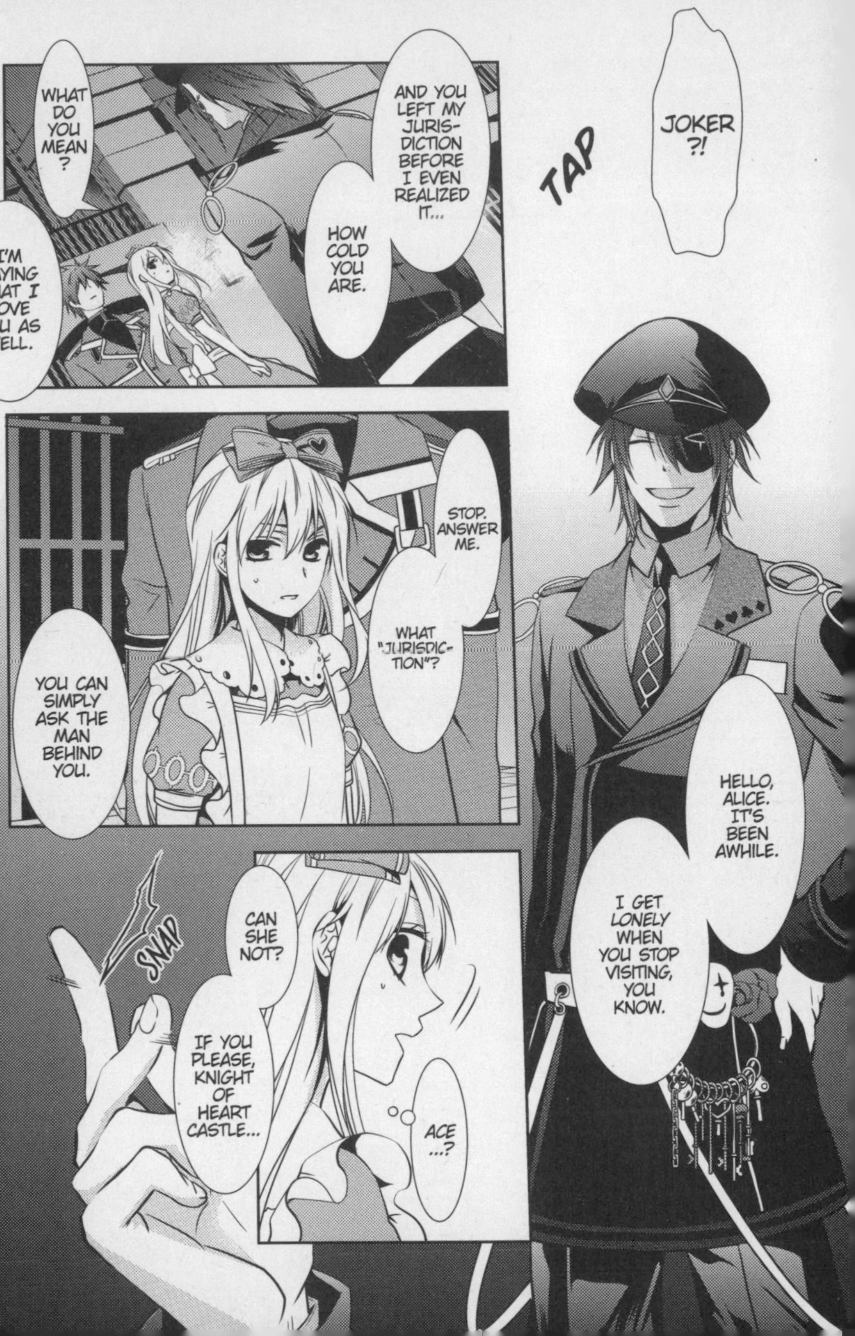
TAP
JOKER?!
HELLO, ALICE. IT'S BEEN AWHILE.
I GET LONELY WHEN YOU STOP VISITING, YOU KNOW.
AND YOU LEFT MY JURIS-DICTION BEFORE I EVEN REALIZED IT...
HOW COLD YOU ARE.
WHAT DO YOU MEAN?
I'M SAYING THAT I LOVE YOU AS WELL.
STOP. ANSWER ME.
WHAT "JURISDIC-TION"?
YOU CAN SIMPLY ASK THE MAN BEHIND YOU.
CAN SHE NOT?
IF YOU PLEASE, KNIGHT OF HEART CASTLE...
ACE ...?
SNAP

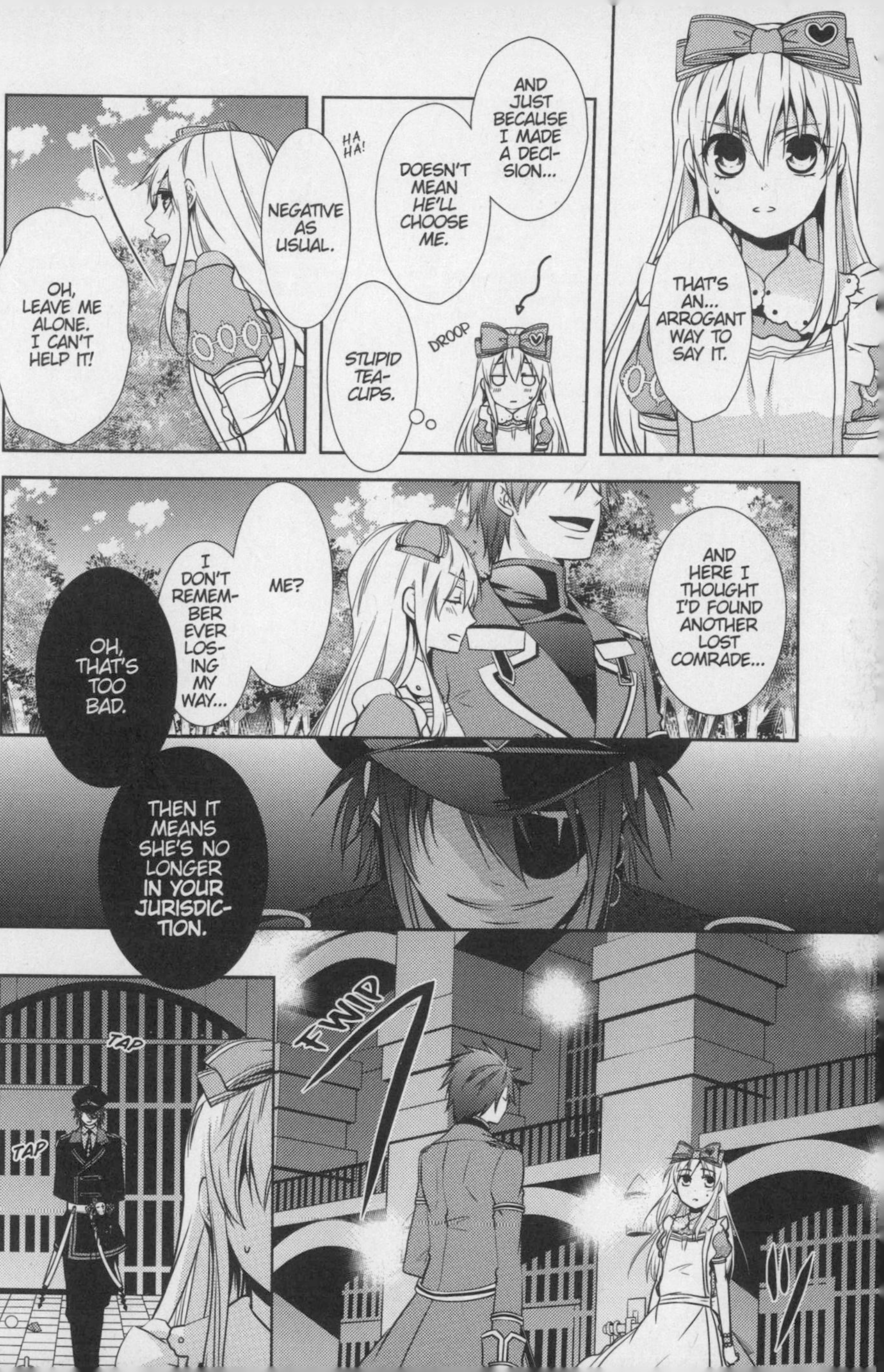
THAT'S AN... ARROGANT WAY TO SAY IT.
AND JUST BECAUSE I MADE A DECI-SION...
DOESN'T MEAN HE'LL CHOOSE ME.
DROOP
STUPID TEA-CUPS.
HA HA!
NEGATIVE AS USUAL.
OH, LEAVE ME ALONE. I CAN'T HELP IT!
AND HERE I THOUGHT I'D FOUND ANOTHER LOST COMRADE...
ME?
I DON'T REMEMBER EVER LOS-ING MY WAY...
OH, THAT'S TOO BAD.
THEN IT MEANS SHE'S NO LONGER IN YOUR JURISDIC-TION.
FWIP
TAP
TAP

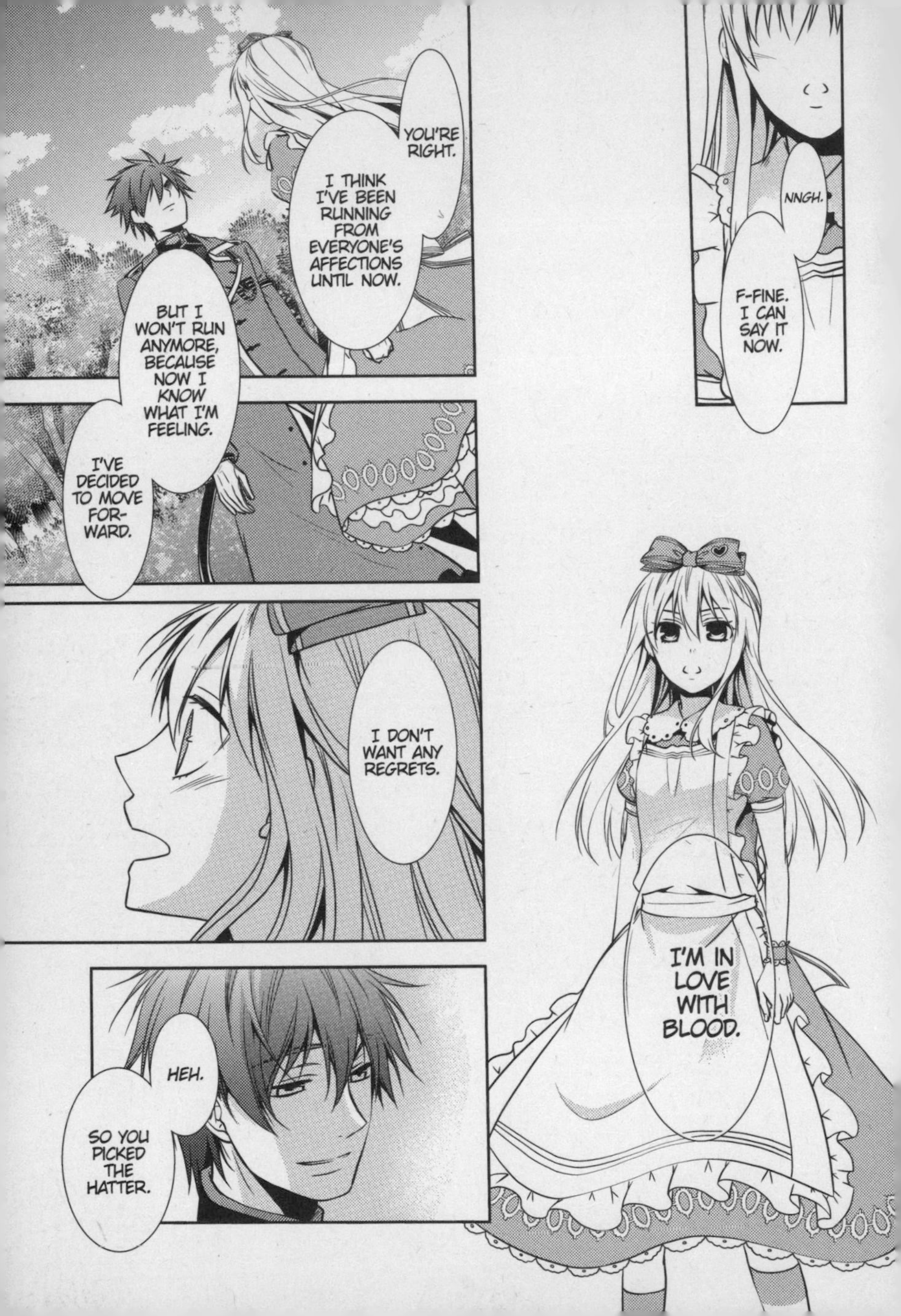
NNGH.
F-FINE. I CAN SAY IT NOW.
YOU'RE RIGHT.
I THINK I'VE BEEN RUNNING FROM EVERYONE'S AFFECTIONS UNTIL NOW.
BUT I WON'T RUN ANYMORE, BECAUSE NOW I KNOW WHAT I'M FEELING.
I'VE DECIDED TO MOVE FOR-WARD.
I DON'T WANT ANY REGRETS.
I'M IN LOVE WITH BLOOD.
HEH.
SO YOU PICKED THE HATTER.

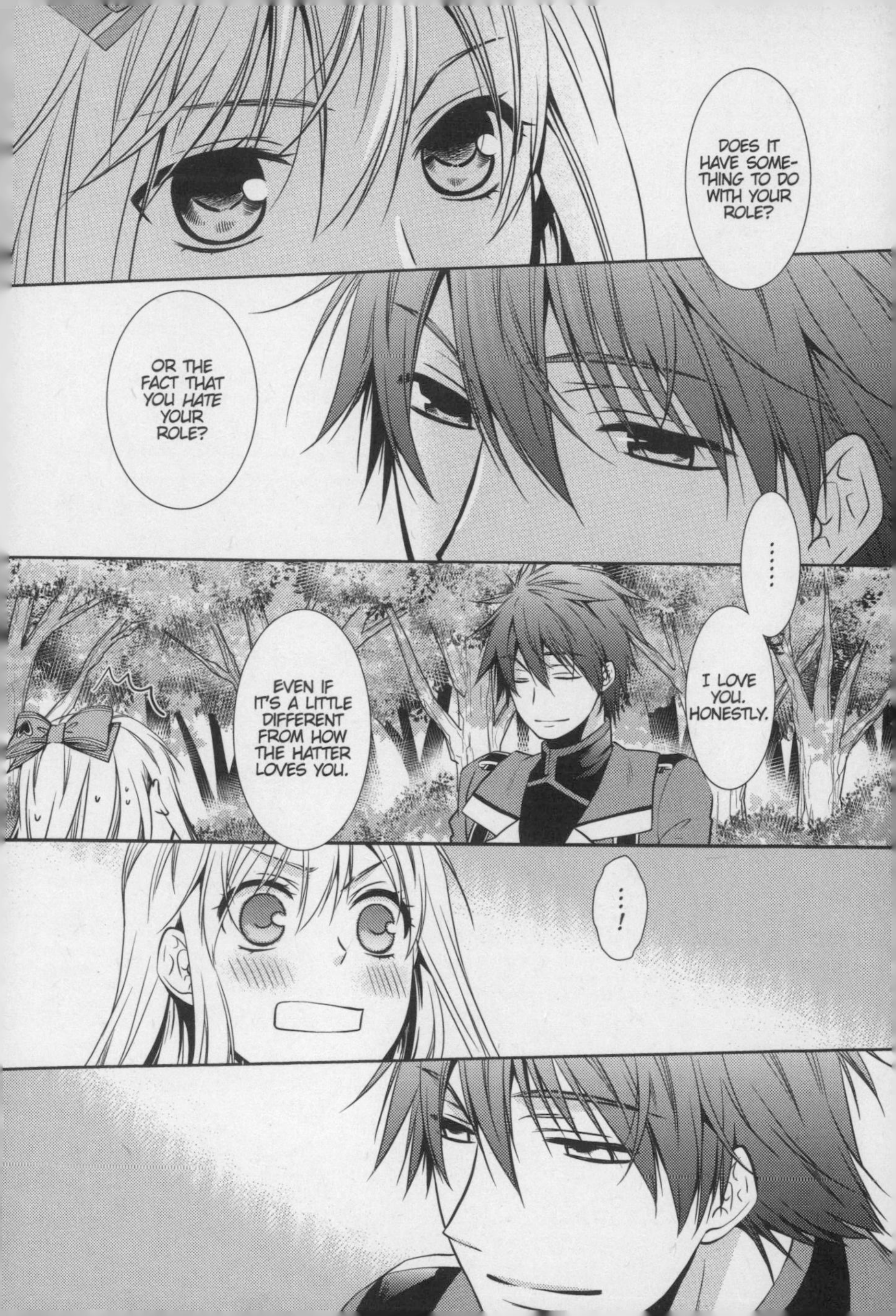
DOES IT HAVE SOME-THING TO DO WITH YOUR ROLE?
OR THE FACT THAT YOU HATE YOUR ROLE?
......
I LOVE YOU. HONESTLY.
EVEN IF IT'S A LITTLE DIFFERENT FROM HOW THE HATTER LOVES YOU.
MM
...!

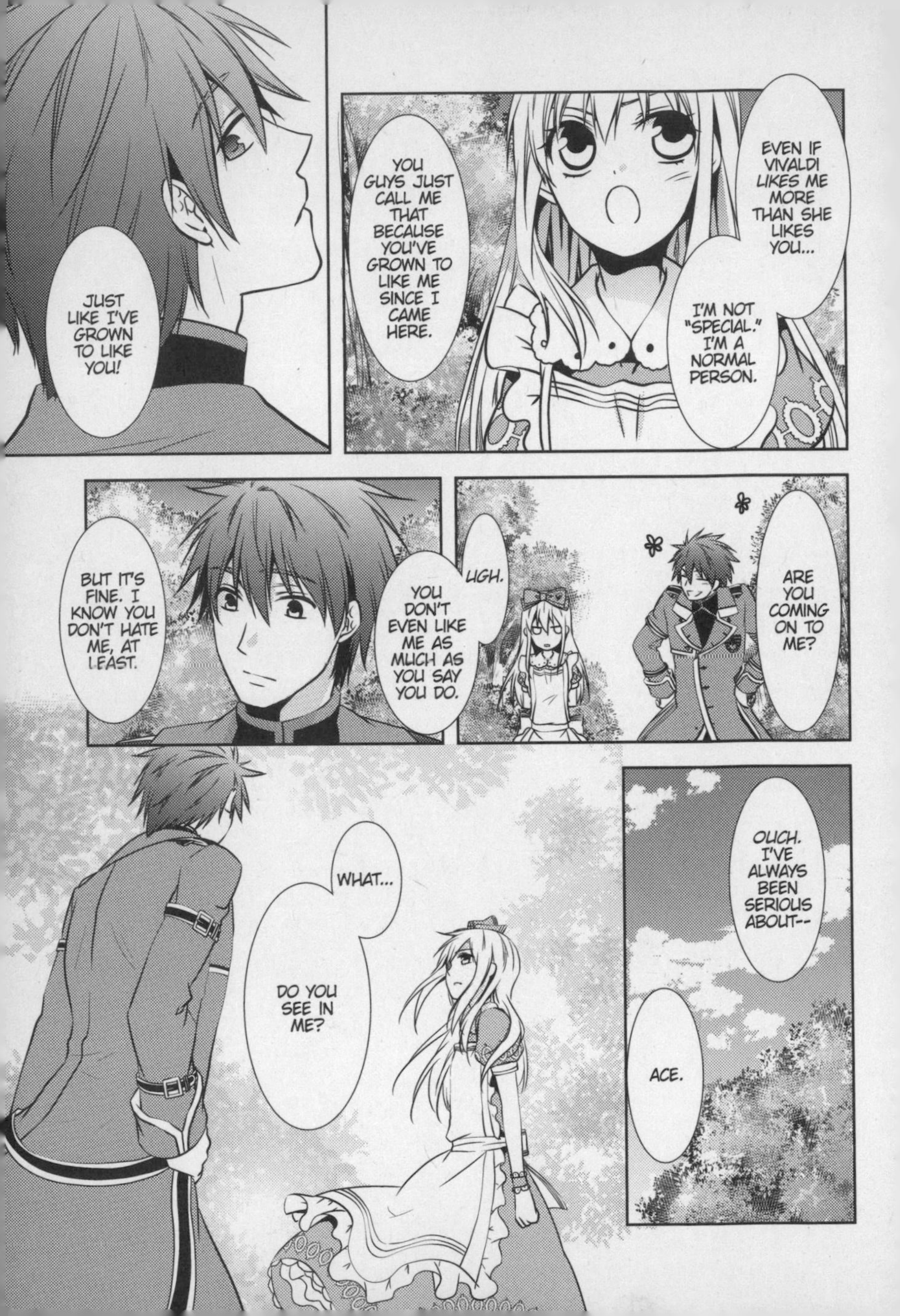
EVEN IF VIVALDI LIKES ME MORE THAN SHE LIKES YOU...
I'M NOT "SPECIAL." I'M A NORMAL PERSON.
YOU GUYS JUST CALL ME THAT BECAUSE YOU'VE GROWN TO LIKE ME SINCE I CAME HERE.
JUST LIKE I'VE GROWN TO LIKE YOU!
ARE YOU COMING ON TO ME?
UGH.
YOU DON'T EVEN LIKE ME AS MUCH AS YOU SAY YOU DO.
BUT IT'S FINE. I KNOW YOU DON'T HATE ME, AT LEAST.
OUCH. I'VE ALWAYS BEEN SERIOUS ABOUT--
ACE.
WHAT...
DO YOU SEE IN ME?

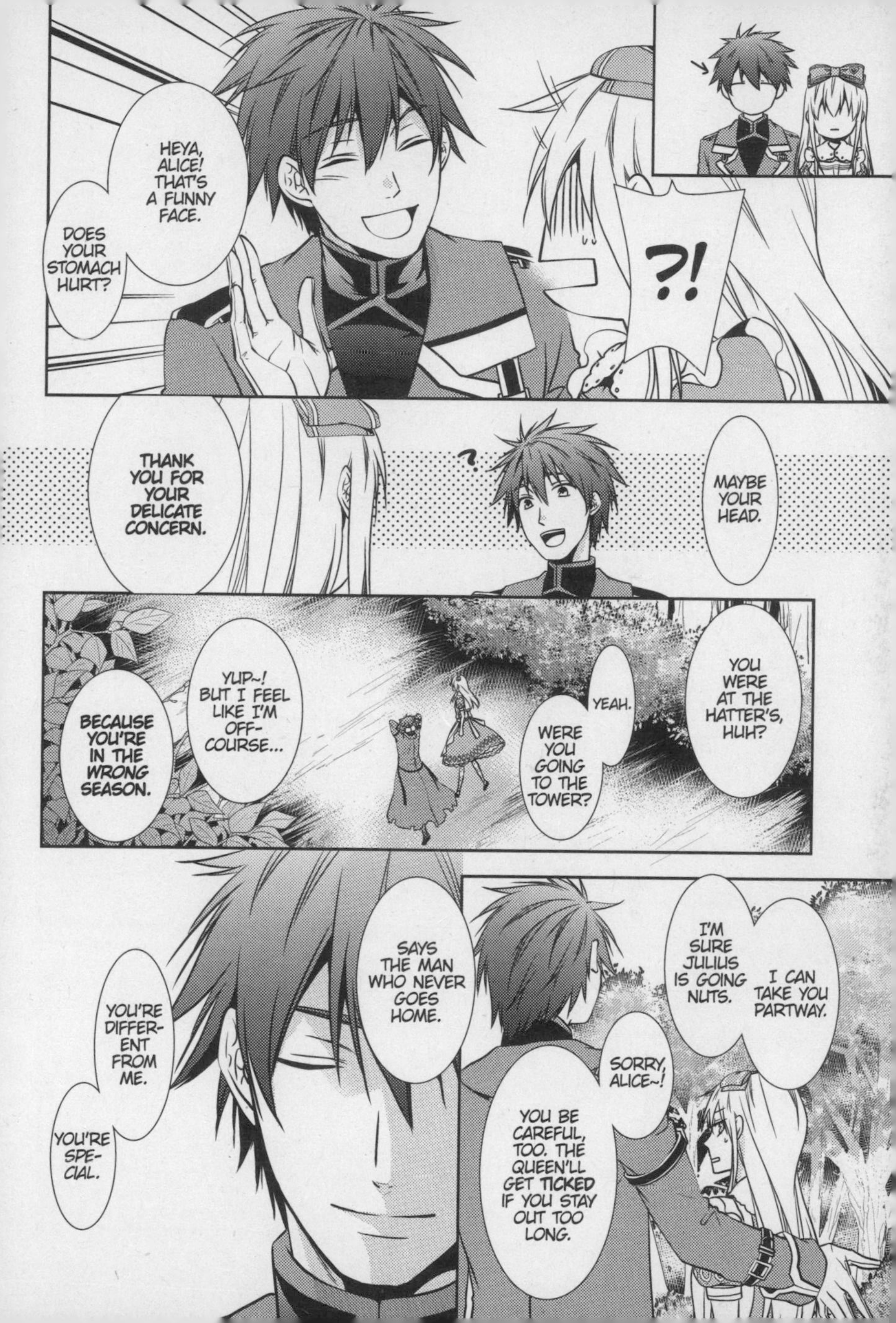
?!
HEYA, ALICE! THAT'S A FUNNY FACE.
DOES YOUR STOMACH HURT?
MAYBE YOUR HEAD.
?
THANK YOU FOR YOUR DELICATE CONCERN.
YOU WERE AT THE HATTER'S, HUH?
YEAH.
WERE YOU GOING TO THE TOWER?
YUP~! BUT I FEEL LIKE I'M OFF-COURSE...
BECAUSE YOU'RE IN THE WRONG SEASON.
I CAN TAKE YOU PARTWAY.
I'M SURE JULIUS IS GOING NUTS.
SORRY, ALICE~!
YOU BE CAREFUL, TOO. THE QUEEN'LL GET TICKED IF YOU STAY OUT TOO LONG.
SAYS THE MAN WHO NEVER GOES HOME.
YOU'RE DIFFERENT FROM ME.
YOU'RE SPECIAL.

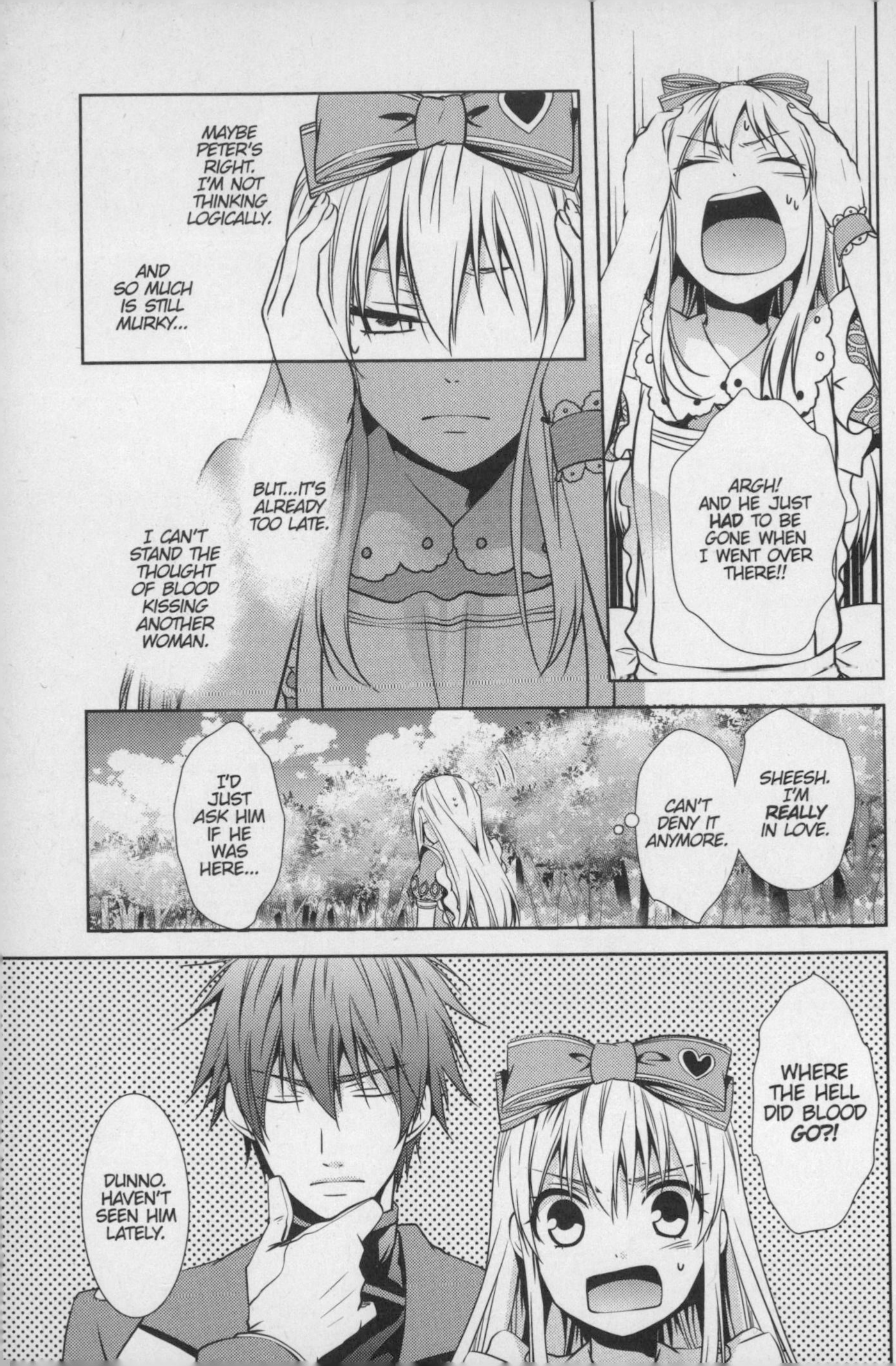
ARGH! AND HE JUST HAD TO BE GONE WHEN I WENT OVER THERE!!
MAYBE PETER'S RIGHT. I'M NOT THINKING LOGICALLY.
AND SO MUCH IS STILL MURKY...
BUT...IT'S ALREADY TOO LATE.
I CAN'T STAND THE THOUGHT OF BLOOD KISSING ANOTHER WOMAN.
SHEESH. I'M REALLY IN LOVE.
CAN'T DENY IT ANYMORE.
I'D JUST ASK HIM IF HE WAS HERE...
WHERE THE HELL DID BLOOD GO?!
DUNNO. HAVEN'T SEEN HIM LATELY.

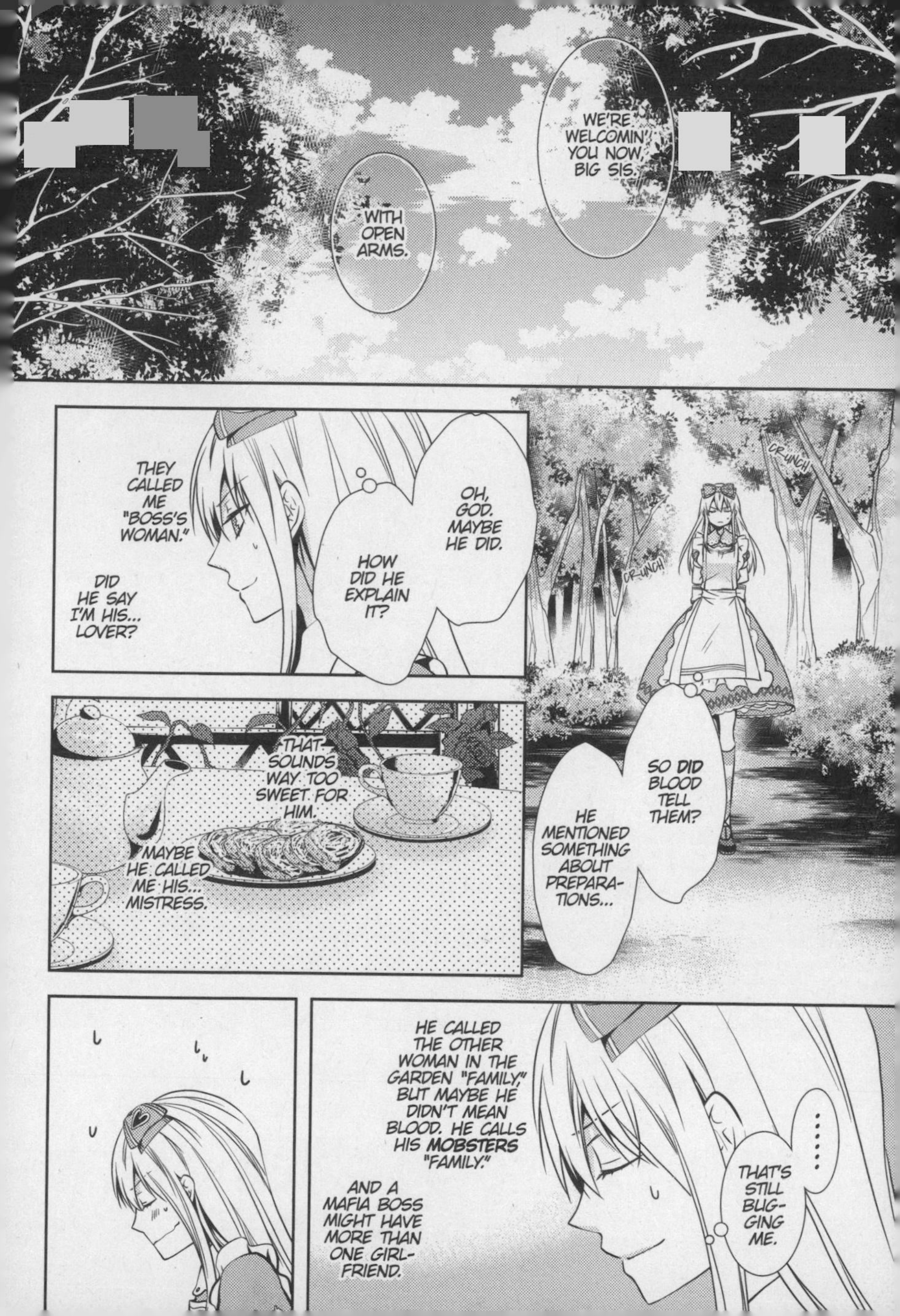
WE'RE WELCOMIN' YOU NOW, BIG SIS.
WITH OPEN ARMS.
CRUNCH
CRUNCH
SO DID BLOOD TELL THEM?
HE MENTIONED SOMETHING ABOUT PREPARATIONS...
OH, GOD. MAYBE HE DID.
HOW DID HE EXPLAIN IT?
THEY CALLED ME "BOSS'S WOMAN."
DID HE SAY I'M HIS... LOVER?
THAT SOUNDS WAY TOO SWEET FOR HIM.
MAYBE HE CALLED ME HIS... MISTRESS.
......
THAT'S STILL BUGGING ME.
HE CALLED THE OTHER WOMAN IN THE GARDEN "FAMILY," BUT MAYBE HE DIDN'T MEAN BLOOD. HE CALLS HIS MOBSTERS "FAMILY."
AND A MAFIA BOSS MIGHT HAVE MORE THAN ONE GIRLFRIEND.

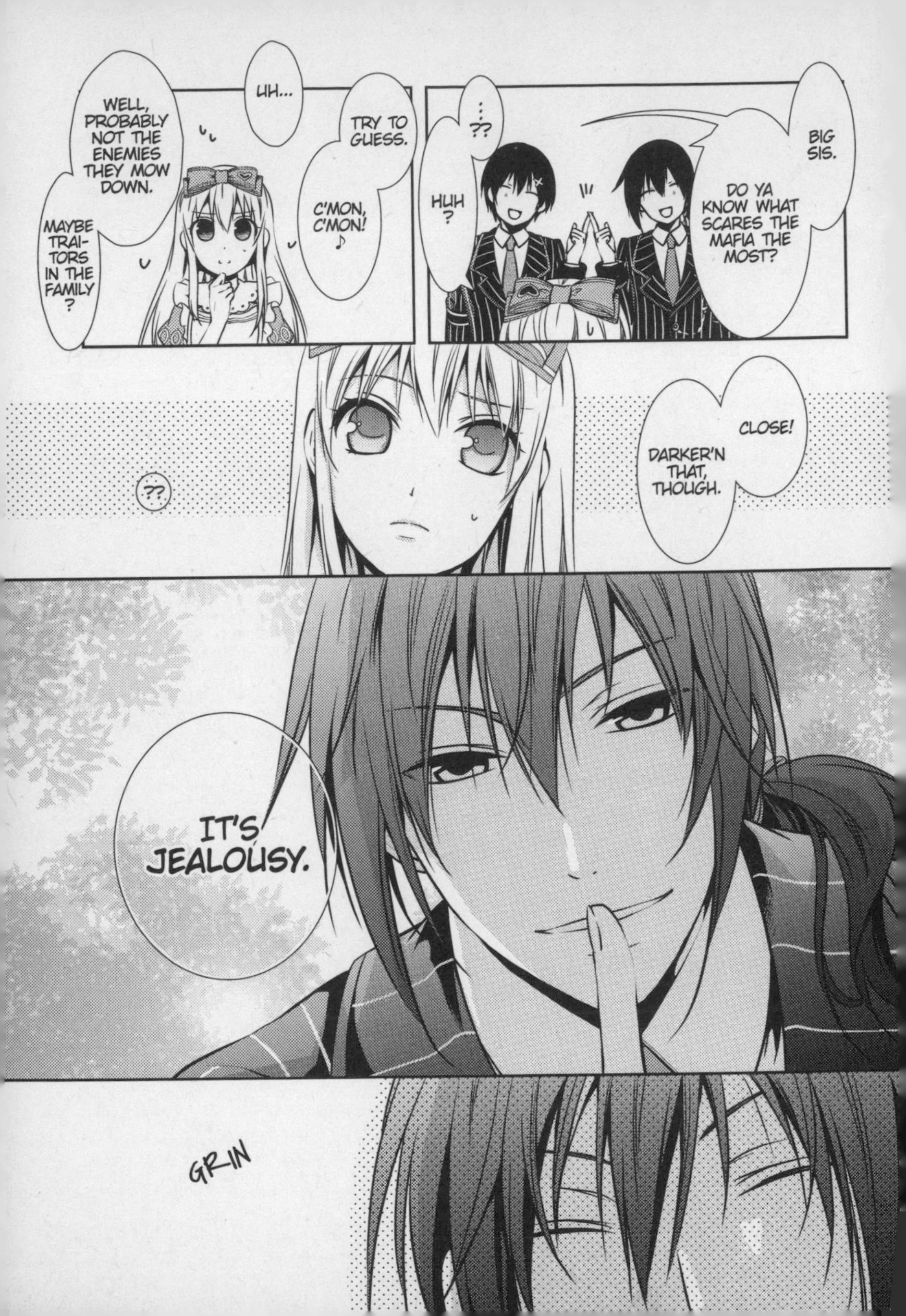
BIG SIS.
DO YA KNOW WHAT SCARES THE MAFIA THE MOST?
...??
HUH?
TRY TO GUESS.
C'MON, C'MON! ♪
UH...
WELL, PROBABLY NOT THE ENEMIES THEY MOW DOWN.
MAYBE TRAI-TORS IN THE FAMILY?
CLOSE!
DARKER'N THAT, THOUGH.
??
IT'S JEALOUSY.
GRIN

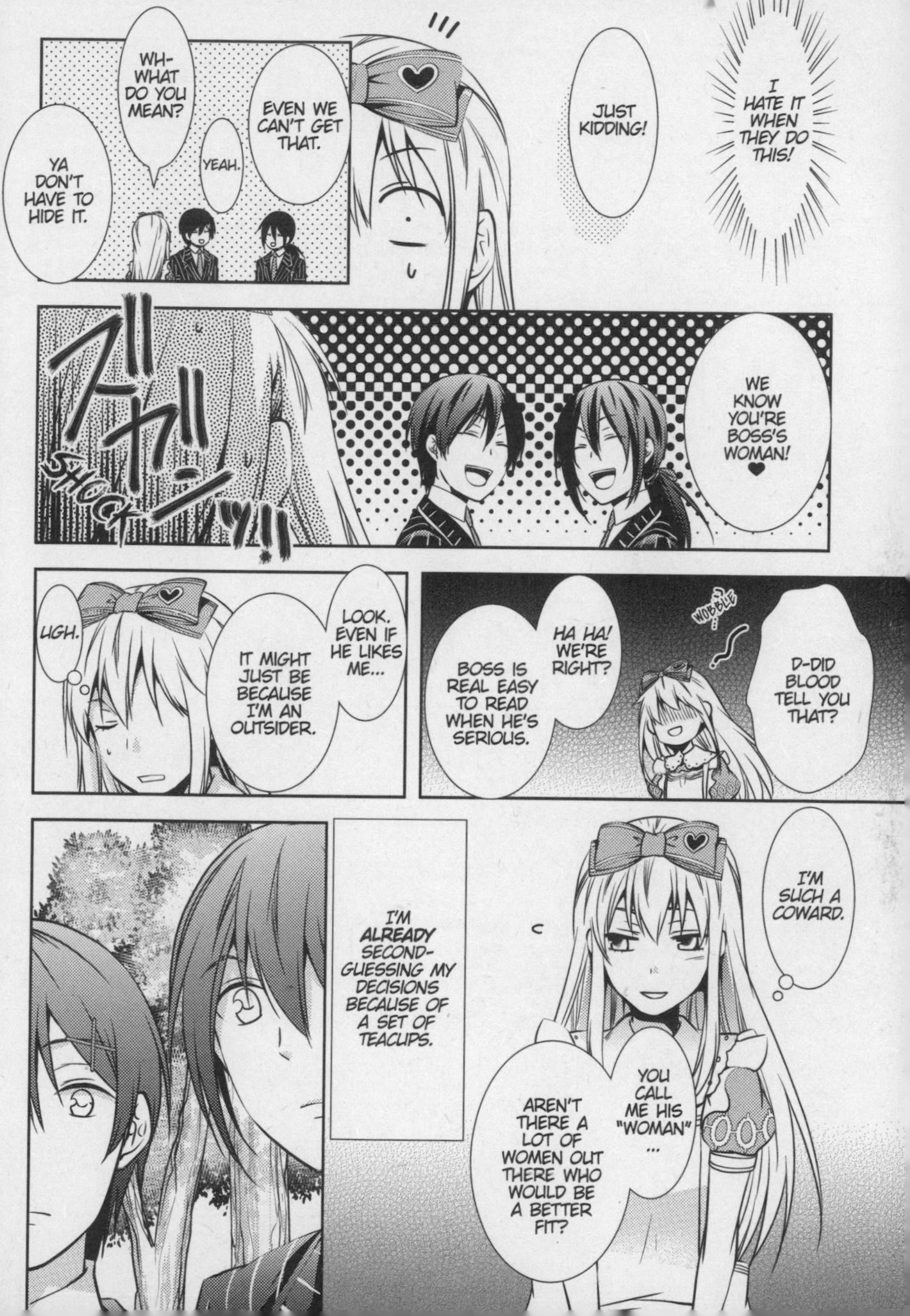
I HATE IT WHEN THEY DO THIS!
JUST KIDDING!
EVEN WE CAN'T GET THAT.
WH- WHAT DO YOU MEAN?
YEAH.
YA DON'T HAVE TO HIDE IT.
WE KNOW YOU'RE BOSS'S WOMAN! ❤
SHOCK
D-DID BLOOD TELL YOU THAT?
WOBBLE
HA HA! WE'RE RIGHT?
BOSS IS REAL EASY TO READ WHEN HE'S SERIOUS.
LOOK. EVEN IF HE LIKES ME...
IT MIGHT JUST BE BECAUSE I'M AN OUTSIDER.
UGH.
I'M SUCH A COWARD.
YOU CALL ME HIS "WOMAN" ...
AREN'T THERE A LOT OF WOMEN OUT THERE WHO WOULD BE A BETTER FIT?
I'M **ALREADY** SECOND-GUESSING MY DECISIONS BECAUSE OF A SET OF TEACUPS.

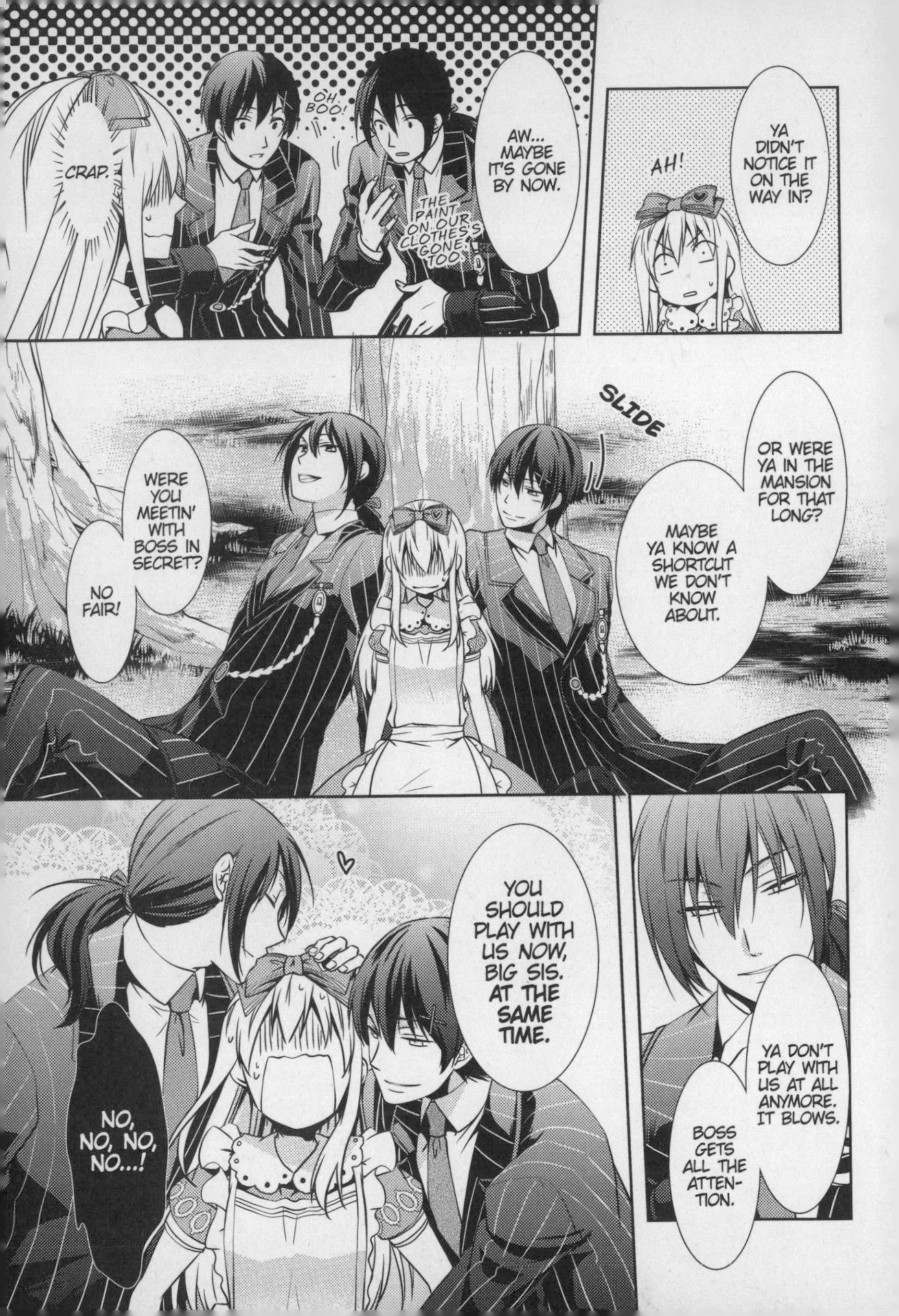
YA DIDN'T NOTICE IT ON THE WAY IN?
AH!
AW... MAYBE IT'S GONE BY NOW.
THE PAINT ON OUR CLOTHES'S GONE, TOO.
OH. BOO!
CRAP.
SLIDE
OR WERE YA IN THE MANSION FOR THAT LONG?
MAYBE YA KNOW A SHORTCUT WE DON'T KNOW ABOUT.
WERE YOU MEETIN' WITH BOSS IN SECRET?
NO FAIR!
YA DON'T PLAY WITH US AT ALL ANYMORE. IT BLOWS.
BOSS GETS ALL THE ATTEN-TION.
YOU SHOULD PLAY WITH US NOW, BIG SIS. AT THE SAME TIME.
NO, NO, NO, NO...!

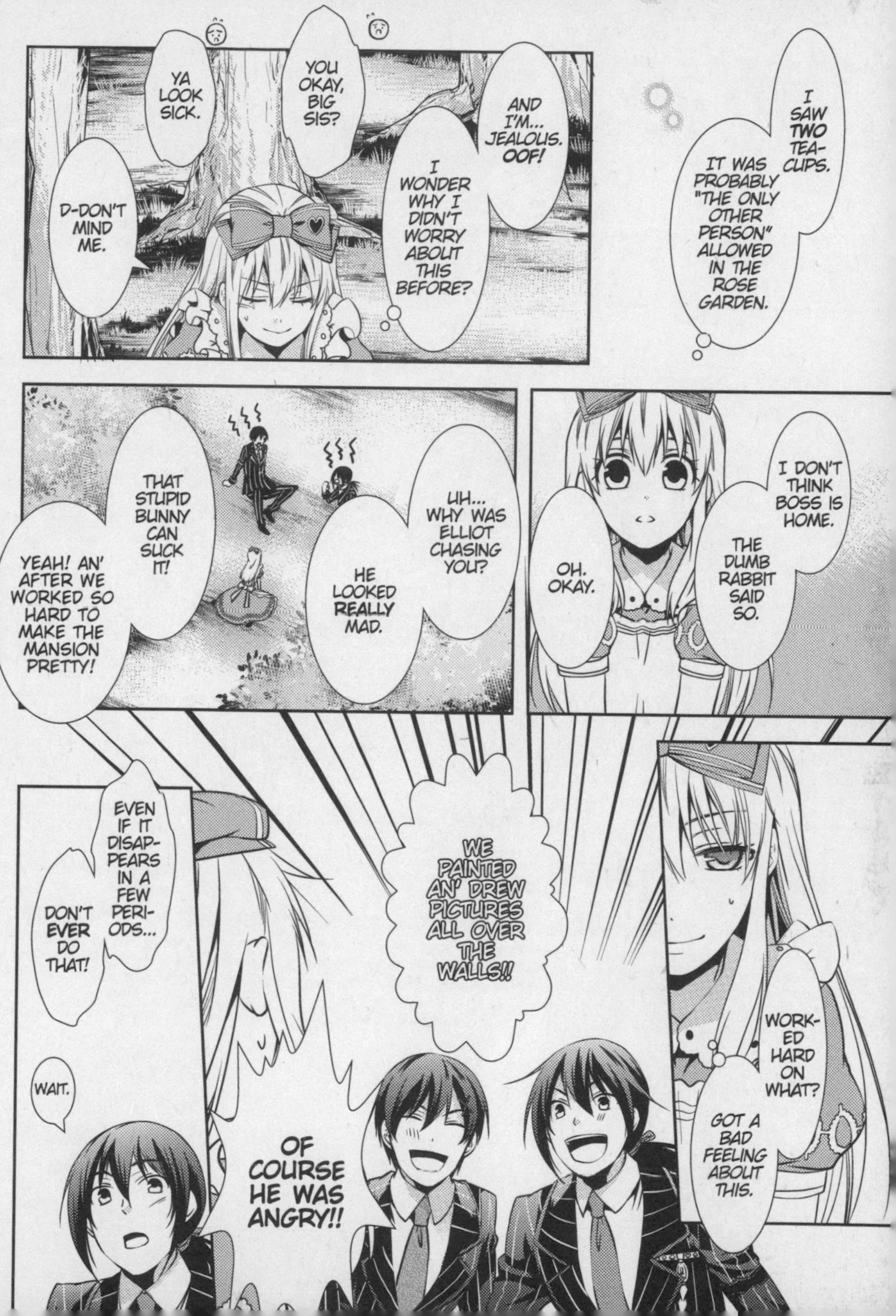
I SAW TWO TEA-CUPS.
IT WAS PROBABLY "THE ONLY OTHER PERSON" ALLOWED IN THE ROSE GARDEN.
AND I'M... JEALOUS. OOF!
I WONDER WHY I DIDN'T WORRY ABOUT THIS BEFORE?
YOU OKAY, BIG SIS?
YA LOOK SICK.
D-DON'T MIND ME.
I DON'T THINK BOSS IS HOME.
THE DUMB RABBIT SAID SO.
OH. OKAY.
UH... WHY WAS ELLIOT CHASING YOU?
HE LOOKED REALLY MAD.
THAT STUPID BUNNY CAN SUCK IT!
YEAH! AN' AFTER WE WORKED SO HARD TO MAKE THE MANSION PRETTY!
WORKED HARD ON WHAT?
GOT A BAD FEELING ABOUT THIS.
WE PAINTED AN' DREW PICTURES ALL OVER THE WALLS!!
OF COURSE HE WAS ANGRY!!
EVEN IF IT DISAPPEARS IN A FEW PERIODS...
DON'T EVER DO THAT!
WAIT.

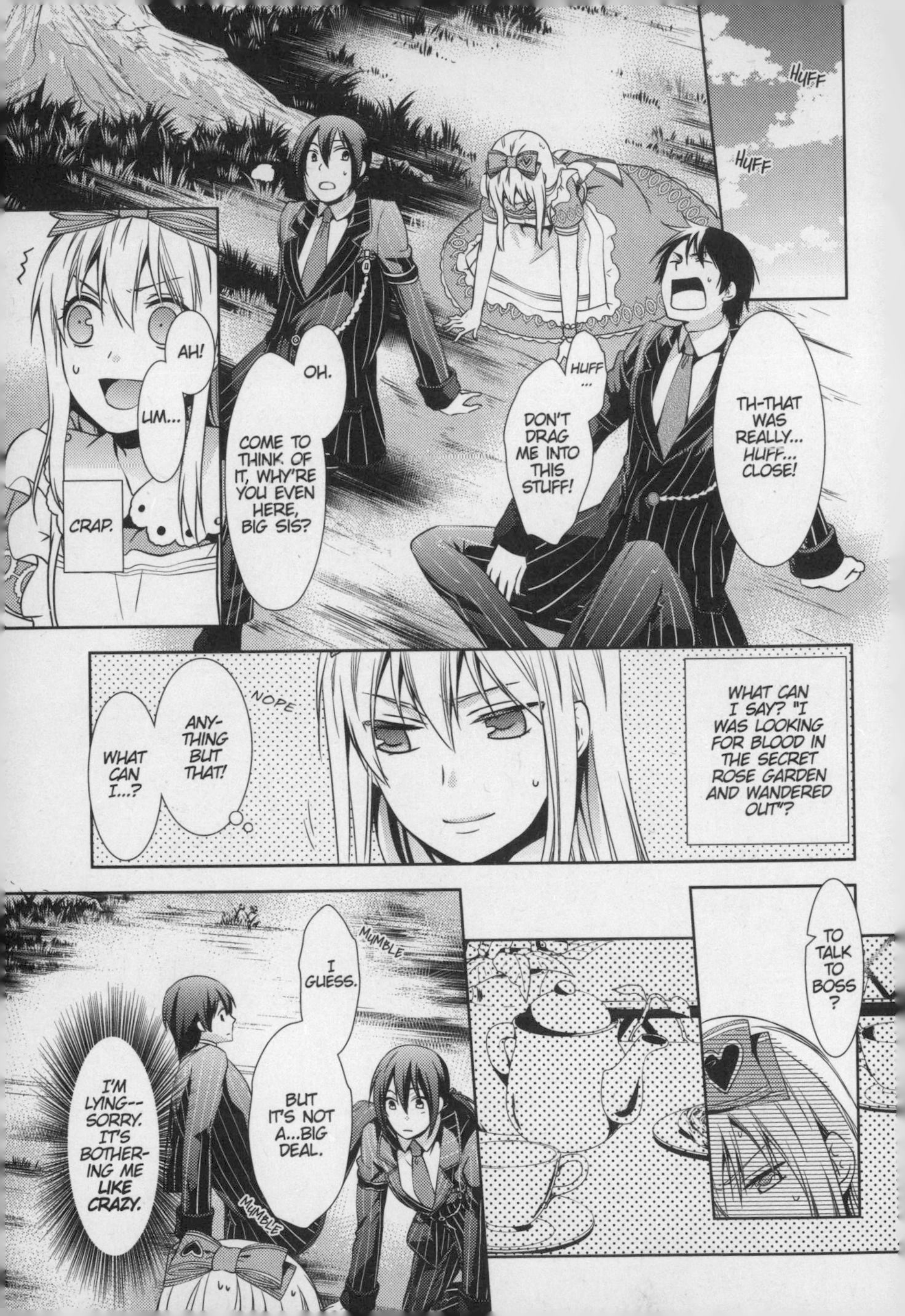
HUFF
HUFF
TH-THAT WAS REALLY... HUFF... CLOSE!
HUFF... DON'T DRAG ME INTO THIS STUFF!
OH.
COME TO THINK OF IT, WHY'RE YOU EVEN HERE, BIG SIS?
AH!
UM...
CRAP.
WHAT CAN I SAY? "I WAS LOOKING FOR BLOOD IN THE SECRET ROSE GARDEN AND WANDERED OUT"?
NOPE
ANY-THING BUT THAT!
WHAT CAN I...?
TO TALK TO BOSS?
MUMBLE
I GUESS.
BUT IT'S NOT A...BIG DEAL.
MUMBLE
I'M LYING--SORRY. IT'S BOTHER-ING ME LIKE CRAZY.

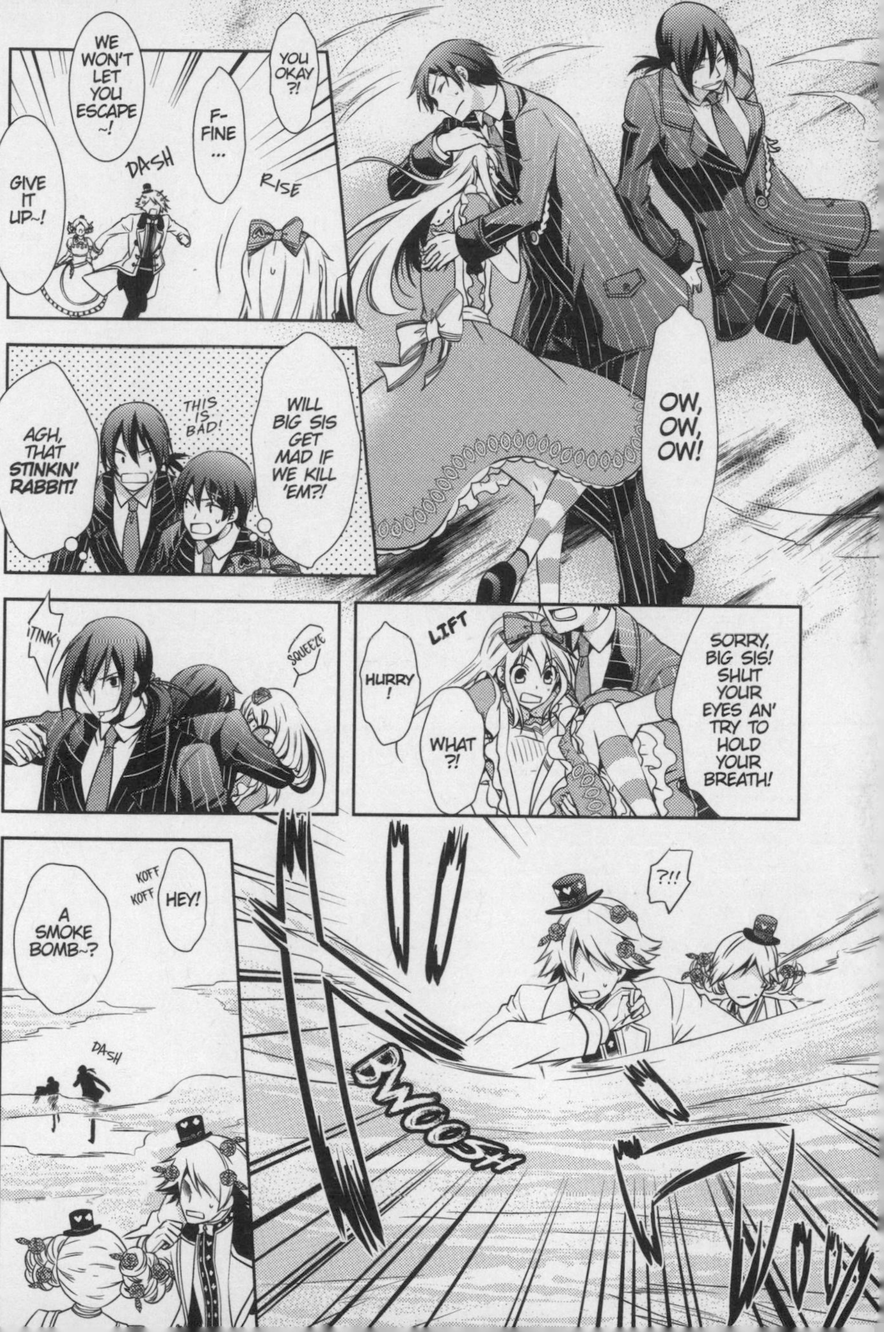
OW, OW, OW!
YOU OKAY?!
F-FINE...
RISE
WE WON'T LET YOU ESCAPE~!
DASH
GIVE IT UP~!
WILL BIG SIS GET MAD IF WE KILL 'EM?!
THIS IS BAD!
AGH, THAT STINKIN' RABBIT!
SORRY, BIG SIS! SHUT YOUR EYES AN' TRY TO HOLD YOUR BREATH!
LIFT
HURRY!
WHAT?!
SQUEEZE
TINK
?!!
BWOOSH
HEY!
KOFF KOFF
A SMOKE BOMB~?
DASH

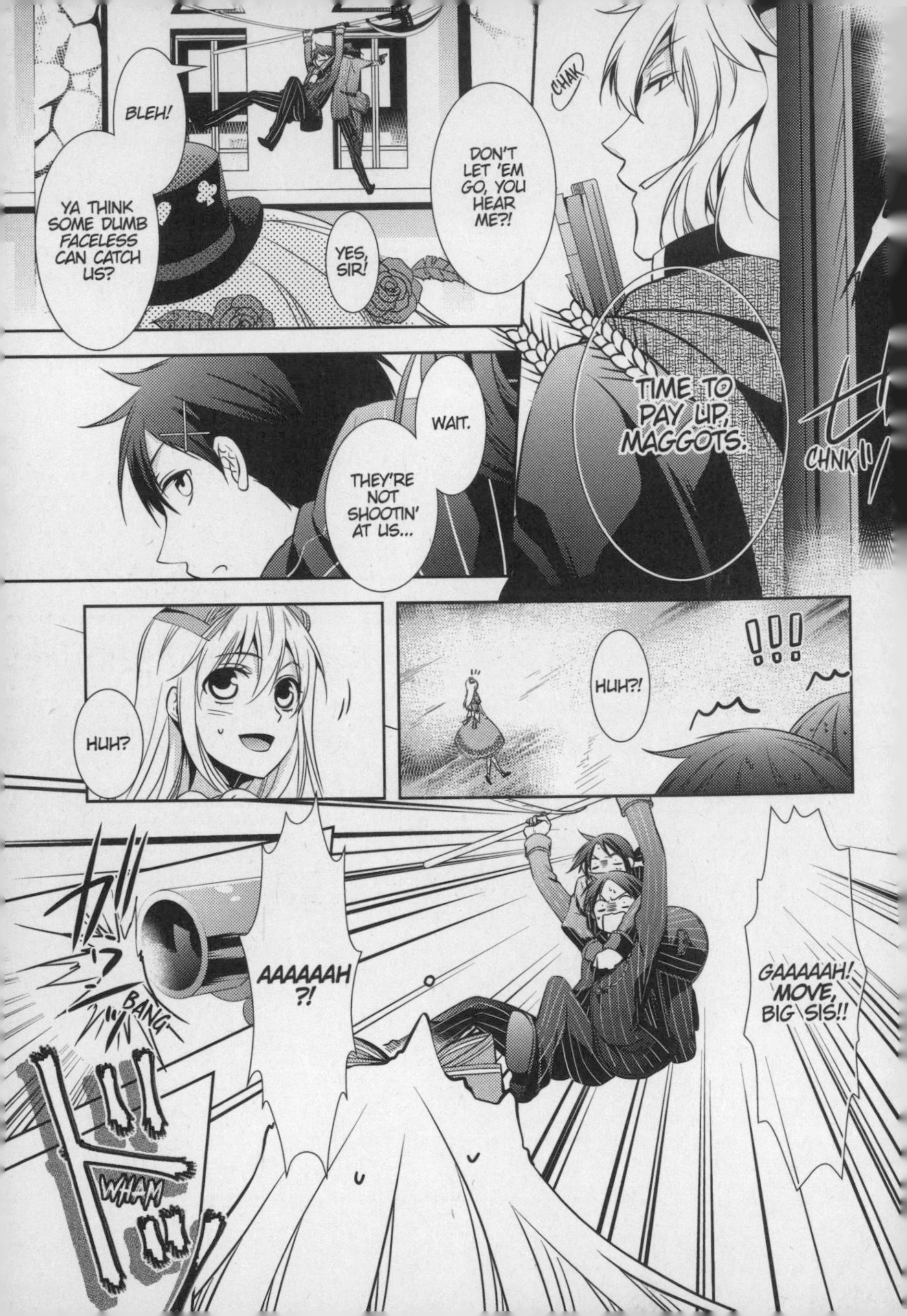
CHAK
DON'T LET 'EM GO, YOU HEAR ME?!
YES, SIR!
BLEH!
YA THINK SOME DUMB FACELESS CAN CATCH US?
TIME TO PAY UP, MAGGOTS.
CHNK
WAIT.
THEY'RE NOT SHOOTIN' AT US...
!!!
HUH?!
HUH?
GAAAAAH! MOVE, BIG SIS!!
AAAAAAH ?!
BANG
WHAM

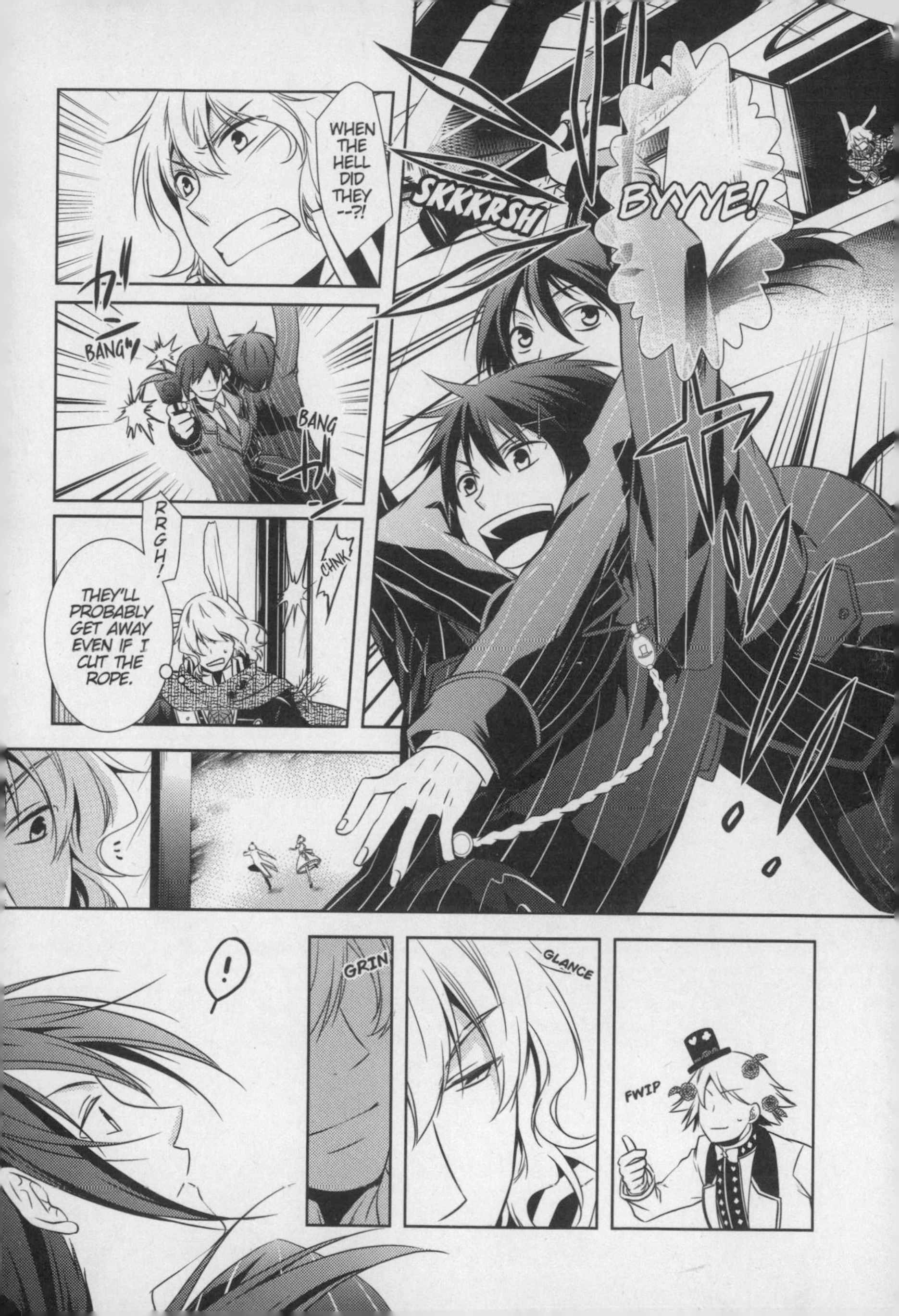

BYYYE!
SKKKRSH
WHEN THE HELL DID THEY --?!
BANG
BANG
RRGH!
CHNK
THEY'LL PROBABLY GET AWAY EVEN IF I CUT THE ROPE.
FWIP
GLANCE
GRIN
!

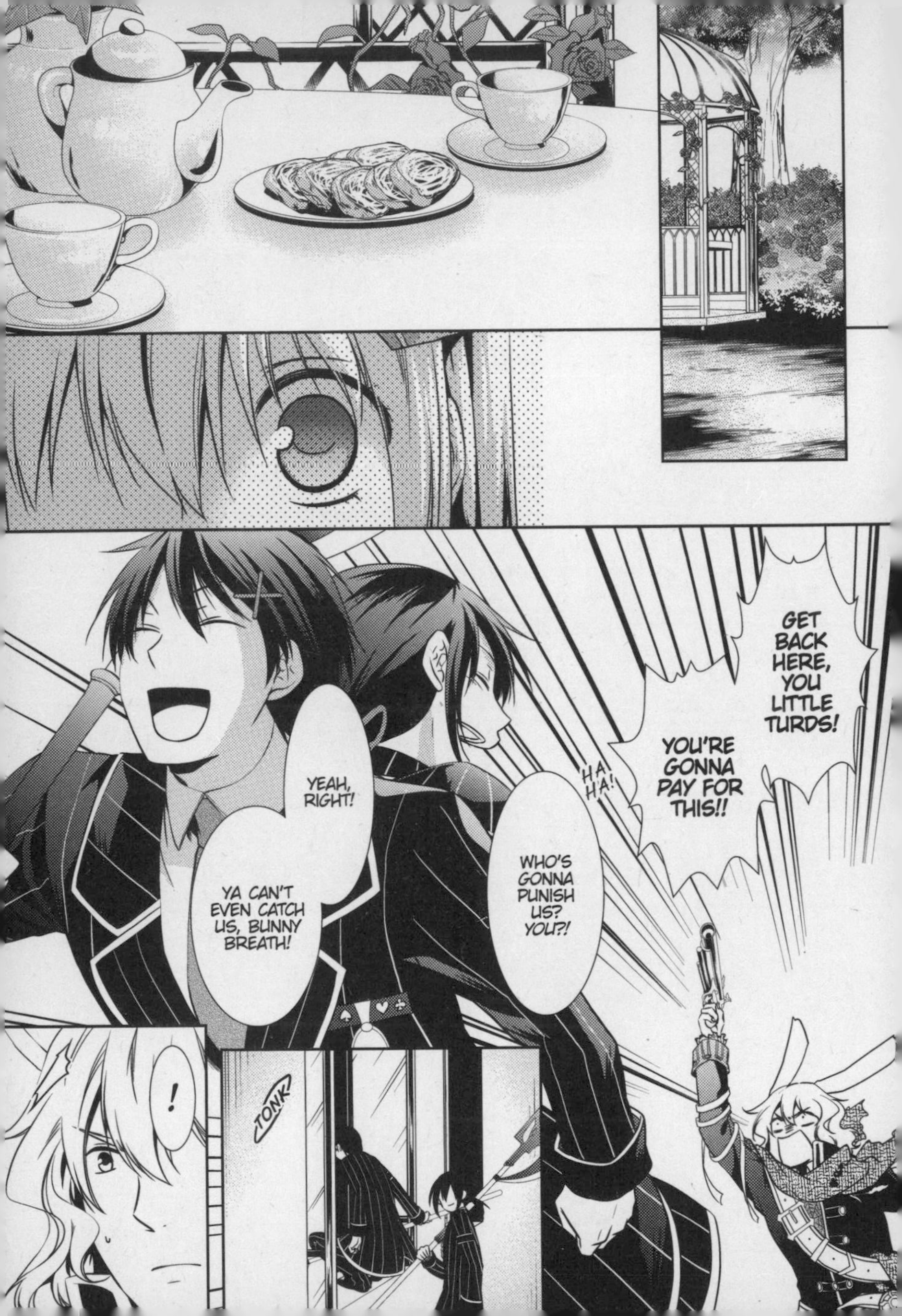
GET BACK HERE, YOU LITTLE TURDS!
YOU'RE GONNA PAY FOR THIS!!
HA HA!
WHO'S GONNA PUNISH US? YOU?!
YEAH, RIGHT!
YA CAN'T EVEN CATCH US, BUNNY BREATH!
TONK
!

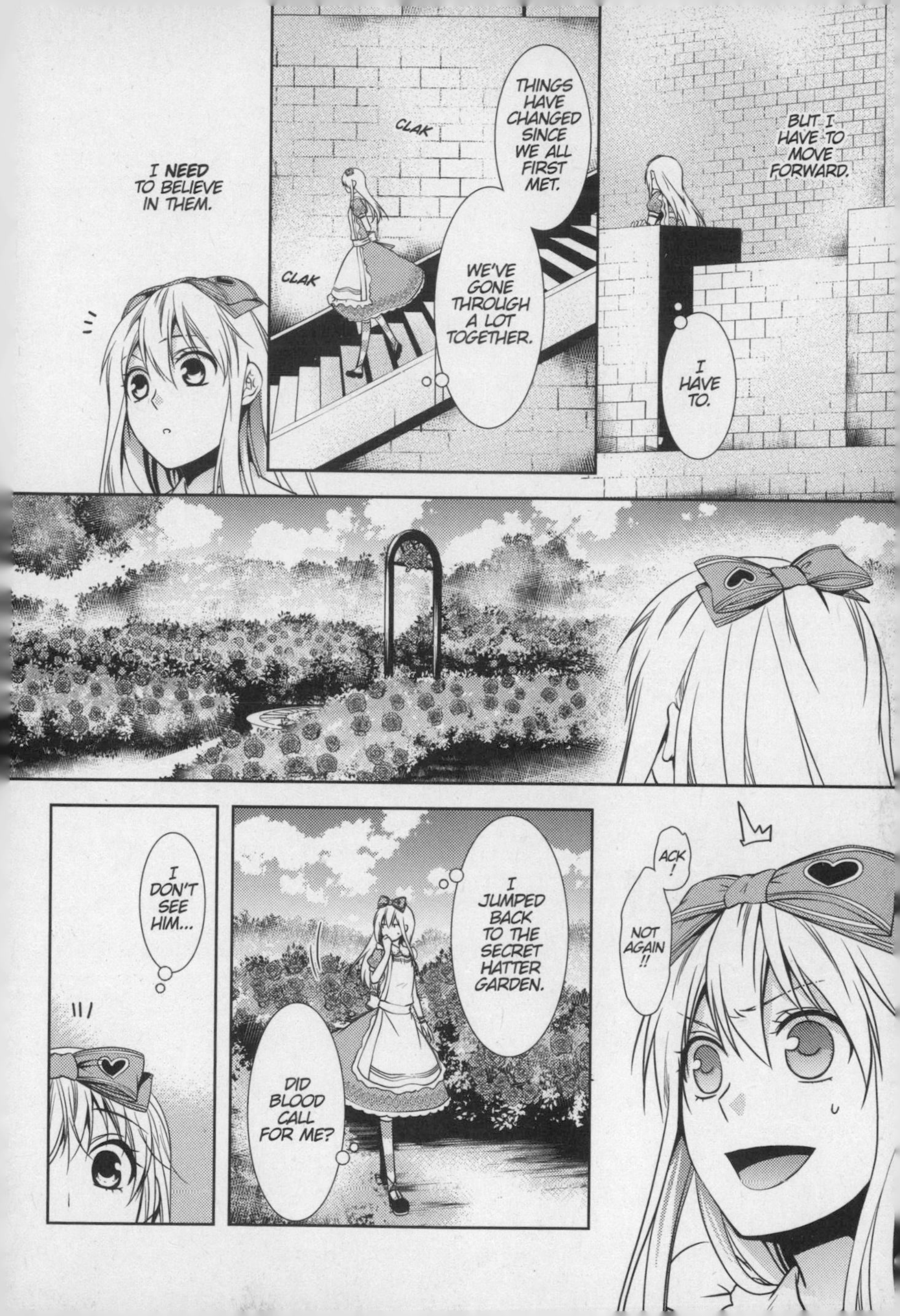
BUT I HAVE TO MOVE FORWARD.
I HAVE TO.
CLAK
THINGS HAVE CHANGED SINCE WE ALL FIRST MET.
WE'VE GONE THROUGH A LOT TOGETHER.
CLAK
I NEED TO BELIEVE IN THEM.
ACK!
NOT AGAIN!!
I JUMPED BACK TO THE SECRET HATTER GARDEN.
DID BLOOD CALL FOR ME?
I DON'T SEE HIM...

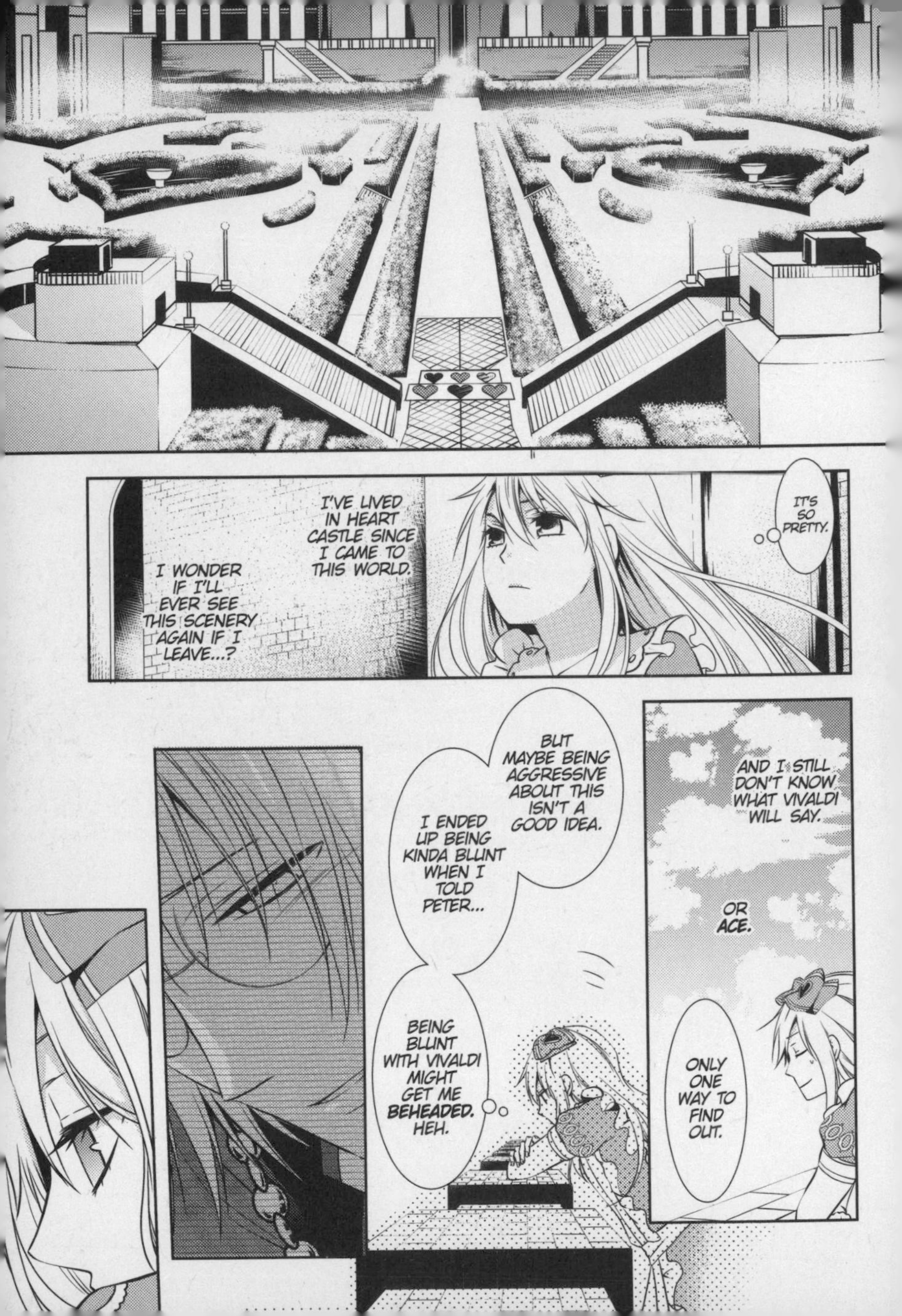
IT'S SO PRETTY.
I'VE LIVED IN HEART CASTLE SINCE I CAME TO THIS WORLD.
I WONDER IF I'LL EVER SEE THIS SCENERY AGAIN IF I LEAVE...?
AND I STILL DON'T KNOW WHAT VIVALDI WILL SAY.
OR ACE.
I ENDED UP BEING KINDA BLUNT WHEN I TOLD PETER...
BUT MAYBE BEING AGGRESSIVE ABOUT THIS ISN'T A GOOD IDEA.
ONLY ONE WAY TO FIND OUT.
BEING BLUNT WITH VIVALDI MIGHT GET ME BEHEADED. HEH.

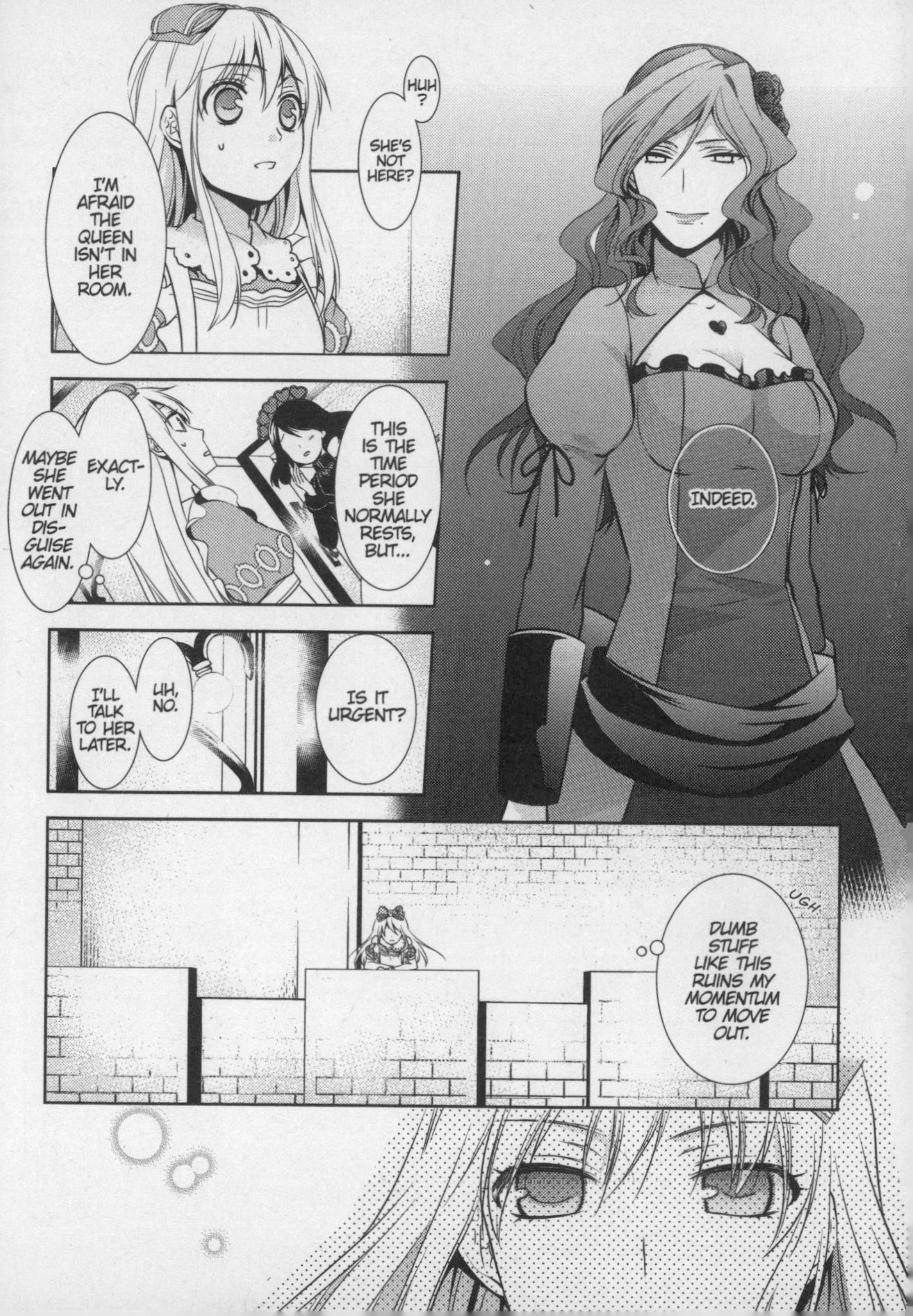
INDEED.
HUH?
SHE'S NOT HERE?
I'M AFRAID THE QUEEN ISN'T IN HER ROOM.
THIS IS THE TIME PERIOD SHE NORMALLY RESTS, BUT...
EXACTLY.
MAYBE SHE WENT OUT IN DISGUISE AGAIN.
IS IT URGENT?
UH, NO.
I'LL TALK TO HER LATER.
UGH
DUMB STUFF LIKE THIS RUINS MY MOMENTUM TO MOVE OUT.

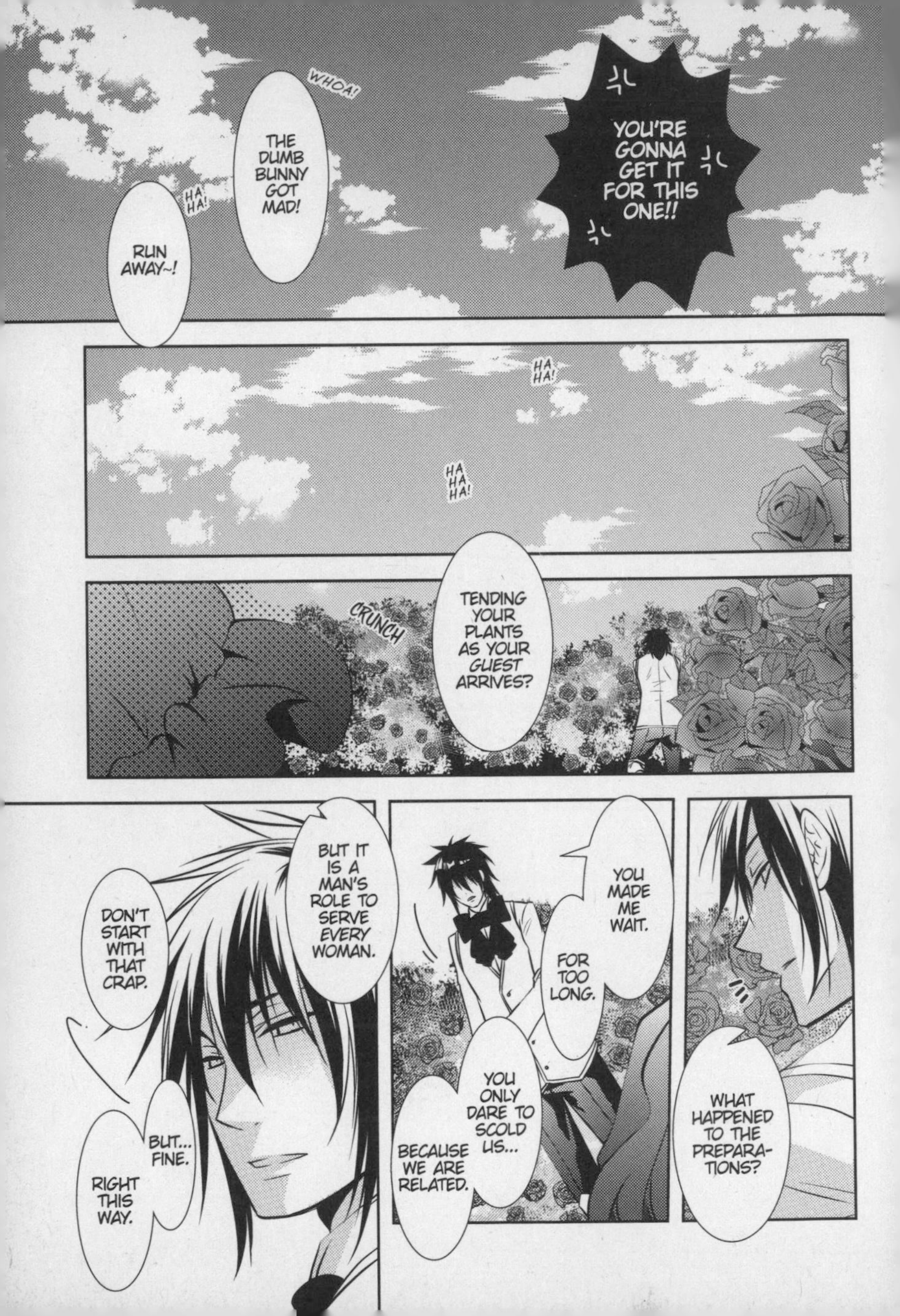
YOU'RE GONNA GET IT FOR THIS ONE!!
WHOA!
THE DUMB BUNNY GOT MAD!
HA HA!
RUN AWAY~!
HA HA!
HA HA HA!
TENDING YOUR PLANTS AS YOUR GUEST ARRIVES?
CRUNCH
WHAT HAPPENED TO THE PREPARATIONS?
YOU MADE ME WAIT.
FOR TOO LONG.
YOU ONLY DARE TO SCOLD US...
BECAUSE WE ARE RELATED.
BUT IT IS A MAN'S ROLE TO SERVE EVERY WOMAN.
DON'T START WITH THAT CRAP.
BUT... FINE.
RIGHT THIS WAY.

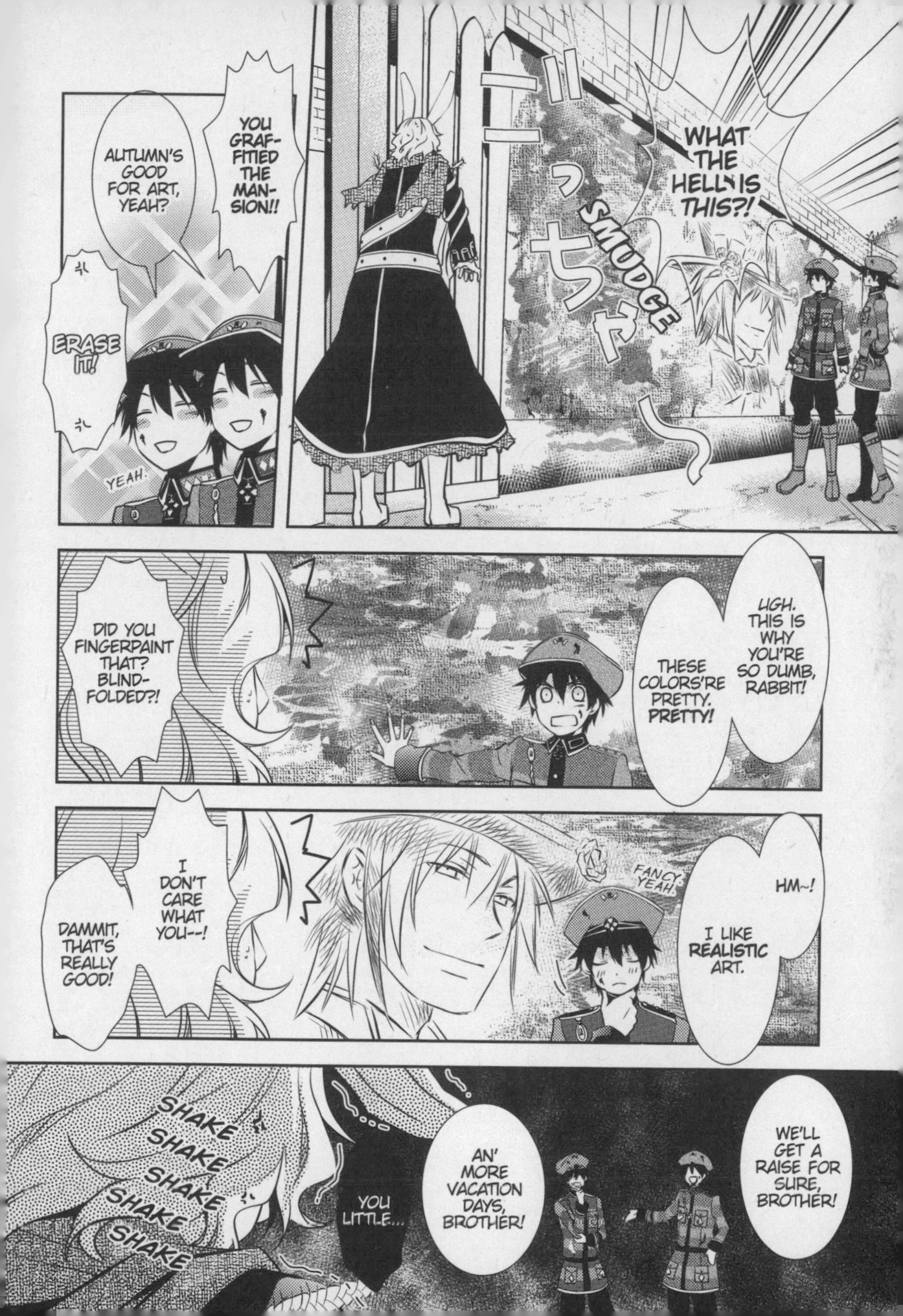
WHAT THE HELL IS THIS?!
SMUDGE
YOU GRAFFITIED THE MANSION!!
AUTUMN'S GOOD FOR ART, YEAH?
ERASE IT!
YEAH.
UGH. THIS IS WHY YOU'RE SO DUMB, RABBIT!
THESE COLORS'RE PRETTY. PRETTY!
DID YOU FINGERPAINT THAT? BLINDFOLDED?!
HM~!
I LIKE REALISTIC ART.
FANCY. YEAH.
I DON'T CARE WHAT YOU--!
DAMMIT, THAT'S REALLY GOOD!
WE'LL GET A RAISE FOR SURE, BROTHER!
AN' MORE VACATION DAYS, BROTHER!
YOU LITTLE...
SHAKE SHAKE SHAKE SHAKE SHAKE

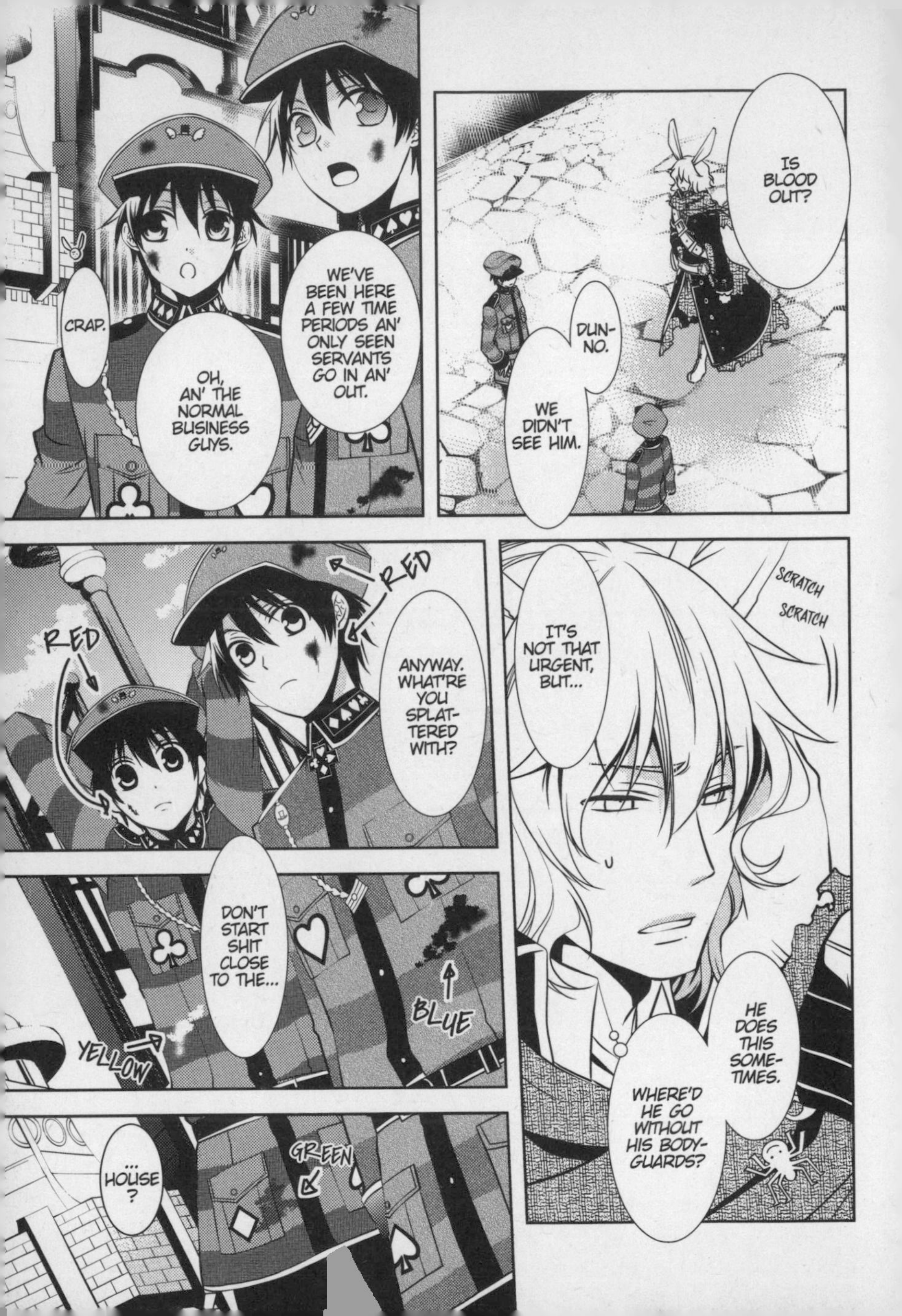
IS BLOOD OUT?
DUNNO.
WE DIDN'T SEE HIM.
WE'VE BEEN HERE A FEW TIME PERIODS AN' ONLY SEEN SERVANTS GO IN AN' OUT.
OH, AN' THE NORMAL BUSINESS GUYS.
CRAP.
SCRATCH
SCRATCH
IT'S NOT THAT URGENT, BUT...
HE DOES THIS SOMETIMES.
WHERE'D HE GO WITHOUT HIS BODYGUARDS?
RED
RED
ANYWAY. WHAT'RE YOU SPLATTERED WITH?
DON'T START SHIT CLOSE TO THE...
BLUE
YELLOW
...HOUSE?
GREEN

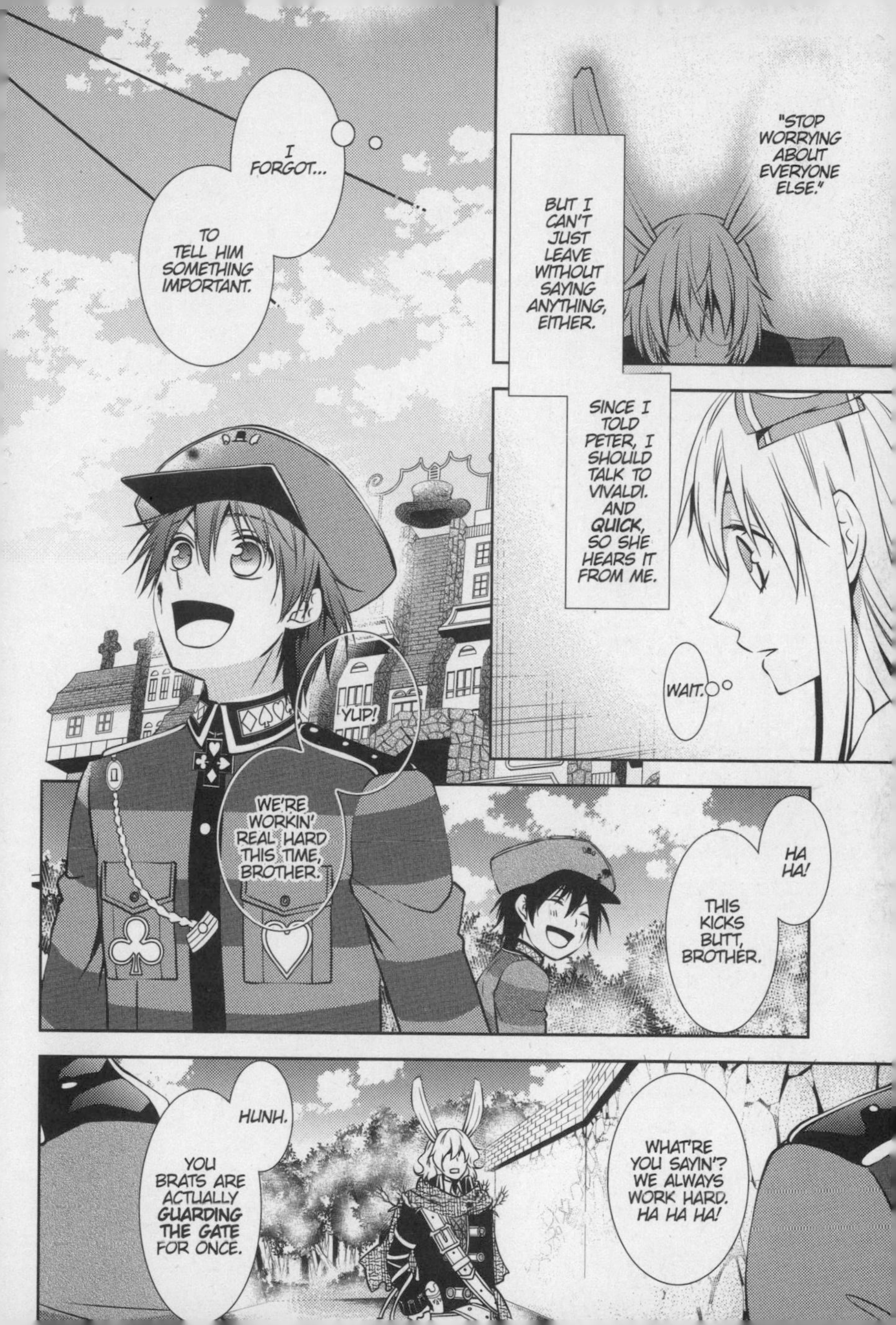
"STOP WORRYING ABOUT EVERYONE ELSE."
BUT I CAN'T JUST LEAVE WITHOUT SAYING ANYTHING, EITHER.
SINCE I TOLD PETER, I SHOULD TALK TO VIVALDI. AND **QUICK**, SO SHE HEARS IT FROM ME.
WAIT.
I FORGOT...
TO TELL HIM SOMETHING IMPORTANT.
HA HA!
THIS KICKS BUTT, BROTHER.
YUP!
WE'RE WORKIN' REAL HARD THIS TIME, BROTHER.
HUNH.
YOU BRATS ARE ACTUALLY **GUARDING** THE GATE FOR ONCE.
WHAT'RE YOU SAYIN'? WE ALWAYS WORK HARD. HA HA HA!

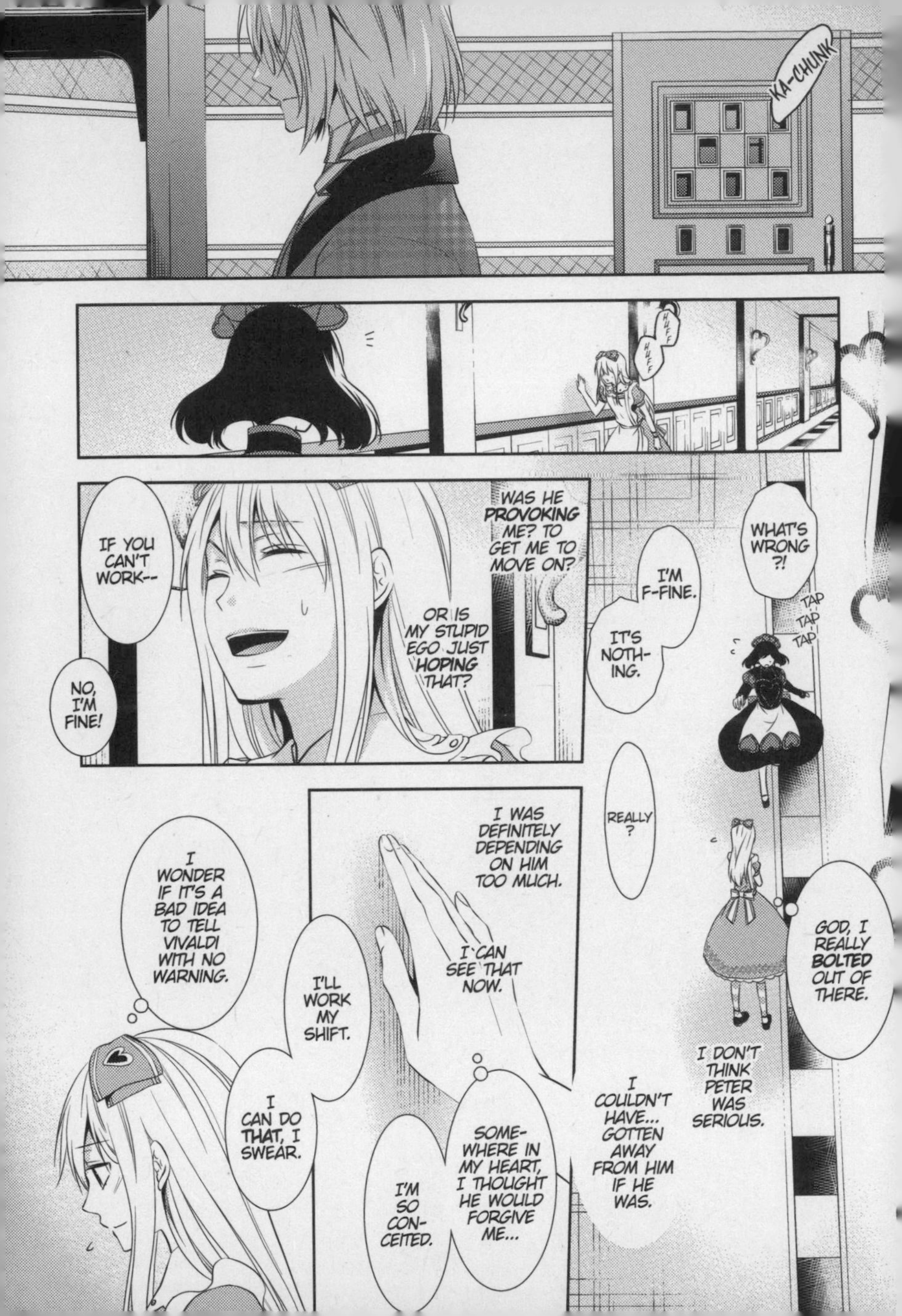
KA-CHUNK
HUFF HUFF
WHAT'S WRONG?!
TAP TAP TAP
I'M F-FINE.
IT'S NOTH-ING.
REALLY?
GOD, I REALLY BOLTED OUT OF THERE.
I DON'T THINK PETER WAS SERIOUS.
I COULDN'T HAVE... GOTTEN AWAY FROM HIM IF HE WAS.
WAS HE PROVOKING ME? TO GET ME TO MOVE ON?
OR IS MY STUPID EGO JUST HOPING THAT?
IF YOU CAN'T WORK--
NO, I'M FINE!
I WAS DEFINITELY DEPENDING ON HIM TOO MUCH.
I CAN SEE THAT NOW.
I WONDER IF IT'S A BAD IDEA TO TELL VIVALDI WITH NO WARNING.
I'LL WORK MY SHIFT.
SOME-WHERE IN MY HEART, I THOUGHT HE WOULD FORGIVE ME...
I'M SO CON-CEITED.
I CAN DO THAT, I SWEAR.

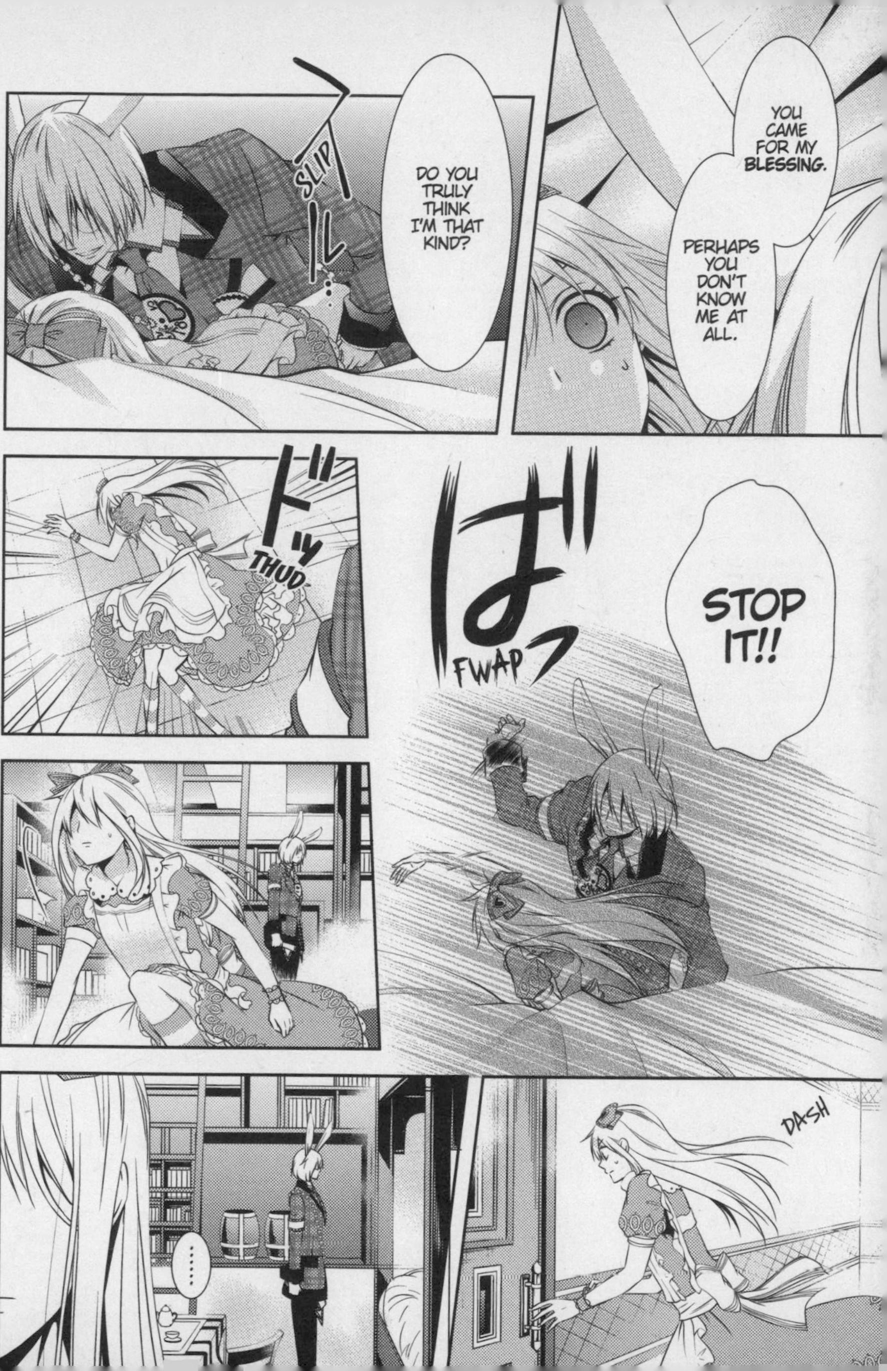
YOU CAME FOR MY BLESSING.
PERHAPS YOU DON'T KNOW ME AT ALL.
DO YOU TRULY THINK I'M THAT KIND?
SLIP
STOP IT!!
FWAP
THUD
DASH
......

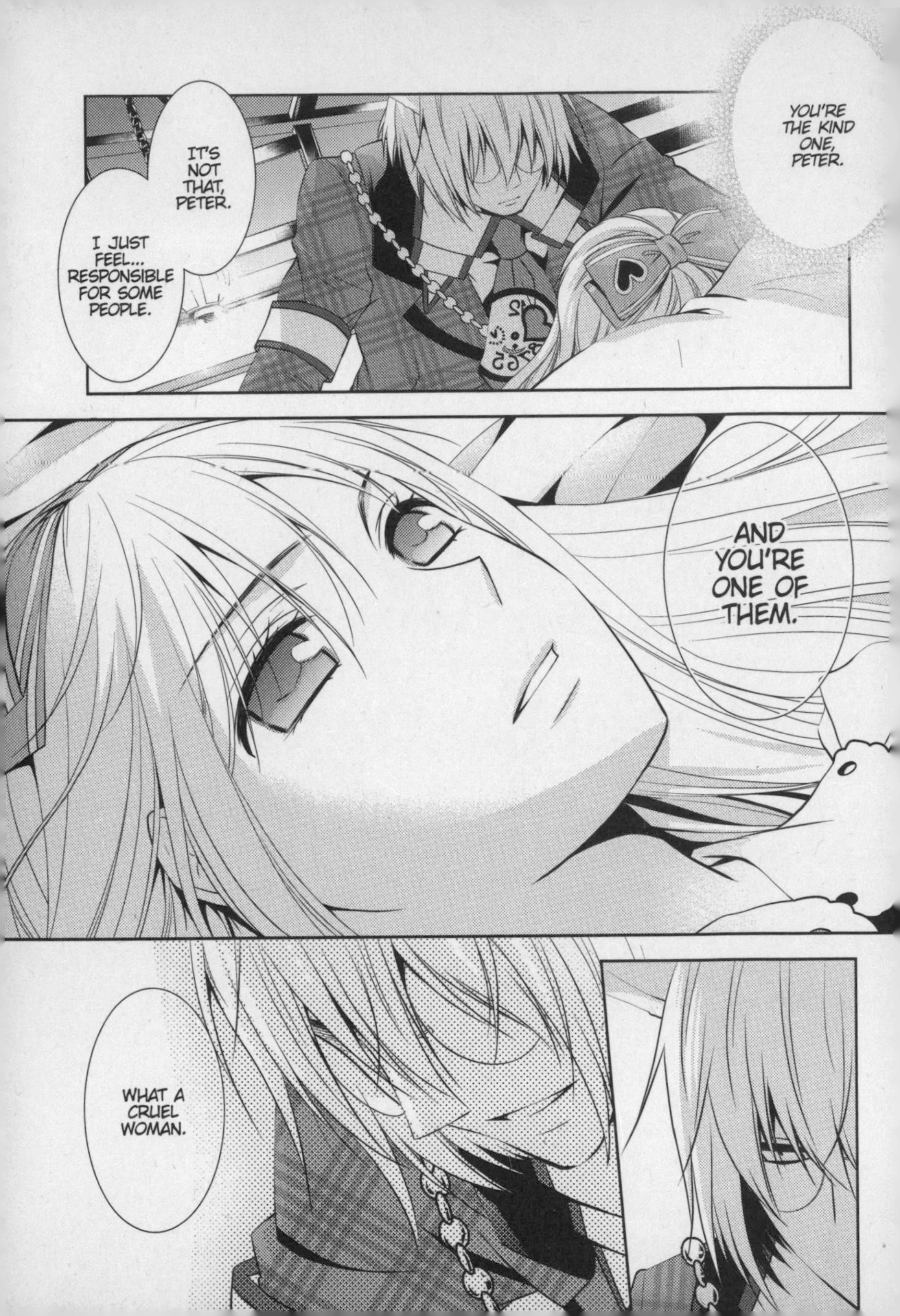
YOU'RE THE KIND ONE, PETER.
IT'S NOT THAT, PETER.
I JUST FEEL... RESPONSIBLE FOR SOME PEOPLE.
AND YOU'RE ONE OF THEM.
WHAT A CRUEL WOMAN.

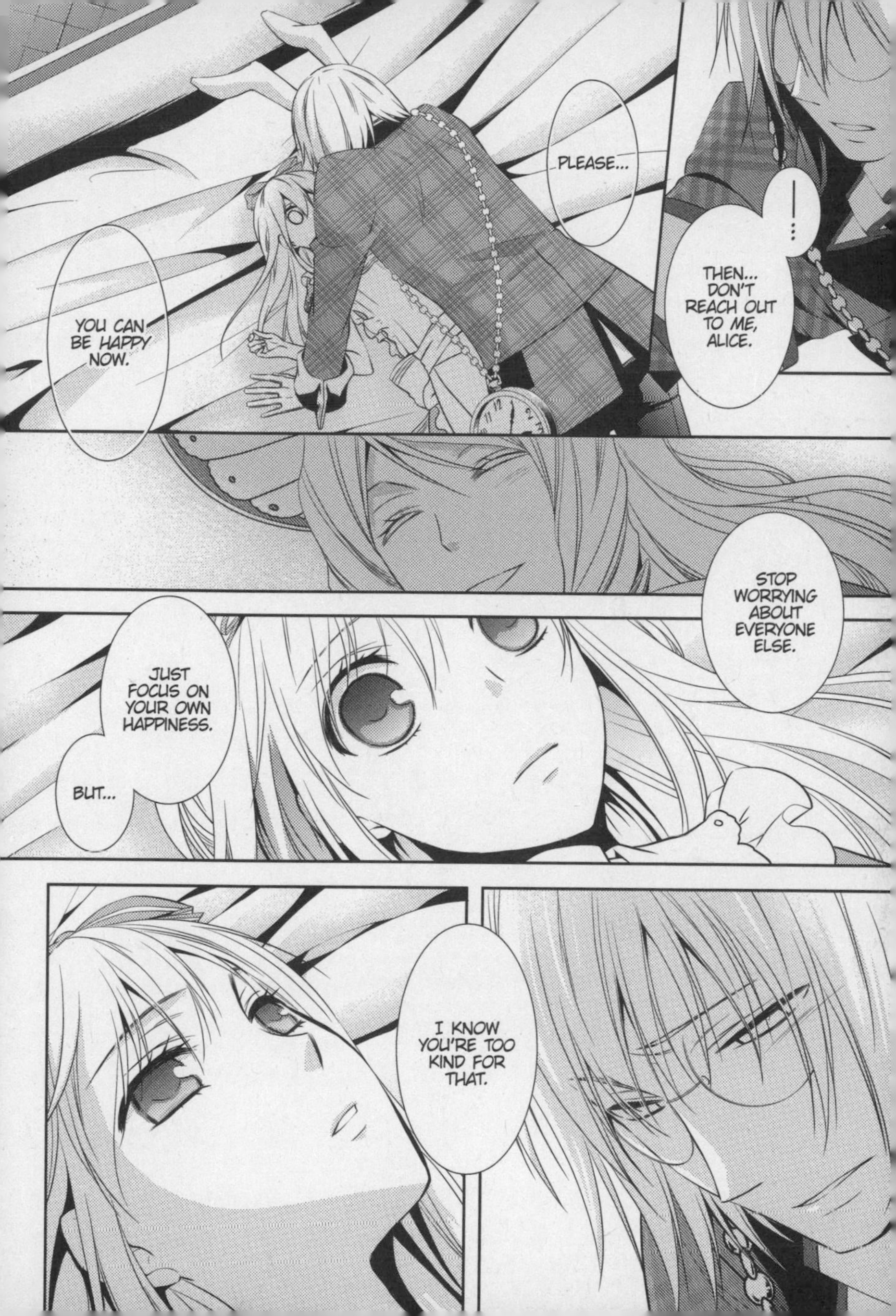
PLEASE...
!...
THEN... DON'T REACH OUT TO ME, ALICE.
YOU CAN BE HAPPY NOW.
STOP WORRYING ABOUT EVERYONE ELSE.
JUST FOCUS ON YOUR OWN HAPPINESS.
BUT...
I KNOW YOU'RE TOO KIND FOR THAT.

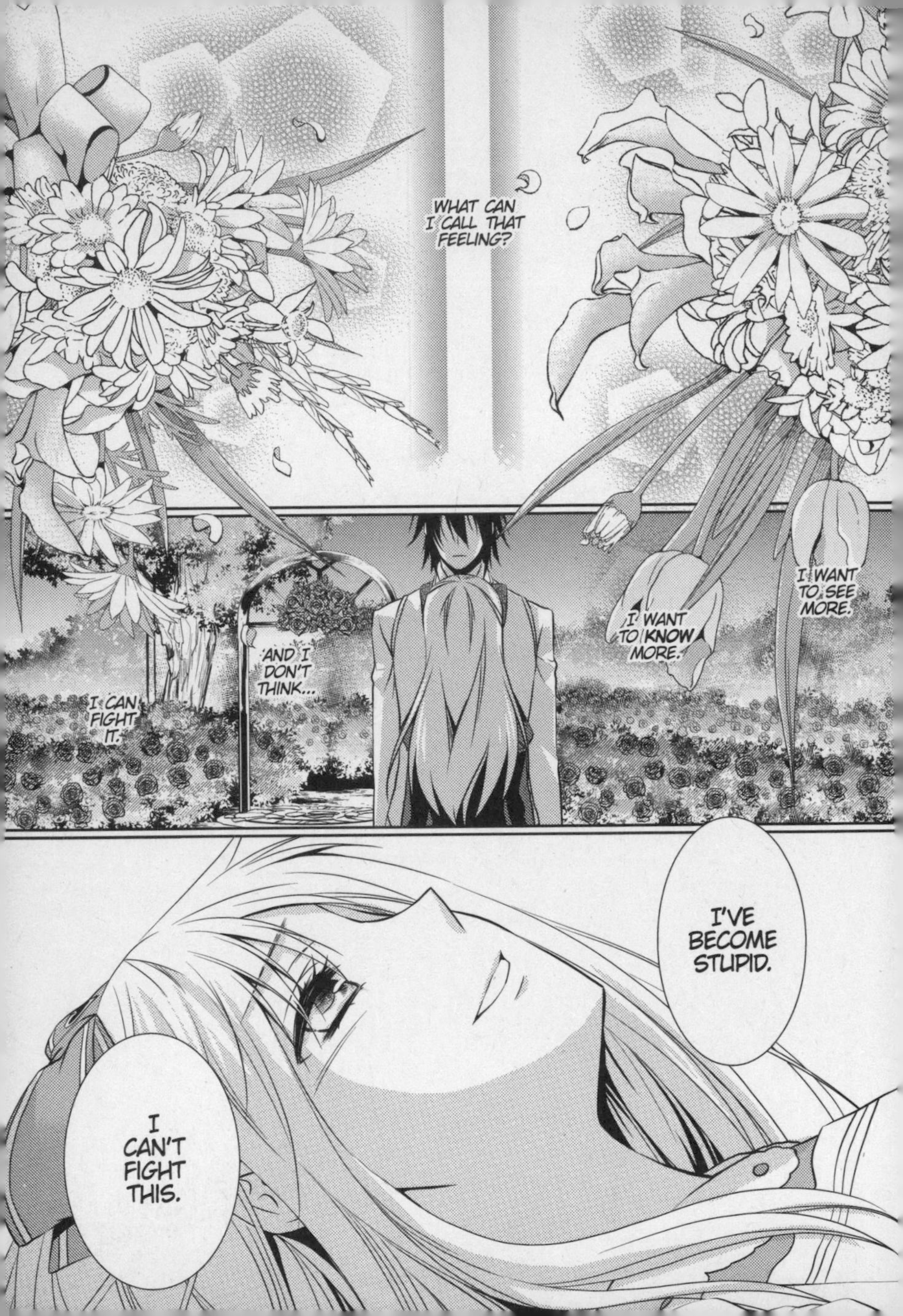
WHAT CAN I CALL THAT FEELING?
I WANT TO SEE MORE.
I WANT TO KNOW MORE.
AND I DON'T THINK...
I CAN FIGHT IT.
I'VE BECOME STUPID.
I CAN'T FIGHT THIS.

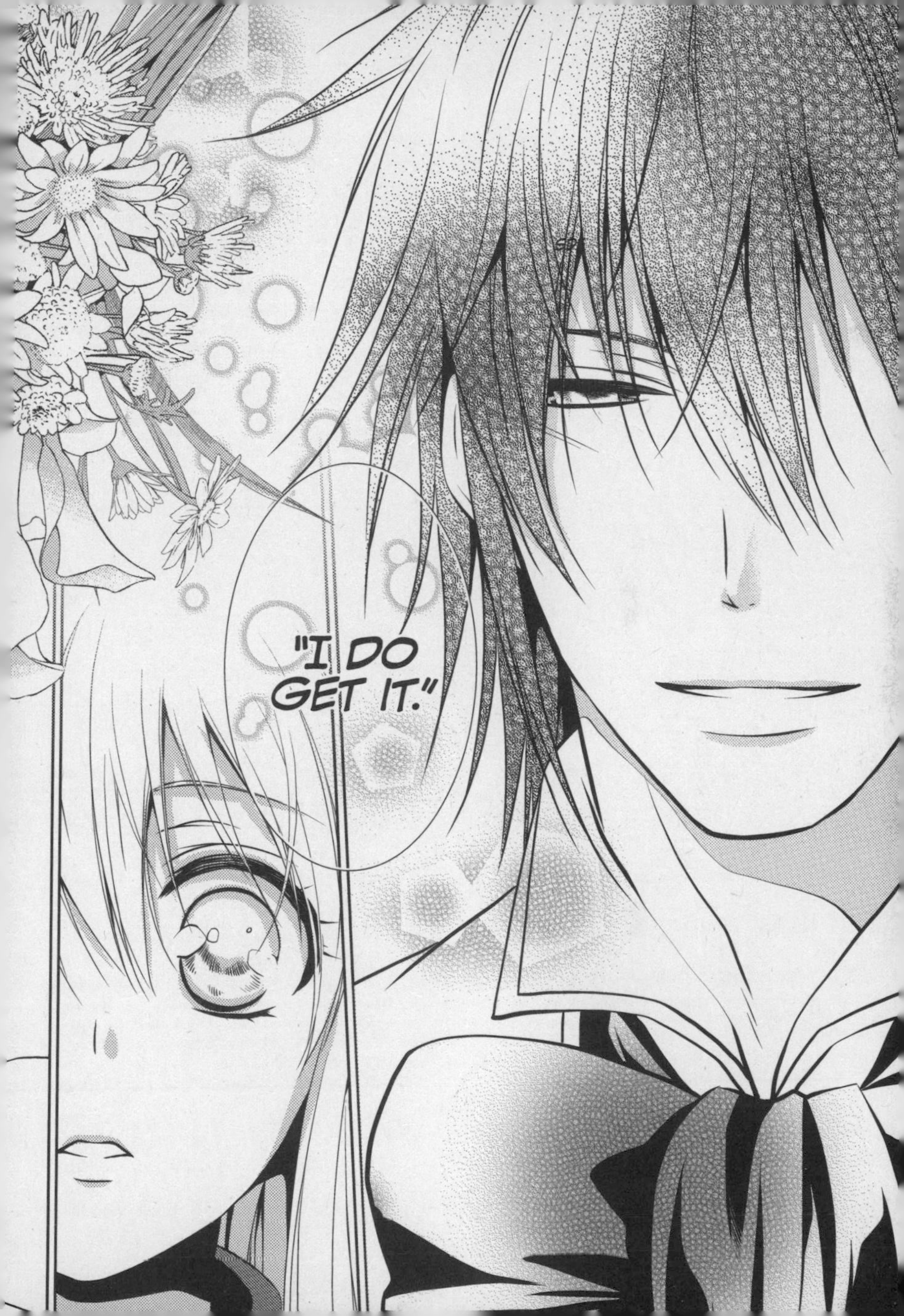
"I DO GET IT."

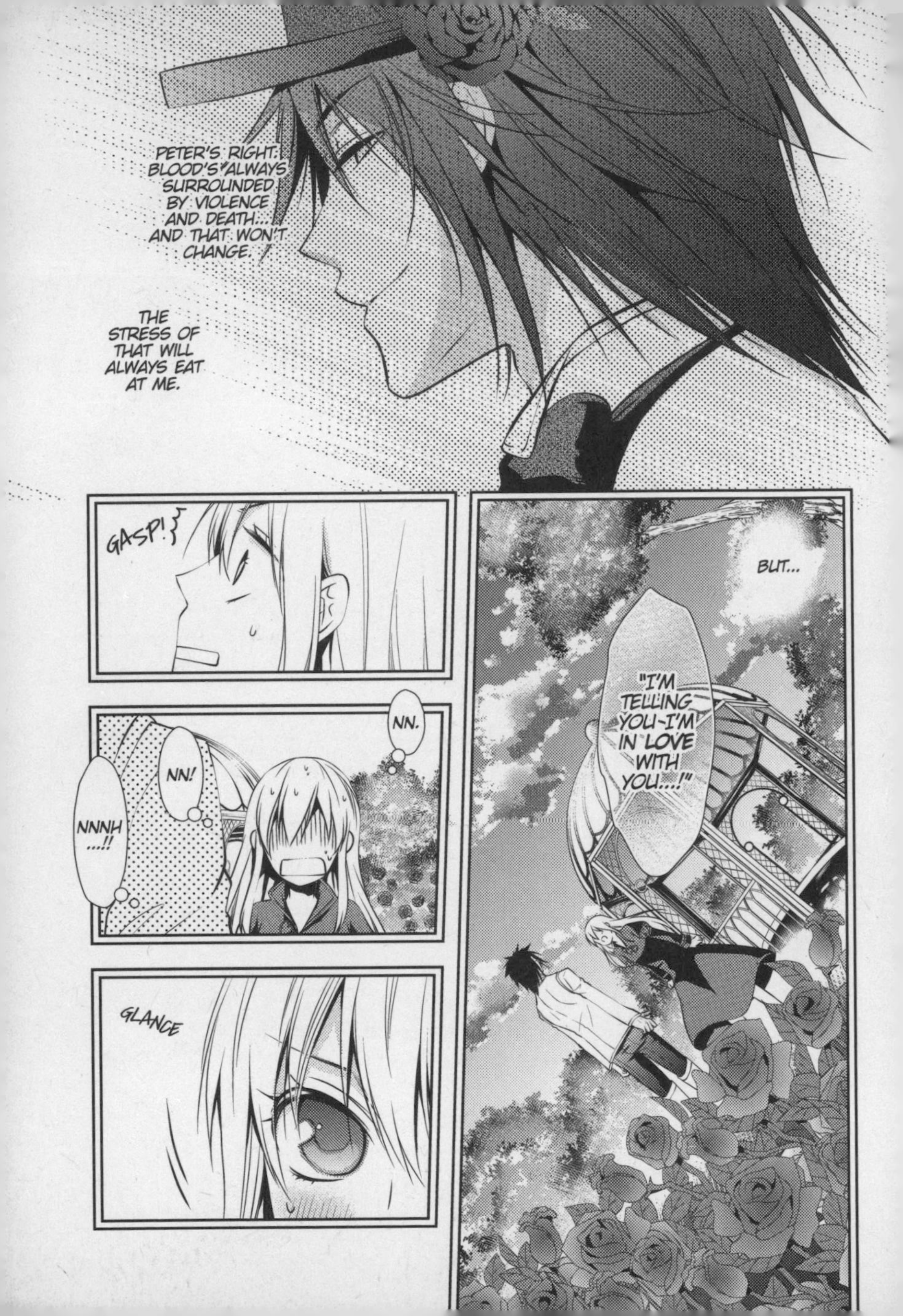
PETER'S RIGHT. BLOOD'S ALWAYS SURROUNDED BY VIOLENCE AND DEATH... AND THAT WON'T CHANGE.
THE STRESS OF THAT WILL ALWAYS EAT AT ME.
BUT...
"I'M TELLING YOU-I'M IN LOVE WITH YOU...!"
GASP!
NN.
NN!
NNNH ...!!
GLANCE

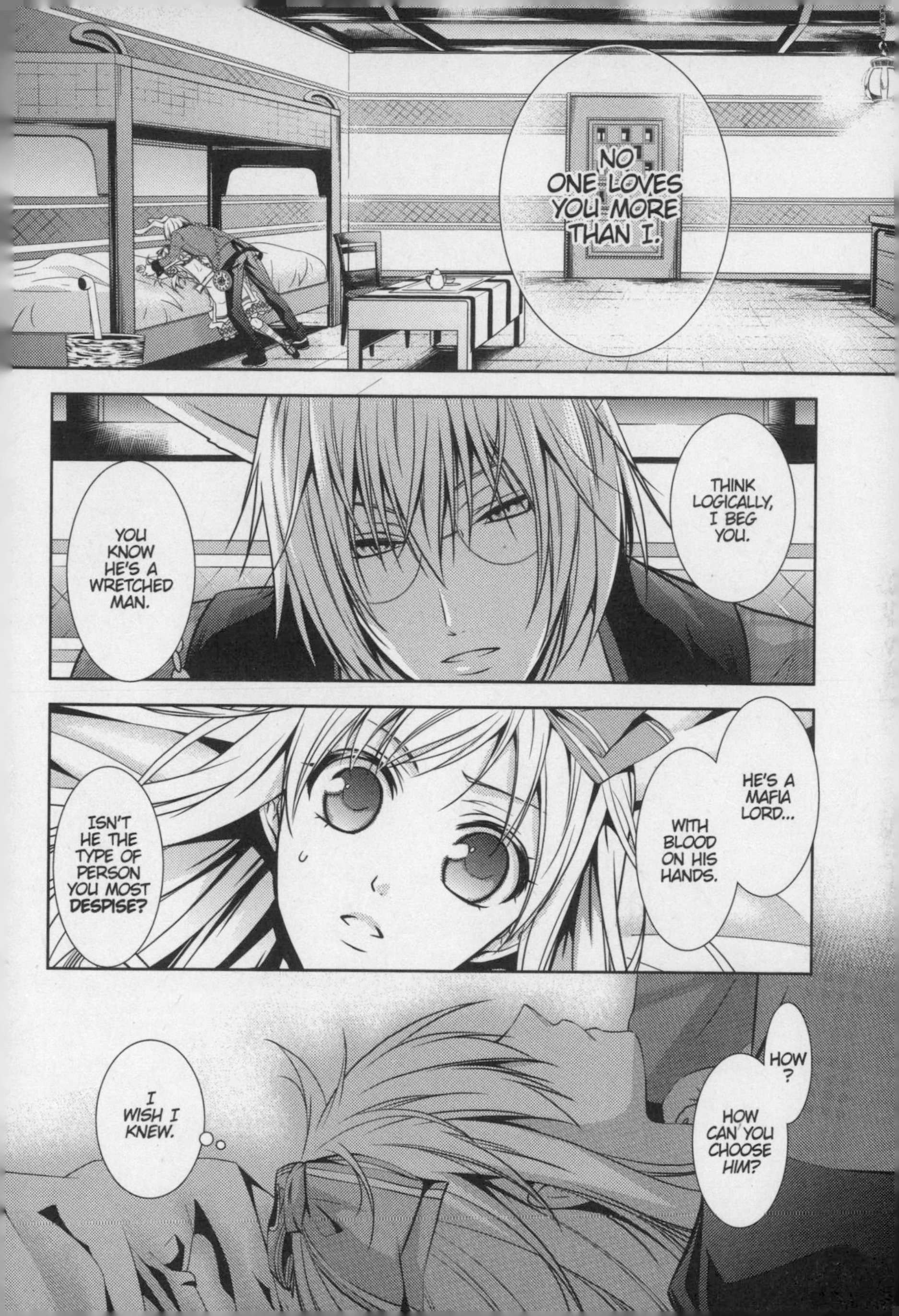
NO ONE LOVES YOU MORE THAN I.
THINK LOGICALLY, I BEG YOU.
YOU KNOW HE'S A WRETCHED MAN.
HE'S A MAFIA LORD...
WITH BLOOD ON HIS HANDS.
ISN'T HE THE TYPE OF PERSON YOU MOST DESPISE?
HOW?
HOW CAN YOU CHOOSE HIM?
I WISH I KNEW.

Hit: 22

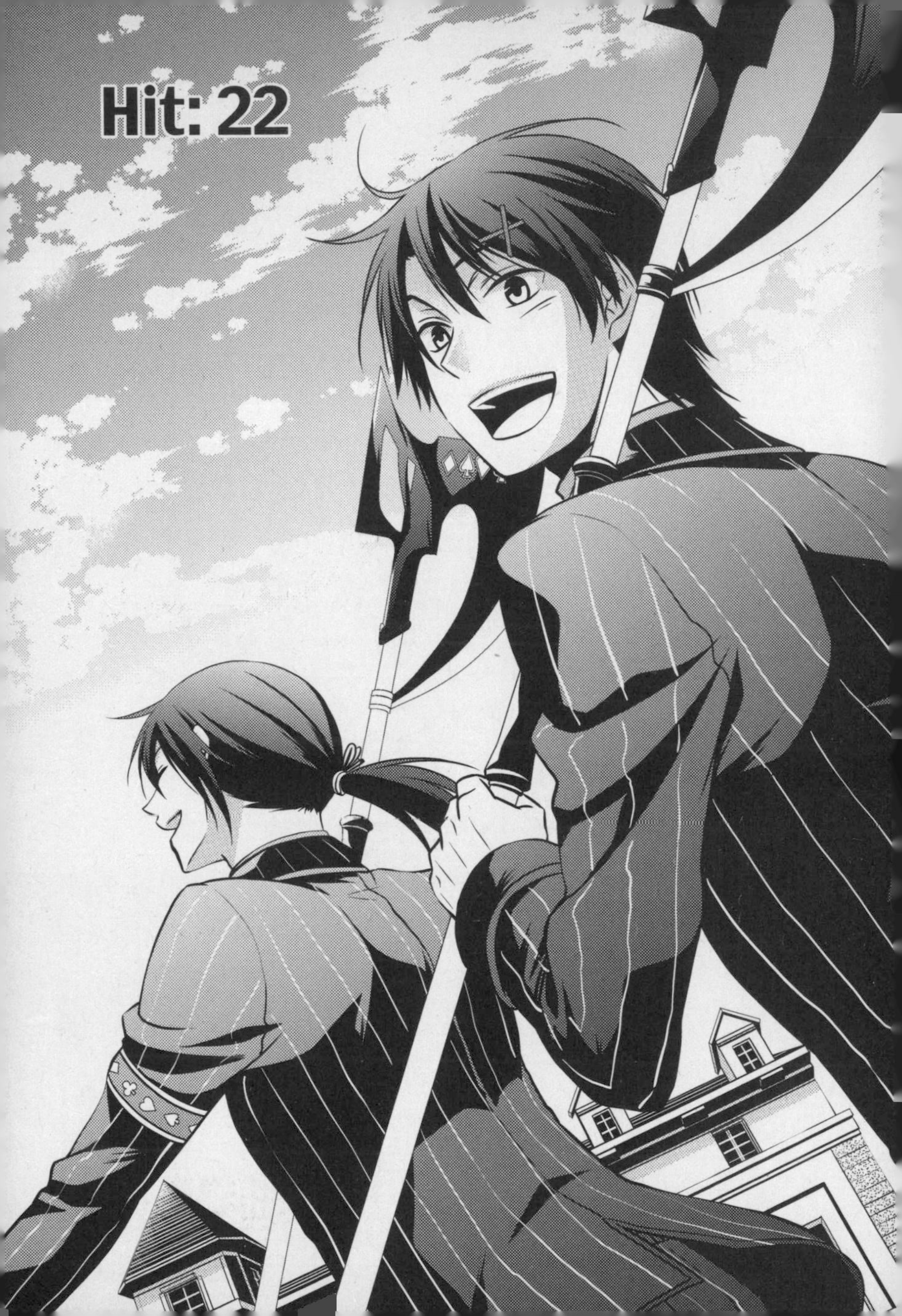

SEVEN SEAS ENTERTAINMENT PRESENTS

Alice IN THE COUNTRY OF Joker
CIRCUS AND LIAR'S GAME

art by **MAMENOSUKE FUJIMARU** / story by **QUINROSE** **VOLUME 6**

TRANSLATION
Angela Liu

ADAPTATION
Lianne Sentar

LETTERING AND LAYOUT
Laura Scoville

LOGO DESIGN
Courtney Williams

COVER DESIGN
Nicky Lim

PROOFREADER
Shanti Whitesides
Lee Otter

MANAGING EDITOR
Adam Arnold

PUBLISHER
Jason DeAngelis

ALICE IN THE COUNTRY OF JOKER: CIRCUS AND LIAR'S GAME VOL. 6

First published in Japan in 2013 by ICHIJINSHA Inc., Tokyo.
English translation rights arranged with ICHIJINSHA Inc., Tokyo, Japan.

ISBN: 978-1-626920-75-0

Printed in Canada

First Printing: October 2014

10 9 8 7 6 5 4 3 2 1

FOLLOW US ONLINE: ***www.gomanga.com***

READING DIRECTIONS

This book reads from ***right to left***, Japanese style. If this is your first time reading manga, you start reading from the top right panel on each page and take it from there. If you get lost, just follow the numbered diagram here. It may seem backwards at first, but you'll get the hang of it! Have fun!!

1
2
3
4
5
6
7
8
9

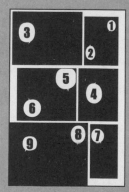

Alice in the Country of Joker

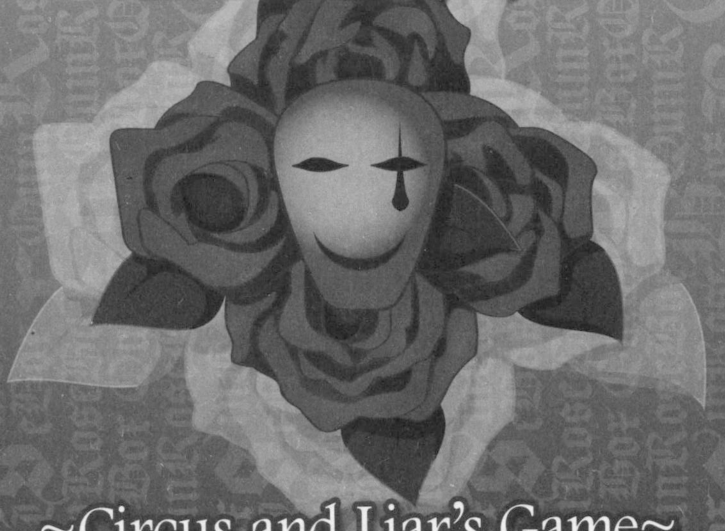

~Circus and Liar's Game~

- STORY -

This is a love adventure game based on Lewis Carroll's *Alice in Wonderland* that develops into a completely different storyline. This Wonderland is a fairy tale gone very wrong—or very *right*, if you like a land of gunfights where the "Hatters" are a mafia syndicate.

The main character is far from a romantic. In fact, she's especially sick of love relationships.

In *Alice in the Country of Joker,* Alice can experience the changing seasons that were absent in the other storylines. The Circus comes along with April Season, the season of lies. The Circus's dazzle and glitter hides its terrible purpose, and as Alice tries to wrap her head around the shifting world, she falls deeper and deeper into a nefarious trap.

When this story begins, Alice is already close to the inhabitants of Wonderland but hasn't fallen in love. Each role-holder treasures Alice differently with their own bizarre love—those who want to *protect* Alice from the Joker are competing with those who would rather be jailers. In the Country of Joker, there's more at stake than Alice's romantic affections...

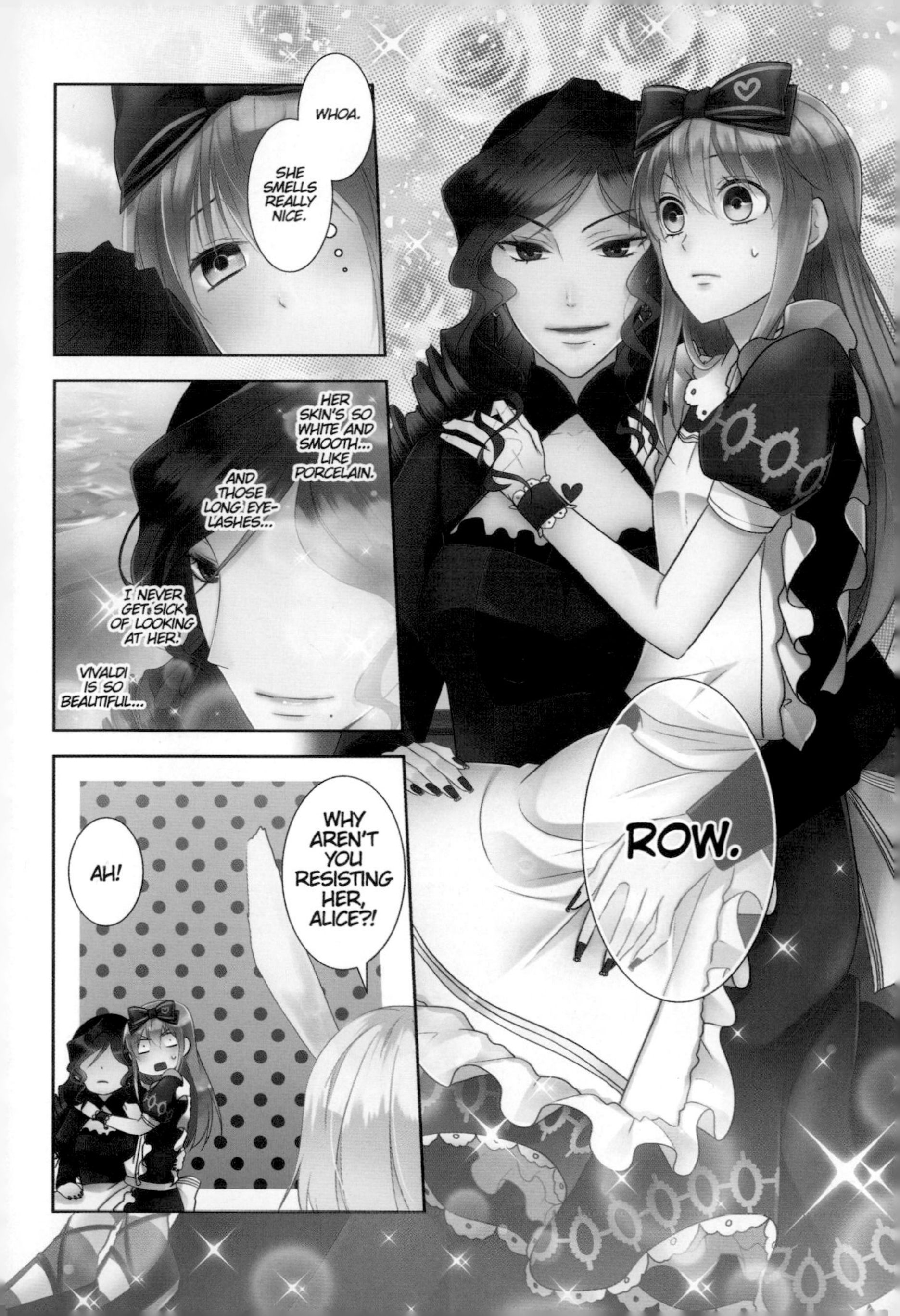
ROW.
WHOA.
SHE SMELLS REALLY NICE.
HER SKIN'S SO WHITE AND SMOOTH... LIKE PORCELAIN.
AND THOSE LONG EYE-LASHES...
I NEVER GET SICK OF LOOKING AT HER.
VIVALDI IS SO BEAUTIFUL...
WHY AREN'T YOU RESISTING HER, ALICE?!
AH!

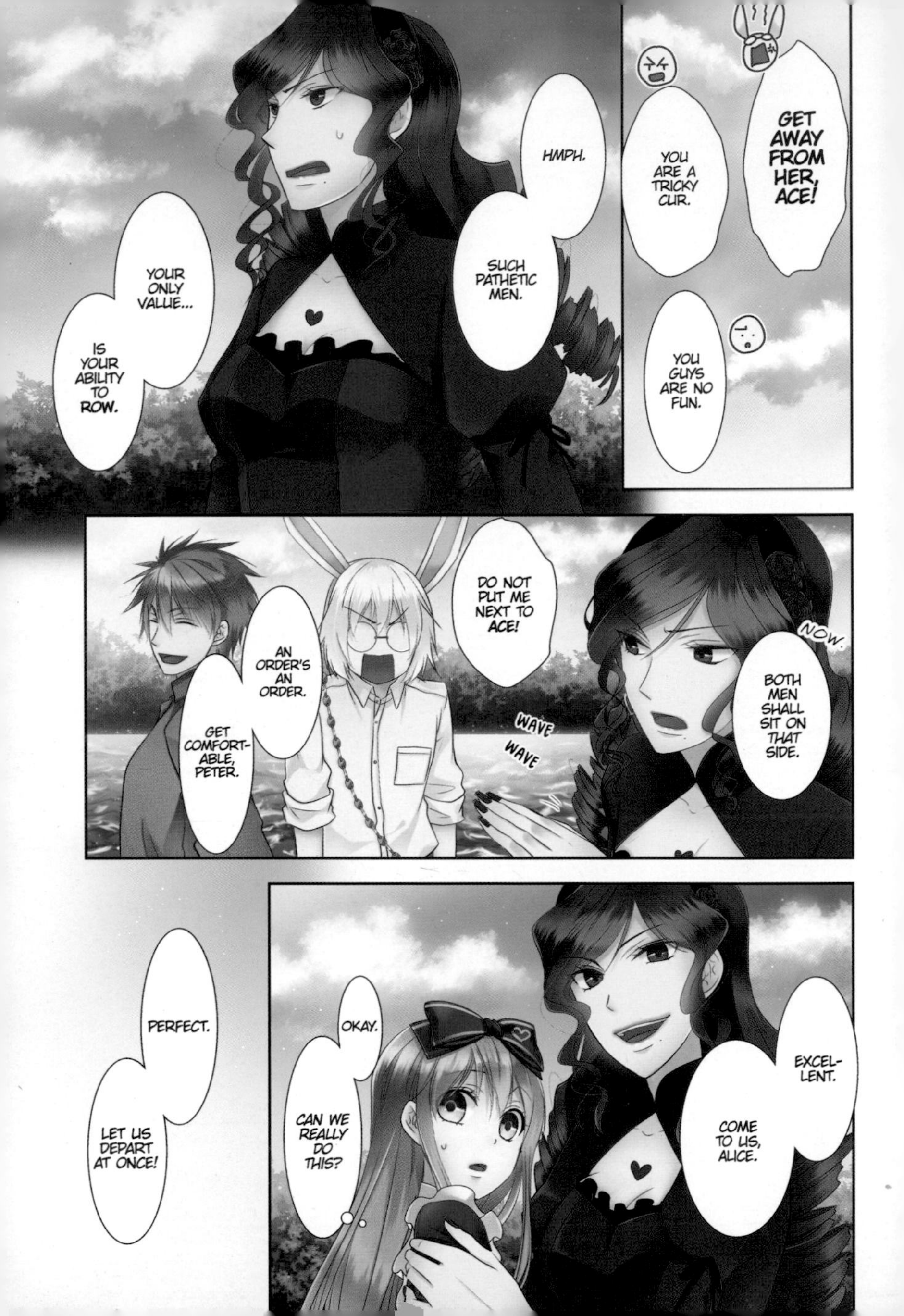
GET AWAY FROM HER, ACE!
YOU ARE A TRICKY CUR.
YOU GUYS ARE NO FUN.
HMPH.
SUCH PATHETIC MEN.
YOUR ONLY VALUE...
IS YOUR ABILITY TO ROW.
NOW.
BOTH MEN SHALL SIT ON THAT SIDE.
WAVE
WAVE
DO NOT PUT ME NEXT TO ACE!
AN ORDER'S AN ORDER.
GET COMFORTABLE, PETER.
EXCELLENT.
COME TO US, ALICE.
OKAY.
CAN WE REALLY DO THIS?
PERFECT.
LET US DEPART AT ONCE!

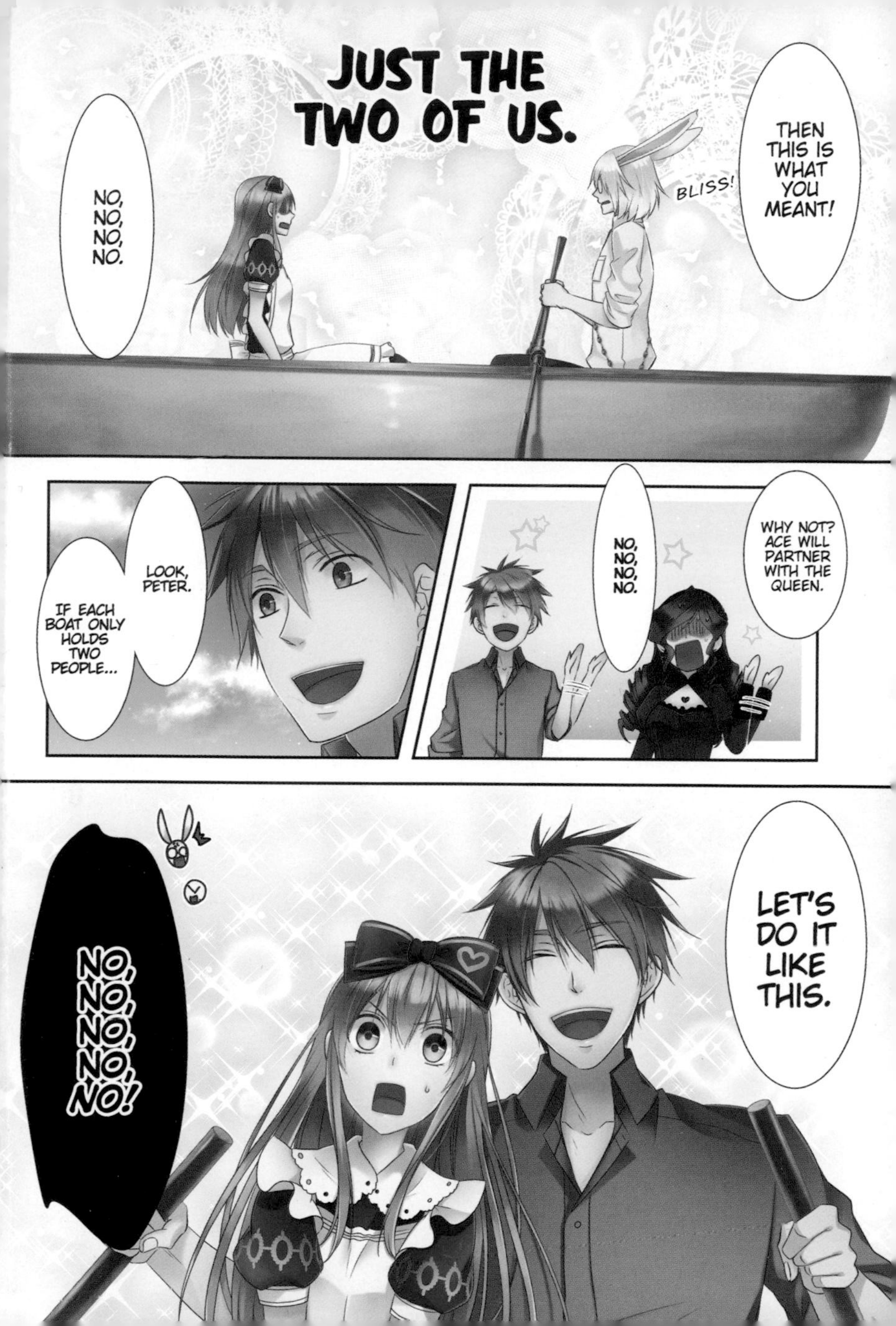
THEN THIS IS WHAT YOU MEANT!
JUST THE TWO OF US.
BLISS!
NO, NO, NO, NO.
WHY NOT? ACE WILL PARTNER WITH THE QUEEN.
NO, NO, NO, NO.
LOOK, PETER.
IF EACH BOAT ONLY HOLDS TWO PEOPLE...
LET'S DO IT LIKE THIS.
NO, NO, NO, NO, NO!

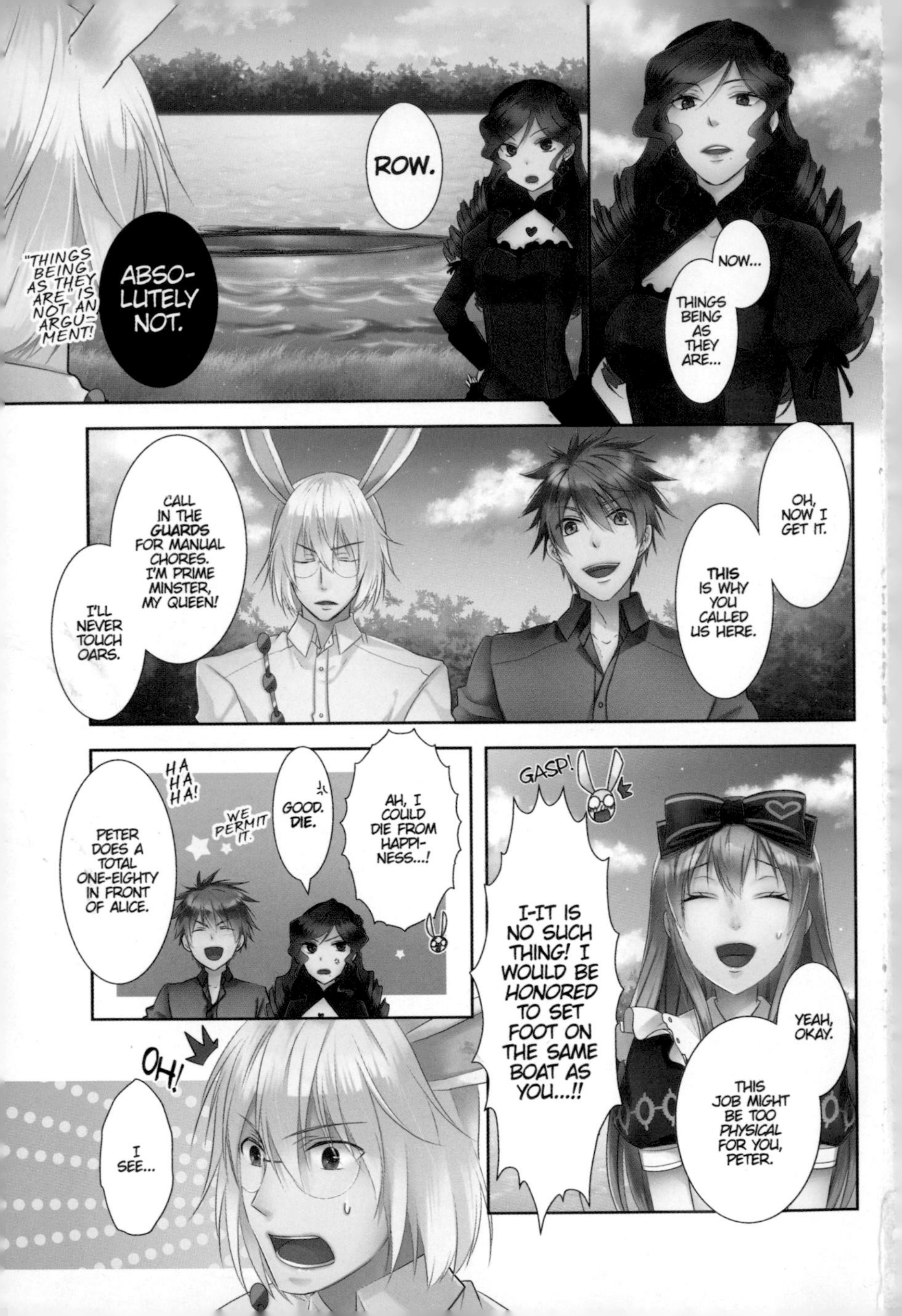

NOW...
THINGS BEING AS THEY ARE...
ROW.
ABSO-LUTELY NOT.
"THINGS BEING AS THEY ARE" IS NOT AN ARGU-MENT!
OH, NOW I GET IT.
THIS IS WHY YOU CALLED US HERE.
CALL IN THE GUARDS FOR MANUAL CHORES. I'M PRIME MINSTER, MY QUEEN!
I'LL NEVER TOUCH OARS.
GASP!
YEAH, OKAY.
THIS JOB MIGHT BE TOO PHYSICAL FOR YOU, PETER.
I-IT IS NO SUCH THING! I WOULD BE HONORED TO SET FOOT ON THE SAME BOAT AS YOU...!!
AH, I COULD DIE FROM HAPPI-NESS...!
GOOD. DIE.
WE PERMIT IT.
HA HA HA!
PETER DOES A TOTAL ONE-EIGHTY IN FRONT OF ALICE.
OH!
I SEE...